1st Joint Workshop on Financial Narrative Processing and MultiLing Financial Summarisation (FNP-FNS 2020)

Held online due to COVID-19

Barcelona, Spain
12 December 2020

ISBN: 978-1-7138-2828-0

FNP-FNS 2020

1st Joint Workshop on Financial Narrative Processing and MultiLing Financial Summarisation

Proceedings of the Workshop

December 12, 2020
Barcelona, Spain (Online)

Preface

Welcome to the 1st Joint Workshop on financial Narrative Processing and MultiLing financial Summarisation (FNP-FNS 2020) held at COLING 2020 in Barcelona, Spain. For future readers, it is worth noting the that workshop as well as the main conference were held as virtual events due to travel restrictions caused by the COVID-19 pandemic.

Following the success of the First FNP 2018 at LREC'18 in Japan, the Second FNP 2019 at NoDaLiDa 2019 in Finland and as well as the Multiling 2019 financial narrative Summarisation task at RANLP in Bulgaria, we have received a great deal of positive feedback and interest in continuing the development of the financial narrative processing field, especially from our shared task participants. This has resulted in a collaborative workshop between the FNP and MultiLing workshop series to co-organise the 1st Joint Workshop on financial Narrative Processing and MultiLing financial Summarisation (FNP-FNS 2020).

The 1st FNP-FNS workshop achieved our aim of supporting the rapidly growing area of financial text mining. We ran three different shared tasks focusing on text summarisation, structure detection and causal sentence detection, namely FNS, FinToc and FinCausal shared tasks respectively. The shared tasks attracted more than 100 teams from different universities and organisations around the globe. The shared tasks resulted in the first large scale experimental results and state of the art methods applied mainly to financial data. This shows the importance and growth of this field and we want to continue to be associated with top NLP venues.

The joint workshop focused mainly on the use of Natural Language Processing (NLP), Machine Learning (ML), and Corpus Linguistics (CL) methods related to all aspects of financial text summarisation, text mining and financial narrative processing (FNP). There is a growing interest in the application of automatic and computer-aided approaches for extracting, summarising, and analysing both qualitative and quantitative financial data. In recent years, previous manual small-scale research in the Accounting and Finance literature has been scaled up with the aid of NLP and ML methods, for example to examine approaches to retrieving structured content from financial reports, and to study the causes and consequences of corporate disclosure and financial reporting outcomes.

The workshop organisers collaborated with two Artificial Intelligence (AI) firms: Fortia financial Solutions (www.fortia.fr) and Yseop (www.yseop.com). Both firms are pioneers in Artificial Intelligence, NLP and Natural Language Generation (NLG). Both firms work on applying those methods to automatically analyse and extract from financial documents and disclosures.

We accepted 36 submissions to be presented in online oral and poster presentations. Each paper was reviewed by up to three reviewers. The submissions distribution is as follows: 6 main workshop papers and 30 shared task papers as follows: 10 papers accepted by the FNS shared task, 14 by the FinCausal shared task and 6 by the FinTOC shared task. Papers accepted in the main workshop were presented orally. All shared task papers were presented in 3 different poster sessions, one for each shared task. The papers covered a diverse set of topics in financial narratives processing reporting work on financial reports from different stock markets around the globe presenting analysis of financial reports and using state of the art NLP methods such as the use of latest word embeddings. The quantity and quality of the contributions to the workshop are strong indicators that there is a continuing and growing interest in the field of financial Natural Language Processing.

I would like to acknowledge all the hard work by the programme committee to make FNP-FNS a great success regardless of the challenging situations. I would also like to thank the submitting authors and the reviewers for the valuable feedback they provided. I hope these proceedings will serve as a valuable reference for researchers and practitioners in the field of financial narrative processing and NLP in general.

Dr Mahmoud El-Haj, General Chair, on behalf of the organizers of the FNP-FNS workshop, December 2020.

Workshop Organizers:

Dr Mahmoud El-Haj, Lancaster University (General Chair)
Dr Vasiliki Athanasakou, Saint Mary's University (FNP-FNS Program Chair and Advisor)
Dr Sira Ferradans (Publication Chair)
Dr Catherine Salzedo, Lancaster University (FNP-FNS Publicity Chair)
Dr Ans Elhag, Lancaster University (FNP-FNS Publication Chair)
Dr Houda Bouamor, CMU, Qatar (FNP Program Chair)
Dr Marina Litvak, Shamoon Academic College of Engineering (FNS Program Chair)
Dr Paul Rayson, Lancaster University (FNP Program Chair)
Dr George Giannakopoulos, NCSR Demokritos (FNS Program Chair)

Shared Task Organizers:

Dr Dialekti Valsamou, Fortia Financial Solutions (FinToc Shared Task Organiser)
Dr Ismail El Maarouf, Fortia Financial Solution (FinToc Shared Task Organiser)
Najah-Imane Bentabet, Fortia Financial Solution (FinToc Shared Task Organiser)
Remi Juge, Fortia Financial Solution (FinToc Shared Task Organiser)
Ahmed AbuRaed, Universitat Pompeu Fabra (FNS Shared Task Organiser)
Nikiforos Pittaras, NCSR Demokritos (Publicity Chair and FNS Shared Task Organiser)
Dominique Mariko, Yseop Lab (FinCausal Shared Task Organizer)
Hanna Abi-Akl, Yseop Lab (FinCausal Shared Task Organizer)
Hugues de Mazancourt, Yseop Lab (FinCausal Shared Task Organizer)
Estelle Labidurie, Yseop Lab (FinCausal Shared Task Organizer)
Stephane Durfort, Yseop Lab (FinCausal Shared Task Organizer)

Table of Contents

FNP-FNS 2020 Workshop Program

Saturday December 12, 2020 - Time zone · Greenwich Mean Time (GMT)

12:00–12:55   *Keynote Speaker*
Dr Ana Gisbert

13:00–13:19   Session 1: Shared Tasks Introduction

13:00–13:05   *The Financial Narrative Summarisation Shared Task (FNS 2020)*
Mahmoud El-Haj, Ahmed AbuRa'ed, Marina Litvak, Nikiforos Pittaras and George Giannakopoulos

13:07–13:12   *The Financial Document Structure Extraction Shared task (FinToc 2020)*
Najah-Imane Bentabet, Rémi JUGE, Ismail El Maarouf, Virginie Mouilleron, Dialekti Valsamou-Stanislawski and Mahmoud El-Haj

13:14–13:19   *The Financial Document Causality Detection Shared Task (FinCausal 2020)*
Dominique Mariko, Hanna Abi-Akl, Estelle Labidurie, Stephane Durfort, Hugues De Mazancourt and Mahmoud El-Haj

13:20–14:50   Session 2: Financial Document Causality Detection (FinCausal)

13:20–14:50   *LangResearchLab_NC at FinCausal 2020, Task 1: A Knowledge Induced Neural Net for Causality Detection*
Raksha Agarwal, Ishaan Verma and Niladri Chatterjee

13:20–14:50   *GBe at FinCausal 2020, Task 2: Span-based Causality Extraction for Financial Documents*
Guillaume Becquin

13:20–14:50   *LIORI at the FinCausal 2020 Shared task*
Denis Gordeev, Adis Davletov, Alexey Rey and Nikolay Arefiev

13:20–14:50   *JDD @ FinCausal 2020, Task 2: Financial Document Causality Detection*
Toshiya Imoto and Tomoki Ito

13:20–14:50   *UPB at FinCausal-2020, Tasks 1 & 2: Causality Analysis in Financial Documents using Pretrained Language Models*
Marius Ionescu, Andrei-Marius Avram, George-Andrei Dima, Dumitru-Clementin Cercel and Mihai Dascalu

13:20–14:50   *NITK NLP at FinCausal-2020 Task 1 Using BERT and Linear models.*
Hariharan R L and Anand Kumar M

14:50–15:50   *SCE-SUMMARY at the FNS 2020 shared task*
Marina Litvak, Natalia Vanetik and Zvi Puchinsky

14:50–15:50   *Knowledge Graph and Deep Neural Network for Extractive Text Summarization by Utilizing Triples*
Amit Vhatkar, Pushpak Bhattacharyya and Kavi Arya

14:50–15:50   *AMEX AI-Labs: An Investigative Study on Extractive Summarization of Financial Documents*
Piyush Arora and Priya Radhakrishnan

14:50–15:50   *Extractive Summarization System for Annual Reports*
Abderrahim Ait Azzi and Juyeon Kang

14:50–15:50   *SUMSUM@FNS-2020 Shared Task*
Siyan Zheng, Anneliese Lu and Claire Cardie

15:50–16:20   Session 4: Financial Document Structure Extraction (FinTOC)

15:50–16:20   *AMEX-AI-LABS: Investigating Transfer Learning for Title Detection in Table of Contents Generation*
Dhruv Premi, Amogh Badugu and Himanshu Sharad Bhatt

15:50–16:20   *UWB@FinTOC-2020 Shared Task: Financial Document Title Detection*
Tomáš Hercig and Pavel Kral

15:50–16:20   *Taxy.io@FinTOC-2020: Multilingual Document Structure Extraction using Transfer Learning*
Frederic Haase and Steffen Kirchhoff

15:50–16:20   *DNLP@FinTOC'20: Table of Contents Detection in Financial Documents*
Dijana Kosmajac, Stacey Taylor and Mozhgan Saeidi

15:50–16:20   *Daniel@FinTOC'2 Shared Task: Title Detection and Structure Extraction*
Emmanuel Giguet, Gaël Lejeune and Jean-Baptiste Tanguy

16:20–16:30   *Break*

16:30–17:10   Session 5: Main Workshop Papers

16:30–16:35   *A Computational Analysis of Financial and Environmental Narratives within Financial Reports and its Value for Investors*
Felix Armbrust, Henry Schäfer and Roman Klinger

16:37–16:42   *Information Extraction from Federal Open Market Committee Statements*
Oana Frunza

16:44–16:49   *Mitigating Silence in Compliance Terminology during Parsing of Utterances*
Esme Manandise and Conrad de Peuter

16:51–16:56   *Hierarchical summarization of financial reports with RUNNER*
Marina Litvak, Natalia Vanetik and Zvi Puchinsky

16:58–17:03   *Predicting Modality in Financial Dialogue*
Kilian Theil and Heiner Stuckenschmidt

17:05–17:10   *Extracting Fine-Grained Economic Events from Business News*
Gilles Jacobs and Veronique Hoste

17:10–17:15   *Short Break*

17:15–18:00   Session 6: Open Discussion

17:15–18:00   *Open Discussion*
Mahmoud El-Haj and Paul Rayson

The Financial Narrative Summarisation Shared Task (FNS 2020)

Mahmoud El-Haj[1]   Ahmed AbuRa'ed[2]   Marina Litvak[3]
Nikiforos Pittaras[4]   and   George Giannakopoulos[4]

[1]Lancaster University, UK, [2]UPF, Spain, [3]SCE, Israel, [4]IIT Demokritos, Greece
[1]m.el-haj@lancaster.ac.uk, [2]ahmed.aburaed@upf.edu,
[3]litvak.marina@gmail.com
[4]{ggianna,pittarasnikif}@iit.demokritos.gr

Abstract

This paper presents the results and findings of the Financial Narrative Summarisation shared task (FNS 2020) on summarising UK annual reports. The shared task was organised as part of the 1st Financial Narrative Processing and Financial Narrative Summarisation Workshop (FNP-FNS 2020). The shared task included one main task which is the use of either abstractive or extractive summarisation methodologies and techniques to automatically summarise UK financial annual reports. FNS summarisation shared task is the first to target financial annual reports. The data for the shared task was created and collected from publicly available UK annual reports published by firms listed on the London Stock Exchange (LSE). A total number of 24 systems from 9 different teams participated in the shared task. In addition we had 2 baseline summarisers and additional 2 topline summarisers to help evaluate and compare against the results of the participants.

1 Introduction

Companies around the world produce a variety of reports containing both narrative and numerical information at various times during their financial year. Such reports are referred to as financial disclosures and usually include quarterly reports, preliminary earnings announcements, conference calls, press releases financial annual reports (El-Haj et al., 2018a). This creates a vast financial information environment which can be impossible to keep track of (Salzedo et al., 2014; El-Haj et al., 2014a; El Haj et al., 2018b; Athanasakou et al., 2019).

The same set of information can be crucial for a number of different reasons. It can help highlight company achievements and gain support from shareholders in the stock exchange. It can identify risks and opportunities that investors need to take into account. Financial reporting is also strongly related to due diligence processes during mergers and acquisitions, as well as during auditing processes. All the above uses, many of which can be critical during a company life-cycle, show the vital need for automatic summarisers, in order to reduce the amount of time and effort required by stakeholders - be they shareholders investors or other parties - to read and analyse those documents.

The financial narrative summarisation (FNS) shared task focuses on annual reports produced by UK firms listed on the London Stock Exchange (LSE). In the UK and elsewhere, annual reports structure is much less rigid than those produced in the US elhaj2019, . Companies usually produce glossy brochures with a much looser structure that is usually disseminated in PDF file format. This makes automatic summarisation of narratives in UK annual reports a challenging task, since the structure of those documents needs to be extracted first in order to summarise the narrative sections of the annual reports. This can be done by detecting narrative sections that usually include the management disclosures (financial narratives) rather than the financial statements of the annual reports (El-Haj et al., 2016). Previously, the 1st and 2nd Financial Narrative Processing Workshops (FNP 2018 and FNP 2019) focused on the process of extracting and analysing financial narratives from multilingual financial statements written in languages such as English, French and Spanish (El-Haj et al., 2018a; El-Haj et al., 2019c).

Proceedings of the 1st Joint Workshop on Financial Narrative Processing and MultiLing Financial Summarisation, pages 1–12
Barcelona, Spain (Online), December 12, 2020.

In this task we ask participants to generate automatic summaries for lengthy UK annual reports (each with more than 60,000 words on average) by focusing on the financial narratives of the reports and producing a summary of no more than 1000 words for each annual report.

This paper presents the results and findings of the Finanical Narrative Summarization shared task, as follows. We begin with an overview of related work in Section 2. We then describe the data, elaborating on the task (Section 3), and continue with the baseline and topline system descriptions (Section 4). After this complete picture of the task and setting, we overview the submitted systems, in section 5. We conclude the paper with the task evaluation and related results as well as an appropriate short discussion of the findings (Section 6).

2   Related Work

The increased availability of financial report data has been met with research interest for applying automatic summarisation methods. The task of automatic text summarisation aims to produce a condensed, informative and non-redundant summary from a single or multiple input texts (Nenkova and McKeown, 2011). This is achieved by either identifying and ranking subsets of the input text (i.e. extractive approaches ((Gupta and Lehal, 2010)), or by generating the summary from scratch (i.e. abstractive methods (Moratanch and Chitrakala, 2016)).

Extractive summarisation methods have received far higher attention than their abstractive counterpart methods. This is mainly due to their relative simple approach when compared to the comparatively high requirements of the abstractive methods, especially when it comes to computational resources and data availability.

Extractive summarisation utilises scoring approaches to identify and reorder parts of the input (e.g. sentences, phrases and/or passages), using a variety of feature extraction/engineering and evaluation methods (Luhn, 1958; Baxendale, 1958; Edmundson, 1969; Mori, 2002; McCargar, 2004; El-Haj, 2012; Giannakopoulos et al., 2008; Koulali et al., 2013). Where adequate data is available, machine learning methods have been employed, such as Hidden Markov Models (Fung and Ngai, 2006), topic-based modelling (Aries et al., 2015), clustering methods (Radev et al., 2000; Liu and Lindroos, 2006; Kruengkrai and Jaruskulchai, 2003), deep neural network classification (Nallapati et al., 2017) and language models (Liu, 2019).

The application of summarisation and natural language processing techniques in general has promising applications in the financial domain (El-Haj et al., 2019b). Recently, statistical features with heuristic approaches have been used to summarise financial disclosure texts (Cardinaels et al., 2019), generating summaries with reduced positive bias and leading to more conservative valuation judgements by investors that receive them.

Furthermore, the financial narrative summarisation task (El-Haj, 2019) of the Multiling 2019 workshop (Giannakopoulos, 2019) involved the generation of structured summaries from financial narrative disclosures. The SummariserPort system (de Oliveira et al., 2002) has been used to produce summaries for financial news. It utilises lexical cohesion (Flowerdew and Mahlberg, 2009), using sentence linkage heuristics to generate the output summary. A summarisation system of financial news was proposed in (Filippova et al., 2009), generating query-based and company-tailored summaries, via unsupervised sentence ranking using simple frequency-based features.

3   Data Description

The financial narrative summarisation (FNS) shared task focuses on annual reports produced by UK firms listed on The London Stock Exchange (LSE). The produced annual reports are written in Corporate language English, which comprises the words and visuals a company uses to communicate internally and externally. This influences corporate communication as a whole, from internal messaging to web content, press releases and including annual reports, which in turn could affect the communication between the corporate and stakeholders (Dawkins, 2004).

In the UK and elsewhere, many registrants publish a glossy report containing graphics, photographs and supplementary narratives such as the letter to shareholders (Dikolli et al. 2017). These documents are typically provided as a digital PDF file and outside the U.S. they represent the primary annual reporting vehicle. This results in barriers to large-scale automated analysis nevertheless mean that little is known about this ubiquitous reporting channel.

3.1 Data Creation

Previous work on analysing UK annual reports provided a methodological through developing, describing and evaluating an automated procedure for retrieving and classifying the narrative component of glossy annual reports presented as digital PDF files (El-Haj et al., 2020). The developed tool, CFIE-FRSE[1], has helped in creating large corpora of by-section text extracted from thousands of UK annual reports[2], which has primarily facilitated the availability and generation of a summarisation dataset that is specific to UK annual reports' financial narratives(El-Haj, 2019).

For the FNS 2020 Shared task we use around 4,000 UK annual reports for firms listed on LSE covering the period between 2002 and 2017 (El-Haj et al., 2014b; El-Haj et al., 2019a). The annual reports have been indirectly summarised by the firms' chairwoman/chairman, the chief executive officer (CEO) and the firm's management. The summaries have been used int he FNS shared task as gold-standard summaries. In addition, those summaries include the financial highlights reported by each firm at the beginning of their annual report. The summaries were extracted from the annual reports using the CFIE-FRSE tool and were then manually converted into a standard summarisation dataset through providing a document and a number of 2 to 3 gold-standard summaries.

3.2 FNS Shared Task Dataset

We divided the annual reports' full text into *training*, *testing* and *validation* sets providing both the full text of each annual report along with the gold-standard summaries.

In total there are 3,863 annual reports divided into training, testing and validation sets. Table 3.2 shows the dataset details.

Data Type	Training	Validation	Testing	Total
Report full text	3,000	363	500	3,863
Gold summaries	9,873	1,250	1,673	12,796

Table 1: FNS 2020 Shared Task Dataset

3.3 Data Availability

The FNS summarisation dataset was delivered to the participating teams at different stages. We provided the training and validation sets first, this included the full text of each annual report along with its gold-standard summaries. On average there are at least 3 gold-standard summaries for each annual report with some reports containing up to 7 gold-standard summaries.

The testing set was provided at a later stage so participants can test their summarisers on unseen test set. We did not provide the gold-standard summaries for the testing set.

The training, testing and validation sets all came in UTF-8 plain text (.txt) file format as shown in Section 3.4.

3.4 Data Sample

Figure 1 shows the structure of the Financial Narrative Summarisation dataset. We provided participants with two sets of directories "training" and "validation". Each contained the full text of the annual reports (*_annual_reports) and the gold standard summaries (*_gold_summaries).

The data was provided in plain text file format in a directory structure similar to the one shown in Figure 1.

Each annual report have a unique identifier (ID) which is used across the datasets in order to link annual reports' full text to their gold-standard summaries.

---

[1] https://github.com/drelhaj/CFIE-FRSE
[2] https://doi.org/10.17635/lancaster/researchdata/271

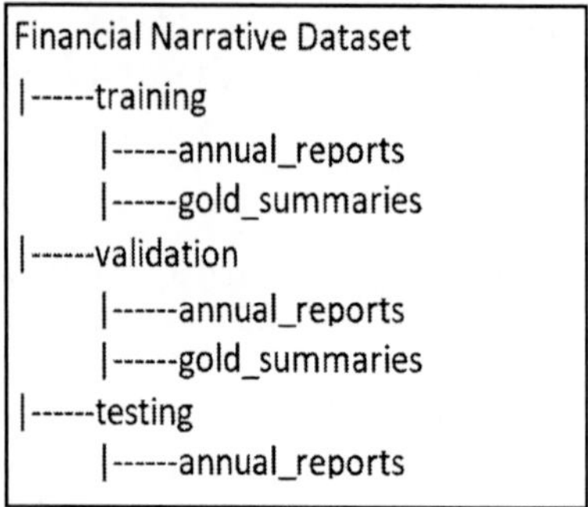

Figure 1: Dataset Structure

For example: The *training/annual_reports* directory contains a file called **19.txt** where 19 is a unique ID and can be used to locate this report's gold standard summaries in the *training_gold_summaries* directory (e.g. **19_1.txt** to **19_3.txt**.

3.5 Task Description

For the purpose of this task we asked each participating team to produce one summary for each annual report. The summary length should not exceed **1000** words[3]. Participants were advised that the summary to be generated/extracted based on the narrative sections of the annual reports, which they could do through training their summarisers to detect narrative sections before creating the summaries.

3.5.1 System Summaries Output

For the output summary we asked each team to produce a no more than 1000 words summary for each annual report in the testing set. Only one summary is allowed for each report, but participating teams are welcome to participate with more than one methodology, each methodology to be evaluated as a separate participating system. The participants were asked to follow a standard file naming process. In the future we aim to provide the human and system summaries free for research purposes. The naming pattern they were asked to follow is: **ID_summary.txt**. Example: 25082_summary.txt. For standardisation and consistency all output summary files should be in UTF-8 file format.

3.5.2 Evaluation

To evaluate the generated system summaries against the human gold-standard summaries we used the JRouge[4] package for ROUGE, using multiple variants (i.e. ROUGE-1, ROUGE-2, ROUGE-L and ROUGE-SU4) (Ganesan, 2015; Litvak et al., 2016).

4 Baseline and Topline Summarisers

All participating systems were evaluated and compared against 2 top performing (topline) systems and 2 baseline systems.

4.1 Baselines

The simplicity and the frequent use of TextRank and LexRank in literature and summarisation tasks make them ideal baselines for our shared task.

4.1.1 TextRank

Rada Mihalcea and Paul Tarau (2004) introduced TextRank as the first graph-based automated text summarisation algorithm. TextRank is a simple application of the PageRank algorithm (Brin and Page, 1998). In order to find the most relevant sentences in text, a graph is constructed where the vertices of the graph

---

[3]We used regex white space delimiter to detect word boundaries.

[4]https://github.com/kavgan/ROUGE-2.0

represent each sentence in a document and the edges between sentences are based on content overlap, namely by calculating the number of words that two sentences have in common.

In order to find relevant keywords, the TextRank algorithm constructs a word network. This network is constructed by looking which words follow one another. A link is set up between two words if they follow one another, the link gets a higher weight if these two words occur more frequently next to each other in the text.

Based on this network of sentences, the sentences are fed into the Pagerank algorithm which identifies the most important sentences.

4.1.2 LexRank

LexRank is another graph-based algorithm for automated text summarisation (Erkan and Radev, 2004). A cluster of documents can be viewed as a network of sentences that are related to each other. Some sentences are more similar to each other while some others may share only a little information with the rest of the sentences. Like TextRank (Section 4.1.1), LexRank too uses the PageRank algorithm for extracting top keywords. The key difference between the two baselines is the weighting function used for assigning weights to the edges of the graph. While TextRank simply assumes all weights to be unit weights and computes ranks like a typical PageRank execution, LexRank uses degrees of similarity between words and phrases and computes the centrality of the sentences to assign weights. (Erkan and Radev, 2004)

4.2 Toplines

To make the shared task more challenging, two topline summarisation algorithms have been used, MUSE and POLY.

4.2.1 MUSE

MUSE is a language-independent approach for extractive summarisation based on the linear optimisation of several sentence ranking metrics using a Genetic Algorithm (GA). We applied the original set of 31 sentence metrics[5], described in (Litvak et al., 2010). The metrics are divided into three main categories—*structure*-, *vector*-, and *graph*-based—according to the text representation model they are based on. Their best combination for the given corpus is calculated by a GA. A typical GA requires (1) a genetic representation of the solution, and (2) a fitness function to evaluate the solution quality. MUSE represents solution as a vector of weights for a linear combination of sentence metrics, and starts with the randomly initialized real values. We applied ROUGE-1 Recall (Lin, 2004) as a fitness function[6], which is maximized during the optimisation procedure. MUSE computation time is directly affected by the number of words in a summarized document. Moreover, its training time is proportional to the number of GA iterations multiplied by the number of individuals in a population times the fitness evaluation (ROUGE) time. As such, training MUSE on the entire training set of FNS 2020 dataset (3000 lengthy files, each with more than 60,000 words on average) is a very time and memory-consuming task. Therefore, we trained MUSE's model on 30 randomly selected reports from the training set and applied it on entire testing set (500 files). All files, from both training and testing sets, were pre-processed before MUSE application. Financial reports usually contain multiple sections, figures, and tables. Because the text files in the FNS-2020 dataset were obtained by converting PDF files into plain text file format, these text files contain a lot of "noise" caused by broken tables and meta-data such as section and page numbers. We cleaned the noise by measuring the ratio between text and numbers and ratio between number of words and white-spaces. Lines with low ratio were removed. Then, regular expressions were applied to find and mark such entities as URLs, phone numbers, dates, time, emails. Finally, non-Unicode characters were filtered out. MUSE is a multilingual summariser which was evaluated on multiple languages[7] and outperformed other systems in multiple MultiLing contests (Litvak and Last, 2013; Litvak et al., 2016). Therefore, it was selected as a topline system.

---

[5]MUSE can be configured with different number of metrics.
[6]MUSE can be configured with different ROUGE metrics.
[7]English, Hebrew, Arabic, and Persian

4.2.2 POLY

POLY (Litvak and Vanetik, 2013a) is unsupervised approach based on linear programming. POLY represent the document as a set of intersecting hyperplanes–polytope. The summary is described by the objective function–hyperplane–and is considered best if the optimal value of objective function is preserved during summarisation. As such, POLY translates the summarisation problem into a problem of finding a point on a convex polytope which is the closest to the hyperplane describing the "ideal" summary. POLY can be run with multiple objective functions describing the distance between a summary (a point on a convex polytope) and the best summary (the hyperplane). We applied POLY with Maximal Weighted Term Sum ($OBJ_1^{POS\_EQ}$ in (Litvak and Vanetik, 2013a)) objective function, which maximizes the information coverage as a term sum, with the same weight for all terms, regardless the term's frequency and position. Because POLY is unsupervised, it was directly (after pre-processing) applied on 500 files from the testing FNS set. All files were pre-processed in the same manner as for MUSE. POLY was selected as a baseline due to its polynomial run-time, no need in training, and comparatively good performance on English and other languages (Hebrew and Arabic), according to MultiLing results from 2013 (Litvak and Vanetik, 2013b) and 2015 (Vanetik and Litvak, 2015). POLY has been chosen as a competitive topline to MUSE and both have been used to assess the quality of the system summaries submitted by the participating summarisation systems.

5   Participating Teams and Systems

A total number of 9 teams participated in the FNS 2020 shared task with a total of 24 system submissions. Table 2 presents the names of the participating teams and their affiliations. In addition we report results from the topline and baseline algorithms (see Section 4).

Team	Affiliation
SRIB2020	Samsung
SUMTO	Politecnico di Torino
HULAT	Universidad Carlos III de Madrid
AMEX-Al Labs	American Express AI Labs, Bangalore
FORTIA	Fortia Financial Solutions
CIST@BUPT	Beijing University of Posts and Telecommunications
SUMSUM	Cornell University
KG-SUMMAR	IIT Bombay, India
SCE	Shamoon college of engineering (SCE)

Table 2: List of the 11 teams that participated in the FNS 2020 Shared Task

Table 5 summarizes the approaches adopted by each team. In the table, ML refers to any non-neural machine learning technique such as multinomial naive Bayes (MNB) and support vector machines (SVM). Neural refers to any neural network based model such as bidirectional long short-term memory (BiLSTM), or convolutional neural network (CNN). In terms of features, word and character ngram features. Language-model based features were also used a lot. A few participants used pre-trained embeddings. Table 3 shows the approaches (techniques and features) adopted by the participating teams. ML refers to any non-neural machine learning technique such as MNB, SVM, etc. Neural refers to any neural network (deep learning) based model such as BILSTM, CNN, GRUs, etc. LM refers to language-model based features. WC corresponds to word and character features. We ordered the teams by Rouge-2 F-measure. Tables 4 and 5 show the results in details for all of the 4 variations of ROUGE scores.

6   Results and Discussion

A number of 24 summarisation systems by 9 different teams have participated and submitted their system summaries to FNS 2020. In addition we report the results of the 4 topline and baseline summarisers (MUSE, POLY, TextRank and LexRank respectively) are reported in Tables 4 and 5.

| | | **Techniques** | | | **Features** | | |
Team	**F1**	ML	Neural	Ensemble	Structure	LM	Embeddings
SUMSUM	0.306		X			X	X
SRIB2020	0.289		X			X	X
FORTIA	0.274		X				X
HULAT	0.261	X			X		X
SUMTO	0.249		X				X
CIST@BUPT	0.248	X					
KG-SUMMAR	0.247	X	X				X
AMEX-Al Labs	0.214		X	X			
SCE	0.138				X		

Table 3: Techniques and Features used by the participating systems

The participating systems used a variety of techniques and methods ranging from rule based extraction methods and more towards high performing deep learning models and word embeddings. In addition the participating teams used methods to investigate the hierarchy of the annual reports to try and detect the structure of the report and extract the narrative sections. The majority of the applied techniques were extractive applying methods such as Determinantal Point Processes (DPPs) sampling algorithm and a combination of Pointer Network and T-5 (Test-to-text transfer Transformer) algorithms. Other extractive summarisers used word embeddings such word2vec, BERT and using CBOW & skip grams. An end-to-end training method using Deep NLP techniques, and a hierarchical summary that visualises as a tree with summaries under different discourse topics and an ensemble based model have also been reported.

This variety of techniques shows the interdisciplinary notion of FNS 2020 and the fact that it attracted such a range of methods, making it a gateway for researchers and practitioners working on summarising lengthy annual reports.

Some of the challenges and limitations reported by the participants is the fact that the average length of those annual reports is 60,000 words, this makes the training process difficult in term of time and performance, which is a problem that we are aware of and it is what prompted us to introduce such a challenging task. In addition, participants explained that it is difficult to detect structure of such reports due to the fact that they come originally in PDF format and extracting information from such files results in a lot of noise. This is a problem that we have been working on since 2012 and though we understand it is challenging, we believe it opens up an interesting research problem that is worth investigating more in the future.

Tables 4 and 5 show the results of the participating systems using ROUGE-1, ROUGE-2, ROUGE-L and ROUGE-SU4 respectively. The results have been sorted in descending order according to the highest F-score. The topline (MUSE and POLY) and baseline (TextRank and LexRank) systems are highlighted in bold font. The results show that the majority of the participating systems produced results that are better on average than our two baselines and POLY topline. On the other hand, our topline MUSE results show a challenging notion making it hard to beat, but even though we are happy to see that many participating systems have managed to produce results that are significantly better than MUSE. Such results will be used as a comparison line in the future through creating a venue of results and techniques for researchers working on financial text summarisation.

System / Metric	R-1 / R	R-1 / P	R-1 / F	R-2 / R	R-2 / P	R-2 / F
SRIB2020-3	0.61	0.39	0.47	0.45	0.22	0.29
SRIB2020-2	0.61	0.39	0.47	0.45	0.22	0.29
SUMSUM-BASE	0.49	0.48	0.46	0.40	0.26	0.29
SUMSUM-BERT	0.45	0.53	0.46	0.37	0.30	0.31
KG-SUMMAR-NN	0.57	0.38	0.44	0.40	0.18	0.25
SUMSUM-1	0.45	0.51	0.44	0.36	0.28	0.29
HULAT-1	0.54	0.39	0.44	0.41	0.20	0.26
KG-SUMMAR-SVM	0.49	0.42	0.44	0.36	0.20	0.25
KG-SUMMAR-S-LSTM	0.51	0.41	0.44	0.36	0.19	0.24
MUSE	0.48	0.41	0.43	0.31	0.20	0.23
CIST-BUPT-3	0.43	0.45	0.43	0.29	0.23	0.25
SUMTO-3	0.45	0.43	0.42	0.30	0.23	0.25
SUMTO-2	0.44	0.43	0.42	0.28	0.22	0.23
SUMTO-1	0.43	0.44	0.42	0.27	0.23	0.24
CIST-BUPT-2	0.42	0.44	0.42	0.27	0.22	0.24
AMEX-ENSEMBLE	0.44	0.41	0.41	0.26	0.19	0.21
AMEX-BILSTM	0.44	0.41	0.41	0.26	0.19	0.21
FORTIA-1	0.43	0.43	0.41	0.30	0.28	0.27
HULAT-2	0.50	0.35	0.40	0.37	0.18	0.23
CIST-BUPT-1	0.40	0.42	0.40	0.26	0.21	0.22
FORTIA-2	0.39	0.41	0.38	0.25	0.26	0.24
FORTIA-3	0.37	0.37	0.35	0.21	0.22	0.20
SCE	0.29	0.40	0.30	0.16	0.16	0.14
AMEX-TEXTRANK	0.35	0.27	0.29	0.18	0.10	0.12
SRIB2020-1	0.24	0.38	0.28	0.11	0.14	0.12
POLY	0.32	0.25	0.27	0.15	0.09	0.11
LEXRANK	0.34	0.27	0.26	0.19	0.11	0.12
TEXTRANK	0.41	0.12	0.17	0.23	0.04	0.07

Table 4: ROUGE-1 and ROUGE-2 Recall, Precision and F-measure scores

System / Metric	R-L / R	R-L / P	R-L / F	R-SU4 / R	R-SU4 / P	R-SU4 / F
SRIB2020-3	0.61	0.38	0.46	0.51	0.21	0.29
SRIB2020-2	0.60	0.38	0.46	0.51	0.21	0.29
MUSE	0.47	0.37	0.41	0.37	0.20	0.25
SUMTO-3	0.41	0.40	0.39	0.35	0.22	0.26
SUMTO-1	0.41	0.39	0.39	0.33	0.22	0.25
HULAT-1	0.44	0.36	0.39	0.46	0.19	0.26
SUMTO-2	0.40	0.38	0.38	0.34	0.21	0.25
FORTIA-1	0.40	0.40	0.38	0.34	0.33	0.32
AMEX-ENSEMBLE	0.41	0.37	0.38	0.33	0.19	0.24
AMEX-BILSTM	0.40	0.36	0.37	0.32	0.19	0.23
HULAT-2	0.39	0.36	0.36	0.43	0.17	0.24
FORTIA-2	0.37	0.37	0.36	0.30	0.31	0.29
FORTIA-3	0.34	0.34	0.33	0.26	0.27	0.25
CIST-BUPT-3	0.32	0.35	0.33	0.35	0.21	0.25
SUMSUM-BASE	0.33	0.35	0.32	0.44	0.24	0.29
CIST-BUPT-2	0.31	0.35	0.32	0.33	0.20	0.24
SUMSUM-BERT	0.30	0.39	0.32	0.41	0.27	0.30
KG-SUMMAR-NN	0.39	0.28	0.32	0.46	0.17	0.24
KG-SUMMAR-S-LSTM	0.34	0.31	0.32	0.42	0.18	0.25
CIST-BUPT-1	0.29	0.36	0.32	0.32	0.19	0.23
SUMSUM-1	0.30	0.38	0.31	0.40	0.25	0.28
KG-SUMMAR-SVM	0.34	0.30	0.31	0.41	0.19	0.25
AMEX-TEXTRANK	0.25	0.24	0.24	0.25	0.11	0.14
SRIB2020-1	0.21	0.25	0.22	0.17	0.15	0.15
SCE	0.22	0.29	0.22	0.21	0.16	0.16
LEXRANK	0.21	0.26	0.22	0.25	0.12	0.14
TEXTRANK	0.24	0.20	0.21	0.30	0.05	0.08
POLY	0.26	0.18	0.20	0.21	0.11	0.13

Table 5: ROUGE-L and ROUGE-SU4 Recall, Precision and F-measure scores

References

Abdelkrime Aries, Djamel Eddine Zegour, and Khaled Walid Hidouci. 2015. Allsummarizer system at multiling 2015: Multilingual single and multi-document summarization. In *Proceedings of the 16th Annual Meeting of the Special Interest Group on Discourse and Dialogue*, pages 237–244. The Association for Computer Linguistics.

Vasiliki Athanasakou, Mahmoud El-Haj, Paul Rayson, Martin Walker, and Steven Young. 2019. Annual report management commentary articulating strategy and business model: Measurement and impact.

Phyllis B Baxendale. 1958. Machine-made index for technical literature—an experiment. *IBM Journal of research and development*, 2(4):354–361.

Sergey Brin and Lawrence Page. 1998. The anatomy of a large-scale hypertextual web search engine. *Computer Networks and ISDN Systems*.

Eddy Cardinaels, Stephan Hollander, and Brian J White. 2019. Automatic summarization of earnings releases: attributes and effects on investors' judgments. *Review of Accounting Studies*, 24(3):860–890.

Jenny Dawkins. 2004. Corporate responsibility: The communication challenge. *Journal of communication management*.

Paulo Cesar Fernandes de Oliveira, Khurshid Ahmad, and Lee Gillam. 2002. A financial news summarization system based on lexical cohesion. In *Proceedings of the International Conference on Terminology and Knowledge Engineering, Nancy, France*.

Harold P Edmundson. 1969. New methods in automatic extracting. *Journal of the ACM (JACM)*, 16(2):264–285.

Mahmoud El-Haj, Vasiliki Athanasakou, Paul Rayson, Steven Young, and Martin Walker. 2014a. Computer-based analysis of the strategic content of uk annual report narratives. In *2014 American Accounting Association Annual Meeting Global Engagement and Perspectives*.

Mahmoud El-Haj, Paul Rayson, Steven Young, and Martin Walker. 2014b. Detecting document structure in a very large corpus of uk financial reports. *European Language Resources Association (ELRA)*.

Mahmoud El-Haj, Paul Edward Rayson, Steven Eric Young, Martin Walker, Andrew Moore, Vasiliki Athanasakou, and Thomas Schleicher. 2016. Learning tone and attribution for financial text mining. In *The 10th edition of the Language Resources and Evaluation Conference (LREC'16). Portoroz, Slovenia*. European Language Resources Association (ELRA).

Mahmoud El-Haj, Paul Rayson, and Andrew Moore. 2018a. The first financial narrative processing workshop (fnp 2018). *LREC 2018*.

Mahmoud El Haj, Paul Edward Rayson, Paulo Alves, and Steven Eric Young. 2018b. Towards a multilingual financial narrative processing system. In *FNP 2018 Workshot at the 11th edition of the Language Resources and Evaluation Conference (LREC'18)*.

Mahmoud El-Haj, Paul Rayson, Paulo Alves, Carlos Herrero-Zorita, and Steven Young. 2019a. Multilingual financial narrative processing: Analysing annual reports in english, spanish and portuguese. *World Scientific Publishing*.

Mahmoud El-Haj, Paul Rayson, Martin Walker, Steven Young, and Vasiliki Simaki. 2019b. In search of meaning: Lessons, resources and next steps for computational analysis of financial discourse. *Journal of Business Finance & Accounting*, 46(3-4):265–306.

Mahmoud El-Haj, Paul Rayson, Steve Young, Houda Bouamor, and Sira Ferradans. 2019c. Proceedings of the second financial narrative processing workshop (fnp 2019). In *Proceedings of the Second Financial Narrative Processing Workshop (FNP 2019)*.

Mahmoud El-Haj, Paulo Alves, Paul Rayson, Martin Walker, and Steven Young. 2020. Retrieving, classifying and analysing narrative commentary in unstructured (glossy) annual reports published as pdf files. *Accounting and Business Research*, 50(1):6–34.

Mahmoud El-Haj. 2012. *Multi-document Arabic Text Summarisation*. Ph.D. thesis, University of Essex.

Mahmoud El-Haj. 2019. MultiLing 2019: Financial narrative summarisation. In *Proceedings of the Workshop MultiLing 2019: Summarization Across Languages, Genres and Sources*, pages 6–10, Varna, Bulgaria, September. RANLP.

Günes Erkan and Dragomir R Radev. 2004. Lexrank: Graph-based lexical centrality as salience in text summarization. *Journal of artificial intelligence research*, 22:457–479.

Katja Filippova, Mihai Surdeanu, Massimiliano Ciaramita, and Hugo Zaragoza. 2009. Company-oriented extractive summarization of financial news. In *Proceedings of the 12th Conference of the European Chapter of the ACL (EACL 2009)*, pages 246–254.

John Flowerdew and Michaela Mahlberg. 2009. *Lexical cohesion and corpus linguistics*, volume 17. John Benjamins Publishing.

Pascale Fung and Grace Ngai. 2006. One story, one flow: Hidden markov story models for multilingual multidocument summarization. *ACM Transactions on Speech and Language Processing (TSLP)*, 3(2):1–16.

Kavita Ganesan. 2015. Rouge 2.0: Updated and improved measures for evaluation of summarization tasks. *arXiv preprint arXiv:1803.01937*.

George Giannakopoulos, Vangelis Karkaletsis, George Vouros, and Panagiotis Stamatopoulos. 2008. Summarization system evaluation revisited: N-gram graphs. *ACM Transactions on Speech and Language Processing (TSLP)*, 5(3):1–39.

George Giannakopoulos. 2019. Proceedings of the workshop multiling 2019: Summarization across languages, genres and sources. In *Proceedings of the Workshop MultiLing 2019: Summarization Across Languages, Genres and Sources*.

Vishal Gupta and Gurpreet Singh Lehal. 2010. A survey of text summarization extractive techniques. *Journal of emerging technologies in web intelligence*, 2(3):258–268.

Rim Koulali, Mahmoud El-Haj, and Abdelouafi Meziane. 2013. Arabic topic detection using automatic text summarisation. In *2013 ACS International Conference on Computer Systems and Applications (AICCSA)*, pages 1–4. IEEE.

Canasai Kruengkrai and Chuleerat Jaruskulchai. 2003. Generic text summarization using local and global properties of sentences. In *Proceedings IEEE/WIC International Conference on Web Intelligence (WI 2003)*, pages 201–206. IEEE.

Chin-Yew Lin. 2004. Rouge: A package for automatic evaluation of summaries. In *Text summarization branches out*, pages 74–81.

Marina Litvak and Mark Last. 2013. Multilingual single-document summarization with muse. In *Proceedings of the MultiLing 2013 Workshop on Multilingual Multi-document Summarization*, pages 77–81.

Marina Litvak and Natalia Vanetik. 2013a. Mining the gaps: Towards polynomial summarization. In *Proceedings of the Sixth International Joint Conference on Natural Language Processing*, pages 655–660.

Marina Litvak and Natalia Vanetik. 2013b. Multilingual multi-document summarization with poly2. In *Proceedings of the MultiLing 2013 Workshop on Multilingual Multi-document Summarization*, pages 45–49.

Marina Litvak, Mark Last, and Menahem Friedman. 2010. A new approach to improving multilingual summarization using a genetic algorithm. In *Proceedings of the 48th annual meeting of the association for computational linguistics*, pages 927–936.

Marina Litvak, Natalia Vanetik, Mark Last, and Elena Churkin. 2016. Museec: A multilingual text summarization tool. In *Proceedings of ACL-2016 System Demonstrations*, pages 73–78.

Shuhua Liu and Johnny Lindroos. 2006. Experiences from automatic summarization of imf staff reports. *Practical Data Mining: Applications, Experiences and Challenges*, page 43.

Yang Liu. 2019. Fine-tune bert for extractive summarization. *arXiv preprint arXiv:1903.10318*.

Hans Peter Luhn. 1958. The automatic creation of literature abstracts. *IBM Journal of research and development*, 2(2):159–165.

Victoria McCargar. 2004. Statistical approaches to automatic text summarization. *Bulletin of the American Society for Information Science and Technology*, 30(4):21–25.

Rada Mihalcea and Paul Tarau. 2004. Textrank: Bringing order into text. In *Proceedings of the 2004 conference on empirical methods in natural language processing*, pages 404–411.

N Moratanch and S Chitrakala. 2016. A survey on abstractive text summarization. In *2016 International Conference on Circuit, power and computing technologies (ICCPCT)*, pages 1–7. IEEE.

Tatsunori Mori. 2002. Information gain ratio as term weight: the case of summarization of ir results. In *COLING 2002: The 19th International Conference on Computational Linguistics*.

Ramesh Nallapati, Feifei Zhai, and Bowen Zhou. 2017. Summarunner: a recurrent neural network based sequence model for extractive summarization of documents. In *Proceedings of the Thirty-First AAAI Conference on Artificial Intelligence*, pages 3075–3081.

Ani Nenkova and Kathleen McKeown. 2011. *Automatic summarization*. Now Publishers Inc.

Dragomir R Radev, Hongyan Jing, and Malgorzata Budzikowska. 2000. Centroid-based summarization of multiple documents: Clustering, sentence extraction, and evaluation. In *Proceedings of the ANLP/NAACL-2000 Workshop on Summarization*.

Catherine Salzedo, Steven Young, and Mahmoud El-Haj. 2014. Does equity analyst research lack rigor and objectivity? evidence from conference call questions and research notes. In *Evidence from Conference Call Questions and Research Notes (May 5, 2014)*.

Natalia Vanetik and Marina Litvak. 2015. Multilingual summarization with polytope model. In *Proceedings of the 16th Annual Meeting of the Special Interest Group on Discourse and Dialogue*, pages 227–231.

The Financial Document Structure Extraction Shared task: FinToc 2020

Najah-Imane Bentabet
Fortia Financial Solutions
Paris, France
najah-imane.bentabet@fortia.fr

Rémi Juge
Fortia Financial Solutions
Paris, France
remi.juge@fortia.fr

Ismail El Maarouf
Fortia Financial Solutions
Paris, France
ismail.elmaarouf@fortia.fr

Virginie Mouilleron
Fortia Financial Solutions
Paris, France
virginie.mouilleron@fortia.fr

Dialekti Valsamou-Stanislawski
Fortia Financial Solutions
Paris, France
dialekti.valsamou@fortia.fr

Mahmoud El-Haj
Lancaster University
Lancaster, UK
m.el-haj@lancaster.ac.uk

Abstract

This paper presents the FinTOC-2020 Shared Task on structure extraction from financial documents, its participants results and their findings. This shared task was organized as part of The 1st Joint Workshop on Financial Narrative Processing and MultiLing Financial Summarisation (FNP-FNS 2020), held at The 28th International Conference on Computational Linguistics (COLING'2020). This shared task aimed to stimulate research in systems for extracting table-of-contents (TOC) from investment documents (such as financial prospectuses) by detecting the document titles and organizing them hierarchically into a TOC. For the second edition of this shared task, two subtasks were presented to the participants: one with English documents and the other one with French documents.

1 Introduction

The use of PDF electronic documents is recurrent in the financial domain. They are used to share and broadcast information concerning investment strategies, policy and regulation. Even with a great layout, long documents can be hard to navigate, hence, the presence of a table-of-contents (TOC) can provide a valuable assistance for potential investors or regulators by increasing readability and facilitating navigation.

In this shared task, we focus on extracting the TOC of financial prospectuses. In these official documents, investment funds accurately depict their characteristics and investment modalities. Depending on their country of origin, they might be edited with or without a TOC, and they might follow a template as well. But even though their format is regulated, the choice of the text format, the layout, the graphics and tabular presentation of the data is in the hand of the editor. Thus, the TOC is of fundamental importance to tackle sophisticated NLP tasks such as information extraction or question answering on long documents.

In this paper, we report the results and findings of the FinTOC-2020 shared task.[1] The Shared Task was organized as part of The 1st Joint Workshop on Financial Narrative Processing and MultiLing Financial Summarisation (FNP-FNS 2020), to be held at The 28th International Conference on Computational Linguistics (COLING'2020).

A total of 5 teams submitted runs and contributed 5 system description papers. All system description papers are included in the FNP-FNS 2020 workshop proceedings and cited in this report.

---

[1] http://wp.lancs.ac.uk/cfie/fintoc2020/

Proceedings of the 1st Joint Workshop on Financial Narrative Processing and MultiLing Financial Summarisation, pages 13–22
Barcelona, Spain (Online), December 12, 2020.

Figure 1: Random pages from the shared task datasets. We observe a strong variability of complex layouts.

2 Previous Work on TOC extraction

There are mainly two concepts in the literature to approach TOC extraction. The first one parses the hierarchical structure of sections and subsections from the TOC pages embedded in the document. This area of research was mostly motivated by the INEX (Dresevic et al., 2009) and ICDAR competitions (Doucet et al., 2013; Beckers et al., 2010; Nguyen et al., 2018) which aim at extracting the TOC of old and lenghtly OCR-ised books. The documents we target in this shared task are very different: they contain graphical elements, and the text is not displayed to respect a linear reading direction but is optimized to condense information and catch the eye of the reader. Apart from these competitions, we find the methods proposed by El-Haj et al (El Haj et al., 2014; El Haj et al., 2019b; El-Haj et al., 2019a), also based on the parsing of the TOC page.

In the second category of approaches, we find algorithms that detect the titles of the document using learning methods based on layout and text features. The set of titles is then hierarchically ordered according to a predefined rule-based function (Doucet et al., 2013; Liu et al., 2011; Gopinath et al., 2018).

Lately, we find systems that address the hierarchical ordering of the titles as a sequence labelling task, using neural networks models such as Recurrent Neural Networks and LSTM networks (Bentabet et al., 2019).

3 Task Description

As part of the FNP-FNS Workshop, we present a shared task on Financial Document Structure Extraction.

Participants to this shared task were given two sets of financial prospectuses with a wide variety of document structure and length. Their systems had to automatically process the documents to extract their document structure, or TOC. In fact, the two sets were specific to two different subtasks:

- **TOC extraction from French documents**: The set of French documents is rather homogeneous in terms of structure, due to the existence of a common template. However, the words and phrasing can differ from one prospectus to another. Also, French prospectuses never include a TOC page that could be parsed.

- **TOC extraction from English documents**: English prospectuses are characterized by a wide variety of structures as there is no template to constrain their format. Contrary to the French documents, there is always a TOC page but the latter is usually highly incomplete as only the higher level section titles are displayed.

For both sets, we observe that:

- some documents contain specific titles that do not appear in any other document

- the same title in two different documents can have a different position in the hierarchy

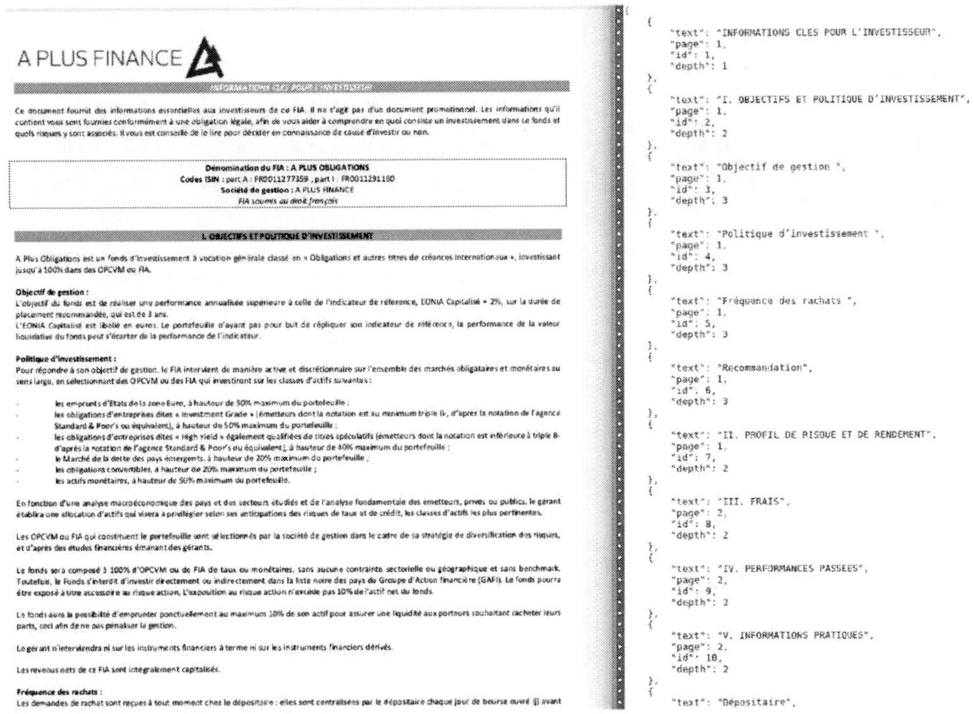

Figure 2: A French prospectus with its JSON annotation file.

- two titles that follow each other can have the same layout but a different position in the TOC

- the font size of a higher-level title can be smaller than the font size of a lower-level one

- and a title can have the exact same layout as its associated paragraph.

For each subtask, all participating teams were provided with a training dataset which included the original PDFs alongside their corresponding JSON file representing the TOC of the document. This JSON represented the TOC by giving the titles, their pages, their depths and their IDs, as shown in Fig. 2. A private test set was used to evaluate the TOCs generated by the participants systems. As stated in Section 2, most of the previous research on TOC generation has focused on short papers such as research publications (*Arxiv* database), or weakly graphical material such as digitalized books. However, the task of extracting the TOC of commercial documents with a complex layout structure in the domain of finance is not much explored in the literature.

4 Shared Task Data

In this section, we discuss the corpus of documents used for the TOC extraction subtasks.

4.1 Corpus annotation

Investment documents can be accessed online in PDF format, and are also made available from asset managers. We compiled a list of 71 French documents, and 72 English documents from Luxembourg, to create the datasets of each subtask. We chose documents with a wide variety of layouts and styles. We provided annotators with the original PDFs and a software that was developed internally to manually annotate the TOC of any PDF document. Once the annotator finishes their annotation task, the software produces a file containing the TOC-entries (title, page number, depth, and id) in a hierarchically structured format.

Techniques et instruments utilisés

Actifs (hors dérivés intégrés)

- Actions

En sa qualité de SICAV éligible au PEA, le portefeuille est investi au minimum à 75 % en titres de sociétés et en parts ou actions d'OPC éligibles au PEA. Les titres de société éligibles au PEA sont ceux dont le siège social est établi dans un État membre de l'Union européenne ou dans un autre Etat partie à l'accord sur l'Espace économique européen (EEE) non membre de l'Union européenne ayant conclu avec la France une convention fiscale contenant une clause administrative en vue de lutter contre la fraude ou l'évasion fiscale.

Les titres sont sélectionnés selon les critères présentés dans la stratégie d'investissement.

La gestion est orientée sur le marché français. Sur opportunité, des investissements peuvent être réalisés sur des valeurs d'autres zones géographiques présentant des perspectives particulièrement attractives.

La sélection des titres s'effectue sans a priori sur la taille des sociétés. La gestion ne s'intéresse pas seulement aux principales capitalisations, même si les grandes capitalisations demeurent majoritaires dans le portefeuille. Le poids accordé aux grandes capitalisations par rapport aux capitalisations plus petites n'est pas figé, il varie en fonction des opportunités de marché et des valorisations relatives entre les différents titres.

- Actions ou parts d'autres placements collectifs de droit français ou d'autres OPCVM, FIA ou fonds d'investissement de droit étranger

La SICAV peut investir jusqu'à 50 % de son actif en parts ou actions d'OPCVM français ou européens ou de fonds d'investissement à vocation générale de droit français, dans des actions ou parts de fonds de capital investissement, d'OPC investissant plus de 10 % en parts ou actions d'un autre véhicule de gestion collective, d'OPC nourriciers, de fonds professionnels à vocation générale, de fonds professionnels spécialisés, de fonds d'investissement constitués sur le fondement d'un droit étranger répondant aux critères prévus aux articles R214-32-42 ou R214-13 du Code monétaire et financier ou de l'article 422-95 du Règlement général de l'AMF, ainsi que des parts ou actions de fonds de fonds alternatifs.

Les OPC sont sélectionnés afin de respecter la politique de gestion ci-dessus présentée.

Afin d'augmenter l'exposition actions ou taux, la SICAV se réserve également la possibilité d'investir dans des OPC indiciels cotés (ETF ou trackers[1]).

La SICAV se réserve la possibilité d'acquérir des parts ou actions d'OPC érés par LA BANQUE POSTALE ASSET MANAGEMENT ou une société liée.

La sélection d'OPCVM et de fonds d'investissement non gérés par LA BANQUE POSTALE ASSET MANAGEMENT ou une société liée repose sur une analyse quantitative des performances passées ainsi que sur une analyse qualitative de leurs processus d'investissement.

Figure 3: In this example, we can see that the titles tagged in green have the same style as the plain text of their paragraphs. Only the indentation is insightful to detect them.

Each annotator was asked to:

1. Identify the title: Locate a title inside the PDF document.

2. Associate the entry level in the TOC: Every title is tagged with an integer representing the depth of the title in the TOC tree. The depth ranges from 1 to 10.

3. Tag the next title.

Each document was annotated independently by two people and a third person would review the annotations to resolve possible conflicts. For each dataset, the agreement scores between annotators are depicted in Table 1 and Table 2. We can observe high agreement scores, allowing us to be confident enough about the quality of our datasets.

	Xerox F1	Inex08 F1
tagger 1 & tagger 2	89.8%	77.0%
tagger 1 & reviewer	92.1%	82.8%
tagger 2 & reviewer	90.1%	79.6%

Table 1: Agreement scores between different annotators of the French investment document dataset (71 documents).

Annotation Challenge: Title identification Investment prospectuses are commercial documents whose complex layout is optimized to highlight specific information such that a potential investor can identify it

	Xerox F1	Inex08 F1
tagger 1 & tagger 2	87.7%	82.4%
tagger 1 & reviewer	95.6%	91.6%
tagger 2 & reviewer	91.8%	90.0 %

Table 2: Agreement scores between different annotators on a validation set of 62 documents from the English investment document dataset (79 documents).

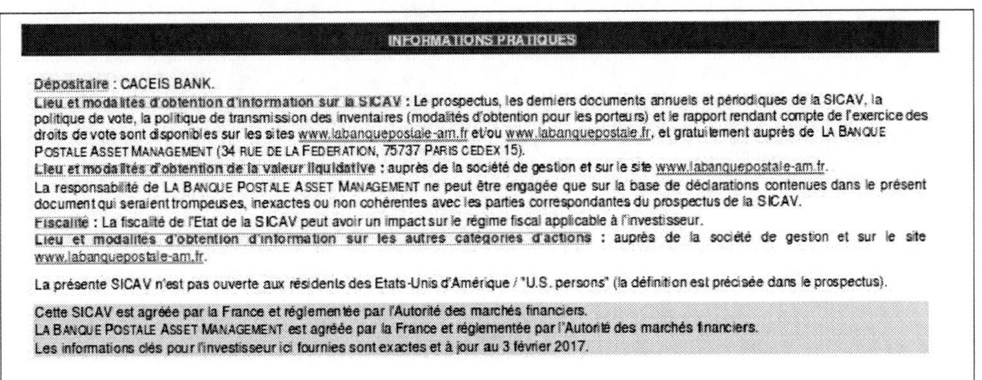

Figure 4: In this second example, the identification of titles tagged in light blue is not evident because they might be followed by plain text in the same line.

quickly. Hence, annotating a title and its level in the TOC hierarchy is a difficult task as one cannot rely on the visual appearance of the title to do so. Some examples can be observed in Fig. 3 and Fig. 4.

Annotation Challenge: Tagging PDF documents. The annotation of PDF documents is not an easy task since they are meant to be displayed. The tool we used for the annotations allows the annotators to directly tag on the PDF, however, the text selection relies on the HTML encoding of the PDF, where the text might slightly differ from what is actually displayed. For instance, it is possible that a piece of text is impossible to select if it is from an image. It is also possible that the tagged text has additional or missing characters.

4.2 Corpus Description

In the following, we provide an analysis of the data used for the shared task.

We simplified greatly the format of the annotation files compared to the first edition of the shared task (Juge et al., 2019). Instead of the XML format inherited from the Structure Extraction Competition (SEC) (Doucet et al., 2013) that implicitly encodes the title level, we used a simple JSON file containing a list of entries, where each entry has the following information: textual content, id, level, page number. An example of a JSON extract is provided in Fig. 2. In particular, the title level is explicitly stated. Statistics about levels on the French and English datasets are presented in Table 3.

In addition to the annotation files, the public dataset provided to the participants contained documents in PDF format. The private dataset on which participants were ranked contained documents in PDF format only. The french subtask (respectively the english substask) had 47 (respectively 50) public documents. The rest was kept private for the final ranking.

5   Participants and Systems

A total of 50 teams registered in the shared task all from different institutions. Eventually, 5 teams participated and submitted a paper with the description of their method, see Table 5 for more information about their affiliation. In Table 4, we show the details on the submissions per task. All the participants that submitted a standard run, sent a paper describing their approach as well.

	French dataset	English dataset
number of documents	71	72
average number of pages	28	91
level 1 (% of titles)	2%	5%
level 2 (% of titles)	11%	21%
level 3 (% of titles)	29%	30%
level 4 (% of titles)	24%	25%
level 5 (% of titles)	21%	11%
level 6 (% of titles)	13%	4%
level 7 (% of titles)	0%	2%
level 8 (% of titles)	0%	1%
level 9 (% of titles)	0%	1%
level 10 (% of titles)	0%	0%

Table 3: Statistics on the subtasks datasets.

	# teams	# std runs
French subtask	4	6
English subtask	5	7
papers	5	-

Table 4: Statistics on the participation on French and English subtasks

Participating teams explored and implemented a wide variety of techniques and features. In this section, we give a brief description of each system. More details could be found in the description papers published in the proceedings of the FNP-FNS 2020 Workshop.

AMEX-AI Labs (Premi et al., 2020):   This team participated in the English subtask only. Several pre-processing steps, including headers and footers removal, are performed to segment the textual content of the documents into elements that are classified later as titles and non-titles. They separately trained two title detectors, one on an external dataset, and the other on the English dataset provided by the FinTOC2020 shared task. Then, they concatenated both models to form their final title detector.

Daniel (Giguet et al., 2020):   Unlike the other teams, this team focused on removing tables to clean the textual content of the documents. They detected titles by looking for numbered lines, leveraging stylistic properties, and checking the existence of a line in the list of training titles. For the hierarchy part, they clustered the titles previously detected to infer their hierarchical level using stylistic features. It is interesting to see that this approach ranked well on the English dataset but not so well on the French dataset.

DNLP (Kosmajac et al., 2020):   The DNLP team participated in both subtasks. They used *tesseract* an open-source OCR tool to extract the text regions. Then, they defined a set of features to use with

Team	Affiliation	Tasks
AMEX-AI Labs (Premi et al., 2020)	American Express AI Labs, Bangalore	E
Daniel (Giguet et al., 2020)	STIH, Sorbonne Univeristy	F and E
DNLP (Kosmajac et al., 2020)	Dalhousie University	F and E
Taxy.io (Haase and Kirchhoff, 2020)	Taxy.io	F and E
UWB (Hercig and Král, 2020)	University of West Bohemia	F and E

Table 5: List of the 5 teams that participated in Subtasks of the FinTOC2020 Shared Task. "F" refers to the French substask and "E" refers to the English subtask

three different algorithms: linear regression, random forest and SVM. For both title detection and TOC extraction steps, their best performing models are random forest models.

Taxy.io (Haase and Kirchhoff, 2020): The Taxy.io team participated in both subtasks, with a multilingual pipeline. They used an unsupervised learning approach to tackle text block detection. They first run a DBSCAN clustering on pages characters to extract features and then run a second DBSCAN clustering to identify the text blocks. Finally, they classify each text block, represented by features from the previous step plus text features extracted with a multilingual BERT model.

UWB (Hercig and Král, 2020): UWB team participated in both subtasks but contributed to the title detection part only. They state title detection as a binary classification on text segments, for which they use a Maximum entropy classifier, on top of a diverse set of features including orthographic characters and character n-grams.

6 Results and Discussion

Evaluation Metric Since both subtasks tackle the same problem but on different corpora, we used the same evaluation metric.

For the TOC generation part, we adapted the metrics proposed by the Structure Extraction Competition (SEC) held at ICDAR 2013 (Doucet et al., 2013): we adapted the script, replaced the customized Levenshtein distance specifically designed for SEC by a standard Levenshtein distance whose edit cost is 1 in all cases, and removed the constraint on first and last 5 characters.

The final ranking is based on the harmonic mean between *Inex F1 score* and *Inex level accuracy*. In the calculation of the *Inex F1 score*, correct entries in the predicted TOC are those which match the title of an entry in the groundtruth TOC *and* have the same page number as this entry. The *Inex level accuracy* evaluates the hierarchy of the predicted TOC. If we denote by E_{ok} an entry in the predicted TOC with a correct page number, and by E'_{ok} an entry in the predicted TOC with a correct page number *and* a correct hierarchical level, then the Inex level accuracy is:

$$\frac{\sum E'_{ok}}{\sum E_{ok}}$$

We also provided scores for the title detection part separately: we used the F1 score, and considered as correct entries the predicted entries which match the titles of groudtruth entries according to the standard Levenshtein distance.

For both parts, the threshold on the Levenshtein *score* was set to 0.85^2. Moreover, the Inex scores and title F1 score are calculated for each document and then averaged over the documents of the private set to produce two performance figures per team submission: one for TOC extraction, and another for title detection (TD).

Baseline For comparison purposes, we implemented a simple baseline TOC extractor consisting of:
- extracting textual content from the PDF documents using `pdftohtml` utility from Poppler library[3]
- assigning groundtruth labels (title or non-title) to text segments by fuzzy string matching with the annotations
- vectorizing text segments into one-dimensional vectors of length 3 encoding the following features: is_bold, is_italic, is_all_capitalized
- training a SVM on the obtained dataset
- assigning to a predicted title the most frequent hierarchy level found in the training set

Table 6 (respectively Table 7) reports the results obtained by the participants and the baseline on TOC extraction from French documents (respectively English documents).

---

[2]The script implementing these metrics can be found here: `https://drive.google.com/file/d/1TzsS2F79af8U5F5ivDEsc9ezUTX97aeW/view?usp=sharing`

[3]see https://poppler.freedesktop.org/

Team	TD
UWB	**0.81**
Taxy.io	0.69
Daniel 1	0.66
DNLP	0.64
Daniel 2	0.64
Daniel 3	0.64
Baseline	0.57

Team	TOC
DNLP	**0.37**
taxy.io	0.32
Baseline	0.32
Daniel 1	0.22
Daniel 2	0.22
Daniel 3	0.20

Table 6: Results obtained by the participants for the first FinTOC2020 subtask : TOC extraction from French documents. The title detection (TD) ranking is based on F1-score, while the Table-Of-Content (TOC) ranking is based on the harmonic mean between Inex F1 score and Inex level accuracy

Team	TD
Amex 1	**0.79**
UWB	0.77
Daniel 1	0.69
Daniel 3	0.63
Daniel 2	0.62
DNLP	0.59
Taxy.io	0.55
Baseline	0.19

Team	TOC
DNLP	**0.34**
Daniel 3	0.28
Daniel 2	0.28
Daniel 1	0.26
taxy.io	0.24
Amex 1	0.23
Amex 2	0.23
Baseline	0.18

Table 7: Results obtained by the participants for the second FinTOC2020 subtask : TOC extraction from English documents. The title detection (TD) ranking is based on F1-score, while the Table-Of-Content (TOC) ranking is based on the harmonic mean between Inex F1 score and Inex level accuracy

Discussion. Title detection is the easiest problem encountered in this competition. All the submitted models show a high increase of performance from the baseline. In addition, the numbers show that it is slightly easier to detect titles from French investment documents than it is from English investment documents. Clearly, supervised methods from UWB, Taxy.io, and AMEX-AI Labs perform better than heuristic methods such as the one proposed by team Daniel. Nevertheless, the supervised multi-lingual model from team Taxy.io performed well on the French documents only.

Concerning TOC extraction on French documents, we observe that the baseline, which naively assigns the most frequent label found in the training set, performs as well as the BERT model used by team Taxy.io, and that the unsupervised approach from team Daniel scores worse than the baseline. This probably indicates that the number of training documents provided is not enough for the diversity encountered among these documents, and that TOC extraction problem on this data is hard. TOC extaction on the English documents is an even harder task as can be inferred from the figures in Table 7. However, team DNLP stands out from the rest of the participants with a 6% to 11% increase in performance.

7 Conclusions

In this paper we presented the setup and results for the Financial Document Structure Extraction task (FinToc) 2020, organized as the 1st Joint Workshop on Financial Narrative Processing and MultiLing Financial Summarisation (FNP-FNS 2020) collocated with the 28th International Conference on Computational Linguistics(COLING'2020). A total of 50 teams registered and 5 teams participated in the shared task with a wide variety of techniques. All participating teams contributed with a paper describing their system.

This edition introduced the community to a new dataset, composed of French investment documents, and annotated for the TOC extraction problem. This dataset supplements previously released datasets for English (Juge et al., 2019). TOC extraction for PDF documents is a realistic problem in everyday applications which explain the interest from and participation of both public universities and profit organizations.

Acknowledgments

We would like to thank our dedicated annotators who contributed to the building of the corpora used in this Shared Task: Anais Koptient, Aouataf Djillani, and Lidia Duarte, and Fortia's DLA team.

References

Thomas Beckers, Patrice Bellot, Gianluca Demartini, Ludovic Denoyer, Christopher M. De Vries, Antoine Doucet, Khairun Nisa Fachry, Norbert Fuhr, Patrick Gallinari, Shlomo Geva, Wei-Che Huang, Tereza Iofciu, Jaap Kamps, Gabriella Kazai, Marijn Koolen, Sangeetha Kutty, Monica Landoni, Miro Lehtonen, Véronique Moriceau, Richi Nayak, Ragnar Nordlie, Nils Pharo, Eric Sanjuan, Ralf Schenkel, Xavier Tannier, Martin Theobald, James A. Thom, Andrew Trotman, and Arjen P. De Vries. 2010. Report on INEX 2009. *Sigir Forum*, 44(1):38–57, June. Article disponible en ligne : http://www.cs.otago.ac.nz/homepages/andrew/papers/2010-4.pdf.

Najah-Imane Bentabet, Rémi Juge, and Sira Ferradans. 2019. Table-of-contents generation on contemporary documents. In *Proceedings of ICDAR 2019*.

Antoine Doucet, Gabriella Kazai, Sebastian Colutto, and Günter Mühlberger. 2013. Icdar 2013 competition on book structure extraction. In *Document Analysis and Recognition (ICDAR), 2013 12th International Conference on*, pages 1438–1443. IEEE.

Bodin Dresevic, Aleksandar Uzelac, Bogdan Radakovic, and Nikola Todic. 2009. Book layout analysis: Toc structure extraction engine. In Shlomo Geva, Jaap Kamps, and Andrew Trotman, editors, *Advances in Focused Retrieval*, pages 164–171, Berlin, Heidelberg. Springer Berlin Heidelberg.

Mahmoud El Haj, Paul Rayson, Steven Young, and Martin Walker, 2014. *Detecting document structure in a very large corpus of UK financial reports*. LREC'14 Ninth International Conference on Language Resources and Evaluation. Proceedings of the Ninth International Conference on Language Resources and Evaluation (LREC-2014) . European Language Resources Association (ELRA), Reykjavik, Iceland, pp. 1335-1338.

Mahmoud El-Haj, Paulo Alves, Paul Rayson, Martin Walker, and Steven Young. 2019a. Retrieving, classifying and analysing narrative commentary in unstructured (glossy) annual reports published as pdf files. *Accounting and Business Research*, pages 1–29.

Mahmoud El Haj, Paul Edward Rayson, Steven Eric Young, Paulo Alves, and Carlos Herrero Zorita, 2019b. *Multilingual Financial Narrative Processing: Analysing Annual Reports in English, Spanish and Portuguese*. World Scientific Publishing, 2.

Emmanuel Giguet, Gael Lejeune, , and Jean-Baptiste Tanguy. 2020. Daniel@fintoc'2 shared task: Title detection and structure extraction. In *The 1st Joint Workshop on Financial Narrative Processing and MultiLing Financial Summarisation of COLING 2020*.

Abhijith Athreya Mysore Gopinath, Shomir Wilson, and Norman Sadeh. 2018. Supervised and unsupervised methods for robust separation of section titles and prose text in web documents. In *Proceedings of the 2018 Conference on Empirical Methods in Natural Language Processing*, pages 850–855.

Frederic Haase and Steffen Kirchhoff. 2020. Taxy.io@fintoc'2: Multilingual document structure extraction using transfer learning. In *The 1st Joint Workshop on Financial Narrative Processing and MultiLing Financial Summarisation of COLING 2020*.

Tomas Hercig and Pavel Král. 2020. Uwb@fintoc-2020 shared task: Financial document title detection. In *The 1st Joint Workshop on Financial Narrative Processing and MultiLing Financial Summarisation of COLING 2020*.

Remi Juge, Imane Bentabet, and Sira Ferradans. 2019. The FinTOC-2019 shared task: Financial document structure extraction. In *Proceedings of the Second Financial Narrative Processing Workshop (FNP 2019)*, pages 51–57, Turku, Finland, September. Linköping University Electronic Press.

Dijana Kosmajac, Stacey Taylor, and Mozhgan Saeidi. 2020. Table of contents detection in financial documents. In *The 1st Joint Workshop on Financial Narrative Processing and MultiLing Financial Summarisation of COLING 2020*.

Caihua Liu, Jiajun Chen, Xiaofeng Zhang, Jie Liu, and Yalou Huang. 2011. Toc structure extraction from ocr-ed books. In *International Workshop of the Initiative for the Evaluation of XML Retrieval*, pages 98–108. Springer.

Thi Tuyet Hai Nguyen, Antoine Doucet, and Mickael Coustaty. 2018. Enhancing table of contents extraction by system aggregation. In *Proceedings of the International Conference on Document Analysis and Recognition, ICDAR*.

Dhruv Premi, Amogh Badugu, and Himanshu Sharad Bhatt. 2020. Amex-ai-labs: Investigating transfer learning for title detection in table of contents generation. In *The 1st Joint Workshop on Financial Narrative Processing and MultiLing Financial Summarisation of COLING 2020*.

Financial Document Causality Detection Shared Task (FinCausal 2020)

Dominique Mariko[1]   Hanna Abi-Akl [1]   Estelle Labidurie[1]

Stéphane Durfort[1]   Hugues de Mazancourt[1]   Mahmoud El-Haj[2]

[1]YseopLab, FR, [2]Lancaster University, UK,
[1]lab@yseop.com, [2]m.el-haj@lancaster.ac.uk

Abstract

We present the FinCausal 2020 Shared Task on Causality Detection in Financial Documents and the associated FinCausal dataset, and discuss the participating systems and results. Two sub-tasks are proposed: a binary classification task (Task 1) and a relation extraction task (Task 2). A total of 16 teams submitted runs across the two Tasks and 13 of them contributed with a system description paper. This workshop is associated to the Joint Workshop on Financial Narrative Processing and MultiLing Financial Summarisation (FNP-FNS 2020[1]), held at The 28th International Conference on Computational Linguistics (COLING'2020[2]), Barcelona, Spain on September 12, 2020.

1 Introduction

In an effort to automatically interpret the semantics of written languages, the analysis and understanding of causal relationships between facts stand as a key element. A major difficulty regarding automation is that causality can be expressed using many different syntactic patterns as well as contrasted semantic representations. This difficulty is reinforced by the existence of both explicit and implicit cause-effect links. Early works in this field, such as (Khoo et al, 1998), aim at detecting causal relations using linguistic patterns. However, these applications are often restricted to a specific domain, limited to explicit causal relationships only (causal links, causative verbs, resultative constructions, conditionals and causative adverbs and adjectives), and do not take into account the ambiguities of the connectors. The semi-automatic method developed by (Girju and Moldovan, 2002) goes a step further by creating lexico-syntactic patterns based on WordNet semantic relations between nouns, then using semantics constraints to test ambiguous causal relations. Despite better results, the exclusive use of linguistic patterns prevents a fully efficient coverage of all cause-effect links. Consequently, various machine learning techniques were tested for this task. (Chang and Choi, 2004) developed Naive Bayes causality extraction models based on lexical pair probability and cue phrase probability. By focusing on the dynamics of causal relationships, the system PREPOST developed by (Sil et al., 2010) stands as a viable system to detect causal relationships between one event and a consequent state of this event, training a classifier to identify events' preconditions and/or postconditions. In parallel, hybrid methods were also developed such as the expanded semantic parsing of (CMU, 2018). This system combines an SCL approach, pattern-based methods and a neural network architecture, offering more flexibility than exclusive pattern based approaches. Overall, the management of linguistic ambiguities as well as the existence of implicit connections appear to be the main brakes in the identification and extraction of causal relationships.

In this paper, we present the FinCausal Corpus and the associated featured Tasks, as a contribution to the research effort addressing implicit and multiple causalities detection automation in financial documents. All the datasets created for this shared task are publicly available to support further research on Causality modelling[3], and the detailed annotation scheme is provided in the Appendix A. Next, Sec-

---

[1]http://wp.lancs.ac.uk/cfie/fnp2020/
[2]https://coling2020.org
[3]https://competitions.codalab.org/competitions/25340

Proceedings of the 1st Joint Workshop on Financial Narrative Processing and MultiLing Financial Summarisation, pages 23–32
Barcelona, Spain (Online), December 12, 2020.

tion 2 describes the FinCausal Corpus and Section 3 presents the Tasks. Section 4 provides the baseline proposed to participants and details their results, with a high-level description of the approaches they adopted. Finally, Section 5 concludes this report and discusses some future directions.

2 FinCausal Corpus

The data are extracted from a corpus of 2019 financial news provided by Qwam, collected on 14.000 economics and finance websites. The original raw corpus is an ensemble of HTML pages corresponding to daily information retrieval from financial news feed. These news mostly inform on the 2019 financial landscape, but can also contain information related to politics, micro economics or other topic considered relevant for finance information. Data are released under the CC0 License[4].

All collected HTML files were initially split into sentences according to their punctuation, then were grouped into text sections of 1 to 3 sentences after the data annotation process has been completed. Below are the principle global metrics gathered during the annotation process. The metrics are defined with respect to the annotation scheme.

For consistency in our references, we refer to a **file** as the original document to process, a **text section** as a multi-sentenced text string (1 to 3 sentences that may or may not contain causality) and a **chunk** as a substring (consisting either of a part of a sentence, a whole sentence or multiple sentences) within a text section. We also retain statistics related to the main tags used in our annotation scheme during the preparation of the datasets. These tags are defined as follows:

- **Cause**: Indicates the presence of causality

- **QFact**: Qualifies the causal chunk as quantitative (i.e., containing numerical entities like amounts)

- **Fact**: Qualifies the causal chunk as non-quantitative

- **Discard/Remove**: Indicates text that is not retained for the final datasets (non financial texts)

In addition, metrics related to **fact alignment** (i.e., trimming sentences according to preset priority rules in the annotation scheme) are also included to consistently reflect the preprocessing carried out at this step. All statistics are provided for the 3 datasets provided to participants: Trial, Practice, Evaluation as well as global statistics to present a general outlook on the overall annotation phase. The resulting statistics are collected in Table 1.

Metric	Trial	Practice	Evaluation	Global
Total annotated files	695	832	1878	3405
Total sentences in files before definition of text sections	25326	29381	74951	129658
Total **Cause** tags in files	657	1128	2244	4029
Total **QFact** tags in files	937	1824	2589	5350
Total **Fact** tags in files	449	999	2514	3962
Total **Discard/Remove** tags in files	1030	612	2462	4104
Total files in review for **fact alignment**	375	560	705	1640
Total files modified in **fact alignment**	116	182	259	557
Average causalities per file	2.73	3.06	2.98	2.92
Average offset of 2nd sentence in text sections	137	139	141	139
Average offset of 3rd sentence in text sections	270	277	282	276
Percentage of multi-sentenced text sections	59.23	51.02	37.52	49.26

Table 1: Global Distribution of Annotated files

After fact alignment and inter annotator agreement (see Appendix A), a Trial and Training sets with Gold annotations were released, along with a blind Evaluation set for systems evaluation.

---

[4]https://creativecommons.org/publicdomain/zero/1.0/deed.en

3 Tasks

Both substaks are intented as a pipeline. The first one aims at detecting if a text section contains a causal scheme (as defined in Appendix A.1), the second one aims at identifying cause and effect in a causal text section. Participants were allowed to concatenate and split the Trial and Practice datasets as they saw fit to train their system.

3.1 Task1

Task 1 is a binary classification task. The dataset consists of a sample of text sections labeled with 1 if the text section is considered containing a causal relation, 0 otherwise. The dataset is by nature unbalanced, as to reflect the proportion of causal sentences extracted from the original news, following the distribution displayed in Table 2.

Metric	Trial	Practice	Evaluation	Global
Total number of text sections	8580	13478	7386	29444
Total number of causal text sections	569	1010	567	2136
Percentage of causal text sections	6.63	7.49	7.68	7.24

Table 2: Task 1 Distribution

The trial and practice samples were provided to participants as csv files with headers *Index; Text; Gold*.

- Index: ID of the text section. Is a concatenation of [file increment . text section index]

- Text: Text section extracted from a 2019 news article

- Gold: Gold Label provided from manual annotation

Index	Text	Gold
23.00005	Electric vehicle manufacturers, components for the vehicles, batteries and producers for charging infrastructure who invest over Rs 50 crore and create at least 50 jobs stand eligible for total SGST (State GST) refund on their sales till end of calendar year 2030.	0
23.00006	In case where SGST refund is not applicable, the state is offering a 15% capital subsidy on investments made in Tamil Nadu till end of 2025.	1

Table 3: Two examples from FinCausal Task 1 Corpus - Practice dataset

3.2 Task2

The purpose of this task is to extract, in provided text sections, the chunks identifying the causal sequences and the chunks describing the effects. The text sections correspond to the ones labeled as 1 in the Task 1 datasets, except in the blind Evaluation set.

The trial and practice samples were provided to participants as csv files with headers: *Index; Text; Cause; Effect*

- Index: ID of the text section. Is a concatenation of [file increment . text section index]

- Text: Text section extracted from a 2019 news article

- Cause: Chunk referencing the cause of an event (event or related object included)

- Effect: Chunk referencing the effect of the cause

Average statistics on the causes and effects chunks detected in the causal text sections are provided in Table 4. As explained in section 3, complex causal chains are considered during the annotation process, leading to one text section possibly containing multiple causes or effects.

Metric	Trial	Practice	Evaluation	Global Average
Average character length of causal chunks	113.73	109.13	112.48	111.78
Average character length of effect chunks	107.79	104.78	99.66	104.08
Total number of text sections	641	1109	638	796
Total number of unicausal text sections	500	913	452	621.67
Total number of multicausal text sections	141	196	186	174.33

Table 4: Task 2 Distribution

Index	Text	Cause	Effect
0009.00052.1	Things got worse when the Wall came down. GDP fell 20% between 1988 and 1993. There were suddenly hundreds of thousands of unemployed in a country that, under Communism, had had full employment.	Things got worse when the Wall came down.	GDP fell 20% between 1988 and 1993.
0009.00052.2	Things got worse when the Wall came down. GDP fell 20% between 1988 and 1993. There were suddenly hundreds of thousands of unemployed in a country that, under Communism, had had full employment.	Things got worse when the Wall came down.	There were suddenly hundreds of thousands of unemployed in a country that, under Communism, had had full employment.
23.00006	In case where SGST refund is not applicable, the state is offering a 15% capital subsidy on investments made in Tamil Nadu till end of 2025.	In case where SGST refund is not applicable	the state is offering a 15% capital subsidy on investments made in Tamil Nadu till end of 2025

Table 5: Three examples from FinCausal Task 2 Corpus - Practice dataset

4   Evaluation

A baseline was provided on the trial samples for both Tasks 1 and 2[5]. Participating systems were ranked on blind Evaluation datasets based on a weighted F1 score, recall, precision for Task 1, plus an additional Exact Match for Task 2. Regarding official ranking, weighted metrics from the scikit-learn package[6] were used for both Tasks, and the official evaluation script is available on Github[7]. Participating teams were allowed to submit as many runs as they wished, while only their highest score was withheld to represent them during evaluation. In addition, they were proposed to enhance their system in a post-evaluation phase[8]. Only the scores validated during the evaluation phase of the competition are displayed below. Amongst the 13 participating teams, six choose to address Tasks 1 and 2 and one (ProsperAMnet) proposed an integrated pipeline for both. Details on the methods and features used by different systems are provided in Table 8 for both Tasks. Noticeably, 7 teams plan to release the code associated to their system publicly.

4.1   Task1

Results for participating teams are provided in Table 6. Last line displays the baseline that had been provided for the task. The baseline was computed using the BERT-base-uncased language model[9] and fine tuned on the Task data using the Hugging Face transformers library (Wolf et al. ., 2019)[10], on a GeForce GTX 1070 8Gb RAM GPU. For Task 1, 6 participants out of 10 took advantage of large Transformers architectures (Vaswani et al. ., 2017) and fine-tuned their systems using the same library as the baseline. Four used Ensemble strategies to aggregate their results and enhance the robustness of their model. Additional strategies such as Data Augmentation and Oversampling are also proposed to work around the unbalanced nature of the data. The best result in terms of weighted-averaged F1-score

---

[5]https://github.com/yseop/YseopLab/tree/develop/FNP_2020_FinCausal/baseline
[6]https://scikit-learn.org/stable/modules/model_evaluation.html#multiclass-and-multilabel-classification
[7]https://github.com/yseop/YseopLab/tree/develop/FNP_2020_FinCausal/scoring
[8]https://competitions.codalab.org/competitions/25340
[9]https://huggingface.co/bert-base-multilingual-uncased
[10]https://huggingface.co/transformers/model_doc/bert.html

is achieved by the winning team LIORI (97.75%), closely followed by UPB and ProsperAMNet with F1 scores of 97.55% and 97.23%, respectively. The top five systems all leveraged Transformers architectures with associated language models features, evaluating at least on a fine-tuned BERT-base model and providing a comparison with similar models (BERT-large, RoBERTa, and specialized BERT such as FinBERT). The top 2 systems used Ensemble methods (See Table 8). BERT-like systems weighted-F1 ratings are in range [97.75 , 95.78], whereas systems using more traditional Machine Learning models have scores in range [95.00 , 93.09], including systems using BERT-like embeddings in their processing.

Team	F1 Score	Recall	Precision
LIORI	97.75 (1)	97.77 (1)	97.73 (1)
UPB	97.55 (2)	97.59 (2)	97.53 (2)
ProsperAMnet	97.23 (3)	97.20 (3)	97.28 (3)
FiNLP	96.99 (4)	97.03 (4)	96.96 (4)
DOMINO	96.12 (5)	96.06 (5)	96.19 (5)
IIT_kgp	95.78 (6)	95.83 (6)	95.74 (6)
LangResearchLab_NC	95.00 (7)	94.92 (7)	95.08 (7)
NITK NLP	94.35 (8)	94.87 (8)	94.32 (8)
fraunhofer_iais	94.29 (9)	94.76 (9)	94.20 (9)
ISIKUN	93.09 (10)	94.33 (10)	93.89 (10)
baseline	95.23	95.21	95.26

Table 6: Task 1 Results

4.2 Task2

Results for Task 2 are provided in Table 7. Last line displays the baseline that has been provided for Task 2, computed with a CRF model using the pycrfsuite package[11]. One of the challenge of this task was to rebuilt the correct span of causal chunks, according to the annotation scheme. The baseline has been kept deliberately low as is does not take this specific problem into account, nor does it focuses on parameter-tuning strategies, though tuning examples are proposed with the code baseline. All participants decided for sequence labelling strategies and used specific penalization methods and/or heuristics to work around the chunks reconstitution problem. The best performer in this subtask (NTUNLP) uses a BERT-CRF system and a Viterbi decoder for span optimization, achieving (94.72%) weighted F1, closely followed by a BERT-SQUAD augmented system with heuristics for span achieving 94.66% F1 (Gbe).

Team	F1 Score	Recall	Precision	Exact match
NTUNLPL	94.72 (1)	94.70 (1)	94.79 (1)	82.45 (1)
GBe	94.66 (2)	94.66 (2)	94.67 (2)	73.67 (2)
ProsperAMnet	83.71 (3)	83.63 (3)	83.92 (3)	70.38 (4)
LIORI	82.60 (4)	82.80 (4)	82.48 (4)	70.53 (3)
DOMINO	79.60 (5)	78.90 (5)	81.90 (5)	00.00 (7)
fraunhofer_iais	76.00 (6)	74.89 (7)	79.95 (6)	19.12 (5)
JDD	75.61 (7)	75.57 (6)	75.95 (7)	00.00 (7)
UPB	73.10 (8)	72.14 (8)	75.61 (8)	18.34 (6)
baseline	51.06	51.74	50.99	11.11

Table 7: Task 2 Results

---

[11]https://python-crfsuite.readthedocs.io/en/latest/

Team	F1	Techniques								
		ML	Neural	TF	Ens	AGM	RS	LM	WCS	HS
Task 1										
LIORI	97.75			X	X			X		
UPB	97.55			X	X			X		
ProsperAMnet	97.23			X				X		
FiNLP	96.99			X	X	X	X	X		
DOMINO	96.12			X				X		
IIT_kgp	95.78			X				X		
LangResearchLab_NC	95.00		X				X	X	X	
NITK NLP	94.35	X							X	
fraunhofer_iais	94.29	X				X			X	
ISIKUN	93.09	X							X	
Task 2										
NTUNLPL	94.72	X		X				X	X	
GBe	94.66			X				X		X
ProsperAMnet	83.71			X				X		
LIORI	82.60			X				X		
DOMINO	79.60			X				X		X
fraunhofer_iais	76.00	X	X					X		X
JDD	75.61	X	X					X	X	
UPB	73.10	X						X		X

Table 8: Approaches adopted by the participating teams in Tasks 1 and 2. ML refers to any non-neural machine learning technique such as XGBoost, SVM, etc. Neural refers to any neural network architecture such as BILSTM, CNN, GRUs,etc, except Transformers. TF refers to Transformers architecture. Ens corresponds to Ensemble Learning method. RS is resampling method. HS implies some heuristics has been used in the final computation, mostly to adapt the span in Task 2. LM refers to any language model embedding features. WCS refers to Word, Character or Syntax based features.

5   Conclusion

In this paper, we present the framework and the results for the FinCausal Shared Task. In addition , we present the new FinCausal dataset built specifically for this shared task. We plan to run similar shared tasks in the near future, possibly with some augmented data, in association with the FNP workshop.

Acknowledgements

We would like to thank our dedicated annotators who contributed to the building the FinCausal Corpus: Yagmur Ozturk, Minh Anh Nguyen, Aurélie Nomblot and Lilia Ait Ouarab, as well as the FNP Committee for their gracious support.

References

Avirup Sil, Fei Huang and Alexander Yates. 2010. *Extracting action and event semantics from web text*. AAAI Fall Symposium: Commonsense Knowledge.

Beth Levin and Malka R. Hovav. 1994. *A Preliminary Analysis of Causative Verbs in English*. Lingua 92, 35-77.

Christopher S.G. Khoo, Jaklin Kornfilt, Sung Hyon Myaeng and Robert N. Oddy. 1998. *Automatic Extraction of cause-effect information from newspaper text without knowledge-based inferencing*. Literary Linguistic Computing 13, 177-186.

Du-Seong Chang and Key-Sun Choi. 2004. *Causal Relation Extraction Using Cue Phrase and Lexical Pair Probabilities*. Natural Language Processing–IJCNLP, 61–70.

Erika Nazaruka. 2019. *Identification of Causal Dependencies by using Natural Language Processing: A Survey.* ENASE 2019.

Jesse Dunietz. 2018. *Annotating and Automatically Tagging Constructions of Causal Language.* Carnegie Mellon University.

Jesse Dunietz, Lori Levin, Jaime Carbonell. 2017. *The BECauSE Corpus 2.0: Annotating Causality and Overlapping Relations.* Proceedings of the 11th Linguistic Annotation Workshop, ACL Anthology 2017.

Nabiha Ashgar. 2016. *Automatic Extraction of Causal Relations from Natural Language Texts: A Comprehensive Survey.* Arxiv 2016.

Roxana Girju and Dan Moldovan. 2002. *Text mining for causal relations.* FLAIRS Conference, 360–364.

Ashish Vaswani, Noam Shazeer, Niki Parmar et al. 2017. *Attention is All you Need.* Advances in Neural Information Processing Systems 30, 5998–6008.

Thomas Wolf, Lysandre Debut, Victor Sanh et al. 2019. *HuggingFace's Transformers: State-of-the-art Natural Language Processing.* Arxiv, abs/1910.03771.

Appendix A. Annotation scheme

In this appendix, we provide detailed information on the concepts guiding the annotation. The annotation process was iterative: Annotations were proposed on a BRAT annotation server[12] by a first annotator then revised by two others until agreement. These agreement sessions were the opportunity to define and iterate on the following annotation scheme.

A.1. Defining causatives

A causal relationship involves the statement of a **cause** and its **effect**, meaning that two events or actors are related to each other with one triggering the other. We focused our annotation on text sections[13] that state causal relationships involving a quantified fact, which was necessary to reduce the complexity of the task. Table 9 displays the terms used in the context of the Shared Task.

FACT	
Empirical Fact	Past event, acknowledged
Process	Concrete event in duration
State of Affairs	In being situation (will become true or false)
Looking Forward Statement	Expectation (often a declaration made by CPY board member)
Hypothesis	Projection based on facts
QUANTIFIED FACT (QFact)	
Explicit	Has a direct connection to an explicit measure
Measurable	Measure is either a quantity or a number that can be precisely identified in a text section
Verifiable	Is a State of Affairs at least

Table 9: Representation of events terminology

In this scheme, an effect can only be a quantified fact. The cause can either be a fact or a quantified fact. The causality between these two elements can be implicit as well as explicitly stated with a triggering linguistic mark also called a connective. The place of these chunks in the text section can vary according to the connective used or simply according to the author's style.

In order to delimit the process, the distance between a cause fact and an effect fact was restricted to **a 3-sentences distance**. In other words, we only annotated a causal relationship when there was a maximal gap of 1 untagged sentence between the two facts. For instance, in the text section <cause>*Previous*

---

[12]https://brat.nlplab.org/installation.html

[13]We are using the term *text section* since it could be a phrase, a sentence as well as a paragraph in which the cause and the effect are split in different sentences. For instance "Selling and marketing expenses decreased to $1,500,000 in 2010. This was primarily attributable to employee-related actions and lower travel costs". However, in order to have a reproducible annotation process, we reduced the context to a paragraph of maximum three sentences.

management sought to transform the company from a simple milk processor into a producer of value-added dairy products as it chased profits offshore<cause>.<effect>Among Fonterra's biggest missteps was the 2015 purchase of an 18.8 per cent stake in Chinese infant formula manufacturer Beingmate Baby & Child Food for $NZ755 million, just as the China market became hyper-competitive and demand slowed <effect>. Fonterra last month announced it would cut its Beingmate stake by selling shares after failing to find a buyer. Meanwhile, back home, Fonterra's share of the milk processing market dropped from 96 per cent in 2001 to 82 per cent currently, with consultants TDB Advisory expecting it to be about 75 per cent by 2021. In this example, "the 2015 purchase of an 18.8 per cent stake in Chinese infant formula manufacturer Beingmate Baby & Child Food for $NZ755 million" was annotated because the cause and the effect have a 2-sentences distance. On the other hand, "Fonterra's share of the milk processing market dropped from 96 per cent in 2001 to 82 per cent currently" was not annotated because this effect is at a 4-sentences distance from the cause.

A.2. Connectives

A connective can be a verb, a preposition, a conjunction, an element of punctuation, or anything else, which explicitly introduces a causal relationship. Among those, there is a specific type of connective that is not taken into account in this Shared Task called lexical causative (Levin and Hovav, 1994) . A lexical causative is a causal relationship stated through connectives (generally predicates) which, from a semantic point of view, also bear the effect of the cause. We will not consider those as causal references, since the effects are *implied* in the connectives' definition. For instance in "The company raised its provisions by 5% in 2018.", *raise* is a lexical causative that can be glossed as *The company caused the provisions to rise by 5%.*

Causal relationships can be introduced by other types of connectives in the identified text section. It is often rendered with the use of polysemous connectives which main function is not to introduce a causal relationship. For example, in this sentence: "Zhao found himself 60 million yuan indebted after losing 9,000 BTC in a single day (February 10, 2014)", the main function of the connective *after* is to express a temporal relation between the two clauses. But we also have a causal relationship between them, since one triggers the other.

In the tagging process, the connectives involved in the causal relationship **were not annotated as part of the facts**. For example: <effect>*Titan has acquired all of Core Gold's secured debt for $US2.5 million*<effect>*in order to* <cause>*ensure the long-term success of its assets.*<cause>. The only exception would be when the connective is inserted in the fact. In that case, the connective was annotated. For instance: <cause>*On August 30, 2013, ST Yushun, in order to strengthen its competitive strength*<cause>, <effect>*acquired a 100% stake in ATV Technologies for 154 billion yuan*<effect>.

A.3. Complex causal relationships

In a text section, complex causal relationships can be rendered with conjoined relationships. A conjoined causal relationship can be one cause related to several effects, or one effect caused by several causes. This is often the case when the facts are not repeated and a conjunction is used as a link for the different effects or causes. This phenomenon can be also found in an implicit causal relationship and/or at sentence level. Here is an instance of a conjoined effect related to two causes: <cause>*India's government slashed corporate taxes on Friday* <cause>, <effect>*giving a surprise $20.5 billion break*<effect><cause>*aimed at reviving private investment and lifting growth from a six-year low that has caused job losses and fueled discontent in the countryside*<cause>. In the tagging process, they were all annotated as separate facts apart if a priority rule was to be taken into account.

A.4. Priority rules

The priority rules allow the annotation process of causal relationships to be more accurate and harmonious.

<u>First rule.</u> If a sentence contained **only one fact** (cause or effect), we **tagged the entire sentence** (even if it contains some noise or a connective). For instance: <cause>*Hurricane Irma was the*

most powerful storm ever recorded in the Atlantic and one of the most powerful to hit land, Bonasia said. <cause><effect>It cause $50 billion in damages.<cause>

<u>Second rule.</u> The **annotation of sentence-to-sentence causal relationships is prioritized**. When the annotator had the choice between linking two full sentences together or subdividing a sentence, he chose the sentence-to-sentence annotation. To illustrate this point, let's look at the text section: *"Finally, Seizert Capital Partners LLC increased its holdings in shares of BlackRock Enhanced Global Dividend Trust by 17.2% during the second quarter. Seizert Capital Partners LLC now owns 138,020 shares of the financial services provider's stock valued at $1,481,000 after acquiring an additional 20,223 shares in the last quarter.* In this text section, there are two causal relationships. The first one links *"Seizert Capital Partners LLC increased its holdings in shares of BlackRock Enhanced Global Dividend Trust by 17.2% during the second quarter"* and *"Seizert Capital Partners LLC now owns 138,020 shares of the financial services provider's stock valued at $1,481,000"*. Since the two facts are located into different sentences, we would have to annotate the full sentences each time (rule 1). The second causal relationship links *"Seizert Capital Partners LLC now owns 138,020 shares of the financial services provider's stock valued at $1,481,000"* and *"acquiring an additional 20,223 shares in the last quarter"*. Here, a sentence is subdivided.

Considering the priority of sentence-to-sentence annotation, the final annotation of this text section was: *"*<cause>*Finally, Seizert Capital Partners LLC increased its holdings in shares of BlackRock Enhanced Global Dividend Trust by 17.2% during the second quarter*<cause>. <effect>*Seizert Capital Partners LLC now owns 138,020 shares of the financial services provider's stock valued at $1,481,000 after acquiring an additional 20,223 shares in the last quarter.*<effect>"*.

This rule also highlights the fact that **two different annotations cannot overlay**. It is impossible to annotate *"acquiring an additional 20,223 shares in the last quarter"* and *"Seizert Capital Partners LLC now owns 138,020 shares of the financial services provider's stock valued at $1,481,000 after acquiring an additional 20,223 shares in the last quarter."* because the same text segment would be part of two different annotations.

<u>Third rule.</u> If a sentence contained **both a cause and an effect**, the **sentence was subdivided**. The spanning was realized so that the exact segments corresponding to the cause and the consequence were selected. For instance: *This week's bad news comes from Rothbury, Michigan, where* <cause>*Barber Steel Foundry will close at the end of the year* <cause>, <effect>*leaving 61 people unemployed*<effect>. However, in the dataset, the spans were extended in order to cover the entirety of the sentence. Only the connector, when located in between the cause and the effect, was left out of the extraction. As a result, in the final dataset we have: <cause>*This week's bad news comes from Rothbury, Michigan, where Barber Steel Foundry will close at the end of the year* <cause>, <effect>*leaving 61 people unemployed*<effect>. The spanning extension facilitate the consistency of the annotation process.

<u>Fourth rule.</u> If **two facts of the same type were located in the same sentence and were related to the same effect or cause**, then **we annotated these two facts as one unit**. For instance, in the text section *"Thomas Cook's demise leaves its German operations hanging. More than 140,000 German holidaymakers have been impacted and tens of thousands of future travel bookings may not be honored."*, the cause fact is *"Thomas Cook's demise"*. Since it was the only fact in the sentence, we annotated the full sentence as the cause (see priority rule number 1). The cause fact has two consequences: *"More than 140,000 German holidaymakers have been impacted"* and *"tens of thousands of future travel bookings may not be honored"*. Since both effect facts are in the same sentence and related to the same cause, we annotated the text section as follow: <cause>Thomas Cook's demise leaves its German operations hanging.<cause><effect>More than 140,000 German holidaymakers have been impacted and tens of thousands of future travel bookings may not be honored<effect>.

This rule was also applied to the annotation of cause.s and effect.s inside a sentence. For instance:

"<effect>*Our total revenue decreased to $31 million*<effect>due to <cause>*decrease in orders from approximately $91,000 to $82,000, and a decrease in total buyers, which includes both new and repeat buyers from approximately 62,000 to 56,000.*<cause>". The two causes were put together since they are related to the same effect.

This rule was only used in the two cases presented above. When more than two sentences were involved it was not taken into account. For example: "<cause>*Let's say Shirley reduced her assets of $165,000 through a gift of $10,000 and pre-paying her funeral expenses for $15,000.*<cause><effect1>*Her DAC would reduce from $55 a day to $43 a day (a saving of just over $4,300 a year).*<effect1><effect2>*Her equivalent lump sum would reduce by almost $88,000!*<effect2>". Consequently, the same text section may appear twice in the release dataset.

Fifth rule. The annotation of **causal chains** inside a sentence. A segment of text that is a cause can also be the effect of another cause. For instance, the sentence *"BHP emitted 14.7m tonnes of carbon dioxide equivalent emissions in its 2019 fiscal year, down from 16.5m tonnes the previous year due to greater use of renewable energy in Chile."* contains three facts. *"greater use of renewable energy in Chile* is the cause of *down from 16.5m tonnes the previous year* which is also the cause of *BHP emitted 14.7m tonnes of carbon dioxide equivalent emissions in its 2019 fiscal year.*

In that case, we **isolated the rightmost fact and tagged it according to its nature. All the remaining facts were gathered as one unit and annotated with the remaining tag**. In our example it gave the final annotation: "<effect>*BHP emitted 14.7m tonnes of carbon dioxide equivalent emissions in its 2019 fiscal year, down from 16.5m tonnes the previous year*<effect><cause>*greater use of renewable energy in Chile*<cause>"

A.5. Other annotation levels

The cause or the effect can sometimes be found as pronouns, relative pronouns included. In that case, the reference (the antecedent) of the pronoun, is the extracted element. For instance, in the text: "The tax revenues decreased by 0.3%, which was caused by fiscal decentralization reform." *The tax revenue decreased by 0.3%* corresponds to the effect and *fiscal decentralization reform* is the cause. In some cases, the pronoun can be added to the opposite fact where the antecedent is.

The role of a clause in a causal sentence can be ambiguous to identify. For example, it can be precarious to tell whether the clause corresponds to the cause, the means or the goal. If so, the sequence was annotated as the cause.

The ambiguity can also exist between two facts - which is the cause? which is the effect? In that case, when there was only one Qfact, the latter was annotated as the effect. When both facts were Qfacts, the annotation order was left to the annotator's appreciation. The annotator was encouraged to use reformulation in order to decide which fact was the cause and which fact was the effect.

If the cause is in the middle of the effect or vice versa, the sentence is not annotated because of the conflict process. Here is an example: "The take-home pay after necessary deductions is S$4,137." where *after necessary deductions* is a cause inserted in the effect.

We decided not to annotated causal relationships with structures identical to a calculation structure. For instance, in the text section *"Google has 100K+ people and $136B in revenue (2018), earning over $1.3M per person."*, we considered that, since the quantified data in the effect fact is the result of a calculation based on the data present in the cause fact, there was no new information. Consequently, there was no need to annotate.

Finally, dates are also to be included in the fact annotated if it is related to it and is placed next to it in the sentence.

LangResearchLab_NC at FinCausal 2020, Task 1:
A Knowledge Induced Neural Net for Causality Detection

Raksha Agarwal
Indian Institute of
Technology Delhi
Raksha.agarwal@maths.ii
td.ac.in

Ishaan Verma
Manipal University
Jaipur
Ishaanverma97@gma
il.com

Niladri Chatterjee
Indian Institute of
Technology Delhi
niladri@maths.iit
d.ac.in

Abstract

Identifying causal relationships in a text is essential for achieving comprehensive natural language understanding. The present work proposes a combination of features derived from pre-trained BERT with linguistic features for training a supervised classifier for the task of Causality Detection. The Linguistic features help to inject knowledge about the semantic and syntactic structure of the input sentences. Experiments on the FinCausal Shared Task1 datasets indicate that the combination of Linguistic features with BERT improves overall performance for causality detection. The proposed system achieves a weighted average F1 score of 0.952 on the post-evaluation dataset.

1 Introduction

The understanding of cause-effect relation is an important NLP task because it appeals to human perception, reasoning, and decision-making. It has vast applications in the field of Information Extraction (Chan et al., 2002), Question Answering (Girju, 2003), and Event Prediction (Radinsky et al., 2012), among others. However, modeling causality relations between events is a non-trivial task because it requires a deeper analysis of the discourse and sometimes external knowledge to forge the relationship between separate events and entities.

In the present work, the focus is on detection of causal relationships in a given text, which is modeled as a binary classification task. Sometimes the presence of causal connectives, such as causes, *because of, leads to, after, due to* indicates causality. However, there may be cases when the causal relation is more implicit making the task of causality detection more challenging.

A causal relationship in a sentence involves the presence of a *cause* and an *effect*, where the cause triggers the effect. In other words, two events X and Y are considered to be causally related if the occurrence of X is triggered by the occurrence of Y, or vice versa. For illustration, consider the following: (1) *Fluctuations in exchange rates added to the risk factors.*

(2) *The company withdrew from bidding.*

It can be observed that the occurrence of (1) resulted in the occurrence of (2). Although there is no explicit marker, the association between the *risk* and *bidding* helps to forge a causal relationship.

Past studies revealed that two major approaches for causality detection involve the use of handcrafted features (Riaz and Girju, 2014) or deep neural networks (Liang et al., 2019). The proposed work integrates syntactic and semantic features of the input text with pre-trained embedding vectors to train a supervised neural network for the classification of causal relations.

The rest of the paper is organized as follows. The proposed system is described in Section 2, Section 3 contains implementation details, and experimental results are presented in Section 4.

2 Model Architecture

The proposed model aims to supplement pre-trained BERT (Devlin et al., 2019) embeddings with linguistic features in order to induce knowledge about the syntactic and semantic peculiarities of the

33

Proceedings of the 1st Joint Workshop on Financial Narrative Processing and MultiLing Financial Summarisation, pages 33–39
Barcelona, Spain (Online), December 12, 2020.

input in the model. The model architecture is presented in Figure 1. The Linguistic feature vector and the BERT embeddings are concatenated together to generate a linguistically informed representation of the input text. The enhanced representations are processed using two identical layers of fully connected feed-forward network before applying a softmax classifier. The details of linguistic features are presented in Sec 2.1, and BERT features is described in Sec 2.2.

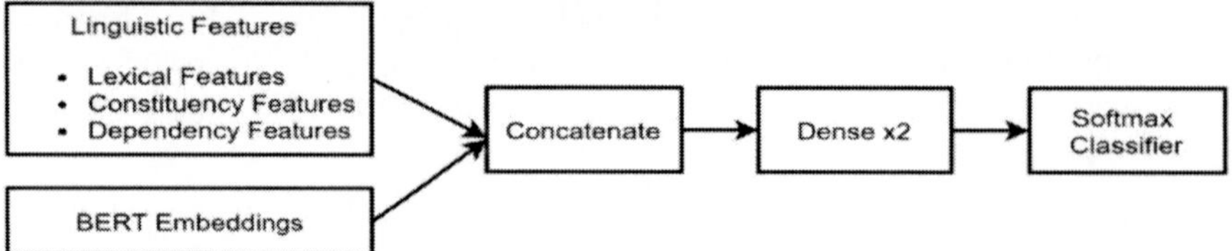

Figure 1: Proposed Model Architecture

2.1 Linguistic features

A combination of lexical and syntactical features is employed for the task of causality detection. These features enable us to encode the semantic information of the input tokens and the structural information of the input sentences.

Lexical Features

The lexical features proposed by Pitler et al. (2009) proved to be effective in sense prediction of implicit discourse relations (Prasad et al., 2008) between pair of input sentences. In the present work, a subset of lexical features is adapted for the task of detecting causality in an input text.

- **Polarity Tags:** The sentiment of each word in the input text is assigned according to the Multi-perspective Question Answering Opinion (MPQA) corpus (Wilson et al., 2005). The number of positive, negative, and neutral words in the input text were considered as features.
- **Inquirer Tags:** The General Inquirer lexicon (Stone et al., 1966) is used to assign semantic categories to the verbs present in the input text. The association between the different verb categories acts as an indicator of causality.
- **Money/Percent/Num:** This feature is used to determine whether the input text contains numbers, monetary amounts, or percentages. These entities frequently occur in financial texts and are useful in determining causality. The count of each such occurrence in the input is considered as a feature.
- **Verbs:** Levin Verb Classes (Levin, 1993) are used to identify verbs that belong to the same verb class. The average verb phrase lengths in the input text are also considered as a feature.
- **Modality:** Pitler et al. (2009) demonstrated that the presence of modal words such as *can, should, may* most likely relate to a contingency or causal relation between sentences. Therefore, a feature indicating the presence of a modal word is used in the present application.
- **Connective:** Text containing connectives belonging to the contingency class such as *because, as a result, consequently* are more likely to indicate causal relationships. A list of connectives is extracted from the Penn Discourse Treebank (Prasad et al., 2008), and a feature indicating the presence of connective in the input text is created.

Syntactical Features

Lin et al. (2009) demonstrated the features extracted from syntactical trees of sentences helps in recognizing implicit discourse relations between pairs of sentences. Since the structure of a text can also indicate the presence of causal relations, two kinds of syntactical features are extracted from the input text.

- **Constituency Parse Features:** Production rules are extracted from the constituency tree of each sentence of the input text. A binary feature represents the presence of each production rule in a given input text.
- **Dependency Parse Features:** Dependency rules are extracted from the dependency parse trees of each sentence of the input text. For each word of the sentence, the dependency rule consists of the POS tag of the word along with a list of all dependency types from the dependents of the word. The presence of each dependency rule is indicated using a binary feature.

The rationale behind using both dependency and constituency features is that that precision and recall are increased when both parsing based features are used as the dependency trees encode additional information about the relationship between words of the sentences.

For illustration, consider the sentence *The New York Times estimates that at least 10,000 people became millionaires just from plunking a few dollars in the wildly profitable stock*[2]. A subset of linguistic features is described in Figure 2. Here, *Econ@, ComForm, EndLw, FormLw, COM* are the Inquirer tags for the word *estimate*. Figure 3 depicts a subset of constituency and dependency features extracted from the respective constituency and dependency parse trees.

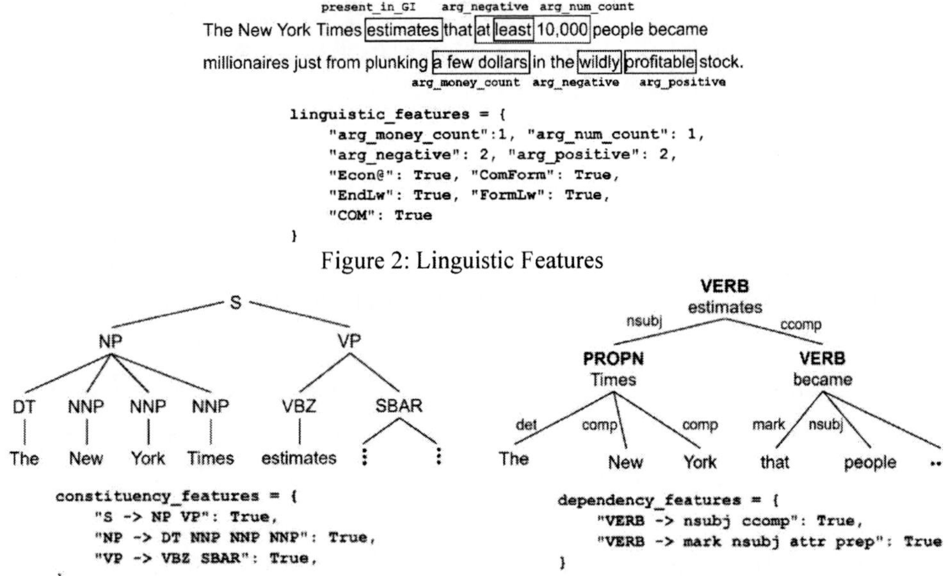

Figure 2: Linguistic Features

Figure 3: Syntactic Features

It was observed that the linguistic features resulted in the creation of sparse feature space. Therefore, Singular Value Decomposition (SVD) is applied on three subsets of linguistic features, namely Lexical features, Constituency Parse Features, and Dependency Parse features. The Lexical features are reduced to a 100-dimensional space, and the Constituency and Dependency Parse features are reduced to 2000 dimensional space each, resulting in a 4100-dimensional feature vector.

2.2 BERT Embeddings

Bidirectional Transformers for Language Understanding (BERT) was introduced by Devlin et al. (2019), and the usage of BERT features has resulted in state-of-the-art performance for various downstream NLP tasks such as Question Answering, Textual Entailment and Paraphrase detection. In the present work, input embeddings are extracted from the pre-trained BERT-base-uncased[3] model. The output from the last layer corresponding to the [CLS] token is considered as the input text embedding.

3   Implementation Details

Pre-processing: In the pre-processing step, SpaCy[4] library is used to perform Tokenization, Lemmatization, Sentence Segmentation, Part-of-Speech (POS) tagging and Dependency Parsing. SpaCy's Named Entity Recognizer is employed to identify entities belonging to Cardinals, Monetary amounts, and Percentages. Constituency parsing is derived using the benepar_en2 model (Kitaev and Klein, 2018).

---

[2] present at Index 0026.00057 in the validation data
[3] https://storage.googleapis.com/bert_models/2018_10_18/uncased_L-12_H-768_A-12.zip
[4] https://github.com/explosion/spaCy

Dataset: The FinCausal Shared Task (Mariko et al., 2020) provides three datasets for Task1 viz., the *Practice-Task1*, the *Trial-Task1* and the blind dataset *Evaluation-Task1*. The aforementioned datasets are used for training, validation and testing, respectively. Oversampling of positive samples was performed during the training process to balance the dataset.

The proposed model is implemented on Python using keras[5] framework. ReLU activation is applied on the intermediate Dense layers along with dropout regularization. The proposed model is trained to minimize the cross entropy loss using the Adam optimizer (Kingma and Lei Ba, 2015). Hyperparameter optimization is performed using keras-tuner[6]. The encoding dimensions of the Dense layers are tuned on the set {256, 512, 1024, 2048, 4096} and dropout ratio is tuned between {0.1, 0.2, ..., 0.9}. The optimal encoding dimension and dropout ratio was found to be 2048 and 0.1, respectively. All the experiments were conducted on Google Colab[7] using the Intel Xeon CPU @ 2.3GHz, the Nvidia Tesla P100 GPU and 25GB available RAM

4 Results and Analysis

In this section we present the results of our experiments on the blind Evaluation-Task1 dataset. The evaluation metrics are Precision, Recall and Weighted F1 score. Weighted F1 score is calculated by multiplying the class wise F1-scores with the class *support*, i.e. the number of examples in that class. The results corresponding to different subsets of the feature space is given in Table 1. It can be observed that linguistically enhanced input representations improve the ability of the supervised model to detect causal relationships in a given text.

Features	Precision	Recall	Weighted F1 score
Only Lexical Features	0.943	0.946	0.936
Only Constituency Features	0.934	0.940	0.936
Only Dependency Features	0.934	0.941	0.930
Only Syntactical Features	0.942	0.946	0.935
Only BERT Features	0.943	0.935	0.938
Only Linguistic Features	0.947	0.950	0.942
Linguistic + BERT Features(Evaluation)	0.950	0.949	0.951
Linguistic + BERT Features (Post Evaluation)	**0.951**	**0.954**	**0.952**

Table 1: Test Results on the blind dataset

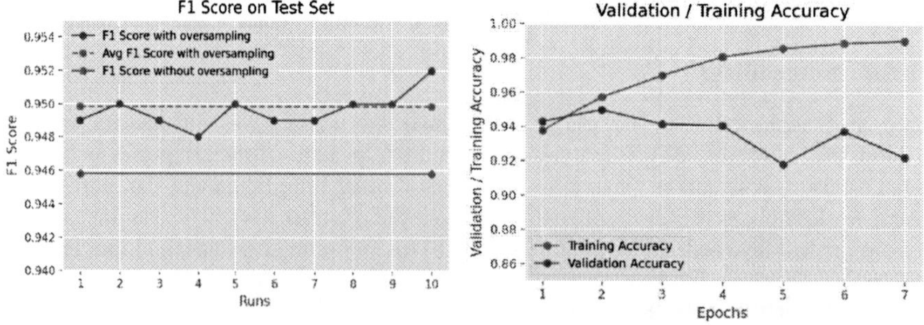

Figure 4:(a) F1 Score of the proposed model on Test Set with and without oversampling with different sampling seeds (b) Validation and Training accuracy for the proposed model (Early Stopping returns the weights of second epoch)

---

[5] https://keras.io/
[6]https://keras-team.github.io/keras-tuner/
[7]https://colab.research.google.com/

The effect of oversampling in the proposed model is demonstrated in Figure 4(a) by using different sampling seeds. The F1 score on the test set of the model trained without oversampling is lower than the average F1 score of the model trained with oversampling[8]. Training and Validation accuracies are shown in Figure 4(b). Early Stopping[9] call back is used to get the weights of the second epoch to avoid overfitting because validation accuracy stops increasing after this epoch.

Predictions of the proposed model for samples taken from the Validation set are described in Table 2. Example 1 and 2 are correctly classified while Examples 3-8 are incorrectly classified. The causality in Example 3 is between *capital out* (withdrawal of capital) and *refinancing*. However, the lexical and syntactical structures of the input sentence conceal the underlying causal relationship. In Examples 4 and 5 the difference in numeric quantities have an underlying causal effect. This indicates that knowledge with respect to variation of numeric quantities may help in improving performance of the model. The reason for unemployment in Example 6 is excluded from the input text and thus, the gold label is not causal. However, due to the presence of the connective phrase *as result* the proposed model assigns causality. The proposed model picks up on the complementary relationship between verbs *earn* and *pay* to predict causality in Example 7. The gold label for Example 8 indicates the absence of causality which is incorrect because the presence of the connective *as* strongly suggest the presence of a causal relation indicating that since 67 persons sold their share it dived. Thus, the proposed system is able to pick up on linguistic clues for meaningful predictions.

Input Text	Index	Gold	Predicted
1 Choice Hotels International has a consensus target price of $85.12, suggesting a potential downside of 8.49%.	0194.00006	Causal	Causal
2 Around the world fiduciaries are struggling with the challenging investment outlook.	0016.00011	Not Causal	Not Causal
3 I refinanced my apartment and took almost 30,000 euros of capital out of my home.	0311.00009	Causal	Not Causal
4 The S&P 500 returned 4.3%, after a 13.6% gain in the March quarter.	0088.00025	Causal	Not Causal
5 Keep in mind that an 8% annual return is really only a 5% annual return after 3% inflation.	0126.00018	Causal	Not Causal
6 It said 1,300 jobs would be lost as result, with a further 3,400 in the supply chain put at risk.	0366.00003	Not Causal	Causal
7 Anyone earning below $2 million a year will not pay a dime.	0102.00016	Not Causal	Causal
8 It dived, as 67 investors sold RTN shares while 352 reduced holdings.	0288.00031	Not Causal	Causal

Table 2: Predictions of the Proposed Model on the Validation Set (*Trial-Task1*)

5   Conclusion

Causality detection in a text is a challenging task due to the semantic peculiarities of the English language and also because it requires a deeper domain understanding. In the present work, semantic and structural knowledge of the input text is induced on the top of input embeddings to generate enhanced representation. The results indicate that the enhanced representations improve the performance across all the evaluation metrics. In future work we would like to experiment with more complex architectures such as LSTMs and Transformers. Additionally, we would also like to experiment with CNN and max-pooling based dimensional reduction for treatment of the sparse linguistic feature space.

---

[8]Best results are obtained for sampling seed 5050
[9] https://www.tensorflow.org/api_docs/python/tf/keras/callbacks/EarlyStopping

Acknowledgements

Raksha Agarwal acknowledges Council of Scientific and Industrial Research (CSIR), India for supporting the research under Grant no: SPM-06/086(0267)/2018-EMR-I

References

Ki Chan, Boon Toh Low, Wai Lam, and Kai Pui Lam. 2002. Extracting causation knowledge from natural language texts. *International Journal of Intelligent Systems*, 20:327–358.

Jacob Devlin, Ming-Wei Chang, Kenton Lee, and Kristina Toutanova. 2019. BERT: Pre-training of Deep Bidirectional Transformers for Language Understanding. In *Proceedings of the North American Chapter of the Association for Computational Linguistics: Human Language Technologies*, pages 4171–4186.

Roxana Girju. 2003. Automatic Detection of Causal Relations for Question Answering. In *Proceedings of ACL 2003 Workshop on Multilingual Summarization and Question Answering*, pages 76–83.

Diederik P Kingma and Jimmy Lei Ba. 2015. Adam: A Method For Stochastic Optimization. In *Proceedings of the 3rd international conference for learning representations (ICLR'15)*, San Diego, California.

Nikita Kitaev and Dan Klein. 2018. Constituency Parsing with a Self-Attentive Encoder. In *Proceedings of the 56th Annual Meeting of the Association for Computational Linguistics*, pages 2676–2686.

Beth Levin. 1993. *English Verb Classes and Alternations: A Preliminary Investigation*. University of Chicago Press.

Shining Liang, Wanli Zuo, Zhenkun Shi, and Sen Wang. 2019. A Multi-level Neural network for Implicit Causality Detection in Web Texts. arXiv: 1908.07822 v2 *http://arxiv.org/abs/1908.07822*

Ziheng Lin, Min-Yen Kan, and Hwee Tou Ng. 2009. Recognizing Implicit Discourse Relations in the Penn Discourse Treebank. In *Proceedings of the 2009 Conference on Empirical Methods in Natural Language Processing (EMNLP)*, pages 343–351, Singapore.

Dominique Mariko, Hanna Abi Akl, Estelle Labidurie, Stephane Durfort, Hugues de Mazancourt, and Mahmoud El-Haj. 2020. The Financial Document Causality Detection Shared Task (FinCausal 2020). In *The 1st Joint Workshop on Financial Narrative Processing and MultiLing Financial Summarisation (FNP-FNS 2020)*, Barcelona, Spain.

Emily Pitler, Annie Louis, and Ani Nenkova. 2009. Automatic sense prediction for implicit discourse relations in text. In *Proceedings of the 47th Annual Meeting of the Association for Computational Linguistics and the 4th International Joint Conference on Natural Language Processing of the AFNLP*, pages 683–691, Singapore.

Rashmi Prasad, Nikhil Dinesh, Alan Lee, Eleni Miltsakaki, Livio Robaldo, Aravind Joshi, and Bonnie Webber. 2008. The Penn Discourse TreeBank 2.0. In *Proceedings of the Sixth International Conference on Language Resources and Evaluation (LREC)*, Marrakech, Morocco.

Kira Radinsky, Sagie Davidovich, and Shaul Markovitch. 2012. Learning to Predict from Textual Data. *Journal of Artificial Intelligence Research*, 45:641–684.

Mehwish Riaz and Roxana Girju. 2014. In-depth Exploitation of Noun and Verb Semantics to Identify Causation in Verb-Noun Pairs. In *Proceedings of the SIGDIAL 2014 Conference, The 15th Annual Meeting of the Special Interest Group on Discourse and Dialogue*, pages 161–170.

Philip J. Stone, Dexter C. Dunphy, Marshall S. Smith, and Daniel M. Ogilvia. 1966. The General Inquirer: A Computer Approach to Content Analysis. *MIT Press*.

Theresa Wilson, Janyce Wiebe, and Paul Hoffmann. 2005. Recognizing contextual polarity in phrase-level sentiment analysis. In *Proceedings of the HLT/EMNLP 2005, Human Language Technology Conference and Conference on Empirical Methods in Natural Language Processing*, pages 347–354.

GBe at FinCausal 2020, Task 2: Span-based Causality Extraction for Financial Documents

Guillaume Becquin `guillaume.becquin@gmail.com`

Abstract

This document describes a system for causality extraction from financial documents submitted as part of the FinCausal 2020 Workshop. The main contribution of this paper is a description of the robust post-processing used to detect the number of cause and effect clauses in a document and extract them. The proposed system achieved a weighted-average F1 score of more than 95% for the official blind test set during the post-evaluation phase and exact clauses match for 83% of the documents.

1 Introduction

The FinCausal 2020 shared task (Mariko et al., 2020) focuses on the identification of causality in financial documents. Beyond factual data, causality detection and characterization in financial documents help to identify the reasons leading to a given quantified financial event. FinCausal 2020 proposes two shared tasks: the first one focuses on the detection of causality in documents (binary classification), while the second task consists of the actual extraction of the cause and effect spans from a document expressing causality (token classification or span extraction).

This document describes a system submitted for the second task. Based on a deep learning language model, it leverages an architecture similar to question answering and therefore addresses the task as a span extraction problem. The post-processing and filtering of unrealistic spans are of high importance given that several clauses (at least a cause and an effect) need to be extracted from the documents. The extracted clauses are further refined to align with the task labeling guidelines.

The proposed system ranked 2nd for the FinCausal 2020 Task 2, achieving a weighted-average F1 score of 94.7% and predicted exact matches for the cause and effect clauses for 73.7% of documents. Further training refinement led to an improved F1 score of 95% and exact match for 83.3% of the documents in the official blind test set in the post-evaluation phase. The code for the proposed solution is available at `https://github.com/guillaume-be/Financial-Causality-Extraction`

2 System Description

The core system used for all submissions is described in Figure 1. Features are generated from an input text using the Transformers library (Wolf et al., 2019) with high-performance tokenizers (Hugging Face, 2020). While the task dataset contains only rather short (2 to 3 sentences) texts, the system can handle longer documents exceeding the language model context using a sliding window mechanism. The tokenized input is then passed through a language model based on the Transformers (Vaswani et al., 2017) architecture. The last layer of hidden states is connected to a dense layer with 4 output dimensions to generate logits for the start and end positions of the cause and effect span. This mechanism is similar to Question Answering state-of-the-art architectures with two spans extracted instead of one.

The output of the model is an array of 4 vectors per document representing the logits for the start and end of the cause and effect. A first step cuts-off the logits vectors to the top-N elements, limiting the potential solution space to a size of N^4. Several of these solutions are unrealistic and must be

Proceedings of the 1st Joint Workshop on Financial Narrative Processing and MultiLing Financial Summarisation, pages 40–44
Barcelona, Spain (Online), December 12, 2020.

filtered out. Some of these filtering steps are leveraged from the BERT (Devlin et al., 2019) Question Answering system for SQuAD (Rajpurkar et al., 2016). This includes for example filtering out start and end combinations where the end is before the start or the span length is longer than the maximum allowed length. The cause and effect extraction tasks add complexity in that two spans need to be extracted. Additional filters ensuring that the cause and effect clauses do not overlap have been added (for example $start_{cause} < start_{effect} < end_{cause}$ would be filtered out).

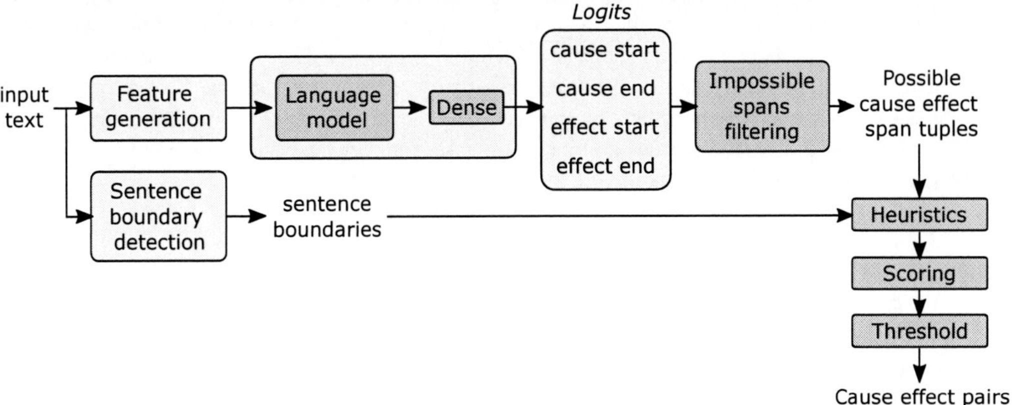

Figure 1: System architecture.

Finally, task-specific heuristics aligned with the labeling guidelines (Mariko et al., 2020) have been implemented. In addition to the filtered logits, these heuristics take the sentence boundaries as an input (these are extracted with the PySBD library (Sadvilkar and Neumann, 2020)). The following heuristics have been implemented:

- **H1**: A clause (cause or effect) may not span over multiple sentences.

- **H2**: If a sentence contains only one clause (cause or effect), extend the clause to the entire sentence

The filtered and improved (via heuristics) possible cause-effect span combinations are then ranked based on the sum of their 4 corresponding logits for start and end of cause and effect. The number of cause/effect combinations to return is either set externally (via the number of duplicated entries in the shared task dataset implicitly defining the number of cause/effects combinations to extract) or dynamically based on the span probability and a threshold.

3 Experimental Results

3.1 Data

The data used for all experiments is the data for the FinCausal 2020 shared task (Mariko et al., 2020). This data was extracted from 2019 financial news (QWAM, 2020). The task 2 dataset contains a subset of documents containing at least one cause and effect relationship. When several cause/effect relationships exist in a sample, this sample is duplicated for each additional cause/effect pair to be found. The data contains two labeled subsets called *Trial* (641 samples, 500 unique), *Practice* (1109 samples, 913 unique) and a blind test dataset *Evaluation* (638 samples, 452 unique). All models have been trained by merging the *Trial* and *Practice* dataset and performing a random split keeping 90% of the data for training and 10% for validation.

3.2 Experiments

The proposed system was trained for 20 epochs using the AdamW (Loshchilov and Hutter, 2017) optimizer. The learning rate is set to a maximum value of $2.5e - 5$ and follows a cosine annealing schedule (Loshchilov and Hutter, 2016) with 100 warm-up steps. The effective batch size was kept constant at

12, using gradient accumulation when necessary. Experiments were performed on a RTX2070 GPU and Google Colaboratory notebooks.

Five different language models have been investigated: DistilBERT (Sanh et al., 2019), BERT-base and BERT-large (Devlin et al., 2019), RoBERTa-base and RoBERTa-large (Liu et al., 2019) using the implementation available in the Transformers library (Wolf et al., 2019). For each of these, the impact of pre-training on a question answering task (SQuAD dataset (Rajpurkar et al., 2016)) is evaluated. The rationale is that question answering is also a span extraction task and that the causality extraction architecture proposed is similar to that of extractive question answering systems. The impact of the language model and its pre-training setup is available in Figure 2. The average for three runs of the weighted-averaged F1 score over the token categories (cause, effect, other) and the fraction of documents with exact spans extractions are shown by the dots. The range represents the minimum and maximum values. The metrics are reported for the bind test dataset following an early stopping on the hold-out validation dataset.

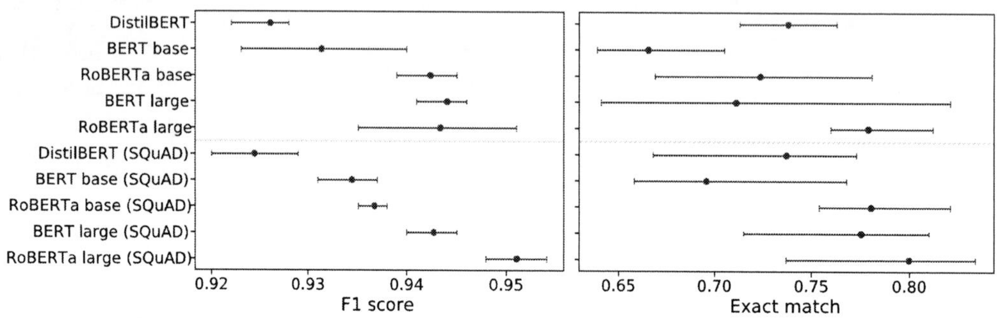

Figure 2: Language model selection and impact on performance.

The training of the system was more stable using models pre-trained for question answering: the weighted-averaged F1 score spread is significantly smaller for these models compared to the unsupervised pre-trained version. The larger models (BERT-large and RoBERTa-large) perform better than smaller models (base versions and DistilBERT) for a significantly higher computational cost. The impact of the model architecture and pre-training for the fraction of exact matches is less significant, probably because the metric is very sensitive to single token prediction changes.

3.3 Ablation study

An ablation study was conducted to identify significant contributions to the proposed model performance. For all ablations, the weighted-average F1 score and exact matches fraction on the blind test set is reported. The reported value is the average over 3 runs and subscripts show the standard deviation. The pre-training on a question answering task has a significant impact on both the weighted average F1 score and the standard deviation, indicating a more stable training regime. The question answering pre-training also improves the number of exact matches significantly, further highlighting the value of pre-training on a similar span extraction task.

Model	F1 score (%)	Exact match (%)	$\Delta_{F1}(\%)$
Full model	**94.68$_{0.3}$**	**79.94$_{4.4}$**	
without SQuAD pre-training	93.92$_{0.6}$	77.90$_{2.3}$	-0.76
Single cause/effect returned	82.86$_{0.2}$	75.29$_{0.1}$	-11.81
without Heuristic 1 (max. 1 sentence per clause)	94.60$_{0.1}$	79.89$_{4.4}$	-0.08
without Heuristic 2 (clause extended to full sentence)	93.24$_{0.1}$	78.53$_{2.8}$	-1.44

The *Single cause/effect return* represents a system that outputs a single cause and effects for all documents provided (instead of returning multiple feasible causes and effects). Since the dataset contains a significant amount of documents with multiple causes and effects this severely impacts the performance. The impact of the first heuristic is marginal and within the uncertainty margins. The second heuristic, extending the clause to the entire sentence, has a significant impact (more than 1% point weighted-average F1 score). Additional training data would likely allow the model to learn more accurate span predictions and reduce the impact of this heuristic.

3.4 Multiple cause/effect predictions

A document may contain multiple cause/effect pairs to extract (for example 1 cause and 2 effects). For the shared task, the example is duplicated for each cause/effect pair, indicating the number of predictions to output. In a real-world setting the model should be able to assess how many predictions (causes and effects) to output for a given example. The following analysis evaluates if the value of the logits produced by the model can be used as a proxy for the confidence of the model for how many examples to return:

1. Rank possible extracted spans by the sum of the logits of start/end positions of the cause/effect

2. Filter out the spans with a cause or effect fully overlapping with more likely spans

3. Calculate the span probability ($P(cause_{start}) * P(cause_{end}) * P(effect_{start}) * P(effect_{end})$)

4. The ground truth of the number of spans (N) to extract is known from the number of duplicates of the given example. The top-N (excluding the first) extracted spans are stored as valid prediction probabilities, the rest of the extracted spans and their probability are stored as invalid predictions.

Figure 3 shows the results on the combined hold-out evaluation and blind test datasets:

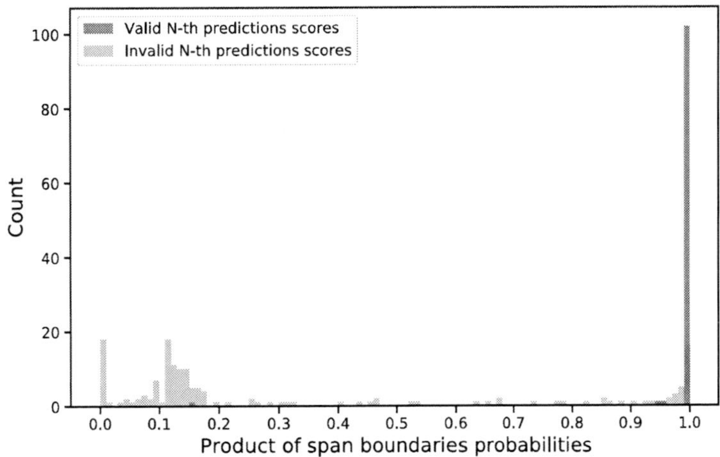

Figure 3: Probability of cause/effect prediction based on actual number of expected predictions.

The distribution of probability scores shows good separation of valid and invalid predictions. Using a confidence threshold of 99%, the model is able to identify the number of cause/effect relationships to extract with a F1 score of 91.4% (precision: 86.4%, recall: 97.1%).

4   Conclusion

A system for the second task of the FinCausal 2020 workshop has been described. The problem was framed as a span extraction task leveraging pre-trained model and post-processing elements from state-of-the-art question answering systems. This strong baseline was complemented with extensions to handle the extraction of two spans per document. The ability of the system to not only extract cause and effect, but also to predict the number of cause/effect relationships in a document was also demonstrated. The proposed model accurately extract causes and effect from documents.

References

Jacob Devlin, Ming-Wei Chang, Kenton Lee, and Kristina Toutanova. 2019. BERT: Pre-training of deep bidirectional transformers for language understanding. In *Proceedings of the 2019 Conference of the North American Chapter of the Association for Computational Linguistics: Human Language Technologies, Volume 1 (Long and Short Papers)*, pages 4171–4186, Minneapolis, Minnesota, June. Association for Computational Linguistics.

Hugging Face. 2020. tokenizers. `https://github.com/huggingface/tokenizers`.

Yinhan Liu, Myle Ott, Naman Goyal, Jingfei Du, Mandar Joshi, Danqi Chen, Omer Levy, Mike Lewis, Luke Zettlemoyer, and Veselin Stoyanov. 2019. Roberta: A robustly optimized BERT pretraining approach. *CoRR*, abs/1907.11692.

Ilya Loshchilov and Frank Hutter. 2016. SGDR: stochastic gradient descent with restarts. *CoRR*, abs/1608.03983.

Ilya Loshchilov and Frank Hutter. 2017. Fixing weight decay regularization in adam. *CoRR*, abs/1711.05101.

Dominique Mariko, Hanna Abi Akl, Estelle Labidurie, Stephane Durfort, Hugues de Mazancourt, and Mahmoud El-Haj. 2020. The Financial Document Causality Detection Shared Task (FinCausal 2020). In *The 1st Joint Workshop on Financial Narrative Processing and MultiLing Financial Summarisation (FNP-FNS 2020, Barcelona, Spain*.

QWAM. 2020. Qwam homepage.

Pranav Rajpurkar, Jian Zhang, Konstantin Lopyrev, and Percy Liang. 2016. SQuAD: 100,000+ questions for machine comprehension of text. In *Proceedings of the 2016 Conference on Empirical Methods in Natural Language Processing*, pages 2383–2392, Austin, Texas, November. Association for Computational Linguistics.

Nipun Sadvilkar and M. Neumann. 2020. Pysbd: Pragmatic sentence boundary disambiguation. *ArXiv*, abs/2010.09657.

Victor Sanh, Lysandre Debut, Julien Chaumond, and Thomas Wolf. 2019. Distilbert, a distilled version of bert: smaller, faster, cheaper and lighter. *ArXiv*, abs/1910.01108.

Ashish Vaswani, Noam Shazeer, Niki Parmar, Jakob Uszkoreit, Llion Jones, Aidan N Gomez, Ł ukasz Kaiser, and Illia Polosukhin. 2017. Attention is all you need. In I. Guyon, U. V. Luxburg, S. Bengio, H. Wallach, R. Fergus, S. Vishwanathan, and R. Garnett, editors, *Advances in Neural Information Processing Systems 30*, pages 5998–6008. Curran Associates, Inc.

Thomas Wolf, Lysandre Debut, Victor Sanh, Julien Chaumond, Clement Delangue, Anthony Moi, Pierric Cistac, Tim Rault, R'emi Louf, Morgan Funtowicz, and Jamie Brew. 2019. Huggingface's transformers: State-of-the-art natural language processing. *ArXiv*, abs/1910.03771.

LIORI at FinCausal 2020, Tasks 1 & 2

Adis Davletov
RANEPA
Lomonosov Moscow State University
`davletov-aa@ranepa.ru`

Denis Gordeev
RANEPA
`gordeev-di@ranepa.ru`

Alexey Rey
RANEPA
`rey-ai@ranepa.ru`

Nikolay Arefyev
Lomonosov Moscow State University,
Samsung R&D Institute Russia,
National Research University
Higher School of Economics
`nick.arefyev@gmail.com`

Abstract

In this paper, we describe the results of team LIORI at the FinCausal 2020 Shared task held as a part of the 1st Joint Workshop on Financial Narrative Processing and MultiLingual Financial Summarisation. The shared task consisted of two subtasks: 1) classifying whether a sentence contains any causality and 2) labelling phrases that indicate causes and consequences. We used Transformer-based models with joint-task learning and their voting ensembles. Our team ranked 1st in the first subtask and 4th in the second one.

1 Introduction

The Financial Document Causality Detection Task was devoted to finding causes and consequences in financial news (Mariko et al., 2020). This task is relevant for information retrieval and economics. This task was focused on causality associated with a financial event while an event was "defined as the arising or emergence of a new object or context in regard to a previous situation".

The shared task consisted of two subtasks:

- Sentence Classification

  It was a binary classification task. The goal of this subtask was to detect whether a sentence displayed any causal meanings or not

- Cause and Effect Detection

  This task was a relation detection task. Participants needed to identify "in a causal sentence or text block the causal elements and the consequential ones" [1]. This task could be considered as a sequence labelling problem because individual words and phrases corresponded to three labels: cause, consequence, empty label. Each word or character corresponded to only one label.

For both tasks simultaneously we used a single Transformer-based model (Vaswani et al., 2017) with two inputs and outputs for each of the tasks respectively. The first task was treated as a classification task with a single label for the input, while for the second the label was predicted for each input word. The training and dataset processing code is published on our GitHub page [2].

Our team ranked 1st in the first subtask and 4th in the second one.

---

[1] http://wp.lancs.ac.uk/cfie/fincausal2020/
[2] https://github.com/InstituteForIndustrialEconomics/fincausal-2020

Proceedings of the 1st Joint Workshop on Financial Narrative Processing and MultiLing Financial Summarisation, pages 45–49
Barcelona, Spain (Online), December 12, 2020.

2   Related Work

There are many works devoted to sequence labelling in various domains as it is one of the most popular tasks in Natural Language Processing (NLP).

Causality detection in texts is also a very old topic. First works date back to the 80s according to the report by Asghar (Asghar, 2016). Recently there have appeared works that leverage neural networks against for causality labelling (Li et al., 2019). The results of neural networks there seem to be in line with the performance for other sequence labelling tasks such as named entity recognition (Ghaddar and Langlais, 2018) for Bi-LSTM models according to paperswithcode.com [3]. For our work, we adopted a Transformer-based approach as it performs the best against current models for sequence labelling and relation extraction. For example, if we look again at named entity recognition (one of the most popular sequence labelling tasks) - at paperswithcode.com[4], we can see that the top 3 best performing use an attention-based model for Ontonotes v5 and CoNLL 2003. Some recent works have also shown that multi-task learning can produce better results if we have several targets for the same input due to eavesdropping and lower task-bias (Ruder, 2017), thus discouraging model from over-fitting. Recent competitions, where multi-task models perform well, also prove this point (Dai et al., 2020; Davletov et al., 2020; Gordeev and Lykova, 2020).

3   Dataset

The task dataset has been extracted from different 2019 financial news provided by Qwam [5]. The corpus consists of HTML-pages of financial news from 2019. It also contains various financial and legal reports from the SEC Edgar Database ticker list, filtered on financial keywords.

The texts have been normalized for the research task in the following way:

- First, the text was split into sentences.

- Then, sentences containing causal elements were identified.

- The document text is then split into passages of consecutive sentences, keeping causally-related sentences in the same passage which are used for binary predictions in the first subtask.

- Passages with positive classes are used as the dataset for the second subtask.

- The organizers provide the start and end indices for causes and effects.

The dataset was split into trial, train and test datasets by the organizers. The trial and train parts contained training labels, while the test part did not include them and was used for ranking. We combined the trial and train parts and used 20% of the combined dataset for validation.

4   Solution

In this work, we went with multitask Transformer-based models for both subtasks. It means that we had two inputs and outputs, for each of the tasks respectively. In this work we tried BERT (Devlin et al., 2018) and ROBERTa (Liu et al., 2019) based models. BERT is a multilingual language model based on self-attention. ROBERTa is a "robustly optimized" BERT variant with larger mini-batches and byte-level BPE (byte-pair encodings). In both cases we used English large model variants (bert-large and roberta-large). On top of pre-trained BERT and ROBERTa models, we added two Linear layers with dropout for each of the tasks. Cross-entropy was used for training the models. Thus, we had two loss functions (for each of the output layers) that were weighted and concatenated. All used models were provided by

---

[3]https://paperswithcode.com/sota/named-entity-recognition-ner-on-ontonotes-v5
[4]https://paperswithcode.com/task/named-entity-recognition-ner
[5]http://www.qwamci.com/

Hugging Face (Wolf et al., 2019). Our combined loss function can be seen below, where L_a is the first subtask loss and L_b is the second subtask loss.

$$L_a = -\frac{1}{m} \sum_{j=1}^{m} \sum_{i=1}^{N_c} y_i \cdot log(\hat{y}_i)$$

where m is the number of samples in the batch, y_i is the target value, $\hat{y}_i$ – our predicted value and N_c is the number of classes.

$$L_b = -\frac{1}{m} \sum_{i=1}^{m} \frac{1}{N_j} \sum_{j=1}^{N_j} \sum_{c=1}^{N_c} y_c \cdot log(\hat{y}_c)$$

where m is the number of samples in the batch, N_j is the number of tokens in the batch, N_c is the number of NER classes, $\hat{y}_c$ – the predicted NER class and y_c is the target value.

$$\mathcal{L} = \lambda_a L_a + \lambda_b L_b, \text{ where } \lambda \text{ are scalar weights for the loss functions.}$$

All padded words and non-labeled words (and their resulting tokens) were excluded from loss function calculation and not included into N_j, while special '[SEP]' and '[CLS]' tokens were included.

While training models for the first subtask we tested a number of weighting schemes ranging between 2 and 0 for sequence labelling subtask loss. However, for the second subtask, the weights for text classification loss were set to zero which makes the model equivalent to a general sequence labelling model. We also tried various sequence labelling formats of the second subtask input: BIO (beginning, inside, outside) and BIEO (beginning, inside, end, outside). Learning rates in the range between $5e - 06$ and $5e - 05$ were tested. Dropout coefficients were tested from 0.1 to 0.2. For the first subtask, there were also provided the results for ensembles of the best 3, 4 and 5 performing models according to the validation dataset. Simple voting ensembles were used.

We used a system with 2 NVidia RTX2080 GPUs and Google Colab to train all models.

5 Results

Test Score	Validation Score	Model	Target Format	Learning Rate	Text Loss Weight	Sequence Loss Weight	Dropout Rate
0.96529	0.960016	bert	bieo	1e-05	1.0	0.2	0.1
0.965454	0.960291	bert	se	7e-06	1.0	0.1	0.1
0.96685	0.961945	bert	se	5e-05	1.0	0.2	0.15
...	...	...	...	...	...	...	...
0.973839	0.961179	roberta	bio	1e-05	1.0	0.1	0.1
0.973839	0.967221	roberta	bio	1e-05	1.0	0.1	0.1
0.975088	*0.9657*	*roberta*	*bio*	*5e-06*	*1.0*	*0.1*	*0.1*
0.975238		top-3 Ensemble					
0.975735		top-4 Ensemble					
0.977467		**top-5 Ensemble**					

Table 1: Model results for Subtask 1: Sentence Classification. In the Table we provide the results for only the best and the worst 3 models and of the ensembles of the top-N performing models. The results are sorted from the bottom to the top.

For the first subtask, the organizers used F1-score. For the second subtask, the metric is a weighted average F1 score, where the F1 score of each class is balanced by the number of items in each class (see (Mariko et al., 2020)).

In the first subtask our final model achieved F1 equal to 0.977 on the leaderboard (the next participant's score is 0.975 F1), in the second subtask our result was 0.826 F1 with the winning solution having 0.947

Test Score	Validation Score	Model	Target Format	Learning Rate	Text Loss Weight	Sequence Loss Weight	Dropout Rate
0.754986	0.872582	roberta	bio	0.0001	0.0	1.0	0.1
0.76584	0.82897	roberta	bio	0.0001	0.0	1.0	0.2
0.794089	0.865707	roberta	bio	9e-05	0.0	1.0	0.2
...	...	...	...	...	...	...	...
0.823952	0.898873	bert	bio	0.0001	0.0	1.0	0.2
0.824818	0.894067	bert	bio	7e-05	0.0	1.0	0.2
0.826049	**0.906328**	**bert**	**bio**	**0.0001**	**0.0**	**1.0**	**0.1**

Table 2: Model results for Subtask 2: Cause and Effect Detection. In the Table, there are provided the results for only the best and the worst 3 models. The results are sorted from the bottom to the top.

F1. The results of individual models and their hyperparameters can be seen in Tables 1 and 2 for each of the subtasks respectively.

As can be seen from Table 1 for subtask 1 ROBERTa robustly outperforms BERT for the first subtask. The best top-3 single models are ROBERTa-based with various hyperparameters. It can also be seen that sequence loss improves model results, but the best models have their weights scaled down by 0.1. It also should be noted that the difference between all individual models is small and the difference between the best and the worst-performing ones is less than 0.1 F-1-score point. For the first subtask, we also tried an ensemble of 3,4 and 5 best performing individual models. The increase in the number of the used best models consistently improved the results. Thus, it may be also beneficial to train other types of models or to increase the number of models in an ensemble.

Paradoxically, for the second subtask BERT-based models consistently outperform ROBERTa based ones. Moreover, the difference is much larger and constitutes more than 0.7 F1-score points. We did not try ensemble-based models for the second subtask. It also can be seen that all our models tend to overfit to the training and validation datasets. A more robust training scheme such as k-fold cross validation might be of benefit here.

6 Conclusion

This paper describes the results of team LIORI at the FinCausal 2020 Shared task held as a part of the 1st Joint Workshop on Financial Narrative Processing and MultiLingual Financial Summarisation. The shared task consisted of two subtasks: classifying whether a sentence contains any causality and labelling phrases which indicate causes and consequences. Transformer-based models with joint-task learning were used. In this paper we show that different model architectures perform better for different subtasks and that joint-task learning might improve results for some subtasks. However, it also results in slight overfitting for sequence labelling task and might require further investigation.

Acknowledgements

We thank the organisers of the competition for such an inspiring task. We are grateful to our reviewers for their useful suggestions. The contribution of Nikolay Arefyev to the paper was partially done within the framework of the HSE University Basic Research Program funded by the Russian Academic Excellence Project '5-100'.

References

Nabiha Asghar. 2016. Automatic extraction of causal relations from natural language texts: a comprehensive survey. *arXiv preprint arXiv:1605.07895*.

Wenliang Dai, Tiezheng Yu, Zihan Liu, and Pascale Fung. 2020. Kungfupanda at semeval-2020 task 12: Bert-based multi-task learning for offensive language detection. *arXiv preprint arXiv:2004.13432*.

Adis Davletov, Denis Gordeev, Alexey Rey, and Nikolay Arefyev. 2020. Renersans: Relation extraction and named entity recognition as sequence annotation. In *Computational Linguistics and Intellectual Technologies*, pages 187–197.

Jacob Devlin, Ming-Wei Chang, Kenton Lee, and Kristina Toutanova. 2018. BERT: Pre-training of Deep Bidirectional Transformers for Language Understanding. oct.

Abbas Ghaddar and Philippe Langlais. 2018. Robust lexical features for improved neural network named-entity recognition. *arXiv preprint arXiv:1806.03489*.

Denis Gordeev and Olga Lykova. 2020. Bert of all trades, master of some. In *Proceedings of the Second Workshop on Trolling, Aggression and Cyberbullying*, pages 93–98.

Zhaoning Li, Qi Li, Xiaotian Zou, and Jiangtao Ren. 2019. Causality extraction based on self-attentive bilstm-crf with transferred embeddings. *arXiv preprint arXiv:1904.07629*.

Yinhan Liu, Myle Ott, Naman Goyal, Jingfei Du, Mandar Joshi, Danqi Chen, Omer Levy, Mike Lewis, Luke Zettlemoyer, and Veselin Stoyanov. 2019. RoBERTa: A Robustly Optimized BERT Pretraining Approach. *arxiv.org*.

Dominique Mariko, Hanna Abi Akl, Estelle Labidurie, Stephane Durfort, Hugues de Mazancourt, and Mahmoud El-Haj. 2020. The Financial Document Causality Detection Shared Task (FinCausal 2020). In *The 1st Joint Workshop on Financial Narrative Processing and MultiLing Financial Summarisation (FNP-FNS 2020, Barcelona, Spain*.

Sebastian Ruder. 2017. An overview of multi-task learning in deep neural networks. *arXiv preprint arXiv:1706.05098*.

Ashish Vaswani, Noam Shazeer, Niki Parmar, Jakob Uszkoreit, Llion Jones, Aidan N Gomez, Łukasz Kaiser, and Illia Polosukhin. 2017. Attention is all you need. In *Adv. Neural Inf. Process. Syst.*, volume 2017-Decem, pages 5999–6009.

Thomas Wolf, Lysandre Debut, Victor Sanh, Julien Chaumond, Clement Delangue, Anthony Moi, Pierric Cistac, Tim Rault, R'emi Louf, Morgan Funtowicz, and Jamie Brew. 2019. HuggingFace's Transformers: State-of-the-art Natural Language Processing. *ArXiv*, abs/1910.0.

JDD @ FinCausal 2020, Task 2: Financial Document Causality Detection

Toshiya Imoto
Japan Digital Design, Inc.
toshiya.imoto@japan-d2.com

Tomoki Ito
The University of Tokyo[*]
m2015titoh@socsim.org

Abstract

This paper describes the approach we built for the Financial Document Causality Detection Shared Task (FinCausal-2020) Task 2: Cause and Effect Detection. Our approach is based on a multi-class classifier using BiLSTM with Graph Convolutional Neural Network (GCN) trained by minimizing the binary cross entropy loss. In the approach, we have not used any extra data source apart from combining the trial and practice dataset. We achieve weighted F1 score to 75.61 percent and are ranked at 7-th place.

1   Introduction

Causal detection is one of the major concrete tasks on Information Extraction (IE) in NLP research. Having a causality in text can be defined as an identification of a pair of sub-strings which explain the cause-effect relationship. How a financial news (political / economical / financial events etc.) links to the other is extremely useful for analysts, investors and risk managers in bank to forecast what will happen in the (near) future in the domestic / global economy and the financial market. FinCausal-2020 Shared Task is associated with a joint workshop on Financial Narrative Processing and MultiLing Financial Summarisation (FNP-FNS 2020). It consists of the two sub-tasks:

- Task 1: Sentence Classification

- Task 2: Cause and Effect Detection

In this paper, we propose a method for solving *Task2: Cause and Effect Detection* (Mariko et al., 2020). To solve this task, we first consider this task to be the sequence labeling task, and then applied the state-of-the-art method for the definition and extraction (DE) (Veyseh et al., 2020) to this task in a reasonable manner. We then evaluate our approach using the shared task 2 dataset. Our approach outperformed most of the other approaches submitted to this shared task. This result demonstrates the effectiveness of our approach.

2   Task and Dataset

We first describe the task setting and dataset organization. The objective of the Task2 is to extract a cause-effect pair from each sample document in the following format.

ID	Text	Cause	Effect
0026.00062	It's risen 106,500% since it came on the scene a split-adjusted $1.50 a share.	it came on the scene a split-adjusted $1.50 a share.	It's risen 106,500%

The below table shows statistics of all the dataset provided by organizer for each in csv file. "Evaluation" dataset is aimed for the bind test; therefore, it has exactly the same format but both the "Cause" and "Effect" columns are left empty.

---

[*]Work started during internship at Japan Digital Design, Inc.

Proceedings of the 1st Joint Workshop on Financial Narrative Processing and MultiLing Financial Summarisation, pages 50–54
Barcelona, Spain (Online), December 12, 2020.

Dataset	#sample	avg #word	avg #word in cause	avg #word in effect
Trial	641	45.20	18.65	18.27
Practice	1109	43.07	17.84	17.56
Evaluation	638	43.07	-	-

Please note that each document can consist of multiple sentences, but limited to less than or equal to five sentences. Also, multiple (different) cause-effect pairs could be found in the same document. In that case, they are distinguished in their IDs by adding an extra separator (ex. 0026.00070.1, 0026.00070.2, 0026.00070.3, and so on).

The prediction results are evaluated using the following weighted F1 score ($= F1_{weighted}$) and the number of exact matches ($= EM$):

$$F1_{weighted} := w_{cause} \times F1_{cause} + w_{effect} \times F1_{effect}$$

$$EM := \frac{\#\textbf{exact match}}{\#\textbf{dataset samples}}$$

where
$$w_{cause} = \frac{\#\textbf{words in cause golds}}{\#\textbf{words in cause golds} + \#\textbf{words in effect golds}} \text{ and } w_{effect} = \frac{\#(\textbf{words in effect golds})}{\#\textbf{words in cause golds} + \#\textbf{words in effect golds}}.$$

3 Approach

3.1 Problem Definition

We first consider the cause and effect detection task to be the sequence labeling task as follows. Given an input sequence $W = w_1, w_2, \cdots, w_N$ where N is the number of terms in the sequence and w_i is the i-th term in the sequence, the task can be defined as to accurately assign a label l_i to each term w_i in a sequence where $l_i \in \{\mathrm{B - Cause, B - Effect, I - Cause, I - Effect, Other}\}$. Here, B-Cause and B-Effect mean the beginning of the cause and effect part, respectively, I-Cause and I-Effect mean the inside of the cause and effect part, respectively, and Other means the other parts of the sequence. These label definitions are followed by the BIO tagging scheme.

3.2 Model Architecture

To solve this task, we utilize a neural network (NN) model that includes the following five components: Embedding Layer, bidirectional Long Short Term Memory (BiLSTM) Layer, Graph Convolutional Network1 (GCN) layer, MLP Layer, and Output Layer (Figure 1). This model is inspired by the NN model proposed in (Veyseh et al., 2020), which was proposed to address the definition extraction (DE) task.

3.2.1 Embedding Layer

This layer converts each w_i to its embedding representation x_i where x_i is the concat vector of the word embedding representation of w_i ($= e_i$) and one-hot representation from the POS (Part-of-Speech) tag of w_i ($= p_i$). Here, we used the open-source Wikipedia 2014 + Gigaword 5 Glove embedding[1] for the word embeddings, and analysis results by spacy[2] for the POS tags.

3.2.2 BiLSTM Layer

This layer converts each e_i to word-level contextual representation $\tilde{h}$ using BiLSTM (Schuster and Paliwal, 1997) and Multi Layer Perceptron (MLP) as follows:

$$h_i := \mathrm{BiLSTM}(x_i), \tilde{h}_i := \mathrm{ReLU}(\mathrm{MLP}(h_i)). \tag{1}$$

3.2.3 GCN Layer

This layer converts each h_i to graph embedding representation g_i using GCN (Xu et al., 2018), and MLP as follows:

$$g_i := \mathrm{GCN}(h_i), \tilde{g}_i := \mathrm{ReLU}(\mathrm{MLP}(g_i)). \tag{2}$$

---

[1] https://nlp.stanford.edu/projects/glove/
[2] https://spacy.io

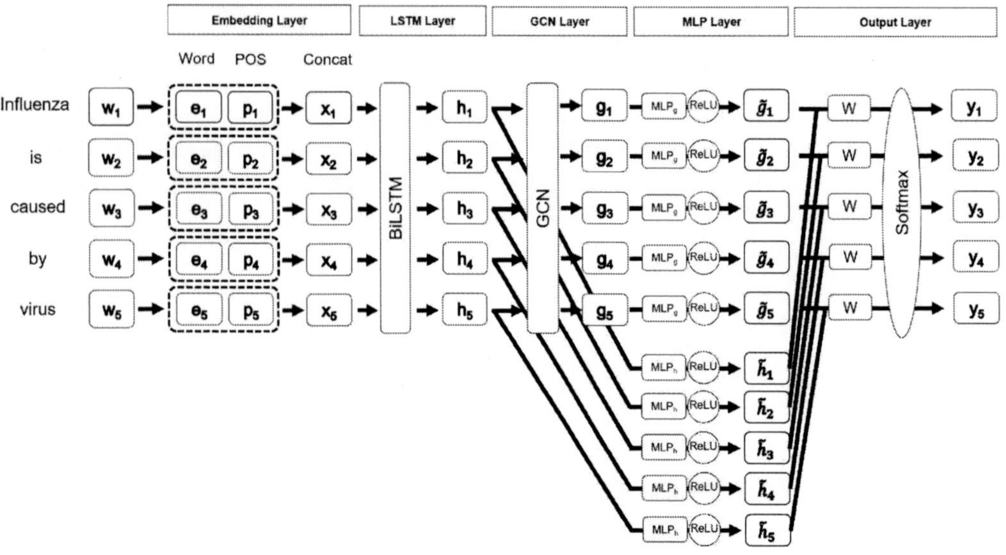

Figure 1: Architecture of our model

3.2.4 Output Layer

Finally, this layer outputs the prediction results as follows:

$$a_i^{B-Cause} := \text{Softmax}(W^{B-Cause}[\tilde{h}_i, \tilde{g}_i]), y_i^{B-Cause} := \text{argmax } a_i^{B-Cause} \tag{3}$$

$$a_i^{I-Cause} := \text{Softmax}(W^{I-Cause}[\tilde{h}_i, \tilde{g}_i]), y_i^{I-Cause} := \text{argmax } a_i^{I-Cause} \tag{4}$$

$$a_i^{B-Effect} := \text{Softmax}(W^{B-Effect}[\tilde{h}_i, \tilde{g}_i]), y_i^{B-Effect} := \text{argmax } a_i^{B-Effect} \tag{5}$$

$$a_i^{I-Effect} := \text{Softmax}(W^{I-Effect}[\tilde{h}_i, \tilde{g}_i]), y_i^{I-Effect} := \text{argmax } a_i^{I-Effect} \tag{6}$$

where $W^{B-Cause} \in \mathbb{R}^{2 \times (d_h + d_g)}$, $W^{B-Effect} \in \mathbb{R}^{2 \times (d_h + d_g)}$, $W^{I-Cause} \in \mathbb{R}^{2 \times (d_h + d_g)}$, and $W^{I-Effect} \in \mathbb{R}^{2 \times (d_h + d_g)}$. Here, d_h and d_g are the dimension sizes of $\tilde{h}_i$ and $\tilde{g}_i$, respectively. In the above, if $y_i^{B-Effect} = 1$ or $y_i^{I-Effect} = 1$, then, we predict that w_i is included in the effect part; whereas if $y_i^{B-Cause} = 1$ or $y_i^{I-Cause} = 1$, then, we predict that w_i is included in the cause part. Moreover, if $y_i^{B-Effect} = y_i^{I-Effect} = y_i^{B-Cause} = y_i^{I-Cause} = 0$, then, l_i is predicted as $Other$.

3.3 Learning

Our model can be trained using the following $\mathcal{L}$ as a loss function:

$$\mathcal{L} = \sum_{i=1}^{N} BCE(a_i^{B-Cause}, l_i^{B-Cause}) + BCE(a_i^{I-Cause}, l_i^{I-Cause})$$
$$+ BCE(a_i^{B-Effect}, l_i^{B-Effect}) + BCE(a_i^{I-Effect}, l_i^{I-Effect})$$

where $BCE(a, b)$ means the binary cross-entropy loss between a and b and l_i^x is defined as follows:

$$l_i^x = \begin{cases} 1 & (x \text{ is } l_i) \\ 0 & (otherwise) \end{cases} \tag{7}$$

Here, it should be noted that we utilize a BCE loss instead of one of the Conditional Random Field (CRF) used in (Veyseh et al., 2020). This is because the BCE loss performed better than the one of CRF in a prior experiment. In addition, it should be noted that utilization of the BCE loss alone could not avoid pathological cases where the predicted B-Cause (Effect) comes after I-Cause (Effect) or the predicted cause phrase overlaps with the effect's one. In the first case, the algorithm gives no cause (effect) label to the document. The second case, the overlap will be labelled as effect phrase. A simple approach to ensure the one and the only one cause-effect pair in a document is to introduce special position embedding used in (Zheng et al., 2017). In Section 4, we evaluate our two models (with and without the position embedding) on the blind dataset.

4 Experimental Evaluation

This section evaluates our approach using the shared task 2 dataset.[3]

4.1 Model Development Setting

We trained our model using the trial and practice datasets, and then submitted the prediction results for the evaluation dataset using the trained model. In this training, we used zero padding where the padding size was 200. Moreover, the number of layers in the BiLSTM layer and dimension size of hidden vectors were 1 and 50, respectively.

4.2 Comparison Approach

To evaluate our approach, we compare the results of the following four approaches:

- Baseline (CRF): CRF based classifier using pycrfsuite provided by organizer [4],

- BiLSTM + GCN + CRF: state-of-the-art DE model (Veyseh et al., 2020) manually adapted to our task.

- BiLSTM + GCN + BCE Loss: our model explained in section 3, and

- BiLSTM + GCN + BCE Loss with Position Embed: our model with the position embedding explained in section 3.

4.3 Results

Table 1 shows the results, demonstrating that our approach outperformed both the Baseline (CRF) and BiLSTM + GCN + CRF at the weighted F1 score. These results indicate the effectiveness of our approach.

Model	Precision	Recall	Weighted F1	EM
Baseline (CRF)	50.99%	51.74%	51.06%	11.11%
BiLSTM+GCN+CRF	72.61%	72.12%	72.29%	0.00%
BiLSTM+GCN+BCE Loss (Ours)	**75.95%**	75.57%	**75.61%**	0.00%
BiLSTM+GCN+BCE Loss with Position Embed (Ours)	75.80%	**76.60%**	75.29%	**53.45%**

Table 1: Evaluation Result for the shared task 2

5 Conclusion

In this paper, we propose a method for extracting cause and effect parts from texts. We first consider this task to be the sequence labeling task and then, applied the method for DE to this task in a reasonable manner. Our approach was ranked at 7-th. In future, our approach can be improved by utilizing the pre-trained language models (e.g., BERT) or transfer learning approaches.

---

[3] For all the experiments in this section, we used the hardware with GPU cores GeForce GTX 1660 and with RAM 16.0GB.
[4] https://github.com/yseop/YseopLab/tree/develop/FNP_2020_FinCausal/baseline/task2

References

Dominique Mariko, Hanna Abi Akl, Estelle Labidurie, Stephane Durfort, Hugues de Mazancourt, and Mahmoud El-Haj. 2020. The Financial Document Causality Detection Shared Task (FinCausal 2020). In *The 1st Joint Workshop on Financial Narrative Processing and MultiLing Financial Summarisation (FNP-FNS 2020)*, Barcelona, Spain.

Mike Schuster and Kuldip K. Paliwal. 1997. Bidirectional recurrent neural networks. *IEEE Transactions on Signal Processing*, 45(11):2673–2681.

Amir Veyseh, Franck Dernoncourt, Dejing Dou, and Thien Huu Nguyen. 2020. A joint model for definition extraction with syntactic connection and semantic consistency. In *Proceedings of The Thirty-Fourth AAAI Conference on Artificial Intelligence (AAAI-20)*, pages 9098–9105.

Keyulu Xu, Chengtao Li, Yonglong Tian, Tomohiro Sonobe, Ken ichi Kawarabayashi, and Stefanie Jegelka. 2018. Representation learning on graphs with jumping knowledge networks. In *Proceedings of ICML 2018*.

Suncong Zheng, Feng Wang, Hongyun Bao, Yuexing Hao, Peng Zhou, and Bo Xu. 2017. Joint extraction of entities and relations based on a novel tagging scheme. In *Proceedings of the 55th Annual Meeting of the Association for Computational Linguistics*, pages 1227–1236.

UPB at FinCausal-2020, Tasks 1 & 2: Causality Analysis in Financial Documents using Pretrained Language Models

Marius Ionescu[1], Andrei-Marius Avram[1,2], George-Andrei Dima[1,3],
Dumitru-Clementin Cercel[1], Mihai Dascalu[1]
University Politehnica of Bucharest[1]
Research Institute for Artificial Intelligence, Romanian Academy[2]
Military Technical Academy Ferdinand I[3]
`{ionescumarius23, avram.andreimarius}@gmail.com,`
`andrei.dima@mta.ro, {dumitru.cercel, mihai.dascalu}@upb.ro`

Abstract

Financial causality detection is centered on identifying connections between different assets from financial news in order to improve trading strategies. FinCausal 2020 - Causality Identification in Financial Documents – is a competition targeting to boost results in financial causality by obtaining an explanation of how different individual events or chain of events interact and generate subsequent events in a financial environment. The competition is divided into two tasks: (a) a binary classification task for determining whether sentences are causal or not, and (b) a sequence labeling task aimed at identifying elements related to cause and effect. Various Transformer-based language models were fine-tuned for the first task and we obtained the second place in the competition with an F1-score of 97.55% using an ensemble of five such language models. Subsequently, a BERT model was fine-tuned for the second task and a Conditional Random Field model was used on top of the generated language features; the system managed to identify the cause and effect relationships with an F1-score of 73.10%. We open-sourced the code and made it available at: `https://github.com/avramandrei/FinCausal2020`.

1 Introduction

Financial news contain various descriptions of causes and effects between financial objects that influence sales, employment, earnings, or stock prices. Causal analysis can be used to detect correlation between news and prices of different assets (Qu and Kazakov, 2019) by identifying different consequence, that in return can lead to major events as a financial crisis (Stavroglou et al., 2017; Tiffin, 2019) or possible arbitrage opportunities (Stavroglou et al., 2017). For example, given the follow-up statement regarding Brexit *"The Leave win led to an 11 percent drop in GBP/USD overnight."*, we can infer that *"The Leave win"* is the cause for *"an 11 percent drop in GBP/USD overnight"*, which represents the effect and indicates a change in price of the GBP/USD currency pair (Mariko et al., 2020).

Nowadays, the high volume of published news and financial documents hinders and renders unfeasible the manual analysis of all articles in order to extract implications on the economy. Thus, a need for developing new tools for causality extraction emerged to facilitate this process. Methods based on pattern detection (Khoo et al., 2000), on combinations of patterns and rules (Sorgente et al., 2013), and on attention mechanisms with different embeddings (Li et al., 2019) were introduced in the field of causal detection. A shared task was proposed at the Financial Narrative Processing Workshops, namely FinCausal-2020 (Mariko et al., 2020), to evaluate the performance of each participant system on two tasks defined on a financial corpus proposed by YseopLab. The *first task* consisted in building a classifier to identify whether a sentence contains a financial causality or not, whereas the *second task* extracted causes and also their corresponding effects from a given text.

The rest of the paper is organized as follows. The second section introduces our proposed methods for tackling the two sub-tasks, while the third section presents our results, together with experimental setup and an error analysis. The paper ends with conclusions and proposals of future work.

Proceedings of the 1st Joint Workshop on Financial Narrative Processing and MultiLing Financial Summarisation, pages 55–59
Barcelona, Spain (Online), December 12, 2020.

2 Dataset

The organizers made available 3 datasets for both tasks: trial, practical, and evaluation. The trial dataset for the first task contained 8580 samples, out of which only 569 (i.e., 6,69% from total samples) included causal events. The practice dataset has approximately the same distribution as trial, with 13478 samples out of which 1010 were labeled as causal (i.e., 7,49% from total samples). The evaluation dataset was kept blind, but it has the same distribution as trial and practice.

The dataset for the second taks largely corresponds to samples from Task 1 that are labelled as causal, with the specification of causal and effect sub-strings. The trial dataset contains 641 samples, while the practical dataset contains 1109 samples. The evaluation dataset contained 638 samples with removed annotations, i.e., the text is revealed, but there are no causal or effect representations.

3 Proposed Solutions

Five Transformer-based language models (Vaswani et al., 2017) were considered for the *the first task* and were fine-tuned on the FinCausal-2020 dataset, namely: BERT (base and large) (Devlin et al., 2018), AL-BERT (base and large) (Lan et al., 2019), RoBERTA (base and large) (Liu et al., 2019), SciBERT (base) (Beltagy et al., 2019), and FinBERT (base) (Araci, 2019). The fine-tuning mechanism was the one proposed by Devlin et al. (2018) who take the embedding of the first token and project it into a scalar that represents a probability. Then, we minimize the Kullback–Leibler divergence between the distribution of the dataset and the distribution predicted by the model by using the Adam optimizer (Kingma and Ba, 2014). We also experimented with various classifier ensembles taking into account different combinations of the fine-tuned language models as these ensembles surpass in general the performance of individual models; majority voting was considered for the final labeling of each sentence.

The *second task* was operationalised as a token labeling, similar to part-of-speech tagging (Bohnet et al., 2018) or named entity recognition (Dumitrescu and Avram, 2019), by marking the corresponding tokens of the causes and effects sequences with *CAUSE* and *EFFECT* labels, whereas the rest of the tokens were marked as *O*. Inside-Outside-Beginning (IOB) format was used for the labels to support the identification of the sequences at inference time. BERT-base models were used to obtain contextualized embeddings for each token, and then a Conditional Random Field (CRF) (Lafferty et al., 2001) was trained to predict the most probable sequence of labels for a given input text.

Although the IOB format and the CRF aided in modeling the problem as a token labeling task, the extraction of causes and effects is harder at inference because the model can make an incorrect prediction in the middle of a cause/effect sequence, or predict a cause/effect token in the middle of *O* tags. Several heuristics were introduced to mitigate this issue when extracting the causes and effects, namely:

- If a cause or effect sequence has a length lower than 4, it is ignored.

- In case that the model does not predict a cause or an effect in a sequence, all the remaining *O* tags become the missing cause or effect.

- If a different predicted sequence (e.g. "EFFECT EFFECT CAUSE CAUSE EFFECT EFFECT") is found inside the initial sequence, the inside predicted sequence has a length lower than 4, and the other part of the initial sequence does not have the beginning tag[1], then the inside predicted sequence is ignored and the two initial sequences are combined.

- After the tokens are labeled as either *CAUSE* or *EFFECT*, the original text is retrieved by identifying the boundary words using the Levenshtein distance (Levenshtein, 1966); a word is considered a boundary word if it has a Levenshtein distance equal to 0 and a length higher than 3. Afterwards, all words between boundary words are labeled as either *CAUSE* or *EFFECT*.

---

[1]The beginning tag can be either B-EFFECT or B-CAUSE.

	Dev Set			Test Set		
Model	**Precision**	**Recall**	**F1 Score**	**Precision**	**Recall**	**F1 Score**
ALBERT-Base	95.71	95.88	95.78	96.75	96.76	96.75
SciBERT-Base	95.67	95.99	95.75	96.77	96.83	96.80
FinBERT-Base	93.88	94.71	93.92	94.08	94.30	94.18
BERT-Large	**95.81**	**96.15**	**95.77**	97.10	97.02	97.05
RoBERTa-Large	95.69	95.29	95.46	97.35	97.30	97.32
Ensemble Model	-	-	-	**97.53**	**97.59**	**97.55**
Baseline	95.26	95.21	95.23	-	-	-
Winning Team	-	-	-	97.73	97.76	97.74

Table 1: Task 1 performance of our methods against the baseline and the winning team solution.

	Dev Set			Test Set		
Model	**Precision**	**Recall**	**F1 Score**	**Precision**	**Recall**	**F1 Score**
BERT-CRF	66.66	74.34	68.85	75.61	72.13	73.10
Baseline	50.98	51.74	51.06	-	-	-
Winning System	-	-	-	94.78	94.70	94.71

Table 2: Task 2 performance of our method against the baseline and the winning team solution.

4 Evaluation

4.1 Experimental Setup

We fine-tune five pretrained models provided by Hugging Face[2]: BERT, RoBERTa, ALBERT, SciBERT, and FinBERT. The models are trained using a Tesla P100-PCIE-16GB GPU. Grid search is performed to determine best hyper-parameters, learning rate, and maximal length of sequence. We use a maximal length of the sequence of 256 for *base* models and 384 for *large* models. Learning rate is set to 2×10^{-6}, with the exception of ALBERT-Base where a learning rate of 2×10^{-5} is preferred. Tests before the evaluation submission were made on a dataset that contained data from trial and practice, separated in 80% train and 20 % validation partitions, while keeping the same distribution as previous datasets.

4.2 Results

Table 1 introduces the results for the first task obtained using the best ensemble of language models, as well as each individual language model, on both the validation and the evaluation sets. The best ensemble contained the following models: ALBERT-Base, SciBERT-Base, BERT-Large, FinBERT-Base and RoBERTA-Large, and it outperformed RoBERTa-Large with 0.23% on the evaluation set, obtaining an 97.55% F1-score, while being marginally behind by 0.19% from the winning model. While considering individual models, BERT-Large obtained the highest score on the validation set with an 95.77% F1-score, surpassing the baseline of the organizers by 0.54%; RoBERTA-Large obtained the highest score on the evaluation set with an 97.32% F1-score.

The results on the second task using BERT-Base and CRF are depicted in Table 2. The model outperformed the baseline by 17.79% in terms of F1-score, but it was surpassed by 21.61% on the evaluation set.

4.3 Error Analysis

Several problems were identified when inspecting the trial and practice datasets, and the errors performed by our models. We observed that false positive examples on the first task exhibit statements containing actions or facts, but these actions or facts do not affect other entities in that sentence. For example, a penalty in the first entry from Table 3 may have effects on individuals with debts, but this is not explicitly mentioned in the sentence; thus, the context is not complete to consider it a cause-effect situation. In

---

[2]https://huggingface.co/transformers/

Index	Text	Pred Label	True Label
0334.00010	The current penalty is 2% per month of the amount of unpaid taxes.	True	False
0360.00009	In the last 90 days, insiders have purchased 817 shares of company stock worth $39,799.	True	False
0588.00013	The average ticket price on TickPick, an online exchange for reselling tickets, plunged 50 percent from $341.19 in 2018 to $170.60 in 2019. With multiple theme park attractions, a film studio tour, and a new exhibit opening in Manhattan, there are other ways for fans of the franchise to consume its content.	False	True
0114.00014	The company had revenue of $64.68 million during the quarter, compared to analyst estimates of $64.51 million. During the same period in the previous year, the business earned $0.73 earnings per share. The firm's quarterly revenue was down 3.9% compared to the same quarter last year.	False	True

Table 3: Misclassified examples for Task1.

the second example, shares purchased by insiders usually have impact on price, but these details are not present. Thus, our models make incorrect predictions because part of these structures are more common in causal statements. In addition, we identified issues in the case of false negative when the cause and the effect are placed in different environments or fields. For example, the cause in the third example is related to attractions located in Manhattan, but the effect is the decrease on an online ticket reselling platform. This is a long dependency and need more specialized knowledge is required to infer these effects. The same situation is encountered in the fourth example, where a company's revenue in this quarter is associate with a 3.9% decrease from same period of last year.

Errors on the second task consist mostly in the incorrect detection of complete sequences of cause or effect. As presented in Table 4, the beginning of our sequences is well identified in most cases, but too few words are considered. This situation may occur from incorrect predictions made by our model or a bad translation from token to text given the post-processing.

Index	Text	Predicted Cause	True Cause	Predicted Effect	True Effect
0332.00009	Net operating profit in the global markets division plunged 26 per cent to 251 billion yen (S$3.19 billion) last year, largely because of a big fall in Europe, and the bank said it struggled in customer business due to sluggish markets.	a big fall in	a big fall in Europe, and the bank said it struggled in customer business due to sluggish markets.	Net operating profit in the global markets division plunged 26 per cent to 251 billion yen	Net operating profit in the global markets division plunged 26 per cent to 251 billion yen (S$3.19 billion) last year
0576.00008	He used the money to help buy a house for his daughter. Now, 229 members of the pension schemes are concerned they may not see their money again.	He used the money to help buy a house for his daughter.	He used the money to help buy a house for his daughter.	Now, 229 members of the pension schemes are concerned they may not see their money	Now, 229 members of the pension schemes are concerned they may not see their money again.

Table 4: Misclassified examples for Task 2.

5 Conclusion and Future Work

As the financial volume of data grows, it becomes harder and harder to analyze chain of events, with corresponding cause and effects. Our solution for the first task at FinCausal-2020 was an ensemble of five Transformer-based language models that placed second on the evaluation leader-board with an 97.55% F1-score. The second task considered a BERT-base model to extract contextualized embeddings for each token, that were further used to train a CRF; an F1-score of 73.10% was achieved on the evaluation set. Possible directions of research include using more powerful language models like XLNet (Yang et al., 2019) or exploring if an additional bidirectional long-short term memory (BiLSTM) on top of the language model to improve the results on either task. In addition, we envision the consideration of specific discourse markers, as well as transfer learning using similar tasks - for example, a model trained on the SNLI corpus from Stanford (Bowman et al., 2015).

References

Dogu Araci. 2019. Finbert: Financial sentiment analysis with pre-trained language models. *arXiv preprint arXiv:1908.10063*.

Iz Beltagy, Kyle Lo, and Arman Cohan. 2019. Scibert: A pretrained language model for scientific text. *arXiv preprint arXiv:1903.10676*.

Bernd Bohnet, Ryan McDonald, Gonçalo Simões, Daniel Andor, Emily Pitler, and Joshua Maynez. 2018. Morphosyntactic tagging with a meta-bilstm model over context sensitive token encodings. In *Proceedings of the 56th Annual Meeting of the Association for Computational Linguistics (Volume 1: Long Papers)*, pages 2642–2652.

Samuel R. Bowman, Gabor Angeli, Christopher Potts, and Christopher D. Manning. 2015. A large annotated corpus for learning natural language inference. In *Proceedings of the 2015 Conference on Empirical Methods in Natural Language Processing (EMNLP)*. Association for Computational Linguistics.

Jacob Devlin, Ming-Wei Chang, Kenton Lee, and Kristina Toutanova. 2018. Bert: Pre-training of deep bidirectional transformers for language understanding. *arXiv preprint arXiv:1810.04805*.

Stefan Daniel Dumitrescu and Andrei-Marius Avram. 2019. Introducing ronec–the romanian named entity corpus. *arXiv preprint arXiv:1909.01247*.

Christopher SG Khoo, Syin Chan, and Yun Niu. 2000. Extracting causal knowledge from a medical database using graphical patterns. In *Proceedings of the 38th annual meeting of the association for computational linguistics*, pages 336–343.

Diederik P Kingma and Jimmy Ba. 2014. Adam: A method for stochastic optimization. *arXiv preprint arXiv:1412.6980*.

John Lafferty, Andrew McCallum, and Fernando CN Pereira. 2001. Conditional random fields: Probabilistic models for segmenting and labeling sequence data. In *ICML*.

Zhenzhong Lan, Mingda Chen, Sebastian Goodman, Kevin Gimpel, Piyush Sharma, and Radu Soricut. 2019. Albert: A lite bert for self-supervised learning of language representations. *arXiv preprint arXiv:1909.11942*.

Vladimir I Levenshtein. 1966. Binary codes capable of correcting deletions, insertions, and reversals. In *Soviet physics doklady*, volume 10, pages 707–710.

Zhaoning Li, Qi Li, Xiaotian Zou, and Jiangtao Ren. 2019. Causality extraction based on self-attentive bilstm-crf with transferred embeddings. *arXiv preprint arXiv:1904.07629*.

Yinhan Liu, Myle Ott, Naman Goyal, Jingfei Du, Mandar Joshi, Danqi Chen, Omer Levy, Mike Lewis, Luke Zettlemoyer, and Veselin Stoyanov. 2019. Roberta: A robustly optimized bert pretraining approach. *arXiv preprint arXiv:1907.11692*.

Dominique Mariko, Hanna Abi Akl, Estelle Labidurie, Stephane Durfort, Hugues de Mazancourt, and Mahmoud El-Haj. 2020. The Financial Document Causality Detection Shared Task (FinCausal 2020). In *The 1st Joint Workshop on Financial Narrative Processing and MultiLing Financial Summarisation (FNP-FNS 2020)*, Barcelona, Spain.

Haizhou Qu and Dimitar Kazakov. 2019. Detecting causal links between financial news and stocks. In *2019 IEEE Conference on Computational Intelligence for Financial Engineering & Economics (CIFEr)*, pages 1–8. IEEE.

Antonio Sorgente, Giuseppe Vettigli, and Francesco Mele. 2013. Automatic extraction of cause-effect relations in natural language text. *DART@ AI* IA*, 2013:37–48.

Stavros K Stavroglou, Athanasios A Pantelous, Kimmo Soramaki, and Konstantin Zuev. 2017. Causality networks of financial assets. *Journal of Network Theory in Finance*, 3(2):17–67.

Mr Andrew J Tiffin. 2019. *Machine learning and causality: the impact of financial crises on growth*. International Monetary Fund.

Ashish Vaswani, Noam Shazeer, Niki Parmar, Jakob Uszkoreit, Llion Jones, Aidan N Gomez, Łukasz Kaiser, and Illia Polosukhin. 2017. Attention is all you need. In *Advances in neural information processing systems*, pages 5998–6008.

Zhilin Yang, Zihang Dai, Yiming Yang, Jaime Carbonell, Russ R Salakhutdinov, and Quoc V Le. 2019. Xlnet: Generalized autoregressive pretraining for language understanding. In *Advances in neural information processing systems*, pages 5753–5763.

NITK NLP at FinCausal-2020 Task 1 Using BERT and Linear models.

Hariharan R L
Dept of Information Technology
National Institute of Technology
Karnataka
hariharanrl.22@gmail.com

Anand Kumar M
Dept of Information Technology
National Institute of Technology
Karnataka
m_anandkumar@nitk.edu.in

Abstract

FinCausal-2020 is the shared task which focuses on the causality detection of factual data for financial analysis. The financial data facts don't provide much explanation on the variability of these data. This paper aims to propose an efficient method to classify the data into one which is having any financial cause or not. Many models were used to classify the data, out of which SVM model gave an F-Score of 0.9435, BERT with specific fine-tuning achieved best results with F-Score of 0.9677.

1 Introduction

The important aspect as far as the financial news is the variability and the impact which it causes. In the information retrieval process, causality is an essential and well-known topic. Several NLP methods can be used to find the relationship between financial data and its effect. The main focus of this work is to come out with a better solution for the FinCausal-2020 shared task (Mariko et al., 2020). This shared task mainly focuses on determining causality associated with the financial object's transformation in quantified facts.

We have applied classification for the financial data using Linear Model and Deep Learning BERT (Devlin et al., 2018) model. In the case of Linear model, an SVM classifier is used, which is further fine tuned to produce better result. The fine-tuned BERT base uncased version was used as a deep learning model.

This paper is presented as follows; the details about the data being used are explained in section 2, system description is being explained in section 3, results and discussion in section 4, which follows the conclusions in the last section 5.

2 Dataset Description

The task organisers provided the data for the shared task as CSV files, namely trial, practice, and evaluation. These data where extracted from a corpus of 2019 financial news provided by Quam. The original data being HTML pages corresponding to the daily financial news feed is extracted. These raw set is being arranged with the column as Index, Text, and Category. Initially, the trial and practice dataset were released to build and train the model, which consists of data as shown in the table 1. The trial data had 8580 sentences with labels indicating whether there is any causality(1) or not(0), similarly 13478 sentences for practice data. The evaluation data had 7386 sentences without any labels and needed to be evaluated and appended with the prediction labels.

Example Sentences from the Dataset:

- Virtually free comprehensive medical care would lead to big increases in the demand for services:0

- Transat loss more than doubles as it works to complete Air Canada deal:1

Proceedings of the 1st Joint Workshop on Financial Narrative Processing and MultiLing Financial Summarisation, pages 60–63
Barcelona, Spain (Online), December 12, 2020.

Data	# of Sentences	Category	
		0(No causality)	1(Causality)
Trial	8580	8011	569
Practice	13478	12468	1010

Table 1: FinCausal 2020 Dataset details

3 System Description

We have developed both linear as well as deep learning models. The SVM classifier was used as a linear model and, BERT was used as a deep learning model. The hardware used for the experiments were Colaboratory by Google with GPU ranging from 10GB to 16GB(Tesla K80/Tesla P100). The description of each system is explained one by one below.

The Linear model SVM classifier was given as a baseline by the task organiser. We have tried with NBSVM model (Wang and Manning, 2012), To apply SVM model for the textual data, some basic preprocessing like removing URL, HTML tags (Richardson, 2007), special symbols, and accented characters were done. Further, these texts were converted to lowercase and TF-IDF vectorizer (Salton and McGill, 1986) was applied. The experiment was conducted in two phases, the first one being training the model using the trial dataset and testing with the practice dataset. The second one was training the model using practice dataset and testing with the trial dataset. The same steps were followed for both the phases. The prediction for the evaluation data provided by the organiser is done by building a model which was trained on both practice and train data.

The first phase of the experiment was done by splitting (Pedregosa et al., 2011) the trial data into 85% and 15% for train and validation, respectively. The TF-IDF was experimented with different n-grams and fixed a range of (1-5). The minimum and the maximum number of occurrences (min_df and max_df) of words to be considered to make a vocabulary were also altered. After grid search, the maximum and minimum occurrences were fixed at 90% (maximum number of sentences) and 2(least number of sentences), which gave better scores for the metrics as in table 2. The same process was repeated for the practice data, which was used to predict the trial data.

The practice and trial data were combined to predict the evaluation data whose scores are also given in table 2.

Task	Trained using	F1	Recall	Precision
Predict Practice Data	Trial	0.926486	0.940867	0.934973
Predict Trial Data	Practice	0.939693	0.943590	0.937448
Predict Evaluation Data	Both	0.943532	0.948687	0.943193

Table 2: SVM Model Results for Trial, Practice and Evaluation Data

The BERT model (Devlin et al., 2018) was used as a deep learning model for the classification task which is based on transformers (Wolf et al., 2019). Here we have used the BERT-base uncased pretrained model and trained FinCausal data on top of it. As the BERT model don't require any preprocessing, it wasn't done. Initially, during the evaluation phase, the BERT model was directly applied with the practice and trial data without any fine-tuning which gave us a result lower than that of the SVM model as shown in table 3.

Task	Trained using	F1	Recall	Precision
Predict Practice Data	Trial	0.868717	0.876911	0.860889
Predict Trial Data	Practice	0.865269	0.870159	0.860506
Predict Evaluation Data	Both	0.851731	0.846872	0.856710

Table 3: BERT Model Results for Trial, Practice and Evaluation Data

The results shown above are done before the evaluation deadline. Post evaluation, the model was fine-tuned with changing important parameters as given below.

- Batch Size: kept as 6 for both training and validation

- Epochs: varied with early stopping keeping lesser validation loss

- Neither attention nor segments were maintained

- Learning rate: Kept at $2e^{-5}$.

- The LR parameter was tried with one fit one cycle and auto-fit learning rate using learning policies (Smith, 2017).

Task	Trained using	F1	Recall	Precision
Predict Evaluation Data	Both Practice and Trial	0.967770	0.967100	0.968712

Table 4: BERT Model Result Post Evaluation Deadline

The cyclic learning rate policy was used as mentioned in (Smith, 2017). This method was adopted for evaluation data, which helped to tune the learning rate and showed improved result than the other two models as shown in table 4.

4 Results and Discussion

Here we will explain the results obtained for the two phases of experiments conducted and the result that the model has given for the evaluation data. As shown in tables 2 and 3, both the models with modified parameters gave better results. These models were used to predict the evaluation data. The leaderboard after the evaluation deadline along with our updated score is as given in table 5. Our result was at 9th position, which was the result obtained from the linear SVM model, as mentioned earlier. On further exploring the BERT model, we could get better results, which shows our proposed fine-tuned BERT model score near the 6th position in the final leaderboard.

Team	F1	Recall	Precision
NITK NLP[1]	0.967770 (6)	0.967100 (6)	0.968712 (6)
NITK NLP	0.943532 (9)	0.948687 (9)	0.943193 (9)

Table 5: Leaderboard Positions

Hence, the results show that BERT model performed if the hyperparameters were well-tuned as it had a large corpus of pretrained data. After the evaluation, it was evident that the model could perform better as the accuracy difference with the first place and the accuracy improvement over the earlier BERT.

5 Conclusions

The FinCausal-2020 shared task was mainly aimed to come up with a model that could analyze the text and say whether it belongs to a particular financial causality or not. The main challenge was the imbalanced dataset and from which we need to develop a model that could produce an accurate result. As per the experiments being conducted and observing the results, the fine-tuned BERT model could perform well for the blind dataset using the k nown data than BERT and the liner SVM model. If we could come up with more balanced data with sampling methods, BERT would outperform most of the existing models.

---

[1] Post Evaluation

References

Jacob Devlin, Ming-Wei Chang, Kenton Lee, and Kristina Toutanova. 2018. Bert: Pre-training of deep bidirectional transformers for language understanding. *arXiv preprint arXiv:1810.04805*.

Dominique Mariko, Hanna Abi Akl, Estelle Labidurie, Stephane Durfort, Hugues de Mazancourt, and Mahmoud El-Haj. 2020. The Financial Document Causality Detection Shared Task (FinCausal 2020). In *The 1st Joint Workshop on Financial Narrative Processing and MultiLing Financial Summarisation (FNP-FNS 2020*, Barcelona, Spain.

Fabian Pedregosa, Gaël Varoquaux, Alexandre Gramfort, Vincent Michel, Bertrand Thirion, Olivier Grisel, Mathieu Blondel, Peter Prettenhofer, Ron Weiss, Vincent Dubourg, et al. 2011. Scikit-learn: Machine learning in python. *Journal of machine learning research*, 12(Oct):2825–2830.

Leonard Richardson. 2007. Beautiful soup documentation. *April*.

Gerard Salton and Michael J McGill. 1986. Introduction to modern information retrieval.

Leslie N Smith. 2017. Cyclical learning rates for training neural networks. In *2017 IEEE Winter Conference on Applications of Computer Vision (WACV)*, pages 464–472. IEEE.

Sida Wang and Christopher D Manning. 2012. Baselines and Bigrams: Simple, Good Sentiment and Topic Classification. Technical report.

Thomas Wolf, Lysandre Debut, Victor Sanh, Julien Chaumond, Clement Delangue, Anthony Moi, Pierric Cistac, Tim Rault, Rémi Louf, Morgan Funtowicz, Joe Davison, Sam Shleifer, Patrick von Platen, Clara Ma, Yacine Jernite, Julien Plu, Canwen Xu, Teven Le Scao, Sylvain Gugger, Mariama Drame, Quentin Lhoest, and Alexander M. Rush. 2019. Huggingface's transformers: State-of-the-art natural language processing. *ArXiv*, abs/1910.03771.

Fraunhofer IAIS at FinCausal 2020, Tasks 1 & 2: Using Ensemble Methods and Sequence Tagging to Detect Causality in Financial Documents

Maren Pielka, Anna Ladi, Clayton Chapman, Eduardo Brito, Rajkumar Ramamurthy, Paul Mayer, Abdul Wahab, Rafet Sifa, and **Christian Bauckhage**
Fraunhofer IAIS, Schloss Birlinghoven, 53757 Sankt Augustin, Germany
Fraunhofer Center for Machine Learning, Germany
`maren.pielka@iais.fraunhofer.de`

Abstract

The FinCausal 2020 shared task aims to detect causality on financial news and identify those parts of the causal sentences related to the underlying cause and effect. We apply ensemble-based and sequence tagging methods for identifying causality, and extracting causal subsequences. Our models yield promising results on both sub-tasks, with the prospect of further improvement given more time and computing resources. With respect to task 1, we achieved an F1 score of 0.9429 on the evaluation data, and a corresponding ranking of 12/14. For task 2, we were ranked 6/10, with an F1 score of 0.76 and an ExactMatch score of 0.1912.

1 Introduction

Despite the many advances in the field of Natural Language Processing (NLP) in recent years, many challenges dealing with contextual relationships still persist, one of which being causality. Causality, as conveyed in written English, relates a textual description of a cause to a description of its effect(s). While the identification of subordinating conjunctions - such as "because", "since" and "if" - can help in identifying relevant pieces of text forming causal relationships, often richer contextual information is needed. The goal of the FinCausal 2020 shared task (Mariko et al., 2020) is to explore causal relationships from financial and economic context and to determine the likelihood of whether or not a given text contains a causal relationship and then detect the cause and effect parts of the sentence.

2 Data

The data sets are composed of 23808 paragraphs from financial news.[1] The data sets contain paragraphs, with an average size of 214 (+/- 161) characters, each with annotations relevant to the corresponding task. For task 1, the size of the complete data is 22058 paragraphs, each of which is annotated with a "1" (a causal relationship exists in this paragraph - 7.2% of the paragraphs), or "0" (no causal relationship in the paragraph - 92.8% of the paragraphs). The data set for task 2 has a size of 1750 paragraphs, with every paragraph containing exactly one cause and one effect character sequence. These are annotated as character ranges. Since we treat task 2 as a sequence tagging task, we transform these annotations to token level annotations, so that every token in the paragraph gets the label CAUSE, EFFECT or, 0 (for all tokens which belong neither to the cause nor the effect part). This yields a label distribution of 40.8% CAUSE, 40.8% EFFECT, and 18.4% "0". For the experimentation and the development of the models for task 1 and task 2, a 70% training - 30% validation split of the respective data-set (joined practice and trial) was used.

3 System

Tasks 1 and 2 were treated independently. The former was treated as a document classification task (a document being a paragraph in this case) and the latter as a sequence tagging task.

---

[1]The data set both for task 1 and task 2 is split into a "trial" and "practice" test. To account for any differences in the distribution of the data in the two subsets, we decided to join the two sub-datasets.

Proceedings of the 1st Joint Workshop on Financial Narrative Processing and MultiLing Financial Summarisation, pages 64–68
Barcelona, Spain (Online), December 12, 2020.

3.1 Task 1: Causality Detection

The goal of task 1 is to identify whether a paragraph contains a causal relation or not. The labels are binary, with a 1 indicating the presence of (a) causal statement(s), and a 0 otherwise. For the best performing models, no data pre-processing was used, other than ignoring punctuation and single-character tokens. We explore two approaches: The first is a paragraph embedding paired with shallow Machine Learning (ML) models, while the second is embedding the individual tokens and using a one-dimensional Convolutional Neural Network (CNN) as a classifier. For the first strategy, the text data is transformed into a feature matrix using the scikit-learn (Pedregosa et al., 2011), version 0.23.1 implementation of TF-IDF. This matrix is then used by several classical ML models, including SVMs, Logistic Regression and Random Forests. The best performers were found to be an SVM Classifier [2] and an XGBoost model. XGBoost, or eXtreme Gradient Boosting, is a fairly recent algorithm based on gradient boosting techniques (Chen and Guestrin, 2016). Additionally, a voting classifier model was made from these two models, which predicts the class label based on the argmax of the sums of the prediction confidence values from the SVM classifier and the XGBoost models. We adjust the parameters of our models using the RandomizedSearchCV class from scikit-learn[3]. These models were trained on an Intel i7-8750H CPU. After training, a Voting Ensemble classifier from scikit-learn was built using the trained models as parameters. This ensemble used "soft" voting, that is, the probabilities output by the SGD and XGBoost were averaged and the result was the output of the ensemble.

The second strategy is based on the idea of using CNNs for NLP (Yin et al., 2017). Adjusting the filter size on a one-dimensional CNN also acts similarly to an N-gram, and CNNs are generally very fast at analyzing problems with large feature matrices. This model was implemented using Tensorflow (Abadi et al., 2015) and Keras (Chollet and others, 2015), versions 2.1.0 and 2.3.1 respectively. The data was processed using the Keras tokenizer and then fed into a one-dimensional CNN. The network consists of an embedding layer that uses the 200-dimensional Word2Vec (Le and Mikolov, 2014) embedding from GoogleNews, a convolutional layer, and 2 dense layers. The models were optimized using manual parameter tuning[4]. This model was trained using an Nvidia GTX 1060 Max-Q with 6GB of GPU memory.

3.2 Task 2: Causality Extraction

The goal of task 2 is to identify the parts of a sentence, that correspond to cause and effect, respectively. It is thus a sequence tagging task in which the tokens of a sentence must be assigned either a CAUSE, EFFECT, or 0 tag. One approach to tackle sequence tagging tasks is the use of sequential models such as a Recurrent Neural Network (RNN). We employ the Flair sequence tagger by (Akbik et al., 2018), using ElMo (Peters et al., 2018) and fine-tuned BERT embeddings. For BERT, the transformers library by (Wolf et al., 2019), version 3.0.2 was used.

Using the Flair Sequence Tagger We utilize the Flair Sequence tagger (Akbik et al., 2018) to produce token-level predictions for the causality extraction task. The framework consists of a recurrent neural model with a Conditional Random Field (CRF) and a Long Short Term Memory (LSTM) layer trained for token classification. Learning rate scheduling is applied during training, meaning that the learning rate will be reduced whenever the validation loss does not decrease after 3 epochs. Once the learning rate falls below 0.0001 following this policy, training is stopped.

As a first fine-tuning step, we evaluate different pre-trained word embeddings (ElMo, BERT, Flair, GloVe, and FastText) that are integrated in the Flair framework. We find that ElMo embeddings obtained from the full-sized model (see (Peters et al., 2018) for implementation details) yield the best results on

---

[2]For the SVM classifier, the scikit-learn implementation was used.

[3]For the TFIDF-SVM the adjusted parameters are: $ngram\_range = (1, 2)$ and $smooth\_idf = false$ for TFIDF, and $alpha = 1e-6$, $loss = log$ for SVM. For TFIDF-XGBoost: $ngram\_range = (1, 1)$ for TFIDF, and $booster = gbtree$, $learning\_rate = 0.3$, $max\_depth = 6$, and $n\_estimators = 100$ for XGBoost.

[4]The best configuration was: a tokenizer that ignored all punctuation and symbols, and set all words to lowercase, and for the CNN: a 1D convolutional layer of 64x3 with relu, a dropout layer with $rate = 0.1$, a global 1D maxpooling layer, a dense layer with an output of 16 with relu, another dropout layer with $rate = 0.1$, and a final dense layer with an output of 1 with sigmoid activation.

Model	F1 score	Recall	Precision
XGBoost	0.942374	0.948957	0.943619
SVM classifier	**0.942909**	0.947604	0.942031
Ensemble	0.937722	**0.949093**	**0.950175**
CNN	0.942066	0.945979	0.940644

Table 1: Task 1 results.

our data, so we use them as word embeddings in the following evaluation steps. The model is being further improved by optimizing the hyperparameters, yielding a batch size of 32, an initial learning rate of 0.1, and a hidden size of 500 neurons. In addition, we adjust the class weights of the model to compensate for the imbalanced label distribution (see section 2). Thus, the weights for the CAUSE and EFFECT classes are decreased to 0.25, and the weight for the 0 class is increased to 0.5. As an alternative embedding method, we also incorporate the fine-tuned BERT model delivered as a baseline for task 1 [5] to the Flair Sequence Tagger. The models were trained on an Nvidia Tesla V100-SXM2 with 32 GB of GPU memory.

Post-processing   In addition to the token classification by the Flair sequence tagger, we apply some post-processing to the output to further improve the results. Our first approach is based on the observation, that the classifier sometimes correctly recognizes large parts of a CAUSE or EFFECT sequence, but still predicts 0 for some single tokens in between. Since in most of the cases, every CAUSE or EFFECT is a coherent sequence, it makes sense to account for that using rule-based post-processing. This is done by filling in every "hole" of up to three tokens in a consequent sequence of CAUSE or EFFECT predictions with the surrounding label. An alternative post-processing approach that was tested, was to smooth the output class probabilities over consecutive tokens, using an average filter with a window size of 3 tokens.

4   Results

The reported results were evaluated on the holdout test set, which was not included in the validation set. The evaluation metrics are reported as defined by the shared task organizers. [6]

4.1   Task 1

For task 1, the best results in terms of F1 score were achieved by the SVM classifier, while the Ensemble of the SVM classifier and the XGBoost classifier performed best in terms of precision and recall (see Table 1). The CNN model performed not significantly different than the less complex ML models.

4.2   Task 2

For task 2, the best scores with respect to the three common metrics are achieved by the Flair sequence tagger model using fine-tuned BERT embeddings, balanced class weights, and applying the first post-processing approach (filling in "holes" of predicted sequences). Interestingly, our baseline model (ElMo) outperforms the tuned models on ExactMatch. Especially adding balanced class weights seems to cause a drop in the ExactMatch metric. This could potentially indicate some overfitting effect of the simpler model. Table 2 shows two examples that illustrate this behavior. In example 1 (Table 2a), while the simpler model predicts the sequence exactly right, the model with fine-tuning added makes one mistake in between. Example 2 (Table 2b), however, shows that the second model is better at separating cause and effect in a non-straightforward formulated sentence, even though it does not get the labels exactly right. Generally, the fine-tuned model tends to leave larger "holes" between "cause" and "effect" sequences, than the simpler model does.

---

[5] `https://github.com/yseop/YseopLab/tree/develop/FNP_2020_FinCausal/baseline/task1`
[6] See website of shared task: `https://competitions.codalab.org/competitions/23748`

Sentence	They	fell	(...)	to	4p	on	Wednesday	as	analysts	lowered	price	targets	and	cut	forecasts.
Model 1 prediction	E	E	(...)	E	E	E	E	0	C	C	C	C	C	C	C
Model 2 prediction	E	E	(...)	E	E	E	0	0	C	C	C	C	C	C	C
True label	E	E	(...)	E	E	E	E	0	C	C	C	C	C	C	C

(a) Example 1

Sentence	Suppose	(...)	they	could	borrow	at	-0.25%	NLY	would	be	getting	paid	$262	million.
Model 1 prediction	E	(...)	E	E	E	E	E	E	E	E	E	E	E	E
Model 2 prediction	C	(...)	0	C	C	C	E	E	E	E	E	E	E	E
True label	C	(...)	C	C	C	C	0	E	E	E	E	E	E	E

(b) Example 2

Table 2: Example predictions of model 1 (ElMo) and model 2 (fine-tuned BERT, balanced, post-processing), on two sentences from our validation split (part of the practice data set). "C" stands for "cause", "E" for "effect". Due to space constraints, only the relevant part of the sentence is displayed.

Model	F1 score	Recall	Precision	ExactMatch
ElMo	0.740380	0.745353	0.741605	**0.231975**
ElMo, balanced	0.726232	0.71307	0.777991	0.184953
ElMo, balanced, post-processing	0.743371	0.734344	0.769642	0.210031
ElMo, balanced, post-processing (probability smoothing)	0.741773	0.734672	0.759757	0.152038
ElMo, task1 data augmentation	0.731066	0.733866	0.729065	0.188088
ElMo, task1 data augmentation , post-processing	0.737836	0.748546	0.735892	0.191223
fine-tuned BERT, balanced, post-processing	**0.759982**	**0.748933**	**0.799503**	0.191223

Table 3: Task 2 results. The Flair sequence tagger model was used to produce all of those results.

5 Discussion

Our present system relies heavily on the choice of embeddings, as well as on large pre-trained language models. This could possibly be changed if we had a more extensive and consistent data set for training. One of our observations in this regard was, that the provided data included a number of irregularly formatted paragraphs (for example headlines or bullet points). We believe that our algorithms would benefit from further analysis and possible cleaning of such instances. Additionally, the current data does not allow us to explore other approaches that are based on syntactic features.

Regarding task 1, the results of the CNN could be potentially improved by additional hyperparameter tuning. The CNN model showed good results already in early epochs, but was not able to outperform the less complex ML models, which were extensively tuned. With respect to task 2, it would have been interesting to test more combinations of embeddings, data augmentation, and post-processing, which was not possible due to limited time and computing resources.

6 Conclusion and Outlook

Identifying causality in text can be a helpful tool for many empirical use cases. In the context of financial document analysis, it could be used to identify important facts and developments in the annual report of a company. We can potentially extend our previous work on various downstream-tasks on financial reports by incorporating causality, for instance for key performance indicator extraction (Brito et al., 2019b) , contradiction detection (Sifa et al., 2019b) , or content-based text classification and consistency checks (Sifa et al., 2019a) . We can also exploit causality detection in the context of text summarization. Causal sentences may indicate content richness, which is useful not only to extract the most relevant sentences of an original text within an extractive summarization setting (as presented in (Brito et al., 2019a)) but also when we evaluate the quality of a generated summary from a wide range of features (Biesner et al., 2020). In our future work, we are planning to address such applications, building on our experiments and insights from this challenge.

References

Martín Abadi, Ashish Agarwal, Paul Barham, Eugene Brevdo, Zhifeng Chen, Craig Citro, Greg S. Corrado, Andy Davis, Jeffrey Dean, Matthieu Devin, Sanjay Ghemawat, Ian Goodfellow, Andrew Harp, Geoffrey Irving, Michael Isard, Yangqing Jia, Rafal Jozefowicz, Lukasz Kaiser, Manjunath Kudlur, Josh Levenberg, Dan Mané, Rajat Monga, Sherry Moore, Derek Murray, Chris Olah, Mike Schuster, Jonathon Shlens, Benoit Steiner, Ilya Sutskever, Kunal Talwar, Paul Tucker, Vincent Vanhoucke, Vijay Vasudevan, Fernanda Viégas, Oriol Vinyals, Pete Warden, Martin Wattenberg, Martin Wicke, Yuan Yu, and Xiaoqiang Zheng. 2015. TensorFlow: Large-scale machine learning on heterogeneous systems. Software available from tensorflow.org.

Alan Akbik, Duncan Blythe, and Roland Vollgraf. 2018. Contextual String Embeddings for Sequence Labeling. In *COLING 2018, 27th International Conference on Computational Linguistics*, pages 1638–1649.

David Biesner, Eduardo Brito, Lars Patrick Hillebrand, and Rafet Sifa. 2020. Hybrid ensemble predictor as quality metric for German text summarization: Fraunhofer IAIS at GermEval 2020 task 3. In *Proceedings of the 5th Swiss Text Analytics Conference (SwissText) & 16th Conference on Natural Language Processing (KONVENS)*.

Eduardo Brito, Max Lübbering, David Biesner, Lars Patrick Hillebrand, and Christian Bauckhage. 2019a. Towards supervised extractive text summarization via RNN-based sequence classification. *arXiv preprint arXiv:1911.06121*.

Eduardo Brito, Rafet Sifa, Christian Bauckhage, Rüdiger Loitz, Uwe Lohmeier, and Christin Pünt. 2019b. A hybrid AI tool to extract key performance indicators from financial reports for benchmarking. In *Proceedings of the ACM Symposium on Document Engineering 2019*.

Tianqi Chen and Carlos Guestrin. 2016. XGBoost: A Scalable Tree Boosting System. *CoRR*, abs/1603.02754.

Francois Chollet et al. 2015. Keras.

Q. V. Le and T. Mikolov. 2014. Distributed representations of sentences and documents. *CoRR*, abs/1405.4053.

Dominique Mariko, Hanna Abi Akl, Estelle Labidurie, Stephane Durfort, Hugues de Mazancourt, and Mahmoud El-Haj. 2020. The Financial Document Causality Detection Shared Task (FinCausal 2020). In *The 1st Joint Workshop on Financial Narrative Processing and MultiLing Financial Summarisation (FNP-FNS 2020, Barcelona, Spain*.

F. Pedregosa, G. Varoquaux, A. Gramfort, V. Michel, B. Thirion, O. Grisel, M. Blondel, P. Prettenhofer, R. Weiss, V. Dubourg, J. Vanderplas, A. Passos, D. Cournapeau, M. Brucher, M. Perrot, and E. Duchesnay. 2011. Scikit-learn: Machine learning in Python. *Journal of Machine Learning Research*.

Matthew E. Peters, Mark Neumann, Mohit Iyyer, Matt Gardner, Christopher Clark, Kenton Lee, and Luke Zettlemoyer. 2018. Deep contextualized word representations. In *Proc. of NAACL*.

Rafet Sifa, Max Lübbering, Ulrich Nütten, Christian Bauckhage, Ulrich Warning, Benedikt Fürst, Tim Khameneh, Daniel Thom, Ilgar Huseynov, Roland Kahlert, Jennifer Schlums, Anna Ladi, Hisham Ismail, Bernd Kliem, Rüdiger Loitz, Maren Pielka, Rajkumar Ramamurthy, Lars Hillebrand, Birgit Kirsch, and Thiago Bell. 2019a. Towards automated auditing with machine learning. In *Proceedings of the ACM Symposium on Document Engineering 2019*. ACM.

Rafet Sifa, Maren Pielka, Rajkumar Ramamurthy, Anna Ladi, Lars Hillebrand, and Christian Bauckhage. 2019b. Towards contradiction detection in German: A translation-driven approach. In *Proc. of IEEE SSCI 2019*.

Thomas Wolf, Lysandre Debut, Victor Sanh, Julien Chaumond, Clement Delangue, Anthony Moi, Pierric Cistac, Tim Rault, Rémi Louf, Morgan Funtowicz, Joe Davison, Sam Shleifer, Patrick von Platen, Clara Ma, Yacine Jernite, Julien Plu, Canwen Xu, Teven Le Scao, Sylvain Gugger, Mariama Drame, Quentin Lhoest, and Alexander M. Rush. 2019. Huggingface's transformers: State-of-the-art natural language processing. *ArXiv*, abs/1910.03771.

Wenpeng Yin, Katharina Kann, Mo Yu, and Hinrich Schütze. 2017. Comparative Study of CNN and RNN for Natural Language Processing. *CoRR*, abs/1702.01923.

NTUNLPL at FinCausal 2020, Task 2: Improving Causality Detection Using Viterbi Decoder

Pei-Wei Kao,[1] Chung-Chi Chen,[1] Hen-Hsen Huang,[2,3] Hsin-Hsi Chen[1,3]

[1] Department of Computer Science and Information Engineering
National Taiwan University, Taiwan
[2] Department of Computer Science, National Chengchi University, Taiwan
[3] MOST Joint Research Center for AI Technology and All Vista Healthcare, Taiwan
{pwgao,cjchen}@nlg.csie.ntu.edu.tw,
hhhuang@nccu.edu.tw, hhchen@ntu.edu.tw

Abstract

In order to provide an explanation of machine learning models, causality detection attracts lots of attention in the artificial intelligence research community. In this paper, we explore the cause-effect detection in financial news and propose an approach, which combines the BIO scheme with the Viterbi decoder for addressing this challenge. Our approach is ranked the first in the official run of cause-effect detection (Task 2) of the FinCausal-2020 shared task. We not only report the implementation details and ablation analysis in this paper, but also publish our code for academic usage.

1 Introduction

Adopting causality information as features can benefit lots of applications such as question answering (Sharp et al., 2016), event prediction (Balashankar et al., 2019), and medical text mining (Khoo et al., 2000). In the financial domain, causality detection can be applied to stock movement prediction (Balashankar et al., 2019) and supporting financial services (Izumi and Sakaji, 2019). To better explain the causality that occurs between financial events, cause-effect detection is a fundamental research issue.

Taking a close look to financial documents, we find that there may exist multiple causal events and multiple causal chains in a paragraph. In such a case, traditional extraction methods like discourse parser are not feasible. In order to deal with this issue, we formulate the cause-effect detection task as a sequence labeling problem and propose an approach using BIO scheme and Viterbi decoder. We find that the proposed approach has the ability to identify multiple causal events and multiple causal chains in a given short paragraph, and also gives a better event span boundary.

Our contributions are two-fold as follows.

1. We propose an approach to cause-effect detection for financial news that could better identify multiple causal events and event spans.

2. We release the code of the best-performing model for future research.[1]

2 Pre-processing

We experiment on the FinCausal-2020 dataset (Mariko et al., 2020), which consists of two subtasks, including causal meanings detection (Task 1) and cause-effect detection (Task 2). The numbers of training instances are 22,058 and 1,750 for Task 1 and Task 2, respectively. This work only focuses on Task 2.

We use the Stanford CoreNLP Stanza (Manning et al., 2014; Qi et al., 2020) toolkit[2] to tokenize each sentence and generate the part-of-speech (POS) tag for each token. For the examples with multiple causal events, we recognize them by their indices and add a special number token before each example to treat them as different model inputs. As for causal relations tagging, we use "B, I, O" (Begin, Inside, and Outside) and "C, E" (Cause and Effect) labels to represent the positional information of the words and the semantic roles of the causal events.

---

[1] https://github.com/pxpxkao/FinCausal-2020
[2] https://github.com/stanfordnlp/stanza

Proceedings of the 1st Joint Workshop on Financial Narrative Processing and MultiLing Financial Summarisation, pages 69–73
Barcelona, Spain (Online), December 12, 2020.

3 Methods

3.1 Baseline Models

- **Conditional Random Field (CRF)**: CRF (Lafferty et al., 2001) is a popular model for sequential labeling, which considers the neighboring labels during calculation. We use the default parameter settings provided by Mariko et al. (2020) to train a baseline model for comparison.

- **Bidirectional Encoder Representations from Transformers (BERT)**: The pretrained text encoder BERT generally performs well in many NLP tasks (Devlin et al., 2018). In this paper, we use the *BERT-base* model, which consists of 12 Transformer layers with the hidden dimension of 768. It is pre-trained on *Masked Language Model Task* and *Next Sentence Prediction Task* via a large cross domain corpus and is well-known for its simplification of fine-tuning downstream tasks. We implement this baseline model by using the package provided by *huggingface*[3] (Wolf et al., 2019).

For clarity of the model structure, we add a linear layer above the BERT-base model, and fine-tune it into a token classifier as our baseline for experiment. Given a sequence of tokens in the source documents $\mathbf{x} = [x_1, x_2, ..., x_n]$, the classifier will generate the target sequence of labels $\mathbf{y} = [y_1, y_2, ..., y_n]$, $y_i \in \{O, C, E\}$ for baseline target, and $y_i \in \{O, B-C, I-C, B-E, I-E\}$ for BIO scheme target.

The training parameters of max length, batch size, and epoch is set as 350, 4 and 4, respectively. The initial learning rate is set to 5e-05, and we use cross entropy as the loss function. The final training time with one GTX TITAN X and Core i7-6700 is approximately 15 minutes, and requires 4GB GPU RAM.

3.2 POS Feature

With the POS tags labeled by the Stanford CoreNLP Stanza (Manning et al., 2014; Qi et al., 2020) toolkit, we first represent the POS information as a one-hot vector and concatenate it with the output of BERT's last hidden state output, and then send it to the final linear layer. The concatenated tensor is subject to predict the final label of the token.

3.3 Viterbi Decoder

Viterbi decoding is a dynamical programming algorithm that allows us to find the path with the global optimal probability. The probability of the most possible path ending in state t with observation i is:

$$p_t(i, x) = e_t(i) \max_k (p_k(j, x - 1) \times p_{kt}), \tag{1}$$

where $e_t(i)$ represents the emission probability to observe element i in state t, $p_k(j, x-1)$ represents the probability of the most possible path ending at position $x-1$ in state k with element j, and p_{kt} represents the transition probability from state k to t.

Our proposed Viterbi decoder is added upon the fine-tuned BERT classifier only during evaluation. We consider the final output of the linear classifier in BERT as the emission matrix, and pre-define the transition matrix based on the BIO scheme. The Viterbi decoder will compute recursively to find the most probable sequence.

4 Results

We perform five-fold cross-validation to verify our experimental results during the self-evaluation period. Table 1 shows the results of the self-evaluation, where exact match stands for the accuracy of both predicted cause and effect are exactly matched with the labels. Table 2 shows the results of the blind test round. The baseline BERT-base model outperforms the CRF model by approximately 0.2 in terms of F1 score and 0.4 in terms of exact match ratio, showing the advantage of the pre-trained model. Compared with CRF, we notice that BERT can better distinguish multiple causal events and causal chains given the

---

[3] https://github.com/huggingface/transformers

same input text. We also find that adding POS features does not significantly improve the performance. Besides, using the BIO tagging scheme alone decreases the performance. However, combining the BIO tagging scheme with the Viterbi decoder achieves a great improvement in exact match ratio by rising 5%.

Extractor	F1	P	R	Exact Match
CRF	0.620	0.620	0.610	0.245
BERT-base	0.871	0.867	0.868	0.673
+ POS	0.873	0.868	0.869	0.673
+ BIO	0.862	0.824	0.832	0.654
+ POS/BIO	0.856	0.816	0.825	0.643
+ BIO/Viterbi	**0.875**	**0.871**	**0.872**	0.708
+ POS/BIO/Viterbi	0.871	0.868	0.869	**0.710**

Table 1: Self-evaluation results.

Extractor	F1	P	R	Exact Match
CRF	0.701	0.694	0.681	0.328
BERT-base	0.942	0.959	0.962	0.773
+ POS	0.942	0.942	0.942	0.779
+ BIO	0.914	0.925	0.912	0.790
+ POS/BIO	0.913	0.923	0.911	0.785
+ BIO/Viterbi	**0.947**	**0.948**	**0.947**	**0.824**
+ POS/BIO/Viterbi	0.942	0.942	0.941	**0.824**

Table 2: Blind test results.

Table 3 shows the performances of the top-3 teams in the official round. The F1-score, Precision, and Recall of the runner-up models are similar to those of the proposed approach. However, the exact match ratio of our proposed approach outperforms those of other participants, which is 8.7% better than that of the method proposed by the second-place team.

Ranking	F1	P	R	Exact Match
1 - Proposed Approach	0.947	0.948	0.947	0.824
2	0.947	0.947	0.947	0.737
3	0.837	0.836	0.839	0.704

Table 3: Results of official round.

5   Error Analysis

Figure 1 shows an instance for error analysis, where our approach outperforms the baseline models in the self-evaluation experiment. Here we use the last partition of the training data as validation set for example. In this case, there are two causal chains. The CRF model does not find any causal event. The BERT model only succeeds in tagging one of the causal chains, but fails to tag the other effect span "That stake...". In contrast, our approach successfully labels the correct causal events, which shows that it can better identify the proper event span and achieve a higher exact match ratio.

Figure 2 shows an instance that our best model fails to correctly identify the causal events. In this example, our model could not extract the two correct causal events in one sentence, suggesting that our system still has room for improvement on detecting multiple causal events in a single sentence.

: Cause : Effect	**(0237.00009.2)**
Baseline BERT-base	Avid Technology (AVID) Impactive Capital disclosed on Sept. 6 an initial position of 3,665,256 shares of the audio- and video-content maker and distributor. That stake counts 2,528,227 shares purchased at $5.98 to $9.97 each during the period of July 8 through Sept. 6. Impactive said that it acquired the shares because it was an attractive investment.
Our Approach	Avid Technology (AVID) Impactive Capital disclosed on Sept. 6 an initial position of 3,665,256 shares of the audio- and video-content maker and distributor. That stake counts 2,528,227 shares purchased at $5.98 to $9.97 each during the period of July 8 through Sept. 6. Impactive said that it acquired the shares because it was an attractive investment.

Figure 1: Instance for error analysis that our approach succeeds.

: Cause : Effect	**(0151.00014.1) & (0151.00014.2)**
Gold	If the total income of a company was in excess of INR 1 Crore but less than INR 10 Crores then applicable surcharge was of 7% and if income exceeded INR 10 Crores, then the surcharge was charged at 12%.
Our Approach	If the total income of a company was in excess of INR 1 Crore but less than INR 10 Crores then applicable surcharge was of 7% and if income exceeded INR 10 Crores, then the surcharge was charged at 12%.

Figure 2: Instance for error analysis that our approach fails.

6 Conclusion

This paper presents our approach to causality detection, which is ranked first in the Task 2 of FinCausal-2020. The ablation analysis shows the effectiveness of the proposed approach. The error analysis also supports that the proposed approach performs better in multiple causal events and multiple causal chains cases.

In the future, we plan to adopt the proposed approach to the documents in other domains. We also plan to adopt the extracted causality from financial documents to improve the performance of downstream tasks such as stock movement prediction and financial argument mining.

Acknowledgements

This research was partially supported by Ministry of Science and Technology, Taiwan, under grants MOST 109-2218-E-009-014, MOST 109-2634-F-002-040, and MOST 109-2634-F-002-034, and by Academia Sinica, Taiwan, under grant AS-TP-107-M05.

References

Ananth Balashankar, Sunandan Chakraborty, Samuel Fraiberger, and Lakshminarayanan Subramanian. 2019. Identifying predictive causal factors from news streams. In *Proceedings of the 2019 Conference on Empirical Methods in Natural Language Processing and the 9th International Joint Conference on Natural Language Processing (EMNLP-IJCNLP)*, pages 2338–2348, Hong Kong, China, November. Association for Computational Linguistics.

Jacob Devlin, Ming-Wei Chang, Kenton Lee, and Kristina Toutanova. 2018. Bert: Pre-training of deep bidirectional transformers for language understanding. *arXiv preprint arXiv:1810.04805*.

Kiyoshi Izumi and Hiroki Sakaji. 2019. Economic causal-chain search using text mining technology. In *Proceed-*

ings of the First Workshop on Financial Technology and Natural Language Processing, pages 61–65, Macao, China, August.

Christopher S. G. Khoo, Syin Chan, and Yun Niu. 2000. Extracting causal knowledge from a medical database using graphical patterns. In *Proceedings of the 38th Annual Meeting of the Association for Computational Linguistics*, pages 336–343, Hong Kong, October. Association for Computational Linguistics.

John Lafferty, Andrew McCallum, and Fernando CN Pereira. 2001. Conditional random fields: Probabilistic models for segmenting and labeling sequence data.

Christopher D. Manning, Mihai Surdeanu, John Bauer, Jenny Finkel, Steven J. Bethard, and David McClosky. 2014. The Stanford CoreNLP natural language processing toolkit. In *Association for Computational Linguistics (ACL) System Demonstrations*, pages 55–60.

Dominique Mariko, Hanna Abi Akl, Estelle Labidurie, Stephane Durfort, Hugues de Mazancourt, and Mahmoud El-Haj. 2020. The financial document causality detection shared task (fincausal 2020). In *The 1st Joint Workshop on Financial Narrative Processing and MultiLing Financial Summarisation (FNP-FNS 2020)*, Barcelona, Spain.

Peng Qi, Yuhao Zhang, Yuhui Zhang, Jason Bolton, and Christopher D. Manning. 2020. Stanza: A Python natural language processing toolkit for many human languages. In *Proceedings of the 58th Annual Meeting of the Association for Computational Linguistics: System Demonstrations*.

Rebecca Sharp, Mihai Surdeanu, Peter Jansen, Peter Clark, and Michael Hammond. 2016. Creating causal embeddings for question answering with minimal supervision. In *Proceedings of the 2016 Conference on Empirical Methods in Natural Language Processing*, pages 138–148, Austin, Texas, November. Association for Computational Linguistics.

Thomas Wolf, Lysandre Debut, Victor Sanh, Julien Chaumond, Clement Delangue, Anthony Moi, Pierric Cistac, Tim Rault, Rémi Louf, Morgan Funtowicz, Joe Davison, Sam Shleifer, Patrick von Platen, Clara Ma, Yacine Jernite, Julien Plu, Canwen Xu, Teven Le Scao, Sylvain Gugger, Mariama Drame, Quentin Lhoest, and Alexander M. Rush. 2019. Huggingface's transformers: State-of-the-art natural language processing. *ArXiv*, abs/1910.03771.

FiNLP at FinCausal 2020 Task 1: Mixture of BERTs for Causal Sentence Identification in Financial Texts

Sarthak Gupta
Munich Re
Munich, Bavaria, Germany
sgupta2@munichre.com

Abstract

This paper describes our system developed for the sub-task 1 of the FinCausal shared task in the FNP-FNS workshop held in conjunction with COLING-2020. The system classifies whether a financial news text segment contains causality or not. To address this task, we fine-tune and ensemble the generic and domain-specific BERT language models pre-trained on financial text corpora. The task data is highly imbalanced with the majority *non-causal* class; therefore, we train the models using strategies such as under-sampling, cost-sensitive learning, and data augmentation. Our best system achieves a weighted F1-score of 96.98 securing 4th position on the evaluation leaderboard. The code is available at https://github.com/sarthakTUM/fincausal

1 Introduction

A causal relation involves two events e_1 and e_2 where one, referred to as 'Cause', is responsible for triggering the other, referred to as the 'Effect'. The causation can be expressed implicitly or explicitly by causal verbs, punctuation, conjunctions, prepositions, or any other linguistic cue that establishes a trigger between the cause and the effect. Explicit causation in a text segment can usually be identified by the presence of causative keywords or characteristic grammatical patterns whereas implicit causality is comparatively harder to detect, usually only through the context. Many studies on Causality Extraction in the text are motivated by (Khoo et al., 1998) in which they identify five different constructs to express explicit cause-effect relation. (Girju, 2003) extended the third construct by identifying lexical syntactic patterns including Noun-Phrases (NP) such as $\langle NP_1, \text{cause-verb}, NP_2 \rangle$ to find causality in the WordNet[1] definitions. (Kim et al., 2007) extends the first and second construct by introducing four categories of the cue phrases for the causality expressions to build an automatic causality extraction framework. More recently, (Dasgupta et al., 2018) proposed an LSTM-CRF architecture for labeling cause and effect tokens in a text segment.

Many prior works on Causality Extraction primarily use the data labeled using weak supervision techniques due to scarcity of the human-labeled data. (Kyriakakis et al., 2019) use Transfer Learning to tackle this issue. To this end, (Mariko et al., 2020) introduced a human-labeled data for causality extraction in financial news text crawled by QWAM.[2]

Shared Task: This shared task consists of two sub-tasks: (i) Binary classification of text segment as *'Causal (C)'* if the text contains causality or *'Non-Causal (NC)'* otherwise, and (ii) Extracting spans of 'cause' and 'effect' within the text segment if it is labelled 'Causal'. The 'effect' can only be a quantified fact, whereas a 'cause' can be a fact or a quantified fact. We propose a system for the first sub-task.

Our Contributions: We augment the data with publicly available Relation Classification and Causality Extraction corpora to increase the number of training instances and leverage Transfer Learning by fine-tuning generic and financial BERT language models (Devlin et al., 2019) on the task data. We train

---

[1] https://wordnet.princeton.edu/
[2] https://www.qwamci.com/

Proceedings of the 1st Joint Workshop on Financial Narrative Processing and MultiLing Financial Summarisation, pages 74–79
Barcelona, Spain (Online), December 12, 2020.

individual models using various strategies to tackle the imbalanced target distribution and propose an ensemble using a second-order classifier. Our best system achieves a weighted F1-score of 96.98 securing 4th position on the evaluation leaderboard out of 14 teams.

2 System Description

2.1 Data

The data consists of English text segments from financial news articles released in three installments namely *Trial*, *Practice*, and *Evaluation*. We combine the *Trial* and the *Practice* data to train, test and fine-tune the models. The results on the leaderboard are obtained on the *Evaluation* data. As shown in table 1, the dataset is imbalanced with approximately 92% Non-Causal class. To increase the number of the training instances, we augment the task data with the publicly available (i) training instances labelled with 'Cause-Effect' Relation in the SemEval 2010 Task-8 Relation Classification Corpus (Hendrickx et al., 2010) (ii) training instances labeled with 'Drug-AE' (Drug-Adverse Effect) relation in the ADE corpus (Gurulingappa et al., 2012), and (iii) training instances in Biomedical causal detection dataset provided by (Kyriakakis et al., 2019).

Corpus	C	NC	Example (Causal)
Task (Trial+Practice)	1579	20479	*"Investors are catching on to B. Riley's growth story, driving up shares more than 70% year-to-date."*
SemEval-2010-Task-8	1331	9386	*"The burst has been caused by water hammer pressure."*
Adverse Drug Effect	4271	16625	*"Pirmenol hydrochloride-induced QT prolongation and T wave inversion on electrocardiogram during treatment for symptomatic atrial fibrillation."*
Causaly	1113	887	*"The obstacle of getting older men to undergo circumcision may also be associated with working schedules that may disclose one's circumcision status."*

Table 1: Number of Causal Instances vs. Non-Causal instances along with examples in the corpus

2.2 Models

Modeling the long-range context is a challenge for the LSTM cell (Hochreiter and Schmidhuber, 1997); Therefore the Transformer architecture based BERT (Devlin et al., 2019) along with its proven superiority for Text Classification[3] is an appropriate choice for this binary classification task containing long texts. We explored 4 different pre-trained BERT language models for this task: (i) generic `BERT-base-uncased` provided by (Wolf et al., 2019)[4], (ii) `FinBert-SEC`[5] (Desola et al., 2019) referred to as `FinBert-Combo` in the original publication trained on 10-K SEC filings, (iii) `FinBert-TRC2`[6] (Araci, 2019) trained on Reuters TRC2 corpus, and (iv) `FinBert-FinCom`[7] (Yang et al., 2020) referred to as `FinBERT-FinVocab-Uncased` in the original publication trained on financial communication text such as 10-K & 10-Q corporate reports, earning calls, and analyst reports. In all the models, we replace the `[CLS]` token representation with the mean-pooled embedding of the last layer tokens as shown in figure 1 (right).

We observed that the individual models specialize in different aspects of the confusion matrix, i.e., some models produce more true positives and others produce less false positives primarily due to the difference in the pre-trained weights and the training strategies. Therefore, we ensemble the individual

---

[3] https://gluebenchmark.com/leaderboard
[4] https://github.com/ThilinaRajapakse/simpletransformers
[5] https://github.com/psnonis/FinBERT
[6] https://github.com/ProsusAI/finBERT
[7] https://github.com/yya518/FinBERT

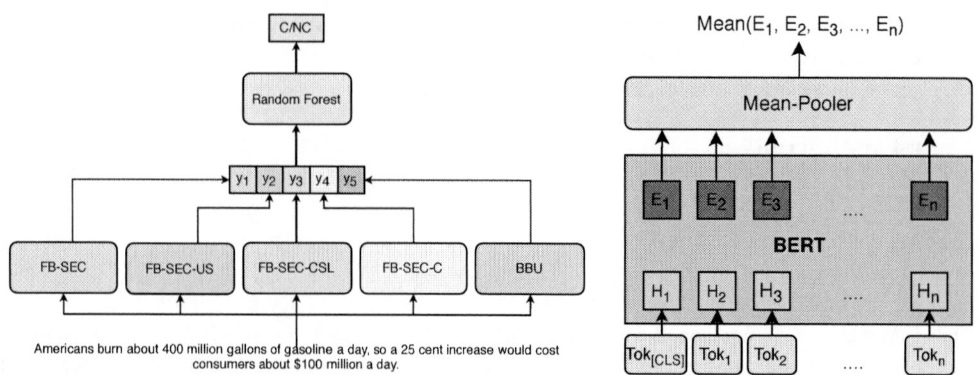

Figure 1: **Left**: Ensemble for the final system consisting of FinBert-SEC trained on task data (FB-SEC), FinBert-SEC with under-sampling on task data (FB-SEC-US), FinBert-SEC with Cost-Sensitive Learning on task data (FB-SEC-CSL), FinBert-SEC trained on task data augmented with Causaly without CSL or US (FB-SEC-C), and Bert-Base-Uncased trained on task data (BBU). *C/NC* refers to *Causal/Non-Causal* and y_n are the predictions by the individual models. **Right**: Demonstration of the Mean-Pooled embeddings calculated using the mean of the last-layer hidden states of the tokens

models to capture their strengths by using the predictions of the individual models as the features for training a second-order Random Forest classifier with 5 estimators and a maximum depth of 100. Our final system is shown in figure 1 (left).

3 Experiments and Results

We split the annotated corpus as 80% for training, 10% for validation, and 10% for testing. The final system is retrained on all the data combined for the number of training epochs obtained from the validation set using Early Stopping (Caruana et al., 2001) with patience of 3 epochs on the F1 score. We use PyTorch (Paszke et al., 2019) models trained on Nvidia GTX1050 GPU. We aim to answer the following Research Questions (RQ) using Precision (P), Recall (R), Weighted F1-score (F1), Confusion Matrix (TP, TN, FP, FN) on our own test set (columns without *-E) and official evaluation set (columns with *-E).

3.1 RQ1: Does further pre-training BERT on financial text affect the Causality Classification performance?

We hypothesize that the BERT models benefit from further pre-training on the financial text corpus before fine-tuning for causality classification. Therefore, we compare the BERT models mentioned in section 2.2, all of which are trained with identical hyperparameters: (i) Maximum Sequence Length of 200, (ii) Batch Size of 8 with Gradient Accumulation of 2 steps, (iii) Adam Optimizer with $4e^{-5}$ Learning Rate that decreases linearly after linearly increasing during a warm-up period of 335 steps. Table 2 shows that the FB-SEC outperforms the other BERT models w.r.t. the weighted F1-score on our own test set and is therefore used as the baseline for comparison in next research questions.

3.2 RQ2: What are the effects of training strategies such as undersampling, data augmentation, and cost-sensitive learning on the classification performance?

We try several strategies to tackle the imbalanced target label distribution.

Undersampling (US): We reduce the number of *non-causal* instances in the training set so that the proportion of the two classes is equal (50-50). Table 3 shows an improvement in the detection of the *causal* class through TP and FN.

Data Augmentation (DA): We select randomly the training instances from the augmenting corpora mentioned in section 2.1 and concatenate with the training set maintaining the target distribution. We see

Model	P	R	F1	TP	TN	FP	FN	P-E	R-E	F1-E
BERT-base-uncased (BBU)	94.42	95.01	94.34	68	**2028**	20	90	95.28	95.64	95.22
FinBert-FinCom (FB-FC)	93.39	94.28	93.40	56	2024	24	102	94.91	95.34	94.87
Finbert-TRC2 (FB-TRC2)	94.24	94.87	94.25	69	2024	24	89	**96.46**	**96.62**	**96.36**
Finbert-SEC (FB-SEC)	**95.19**	**95.55**	**95.29**	**91**	2017	31	**67**	96.19	96.42	96.23

Table 2: Comparison of generic BERT model with the Financial BERTs

Strategy	Configuration	P	R	F1	TP	TN	FP	FN	P-E	R-E	F1-E
Baseline	FB-SEC	95.19	95.55	95.29	91	2017	31	67	96.19	96.42	**96.23**
US	**FB-SEC 50-50 (FB-SEC-US)**	95.30	91.93	93.03	**140**	1888	160	**18**	95.11	90.90	92.23
DA	Training+SemEval (FB-SEC-SE)	94.79	95.01	94.89	95	2001	47	63	94.17	94.05	94.11
	Training+ADE (FB-SEC-ADE)	**95.34**	95.37	95.36	**106**	1998	50	**52**	94.79	94.81	94.80
	Training+Causaly (FB-SEC-C)	95.33	**95.64**	**95.43**	95	**2015**	**33**	63	96.18	96.26	96.22
CSL	**FB-SEC scaled (FB-SEC-CSL)**	95.62	95.92	**95.70**	97	2019	29	**61**	**96.22**	**96.43**	96.19

Table 3: Effect of training strategies on the performance

from Table 3 that augmenting the training set with *Causaly* (FB-SEC-C) outperforms other augmentations w.r.t. the weighted F1-score on our own test set.

Cost-Sensitive Learning (CSL): We scale the loss resulting from incorrect classification of a *Causal* instance during the training of the model using scaling factor $\alpha = \frac{1}{C} * \frac{N(D)}{N(D_{causal})}$ where C is the number of classes, $N(D)$ is the number of samples in data D and $N(D_{causal})$ is the number of samples where label is *causal*. Table 3 shows that the CSL leads to more True Positives than the baseline as expected.

3.3 RQ3: Which models should be combined for an ensemble and how?

Table 4 shows that ensembling using a second-order Random Forest (RF) classifier performs marginally better than majority-voting, and that the overall performance of the ensembled system is higher than the individual models. Our final system is an ensemble of FB-SEC, FB-SEC-CSL, FB-SEC-US, FB-SEC-C, and BBU.

Configuration	Ensemble	P	R	F1	P-E	R-E	F1-E
Final system	Majority Voting	95.89	96.14	95.96	96.90	96.99	96.93
Final system	**Second-Order RF**	**96.10**	**96.19**	**96.14**	**96.95**	**97.03**	**96.98**
Final system w/o BBU	Majority Voting	95.57	95.92	95.54	96.60	96.52	96.56
Final system w/o BBU	Second-Order RF	95.82	96.05	95.89	96.51	96.68	96.55

Table 4: Comparison of various ensemble configurations

4   Conclusion

We proposed a system to detect causality in the financial texts using an ensemble of domain-specific and generic BERT classifiers, trained using various datasets and training strategies to tackle the imbalanced class distribution. Among many other experiments that did not improve the performance and are not mentioned in this paper are the Convolutional Neural Networks (CNNs), RoBERTa language model (Liu et al., 2019), and non-neural classifiers trained on hand-crafted linguistic features. We would like to continue the improvement by jointly training the Causality Classifier (sub-task-1) with the Causal Span Extraction (sub-task-2).

References

Dogu Araci. 2019. Finbert: Financial sentiment analysis with pre-trained language models, 08.

Rich Caruana, Steve Lawrence, and C. Lee Giles. 2001. Overfitting in neural nets: Backpropagation, conjugate gradient, and early stopping. In T. K. Leen, T. G. Dietterich, and V. Tresp, editors, *Advances in Neural Information Processing Systems 13*, pages 402–408. MIT Press.

Tirthankar Dasgupta, Rupsa Saha, Lipika Dey, and Abir Naskar. 2018. Automatic extraction of causal relations from text using linguistically informed deep neural networks. pages 306–316, 01.

Vinicio Desola, Kevin Hanna, and Pri Nonis. 2019. Finbert: pre-trained model on sec filings for financial natural language tasks, 08.

J. Devlin, Ming-Wei Chang, Kenton Lee, and Kristina Toutanova. 2019. Bert: Pre-training of deep bidirectional transformers for language understanding. In *NAACL-HLT*.

Roxana Girju. 2003. Automatic detection of causal relations for question answering. In *Proceedings of the ACL 2003 Workshop on Multilingual Summarization and Question Answering - Volume 12*, MultiSumQA '03, page 76–83, USA. Association for Computational Linguistics.

Harsha Gurulingappa, Abdul Mateen, Angus Roberts, Juliane Fluck, Martin Hofmann-Apitius, and Luca Toldo. 2012. Development of a benchmark corpus to support the automatic extraction of drug-related adverse effects from medical case reports. *Journal of Biomedical Informatics*, http://dx.doi.org/10.1016/j.jbi.2012.04.008, 04.

Iris Hendrickx, Su Nam Kim, Zornitsa Kozareva, Preslav Nakov, Diarmuid Ó Séaghdha, Sebastian Padó, Marco Pennacchiotti, Lorenza Romano, and Stan Szpakowicz. 2010. SemEval-2010 task 8: Multi-way classification of semantic relations between pairs of nominals. In *Proceedings of the 5th International Workshop on Semantic Evaluation*, pages 33–38, Uppsala, Sweden, July. Association for Computational Linguistics.

Sepp Hochreiter and Jürgen Schmidhuber. 1997. Long short-term memory. *Neural Comput.*, 9(8):1735–1780, November.

C. Khoo, Jaklin Kornfilt, R. Oddy, and Sung-Hyon Myaeng. 1998. Automatic extraction of cause-effect information from newspaper text without knowledge-based inferencing. *Literary and Linguistic Computing*, 13:177–186, 12.

Sanghee Kim, Rob Bracewell, and Ken Wallace. 2007. A framework for automatic causality extraction using semantic similarity. 01.

Manolis Kyriakakis, Ion Androutsopoulos, Artur Saudabayev, and Joan Ametllé. 2019. Transfer learning for causal sentence detection. pages 292–297, 01.

Y. Liu, Myle Ott, Naman Goyal, Jingfei Du, Mandar Joshi, Danqi Chen, Omer Levy, M. Lewis, Luke Zettlemoyer, and Veselin Stoyanov. 2019. Roberta: A robustly optimized bert pretraining approach. *ArXiv*, abs/1907.11692.

Dominique Mariko, Hanna Abi Akl, Estelle Labidurie, Stephane Durfort, Hugues de Mazancourt, and Mahmoud El-Haj. 2020. The financial document causality detection shared task (fincausal 2020). In *The 1st Joint Workshop on Financial Narrative Processing and MultiLing Financial Summarisation (FNP-FNS 2020*, Barcelona, Spain.

Adam Paszke, Sam Gross, Francisco Massa, Adam Lerer, James Bradbury, Gregory Chanan, Trevor Killeen, Zeming Lin, Natalia Gimelshein, Luca Antiga, Alban Desmaison, Andreas Kopf, Edward Yang, Zachary DeVito, Martin Raison, Alykhan Tejani, Sasank Chilamkurthy, Benoit Steiner, Lu Fang, Junjie Bai, and Soumith Chintala. 2019. Pytorch: An imperative style, high-performance deep learning library. In H. Wallach, H. Larochelle, A. Beygelzimer, F. dAlché-Buc, E. Fox, and R. Garnett, editors, *Advances in Neural Information Processing Systems 32*, pages 8024–8035. Curran Associates, Inc.

Thomas Wolf, Lysandre Debut, Victor Sanh, Julien Chaumond, Clement Delangue, Anthony Moi, Pierric Cistac, Tim Rault, Rémi Louf, Morgan Funtowicz, Joe Davison, Sam Shleifer, Patrick von Platen, Clara Ma, Yacine Jernite, Julien Plu, Canwen Xu, Teven Le Scao, Sylvain Gugger, Mariama Drame, Quentin Lhoest, and Alexander M. Rush. 2019. Huggingface's transformers: State-of-the-art natural language processing. *ArXiv*, abs/1910.03771.

Yi Yang, Mark Christopher Siy UY, and Allen Huang. 2020. Finbert: A pretrained language model for financial communications.

ProsperAMnet at FinCausal 2020, Task 1 & 2: Modeling causality in financial texts using multi-headed transformers

Zsolt Szántó
Institute of Informatics,
University of Szeged
szantozs@inf.u-szeged.hu

Gábor Berend
Institute of Informatics,
University of Szeged
berendg@inf.u-szeged.hu

Abstract

This paper introduces our efforts at the FinCasual shared task for modeling causality in financial utterances. Our approach uses the commonly and successfully applied strategy of fine-tuning a transformer-based language model with a twist, i.e. we modified the training and inference mechanism such that our model produces multiple predictions for the same instance. By designing such a model that returns $k > 1$ predictions at the same time, we not only obtain a more resource efficient training (as opposed to fine-tuning some pre-trained language model k independent times), but our results indicate that we are also capable of obtaining comparable or even better evaluation scores that way. We compare multiple strategies for combining the k predictions of our model. Our submissions got ranked third on both subtasks of the shared task.

1 Introduction

The dominant strategy for solving natural language processing (NLP) problems these days is by taking some large, task-agnostic pre-trained neural language model and fine-tune it on the set of task-specific training data at disposal. This transfer learning setting has been proven to be highly effective in various NLP problems (Devlin et al., 2019; Yang et al., 2019; Raffel et al., 2020).

Despite having demonstrated its efficacy, the above described approach also comes with inconveniences inherent to the stochasticity of the fine-tuning procedure. As the performance of the fine-tuned model is dependant on random factors such as the order in which the training instances are considered during fine-tuning or the choice of hyper-parameters of the fine-tuning procedure. One could possibly account for this variability by performing fine-tuning multiple times with different hyper-parameter choices and performing model selection using the development set performance of the independently fine-tuned models. Performing fine-tuning $k > 1$ many times, however, naturally increases the computational resources required for model selection by a factor of k.

The models that we propose in our work are such that they make the training of $k > 1$ fine-tuned model possible without a k-fold overhead. We achieve this by simultaneously adding k multiple classification heads to the same pre-trained architecture and performing fine-tuning based on the aggregated loss coming from the individual classification heads. Our experimental results indicate that the above fine-tuning strategy not only provides a more resource efficient way of training multiple fine-tuned models, but it also has the potential of providing an increased performance for the models, since fine-tuning classifiers in a simultaneous manner likely acts as a regularizer. Our source code for replicating our results can be accessed at https://github.com/zsozso21/camuh.

2 Data

The shared task consisted of a Sentence Classification (SC) and a Cause and Effect Detection (CED) subtask, that we briefly describe below. A more detailed overview of the shared task can be found in the summary paper (Mariko et al., 2020).

Proceedings of the 1st Joint Workshop on Financial Narrative Processing and MultiLing Financial Summarisation, pages 80–84
Barcelona, Spain (Online), December 12, 2020.

For the SC subtask, the goal was to classify textual utterances whether they convey some form of causality. As such, we treated the SC subtask as a sentence-level binary classification problem for which one can conveniently fine-tune some pre-trained transformer-based model.

In the CED subtask, systems were provided (blocks of) sentences and the goal was to detect the correct spans of the causal elements and their consequences. As a concrete example, the spans formatted in italics and bold in the below sentence are considered as the effect and cause constituents, respectively:

"Zhao found himself 60 million yuan indebted after **losing 9,000 BTC in a single day (February 10, 2014)"**.

Illustrated by the previous example, the CED subtask can be handled as a token-level sequence classification with three classes, i.e. a token can either belong to a constituent of the cause or the effect or it can be none of the above. We shall refer to these three classes by their initials, i.e. C and E for the cause and effect classes and N for those tokens that are neither the cause or the effect constituent of some text.

3 System

We trained our models using the pre-trained BERT models based on the transformers library (Wolf et al., 2019). During fine-tuning, we relied on the utilization of the cross-entropy loss for both the SC and the CED subtasks. We treated the SC subtask as a binary sequence-level classification task, whereas we framed the CED subtask as an utterance-level classification problem.

3.1 Treatment of subtokens

BERT uses pieces of words (subtokens) as input representations to utilize the information for out-of-vocabulary words. As we mentioned earlier the CED subtask can be handled as token-level sequence classification. To create BERT compatible sequences we split these tokens into subtokens where the subtokens get the label of the original token. We made the classification on this subtoken-level dataset. In the prediction, there will be a label for each subtoken. We merge this subtokens back into tokens and assign the label of the first subtoken to each tokens.

3.2 Strategies for aggregating prediction heads

The main difference in our model – compared to standard single-headed fine-tuning – is that we employ $k \geq 1$ classification heads, resulting in a loss function that needs to be aggregated over k distinct loss terms. A similar method was proposed for LSTM architectures (Kis-Szabó and Berend, 2020), but not in the case of transformers. One of our strategy, that we call *averaging of heads*, calculated k distinct loss terms for each training instance and took their average as the aggregated loss. This strategy also ensures that we are learning k fine-tuned models on top of the same pre-trained architecture simultaneously.

Another strategy for the aggregation that we experimented with was the application of a fully connected layer over the heads. In this case, there are k separated branches in the network too, but these branches are merged in a higher level layer that takes as input the concatenation of the output of the k prediction heads and outputs a single vector of logits. Hence, even though we have k distinct heads, this aggregation strategy ensures that they are merged together into a single prediction and loss term.

3.3 Span-level auxiliary loss

In order to enforce homogeneity of the predicted tags in the case of the CED subtask we added an auxiliary loss to our model which penalizes the changes in the predicted labels within a sentence. We deemed it a useful extension, as our error analysis revealed that each input sequence contained exactly one cause and one effect span (a span being a contiguous sequence of tokens with the same label), whereas our system was not encouraged to behave like that, i.e. it could easily predict spans of label sequences (over the tokens) like ECE, CNCNC, etc. In order to discourage inhomogeneous predictions, we decided to add an auxiliary loss term to our loss function that was calculated as the squared difference between the number of predicted and gold standard spans over some input sequence.

BERT	k	rs 1	rs 2	rs 3	rs 4	rs 5	avg	std
base	1	96.79	96.69	96.77	96.90	96.68	96.77	0.09
large	1	**96.98**	96.89	96.82	97.13	97.01	96.96	0.12
large	5	96.92	**97.39**	97.02	**97.18**	97.03	**97.11**	0.18
large	20	96.82	97.24	**97.11**	97.10	**97.08**	97.07	0.15

Table 1: The effects of employing different BERT models (base/large) and different number of heads (k) on the Sentence Classification subtask for different random seeds (denoted by rs). Performance is reported as F1 scores.

4   Results and discussion

The parameters of the system were optimized by using the shared task's trial dataset for training and the practice dataset for testing[1]. Based on our evaluation on the practice dataset, we fixed the batch size to on the SC and the CED subtasks to 8 and 1, respectively. We also applied dropout with probability 0.1 in all of our experiments. Those models that we used for making predictions over the evaluation data were trained on the concatenation of the practice and trial datasets and later tested on the evaluation dataset during the post evaluation period. Unless stated otherwise, our models described below use averaging-based aggregation strategy of the heads and no span-level auxiliary loss.

As neural methods are prone to achieving results with high variance when being trained with different choices of random seed, we evaluated each architectures five times with only their random seeds set differently. We report the individual results obtained by the different choices of the random seed as well as the average and standard deviation of the performance metrics.

4.1   Experiments on the number of heads

Sentence Classification subtask   Table 1 compares the results of the base-cased and the large-cased BERT models and shows the added value of the extra heads on the SC subtask. There is only a small gap between the performance of the base and the large BERT models, 0.19 percentage point on average, but the base model was outperformed by the large one five out of five times. The usage of more than one heads improved the results in both cases. The five-headed model achieved the best average F1 score if we compare it against the five independent runs of the standard model with a single classification head. Overall, we found that our multi-headed systems were better four out of five times regarding the individual runs.

Cause and Effect Detection subtask   Table 2 contains the results of the same experiments on the CED subtask. The BERT large model outperformed the base once again and the application of $k \geq 1$ heads improved the results too. For that task, the higher value of k made the larger improvement, as we obtained the best results with the twenty-headed model.

---

[1]Our configuration contains an RTX 2080ti GPU, equipped with 11GB RAM.

BERT	k	rs 1	rs 2	rs 3	rs 4	rs 5	avg	std
base	1	81.27	82.96	**82.62**	81.25	81.85	81.99	0.78
large	1	82.54	82.71	82.07	**83.00**	82.04	82.47	0.41
large	5	83.39	83.21	82.25	82.58	82.38	82.76	0.51
large	20	**83.43**	**83.63**	82.00	82.73	**82.68**	**82.90**	0.65

Table 2: The effects of employing different BERT models (base/large) and different number of heads (k) on the Cause and Effect Detection subtask using different random seeds (denoted by rs). Performance is reported as F1 scores.

4.2 Evaluation of the strategies for aggregating prediction heads

Table 3 provides a comparison of the two aggregation strategies, illustrating that backpropagating the loss from the average of the k distinct heads tends to perform better compared to the aggregation of the different heads by applying a fully connected layer on top of their concatenation.

	rs 1	rs 2	rs 3	rs 4	rs 5	avg	std
Using an FC layer	81.91	82.02	**82.64**	**83.27**	82.05	82.38	0.57
Averaging of heads	**83.39**	**83.21**	82.25	82.58	**82.38**	**82.76**	0.51

Table 3: Comparison of the head aggregation strategies on the Cause and Effect Detection subtask using $k = 5$, and the BERT large-cased model. Performance is reported as F1 scores.

4.3 Span number penalization

Table 4 shows that by utilizing the auxiliary loss introduced in Section 3.3, we obtained lower F1 scores on the token level evaluation, but an increased efficiency regarding the fraction of perfectly predicted sequences. By analyzing the results our model predicted 2589 spans on the evaluation dataset by using the original loss function with random seed 1. When using the same architecture with the auxiliary loss that we introduced for encouraging the homogenity of predicted labels, the number of predicted spans decreased to 2018.

In order to see the qualitative effects of the application of our auxiliary loss term, consider the following prediction that we obtained by our original system that did not involve the auxiliary loss term:

> With over $5.2 billion of TRX locked up in staking and an average yield of 13.2%, almost $700 million are made in profits annually from staking on Tron.

Tokens in red were predicted as being part of a *cause*, whereas tokens in blue were predicted as being part of an *effect* by our system. In contrast, the prediction of our model that also incorporated the auxiliary loss produced this more coherent output for the same sequence:

> With over $5.2 billion of TRX locked up in staking and an average yield of 13.2%, almost $700 million are made in profits annually from staking on Tron.

	rs 1	rs 2	rs 3	rs 4	rs 5	avg
Original	83.39 / 61.44	83.21 / 56.58	82.25 / 69.28	82.58 / 14.58	82.38 / 67.08	82.76 / 53.79
+ span	81.62 / 61.91	82.13 / 49.84	83.01 / 61.13	82.50 / 60.50	83.04 / 70.69	82.46 / 60.82

Table 4: The effect of span-level auxiliary loss on Cause and Effect Detection dataset using $k = 5$, and the BERT large-cased model. Performance is reported as F1 / Exact match scores.

4.4 Submission results

We reached the third place in both of the SC and CED subtasks. Our best submission obtained an F1 score of 97.23 in the SC subtask by applying the following parameters: large BERT model, $k = 20$, averaging of heads aggregation, without span penalization. In the CED subtask our top model used BERT large mode, $k = 5$, averaging of heads aggregation, without span penalization, and got 83.71 for F1 score. The reason why the figures that we described in this article slightly differ from our official shared task results is the non-deterministic behavior of GPU computing. We repeated and extended each experiment to get a more detailed image about our system.

5 Conclusions

Our experiments demonstrated that the standard fine-tuning mechanisms work well for modeling causality in financial texts as well. More importantly, we introduced our modified fine-tuning architecture that is capable of training multiple classification model on top of a shared transformer architecture. Our results demonstrate that we did not only obtain multiple classifiers in a less resource intensive manner, but the classifiers also performed better as if we were training them separately of each other. A potential avenue for improving our proposed fine-tuning architecture could focus on more sophisticated aggregation strategies for the predictions of the simultaneously fine-tuned classification models.

Acknowledgements

This research has been conducted in the project "Progressing Service Performance and Export Results of Advanced Manufacturers Networks", no CE1569 ProsperAMnet. The project has been supported by the European Fund for Regional Development in the framework of Interreg CENTRAL EUROPE 2019-2022.

References

Jacob Devlin, Ming-Wei Chang, Kenton Lee, and Kristina Toutanova. 2019. BERT: Pre-training of deep bidirectional transformers for language understanding. In *Proceedings of the 2019 Conference of the North American Chapter of the Association for Computational Linguistics: Human Language Technologies, Volume 1 (Long and Short Papers)*, pages 4171–4186, Minneapolis, Minnesota, June. Association for Computational Linguistics.

Norbert Kis-Szabó and Gábor Berend. 2020. Quasi-multitask learning: an efficient surrogate for obtaining model ensembles. In *Proceedings of the First Workshop on Simple and Efficient Natural Language Processing*, November.

Dominique Mariko, Hanna Abi Akl, Estelle Labidurie, Stephane Durfort, Hugues de Mazancourt, and Mahmoud El-Haj. 2020. The Financial Document Causality Detection Shared Task (FinCausal 2020). In *The 1st Joint Workshop on Financial Narrative Processing and MultiLing Financial Summarisation (FNP-FNS 2020*, Barcelona, Spain.

Colin Raffel, Noam Shazeer, Adam Roberts, Katherine Lee, Sharan Narang, Michael Matena, Yanqi Zhou, Wei Li, and Peter J. Liu. 2020. Exploring the limits of transfer learning with a unified text-to-text transformer. *Journal of Machine Learning Research*, 21(140):1–67.

Thomas Wolf, Lysandre Debut, Victor Sanh, Julien Chaumond, Clement Delangue, Anthony Moi, Pierric Cistac, Tim Rault, Rémi Louf, Morgan Funtowicz, Joe Davison, Sam Shleifer, Patrick von Platen, Clara Ma, Yacine Jernite, Julien Plu, Canwen Xu, Teven Le Scao, Sylvain Gugger, Mariama Drame, Quentin Lhoest, and Alexander M. Rush. 2019. Huggingface's transformers: State-of-the-art natural language processing. *ArXiv*, abs/1910.03771.

Zhilin Yang, Zihang Dai, Yiming Yang, Jaime Carbonell, Russ R Salakhutdinov, and Quoc V Le. 2019. Xlnet: Generalized autoregressive pretraining for language understanding. In H. Wallach, H. Larochelle, A. Beygelzimer, F. d'Alché-Buc, E. Fox, and R. Garnett, editors, *Advances in Neural Information Processing Systems 32*, pages 5753–5763. Curran Associates, Inc.

ISIKUN at the FinCausal 2020: Linguistically informed Machine-learning Approach for Causality Identification in Financial Documents

Hüseyin Gökberk Özenir
Işık University
219MCS8082@isik.edu.tr

İlknur Karadeniz
Işık University
ilknur.karadeniz@isikun.edu.tr

Abstract

This paper presents our participation to the FinCausal-2020 Shared Task whose ultimate aim is to extract cause-effect relations from a given financial text. Our participation includes two systems for the two sub-tasks of the FinCausal-2020 Shared Task. The first sub-task (Task-1) consists of the binary classification of the given sentences as causal meaningful (1) or causal meaningless (0). Our approach for the Task-1 includes applying linear support vector machines after transforming the input sentences into vector representations using term frequency-inverse document frequency scheme with 3-grams. The second sub-task (Task-2) consists of the identification of the cause-effect relations in the sentences, which are detected as causal meaningful. Our approach for the Task-2 is a CRF-based model which uses linguistically informed features. For the Task-1, the obtained results show that there is a small difference between the proposed approach based on linear support vector machines (F-score 94%), which requires less time compared to the BERT-based baseline (F-score 95%). For the Task-2, although a minor modifications such as the learning algorithm type and the feature representations are made in the conditional random fields based baseline (F-score 52%), we have obtained better results (F-score 60%). The source codes for the both tasks are available online (https://github.com/ozenirgokberk/FinCausal2020.git/).

1 Introduction

The causality detection, which is a well-known task in text mining, has a goal of the extraction of the cause-effect relations from a given text. Although the causality detection task has been applied to various types of texts in various domains such as biomedical (Khoo et al., 2000; Mihăilă et al., 2013; Mihăilă and Ananiadou, 2014), clinical (Casillas et al., 2016), and financial (Blanco et al., 2008; Asghar, 2016; Kumar and Ravi, 2016) until now, there is still room for the improvement of these approaches.

The FinCausal-2020 Shared Task is a community-wide effort, which presents an opportunity for the researchers to test their financial causality detection systems on a common platform (Mariko et al., 2020). The FinCausal-2020 Shared Task consists of two sub-tasks, which are called Task-1 (sentence classification) and Task-2 (relation extraction). Task-1 is a binary classification task in which the participants are intended to classify the given financial sentences as 1 if the text section is considered containing a causal relation, and 0 otherwise. Task-2 is a relation extraction task in which the participants are intended to extract the text sections as a cause or an effect from the given text in which it is known that there is at least one causality relation.

In this paper, the two systems that are developed for the two sub-tasks of the FinCausal-2020 Shared Task are explained. For the Task-1, the problem is handled as a binary classification problem. We have used two different linguistically informed machine learning classifiers which are naive bayes (McCallum et al., 1998) and linear support vector machines. For the Task-2, which aims the automatic extraction of cause-effect relations from a given financial text, Conditional Random Fields (Lafferty et al., 2001) are used.

Proceedings of the 1st Joint Workshop on Financial Narrative Processing and MultiLing Financial Summarisation, pages 85–89
Barcelona, Spain (Online), December 12, 2020.

2 Data Set

The data set, which is provided by the organizers, is created from 2019 financial news. The training data set for the Task-1 has entries which are the index of the sentence, the sentence, and the class label which the corresponding sentence belongs to, while the test data set entries consist of the index of the sentence and the sentence only without the class labels.

The test data set that is related with the Task-2 consists of the index of the sentence and the sentence entries, while the training data set has entries which are the index of the sentence, the sentence, as well as the cause mention, and the effect mention of the corresponding sentence.

3 Task-1: Sentence Classification

The workflow of our system for the Task-1 begins with the preprocessing phase of the data, which is followed by the feature representation of the sentences. After obtaining the sentences as feature vectors, different supervised machine learning classifiers are used to predict the given text as containing a causal relation or not-containing a causal relation. In the following subsections, a detailed explanation of the system that we have developed for the Task-1 is provided.

3.1 Preprocessing

For the preprocessing phase, the stop words, the punctuations and the abbreviations are removed to clear the uninformative words. Our assumption is that the uninformative words are the words which do not convey any meaning for the classification of the causality of the given sentences. With this assumption, as uninformative words, any numbers, currency signs and time specifications such as *"am, pm"* are removed. The intuition behind this pre-processing phase is that the sentences which include similar numerical specifications such as dates and the money amount may be classified as different classes. For instance, considering the two sentences in the training data set, one sample sentence begins with *"Third Democratic presidential debate September 12, 2019 at 9:54 PM EDT -* and an another sentence *"It found that total U.S. health care spending would be about $3.9 trillion under Medicare for All in 2019, compared with about $3.8 trillion under the status quo. Part of the reason is that Medicare for All would offer generous benefits with no copays and deductibles, except limited cost-sharing for certain medications.".* Although both sentences include the date mention *"2019"*, the first sentence has a causality relation (class 1), while the second sentence does not carry a causality meaning (class 0).

After the removal of the unnecassary words, the stems of the remaining words in the given text are obtained by utilizing nltk library's tokenizer (Loper and Bird, 2002). Since there are no distinct data sets such as training and development, the training data set is splitted by using 5-fold cross validation.

3.2 Feature Representations

Term frequency-inverse document frequency (TF-IDF) representation is used to represent the text sections which are treated as separate sentences. TF-IDF scoring computes the relative frequency that a word appears in a sentence compared to its frequency across all training data. In TF-IDF scoring, the IDF measure makes the words that are rare in the data set become more informative than the words which are more frequent in the data set. For the realization of the transformation of the given sentences into real-valued vectors, we used the TF-IDFTransformer as a vectorizer, which is provided by Python's scikit-learn library (Pedregosa et al., 2011).

Maximum document frequency value (*max df*) is used for removing terms that appear too frequently, which are also known as "corpus-specific stop words". The value *max df = 0.2* is heuristically used in the submission, where *max df = 0.2* means "ignore terms that appear in more than 20 percentage of the documents". On the other hand, minimum document frequency value (*min df*) is used for removing terms that appear too abundant. The value *min df = 3* is heuristically used in the submission, where *min df = 3* means "ignore terms that appear in less than 3 documents of the document collection".

3.3 Training the model

Two different classifiers such as support vector machines (SVMs) and Multinominal Naive Bayes (MNB) are used to classify the financial sentences in the training data set, whose results are shown at the Table 1. MNB produces an estimation using the frequency of usage of words, which are existed in the dictionary that is created with all sentences in the data set, therefore we need to use Count Vectorizer and TF-IDF that is explained in previous section. SVMs examine inputs to determine hyper-plane which is separate binary class samples.This hyper-plane separation is expected to be as larger as possible to label input correctly.In addition to MNB model, vectorizers and term frequency approaches are also used for training SVMs. For the reason that the data set is limited in size, k-Fold cross validation, where k is heuristically chosen as 5, is used for the validation of the data set. The best results on the training data set are obtained with the system based on SVMs that we submitted the system as the first run for the Task-1 in the shared task.

4 Task-2: Cause-Effect Detection

4.1 Preprocessing & Feature Representations

Firstly, the punctuations and the general stop words in English are removed. The remaining words are converted to lower case.After that, the word tokenizer in NLTK library is used to tokenize the sentences.

For the feature representation, for each word the following features, which are the Part-of-Speech (POS) tags, surface form of the words, the reduced form of the words (the removal of the last three letters and the last two letters), digit or not, title or not,whether each word is at the beginning of the sentence or not, and tuples, which are explained in detail below, are extracted.

A tuple is automatically created for each sentence in the training data set depending on the constituent word which is a part of the followings: a cause mention, an effect mention or none of them. For example, considering the following sentence, *'Transat loss more than doubles as it works to complete Air Canada deal.'* , the cause mention is *'it works to complete Air Canada deal.'* , while the effect mention is *'Transat loss more than doubles '* . If a word is located in the sentence as a cause mention, the word is assigned to *"C"* tuple, while a word is located in the sentence as an effect mention, the word is assigned to *"E"* tuple. Otherwise, If a word is not either a part of a cause mention or an effect mention, the word is assigned to *"_"* tuple. Our sample tuples for the corresponding sentence will be such as *[('Transat','E'), ('work','C'), ('as','"_"),...]* .

4.2 Method

For the Task-2, Conditional random fields (CRFs) ,which are the one of the statistical modeling methods that has been successfully applied to the natural language processing problems previously, are used. The open-source Python library scikit-learn (Pedregosa et al., 2011) is utilzied to train our model on CRF approach for the utilities such as cross-validation, and hyperparameter optimization. We have focused on CRF models by combining with Averaged Perceptron (AP) as learning algorithms of the CRF approach. As far as we know, for the baseline which is provided by the organizers, the stochastic gradient descent algorithm is used.

5 Results

The results for the Task-1 of the FinCausal 2020 Shared task, which are obtained on the training data set with 5-fold cross-validation, are shown at Table 1.

The results of the CRF-based basedline model with the base features and the L-BFGS learning algorithm for the Task-2 are shown at Table 2.

On the other hand, the results of the CRF-based system with the linguistically informed features and the average perceptron learning algorithm for the Task-2 are shown at Table 3 which is above the baseline.

The official evaluation results for the Task-1 of the FinCausal 2020 Shared task, which are obtained on the test data set, are shown in Table 4. The obtained results consist of performance metrics by using linear support vector machines. On the other hand, the post evaluation results for the Task-2 of the FinCausal

Algorithm	Classes	Precision	Recall	F-1 Score
Baseline (BERT)	0	0.96	0.97	0.97
	1	0.64	0.64	0.64
	Macro Avg	0.81	0.81	0.81
	Weighted Avg	0.95	0.95	0.95
Multinomial Naive Bayes	0	0.94	**1.00**	0.97
	1	0.87	0.17	0.28
	Macro Avg	0.91	0.58	0.63
	Weighted Avg	0.94	0.93	0.93
Linear Support Vector Machine	0	**0.97**	0.99	0.98
	1	0.79	0.32	0.57
	Macro Avg	0.89	0.68	0.75
	Weighted Avg	0.95	0.95	**0.96**

Table 1: *Task-1 results.* The results are also obtained in the training data set with 5-fold cross validation.

	Precision	Recall	F-1 Score
Cause	0.53	0.70	0.60
Effect	0.53	0.57	0.53
-	0.65	0.17	0.27
Accuracy			0.52
Macro Avg	0.56	0.48	0.47
Weighted Avg	0.55	0.52	0.49

Table 2: *The results of CRF based model with base feautures and L-BFGS learning algorithm (Baseline) for the Task-2.*

	Precision	Recall	F-1 Score
Cause	0.57	0.72	0.68
Effect	0.53	0.66	0.63
-	0.65	0.13	0.22
Accuracy			0.60
Macro Avg	0.62	0.54	0.52
Weighted Avg	0.60	0.58	0.55

Table 3: *The results of CRF based model with linguistically informed features and the Averaged Perceptron learning algorithm (Our system) for the Task-2.* The results are obtained in the training data set with 5-fold cross validation.

Task (System)	Precision	Recall	F-1 Score	Exact Match
Task-1 (Our system)	0.93	0.94	0.94	1.000
Task-1 (Baseline)	0.95	0.95	0.95	1.000
Task-2 (Our system)	0.62	0.59	0.60	0.006
Task-2 (Baseline)	0.51	0.52	0.51	0.111

Table 4: *The test data test results* The results are obtained in the test data set at the official evaluation (for Task-1) and the post-evaluation (for Task-2) phases.

2020 Shared task, which are obtained on the test data set, are shown in Table 4. The obtained results consist of performance metrics by using averaged perceptron algorithm in CRF. The results show that for both tasks, the obtained results on the training data set with 5-fold cross validation and the results on the test data set are similar.

6   Conclusion

In this study, we have presented two systems that are implemented in the scope of the FinCausal 2020 Shared Task. The aim of the first system is the binary classification of the sentences in a financial text as carrying causality relation or not-carrying causality relation, whereas the goal of the second system is the extraction of the cause-effect relations in the financial text. In conclusion, compared to the baseline, for the Task-1, there is a small difference (1%) between the results of the proposed approach based on linear support vector machines which requires less time compared to the BERT-based baseline. For the Task-2, on the other hand, better results are obtained compared to the baseline.

Acknowledgements

We would like to thank the FinCausal shared task organizers for organizing the shared task and for their help with the questions.

References

Nabiha Asghar. 2016. Automatic extraction of causal relations from natural language texts: a comprehensive survey. *arXiv preprint arXiv:1605.07895*.

Eduardo Blanco, Nuria Castell, and Dan I Moldovan. 2008. Causal relation extraction. In *Lrec*, volume 66, page 74.

Arantza Casillas, Koldo Gojenola, Alicia Pérez, and Maite Oronoz. 2016. Clinical text mining for efficient extraction of drug-allergy reactions. In *2016 IEEE International Conference on Bioinformatics and Biomedicine (BIBM)*, pages 946–952. IEEE.

Christopher SG Khoo, Syin Chan, and Yun Niu. 2000. Extracting causal knowledge from a medical database using graphical patterns. In *Proceedings of the 38th annual meeting of the association for computational linguistics*, pages 336–343.

B Shravan Kumar and Vadlamani Ravi. 2016. A survey of the applications of text mining in financial domain. *Knowledge-Based Systems*, 114:128–147.

John Lafferty, Andrew McCallum, and Fernando CN Pereira. 2001. Conditional random fields: Probabilistic models for segmenting and labeling sequence data.

Edward Loper and Steven Bird. 2002. Nltk: the natural language toolkit. *arXiv preprint cs/0205028*.

Dominique Mariko, Hanna Abi Akl, Estelle Labidurie, Stephane Durfort, Hugues de Mazancourt, and Mahmoud El-Haj. 2020. The Financial Document Causality Detection Shared Task (FinCausal 2020). In *The 1st Joint Workshop on Financial Narrative Processing and MultiLing Financial Summarisation (FNP-FNS 2020, Barcelona, Spain*.

Andrew McCallum, Kamal Nigam, et al. 1998. A comparison of event models for naive bayes text classification. In *AAAI-98 workshop on learning for text categorization*, volume 752, pages 41–48. Citeseer.

Claudiu Mihăilă and Sophia Ananiadou. 2014. Semi-supervised learning of causal relations in biomedical scientific discourse. *Biomedical engineering online*, 13(2):1–24.

Claudiu Mihăilă, Tomoko Ohta, Sampo Pyysalo, and Sophia Ananiadou. 2013. Biocause: Annotating and analysing causality in the biomedical domain. *BMC bioinformatics*, 14(1):2.

F. Pedregosa, G. Varoquaux, A. Gramfort, V. Michel, B. Thirion, O. Grisel, M. Blondel, P. Prettenhofer, R. Weiss, V. Dubourg, J. Vanderplas, A. Passos, D. Cournapeau, M. Brucher, M. Perrot, and E. Duchesnay. 2011. Scikit-learn: Machine learning in Python. *Journal of Machine Learning Research*, 12:2825–2830.

Domino at FinCausal 2020, Task 1 and 2: Causal Extraction System

Sharanya Chakravarthy* Tushar Kanakagiri*
Karthik Radhakrishnan* Anjana Umapathy*
Language Technologies Institute
Carnegie Mellon University
{sharanyc, tkanakag, kradhak2, aumapath}@cs.cmu.edu

Abstract

Automatic identification of cause-effect relationships from data is a challenging but important problem in artificial intelligence. Identifying semantic relationships has become increasingly important for multiple downstream applications like Question Answering, Information Retrieval and Event Prediction. In this work, we tackle the problem of causal relationship extraction from financial news using the FinCausal 2020 dataset. We tackle two tasks - 1) Detecting the presence of causal relationships and 2) Extracting segments corresponding to cause and effect from news snippets. We propose Transformer based sequence and token classification models with post-processing rules which achieve an F_1 score of 96.12 and 79.60 on Tasks 1 and 2 respectively.

1   Introduction

With the rise of the internet came an unprecedented growth in the amount of financial news being produced everyday. In its raw form however, this data though large, has limited utility. From this raw data, identifying relationship mapping between an external cause and its consequence can be of great value.

The simplest way to define a causal relationship is expressing it in the form of "E_1 causes E_2" where E_1 and E_2 are two linked events - E_1 being the cause and E_2 being the effect. Though this forms a simple illustrative example, real world causal relationships are often expressed with different lexical constructs, span across multiple sentences or are coupled together with other effects and causes.

We can now formally define our tasks as follows :

1. Binary classification task of identifying if a snippet of financial news displays a causal meaning. [Measured by weighted F_1]

2. Given a causal snippet, identify the span corresponding to the cause and the span corresponding to the effect displayed in the relation. [Measured by F_1 on span overlap]

Our first task is framed as a text classification task and has been widely studied in the NLP community (Minaee et al., 2020). Long-Short Term Memory networks, Convolutional Neural Networks (Kim, 2014), and more recently pre-trained Transformer models (Devlin et al., 2018) have shown success on a wide range of text classification tasks. Particularly, for the task of Cause-Effect detection, BERT based models have achieved state of the art performance (Soares et al., 2019) on the SemEval task (Hendrickx et al., 2019) on detecting semantic relations in text such as Cause-Effect, Entity-Origin, etc. To further leverage the benefits of pre-training, we use FinBERT (Araci, 2019), a BERT based model fine-tuned on financial data for better language understanding and domain adaptation.

Our second task is concerned with extracting spans corresponding to cause and effect from a causal news snippet. With the advent of large scale Question Answering datasets (Rajpurkar et al., 2016), deep learning models and specifically Transformers have been used extensively to identify answer spans. This task can also be framed as a token classification task where each token is classified as Cause/Effect/Other

---

Proceedings of the 1st Joint Workshop on Financial Narrative Processing and MultiLing Financial Summarisation, pages 90–94
Barcelona, Spain (Online), December 12, 2020.

and the tokens are grouped to form Cause/Effect spans. Additionally, token classification models such as BiLSTM-CRF (Li et al., 2019) and feature-based CRF (Mariko et al., 2020) have demonstrated good performance for causality extraction. We cast our task as a token classification problem and apply certain post-processing rules to reconstruct the spans from individual token outputs.

In this work, we present our results on Task 1 using a variant of BERT - FinBERT pre-trained on financial data. Our FinBERT model achieve F_1 scores of 95.60 and 96.12 on the validation and test set respectively.

For Task 2, we use BERT with a linear layer over token embeddings for token classification. Our model achieves a validation F_1 score of 75.40, beating the baseline CRF model and a test set F_1 score 79.60. The code for our approaches will be made available on GitHub[1].

2 Data

In this work, we use the two datasets provided by FinCausal 2020 Workshop (Mariko et al., 2020) to train and evaluate our models. In comparison to datasets for other NLP tasks, the datasets for Tasks 1 and 2 are relatively small.

2.1 Task 1

The Task 1 dataset consists of approximately 20,000 financial text samples, each annotated for the binary classification task of causality detection. The labels 1 and 0 indicate the presence and absence of a causal relationship respectively. The dataset has a large imbalance with only 7% of the examples labeled as 1.

2.2 Task 2

The dataset for Task 2 consists of 1,100 pieces of text containing causal relations, along with information about sections of the text that correspond to cause and effect. For example -
Text: Zhao found himself 60 million yuan indebted after losing 9,000 BTC in a single day
Cause: losing 9,000 BTC in a single day
Effect: Zhao found himself 60 million yuan indebted

Note that the system is expected to pick maximal spans - In the example shown above, the effect is annotated as "losing 9,000 BTC in a **single day**" although the fact that he lost it in a single day is irrelevant to the effect. Similarly for samples which span multiple sentences, the system is sometimes required to tag whole sentences as cause / effect even if the actual cause / effect is only a part of the sentence. The various rules and heuristics followed by the annotators are documented here [2].

3 Proposed Approach

We now present our systems for cause-effect detection and extraction. Given the small size of our dataset, it might not be possible for deep learning models to completely fit our tasks. We combat this in two ways - pre-training and post-processing. We leverage pre-training by utilizing FinBERT (Araci, 2019) - a BERT model trained on Reuters TRC2 Corpus, Financial Phrasebank and FIQA datasets for easier adaptation to the financial domain and use a post-processing module for Task 2 to incorporate some of the rules followed by the annotators as opposed to relying solely on the model to learn them.

3.1 Task 1

We first tokenize our sentence into sub-tokens (Wu et al., 2016) using the bert-base-uncased tokenizer provided by Hugging Face[3]. These tokens are passed through the FinBERT model[4]. The [CLS] representation from FinBERT is then passed through a 2 layer feed-forward network to output probability scores to indicate whether a cause-effect relation is contained in the sentence.

---

[1] `https://github.com/sharanyarc96/Domino-Fincausal2020`
[2] `https://drive.google.com/drive/folders/1ryH76Z_hqrFaGlxx6SMJRGxK4BeJeg97`
[3] `https://huggingface.co/bert-base-uncased`
[4] `https://prosus-public.s3-eu-west-1.amazonaws.com/finbert/language-model/pytorch_model.bin`

3.2 Task 2

We frame the task of extracting cause-effect spans as a token classification task by labeling each token as Cause/Effect/Other, and use a post-processing module to extract the spans from the predictions.

3.2.1 Pre-Processing

We first apply the bert-base-cased tokenizer[5] to our sentence and gold spans and tag each sub-token as Cause, Effect, and Other. For example,
Tokenized Sentence - "The stock market crashing resulted in multiple lay ##offs"
Labels - "C C C C O O E E E"

We manually corrected 11 instances in the training dataset where the gold Cause and Effect offsets were incorrectly labelled at the second letter of a word or before the end of a word, causing mismatches between the sentence and individual span tokenizations - an example of an incorrectly labelled gold cause is shown below.
Index - 0001.00010
Text - Connecticut, Pennsylvania, New Jersey, Illinois and New York lost about half of their income from people earning more than $200,000 - indicating the wealthy were picking up and leaving.
Gold Cause - *ndicating* the wealthy were picking up and leaving.
Effect - Connecticut, Pennsylvania, New Jersey, Illinois and New York lost about half of their income from people earning more than $200,000

3.2.2 Model

We use a softmax layer over each token representation produced by BERT to classify each token as Cause/Effect/Other. We then merge labels for sub-tokens and align them with the word tokenizations produced by NLTK[6] for compatibility with the evaluation script. For this task, we finetune the bert-base-cased model provided by Hugging Face[7].

3.2.3 Post-Processing Module

Since we framed the task as token classification, the model does not necessarily tag contiguous tokens with the same label. We apply rules based on adjacent tags to modify the tag in case of a mislabelling (A single cause token surrounded by effect tokens is likely mislabeled). Additionally, the task annotators followed various rules whilst tagging the sentences (marking entire sentences as cause/effect if the cause/effect were in different sentences, stretching the spans to cover the entire sentence, etc). We mimic these rules in our post-processing module to produce spans that better match the gold annotations.

Specifically, we check if the predicted tag is different from its previous and next, and if the previous and next tag are the same, we change the label of the predicted tag. In case of multiple cause-effect predictions, we take the dominant prediction (highest contiguous count) and if the cause and effects are predicted in individual sentences, we stretch their spans to encompass the whole sentence.

4 Experimental Setup

We finetune models for Tasks 1 and 2 on an NVIDIA Tesla T4 GPU and use the Adam optimizer (Kingma and Ba, 2014). The data partition and hyperparameters used for the individual tasks are described below.

4.1 Task 1

We finetune FinBERT for 8-10 epochs on the TRIAL set provided by the organizers, and report test set scores on the EVALUATION set. To finetune our hyperparameters, we train and evaluate on the data partition provided with the baseline code[8]. The test set in this partition is used to report validation set results. We experiment with batch sizes of 8, 16, 32 and learning rates in the range 5e-3 to 5e-5. The results reported are obtained using a batch size of 8 and a learning rate of 2e-5.

---

[5]https://huggingface.co/transformers/model_doc/bert.html#berttokenizer
[6]https://www.nltk.org/api/nltk.tokenize.html
[7]https://huggingface.co/bert-base-cased
[8]https://github.com/yseop/YseopLab/tree/develop/FNP_2020_FinCausal/baseline/task1

4.2 Task 2

We finetune BERT on TRIAL and use PRACTICE set as the validation set and report the test set scores on the EVALUATION set. We use a batch size of 8, learning rates in the range of 1.5e-4 to 5e-5 and run the optimization for around 15 epochs. We use the BERT tokenizer and pick the tag predicted for the root sub-token as the prediction for the word.

5 Results and Analysis

We compare our approaches against baselines and models provided by the task organizers. For Task 1, we compare our FinBERT model against a 1D CNN model (Kim, 2014) and vanilla BERT based task baseline. Tables 1, 3 show the strong performance of our model on validation and test splits. Our FinBERT model placed 7th on the official FinCausal leaderboard[9].

For Task 2, we compare our approach against a zero-shot model based on SQuAD BERT[10] (We frame synthetic questions asking for the cause/effect, and extract spans produced by the model), a CRF baseline provided by the organizers and our Sequence Labelling approach. We can see from Table 2 that the post-processing module achieves gains of over 5 F_1 on validation. Our final model scores 79.60 on the official FinCausal leaderboard, placing 5th on the shared task.

Model	F_1 Score
CNN-GloVe300D-FT	94.10
Task Baseline - BERT	95.23
FinBERT w/ fine-tuning	**95.60**

Table 1: Validation set results for Task 1

Model	F_1 Score
SQuAD BERT	43.22
Task Baseline - CRF	60.01
BERT Sequence Labelling	70.00
+ Post-Processing	**75.40**

Table 2: Validation set results for Task 2

Model	F_1 Score
FinBERT w/ fine-tuning	96.12

Table 3: Test set results for Task 1

Model	F_1 Score
BERT + Post-Processing	79.60

Table 4: Test set results for Task 2

5.1 Error Analysis

We randomly sampled from our predictions on Task 2 and analyzed the different kinds of errors made by the model. Errors primarily stemmed from the model's inability to correctly identify boundaries of causes and effects. Additionally, there were a few instances where the gold annotations had noise in tagging.

Some gold annotations appeared to have the cause and effect switched, such as the one shown below:
Index - 0038.00033
Text - CLIMATE - Invest in a 100% renewable electricity grid. Cut federal emission-level goals to 60% below 2005 levels by 2030.
Gold Cause - Cut federal emission-level goals to 60% below 2005 levels by 2030.
Error - Investing in renewable energy is the reasonable choice for the cause in this sentence and cutting emissions is more likely an effect and not the cause.

Some annotations had incorrectly labeled boundaries where the gold span started or ended within a word (§3.2.1). Despite correct prediction by our model, examples such as the one shown below are marked wrong due to switched cause-effect in the dataset.

The model incorrectly predicts the boundaries for causes and effects in multiple cases. On most occasions, the predictions are off by 1-2 words. To discern boundaries better, a larger training set could help the model make more accurate predictions or syntax-aware post-processing rules that identify phrases

---

[9] https://competitions.codalab.org/competitions/23748#results
[10] https://huggingface.co/distilbert-base-cased-distilled-squad

within sentences and ensure that the predicted spans cover entire phrases.

Index - 0047.00024

Text - Landmark 10 is racing four-year-old pacing mare, Hello Love, who races in the top condition events at Woodbine Mohawk Park and has made over $50,000 to date.

Predicted Cause - Landmark 10 is racing four-year-old pacing mare, Hello Love, who races in the top condition events at Woodbine Mohawk Park *and has*

Potential Solution - We can utilize the structural information by parsing the sentence and exclude 'and has' as they occur as part of a different sub-tree in the syntactic parse.

For a few examples with multiple sentences, the model sometimes includes irrelevant sentences as part of the cause/effect. Additionally, when a chain of cause-effect relations are present, our model predicts the final effect instead of the effect immediately following the cause. This increases the number of false positives and impacts the F_1 score. A potential solution would be to examine the individual logits in order to identify if strength of predictions vary significantly across the span and shorten the prediction in such cases.

6 Conclusion

In this work, we leverage BERT for sequence and token classification to detect and extract cause-effect relations in financial documents. We show the efficacy of domain-specific pre-training and address the low resource problem by applying post-processing rules over the model's predictions. In the future, we plan to experiment with data augmentation techniques such as synthetic data created from the cause and effect of different examples, and syntax-aware post-processing rules for more effective span extraction.

References

Dogu Araci. 2019. Finbert: Financial sentiment analysis with pre-trained language models. *ArXiv*, abs/1908.10063.

Jacob Devlin, Ming-Wei Chang, Kenton Lee, and Kristina Toutanova. 2018. Bert: Pre-training of deep bidirectional transformers for language understanding. *arXiv preprint arXiv:1810.04805*.

Iris Hendrickx, Su Nam Kim, Zornitsa Kozareva, Preslav Nakov, Diarmuid O Séaghdha, Sebastian Padó, Marco Pennacchiotti, Lorenza Romano, and Stan Szpakowicz. 2019. Semeval-2010 task 8: Multi-way classification of semantic relations between pairs of nominals. *arXiv preprint arXiv:1911.10422*.

Yoon Kim. 2014. Convolutional neural networks for sentence classification. *arXiv preprint arXiv:1408.5882*.

Diederik P. Kingma and Jimmy Ba. 2014. Adam: A Method for Stochastic Optimization. *CoRR*, abs/1412.6980.

Zhaoning Li, Qi Li, Xiaotian Zou, and Jiangtao Ren. 2019. Causality extraction based on self-attentive bilstm-crf with transferred embeddings. *arXiv preprint arXiv:1904.07629*.

Dominique Mariko, Hanna Abi Akl, Estelle Labidurie, Stephane Durfort, Hugues de Mazancourt, and Mahmoud El-Haj. 2020. The Financial Document Causality Detection Shared Task (FinCausal 2020). In *The 1st Joint Workshop on Financial Narrative Processing and MultiLing Financial Summarisation (FNP-FNS 2020, Barcelona, Spain*.

Shervin Minaee, Nal Kalchbrenner, Erik Cambria, Narjes Nikzad, Meysam Chenaghlu, and Jianfeng Gao. 2020. Deep learning based text classification: A comprehensive review. *arXiv preprint arXiv:2004.03705*.

Pranav Rajpurkar, Jian Zhang, Konstantin Lopyrev, and Percy Liang. 2016. Squad: 100,000+ questions for machine comprehension of text. *arXiv preprint arXiv:1606.05250*.

Livio Baldini Soares, Nicholas FitzGerald, Jeffrey Ling, and Tom Kwiatkowski. 2019. Matching the blanks: Distributional similarity for relation learning. *arXiv preprint arXiv:1906.03158*.

Yonghui Wu, Mike Schuster, Zhifeng Chen, Quoc V Le, Mohammad Norouzi, Wolfgang Macherey, Maxim Krikun, Yuan Cao, Qin Gao, Klaus Macherey, et al. 2016. Google's neural machine translation system: Bridging the gap between human and machine translation. *arXiv preprint arXiv:1609.08144*.

IIT_kgp at FinCausal 2020, Shared Task 1: Causality Detection using Sentence Embeddings in Financial Reports

Arka Mitra
Electronics and
Electrical Communication
Engineering
IIT Kharagpur
`thearkamitra`
`@iitkgp.ac.in`

Harshvardhan Srivastava
Electrical Engineering
IIT Kharagpur
`hvs24`
`@iitkgp.ac.in`

Yugam Tiwari
Mechanical Engineering
IIT Kharagpur
`tiwariyugam`
`@iitkgp.ac.in`

Abstract

The paper describes the work that the team submitted to FinCausal 2020 Shared Task. This work is associated with the first sub-task of identifying causality in sentences. The various models used in the experiments tried to obtain a latent space representation for each of the sentences. Linear regression was performed on these representations to classify whether the sentence is causal or not. The experiments have shown BERT (Large) performed the best, giving a F1 score of 0.958, in the task of detecting the causality of sentences in financial texts and reports. The class imbalance was dealt with a modified loss function to give a better metric score for the evaluation.

1 Introduction

The last few decades have seen an advent in the storage capacities which has inherently increased the amount of data that people can store. This generates a massive amount of data as well. One such type of data which is of utmost importance is financial data comprising mainly of financial reports. It is not possible to go through all the reports as the number of such reports keep on increasing with time and it is expensive to hire people to summarize the main contents. But these data can contain important information which might help in explaining the profits gained or losses incurred by a branch or a company as a whole. It also provides key insights to the company's decisions and it's monetary effect on the stock prices of the company. Thus there is also a need for more and more financial analysis. In order to explain the variability in the data and to draw conclusions from it, we need to identify the causal relationships between various sentences occurring in the document.

A causal relationship implies that there is an underlying dependency between the two clauses of the sentence. If *cause* clause triggers the *effect* clause in the sentence and the effect can be explained by the cause, this implies that sentence is causal. The trigger word that can be used to determine and separate the two clauses can be implicit like verbs, propositions, conjunctions etc. or can be explicit that can be understood from the overall structure of the sentence. But the triggers can be present in multiple positions and all of them might not contribute to the main causal relationship present in the sentence. Also, the presence of these triggers does not always imply that the sentence has causality. Thus it is important to improve from regular expression based methods and introduce a new method.

Causality has already been studied extensively in a general field but it has not been extended to the field of financial data considerably. The FinCausal 2020 tries to extend the same methodologies in the financial domain and see their performance to have a more comprehensive understanding of what works better in the domain of finance. The challenges posed by financial narratives are at the heart of a lot of discussions within the finance industry. As a Natural Language Generation provider with a specialized focus on Financial Reporting, Yseop (D., Mariko and H., Abi Akl and E., Labidurie and S., Durfort and H. de, Mazancourt, and M., El-Haj, 2019) is often faced with the need to deliver a relevant mapping of events, indicators, and facts, making causality one of their main research topics. The task we are tackling here can be considered analogous to a sequence classification task where we are required to assign labels

Proceedings of the 1st Joint Workshop on Financial Narrative Processing and MultiLing Financial Summarisation, pages 95–99
Barcelona, Spain (Online), December 12, 2020.

to a sentence. This motivated us to use a transformer-based architecture which has shown state of the art results in many natural language tasks like text classification, language modelling, neural machine translation, etc. In this Shared Task, the phenomenon of lexical causative (Levin and Hovav, 1994) is not taken into account. A lexical causative is a causal relationship stated through specific connectives (generally predicates) which, from a semantic point of view, also bear the effect of the cause. We will not consider those as causal references, since the effects are implied in the connectives' definition. For instance in "The company decreased its provisions in 2018.", decrease is a lexical causative that can be glossed as make something lower.

There can also be different types of relationships along with the causal relationship in the identified text section. It is often rendered with the use of polysemous connectives whose main function is not to introduce a causal relationship. For example, in this sentence: "Zhao found himself 60 million yuan indebted after losing 9,000 BTC in a single day (February 10, 2014)", the main function of the connective after is to express a temporal relation between the two clauses. But we also have a causal relationship between them, since one triggers the other.

We are using the term text section since it could be a phrase, a sentence or a paragraph in which the cause and the effect are split in different sentences.

2 Data

The data was provided as a part of the Financial Narrative Workshop by the organisers (Mariko et al., 2020). The data was mainly provided as csv files. The training data consisted of about 4200 sentences. The data was divided into two classes depending on whether they had causality in their underlying structure (causal sentence) or not (non-causal sentence). The data mainly consisted of non-causal sentences and the number of non-causal sentences was about 16 times that of causal sentences.

3 Method

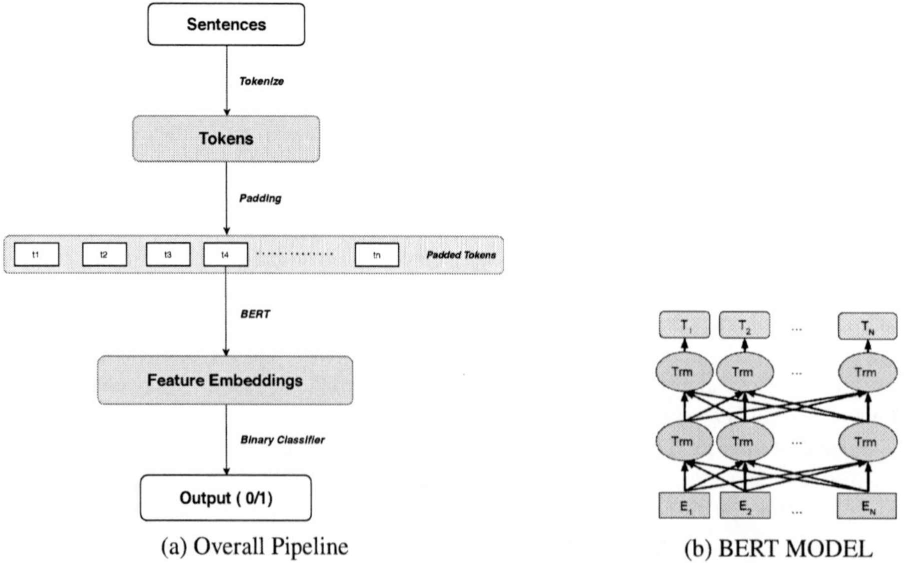

(a) Overall Pipeline

(b) BERT MODEL

Figure 1: (a) shows the overall methodology that has been followed. (b) shows the architecture of the BERT Model that takes in a sentence and output the corresponding embeddings.

3.1 Motivation

Earlier trigger words were identified for classifying sentences into causal and non-causal. However if we consider the word "Since" and the following examples, it will become quite clear why it is not always a correct way to do so.

- "Since the deer could not run slow, the lion was able to catch it."
- "Since morning, the man was not feeling well."

In the first case, the cause-effect relationship is quite visible. However, in the second case, a human can easily identify that the sentence does not have a causal relationship. One of the main reasons due to which humans are capable at doing so is because they can identify the context in which the words are spoken. With the advances in natural language processing, we have models which can also consider contextual representation.

This motivated us to try models like BERT (Devlin et al., 2018), XLNet (Yang et al., 2019) and RoBERTa (Liu et al., 2019). They take into consideration the contextual embedding of each word. We generated the sentence embeddings of each sentence and then passed it through a linear layer to classify whether the sentence is causal or not. 1 shows the overall pipeline of our model.

3.2 Loss

The evaluation metric was taken to be the **F1** score which is the harmonic mean of *precision* and *recall*. When there is a high class imbalance in the dataset, the model generally has a high recall or precision. As stated in the data section, the number of non-causal sentences exceeded the number of causal sentences by an order magnitude and thus it has high precision but low recall. To tackle that, whenever there was a false negative the loss function was configured to penalize it heavily (Ho and Wookey, 2020). The loss L is defined by the following:

$$L = -\alpha * y_{true} * \log(y_{pred}) - (1 - y_{true}) * \log(1 - y_{pred}) \tag{1}$$

The parameter alpha is introduced as a coefficient of the first term in the product. Increasing the value of alpha makes the model adjust it's weights thereby decreasing the number of false negatives. Hence the recall of the system increases but the precision decreases by only a small amount. This increases the overall F1 score.

3.3 Backbone

As a state of the art language model BERT (Bidirectional Encoder Representations from Transformers) has achieved great results in the task of text classification. Models like BERT takes in an input of atmost 512 sequential tokens and generates a vector representation of the sequence. We followed a similar methodology as BERT for text classification (Sun et al., 2019). After obtaining the BERT representation of the sentence, we added a linear classifier on top of it with an output of two nodes. A softmax was applied on the logits and the one with the max score was selected as the predicted output.

$$y_{pred} = argmax(softmax(W * BERT(sentence) + b)) \tag{2}$$

where W is the Linear layer matrix and b is the corresponding bias.

We investigated different masked attention models like the BERT-uncased-base, BERT-cased-base, BERT-cased-large, XLNet-base, RoBERTa-cased-base for this sub-task and it was seen that the best results were obtained for the BERT-cased-large model. Cased models performed better than the uncased ones when tried out with the BERT base and thus in the consequent experiments, we proceeded with the cased versions. Other transformer-based language models like XLNet (large) and RoBERTa (large) were not employed due to their large size and our limited access to computational power.

3.4 Input Tokens Length

Another method that we tried to explore was the relationship between the input dimensions and the overall performance. (Tan and Le, 2019) shows that there exists a correlation between the width of the architecture, height of the architecture and the initial input shape which is fed into the network. Also, the paper had shown that when only one of the individual parameters was changed, the performance saturated very quickly. We had also changed the input dimension and the model height (by using BERT base and large). There was a trade-off between the input shape and the performance. Due to the large hidden dimension size, the Floating Point Operations (FLOPs) of the model is almost linearly proportional to the input length to the transformer (Dai et al., 2020). Decrease in the number of FLOPs also decreases the time for completing the same number of epochs. However, if the input size is decreased, some important information may get lost due to the truncation which decreases the performance of the model. By some analysis of the data that had been provided, we saw that most sentences that were causal were at most 128 words long, and thereby it was chosen as the truncation length for the BERT model.

Table 1: Sequence length variation of BERT-base in experiments

Sequence length	F1 Score	Precision	Recall
64	0.94268	0.942527	0.942835
128	0.948066	0.948282	0.947856
256	0.951081	0.951650	0.950560
512	0.951879	0.953650	0.950717

4   Results

The datasets that had been provided as a part of the competition had been given as Trial1, Practice1, and Evaluation1. To choose the model on which to proceed further, the initial experiments were run on Trail1 dataset. The F1 scores of the different models followed a ranking of BERT Large, XLNET-Base, BERT-Base, and RoBERTa with BERT-Large being the largest and the RoBERTa results being the lowest. The experiments had been run on Google Colaboratory **using a single 12 GB NVIDIA K80 Tesla GPU** and due to computing limitations, XLNet Large and RoBERTa Large could not be calculated. Based on

Table 2: Results of the Different Experiments

Model	F1 Score	Precision	Recall
XLNet (Base)	0.950820	0.952041	0.949788
RoBERTa	0.929485	0.871544	0.921205
BERT (Base)	0.948066	0.948282	0.947856
BERT (Large)	0.957814	0.957408	0.958299

these results, the outputs from BERT-Large-Cased had been sent into the final evaluation system which resulted in an **F1** score of **0.958** resulting in us securing the 8th position.

5   Discussion

This method uses contextual word embeddings and removes most of the problems a regular expression based method would have had. Based on the results, a comparative study was done on the performance of various models like BERT, XLNet and RoBERTa. The BERT-large model performs better than BERT-base as expected as it can have more hidden features to explore. XLNet performs better than BERT as the former is a mix of both masked and permutation language modeling. RoBERTa performed worse than BERT despite it being trained on more data. One of the reasons for that might be as RoBERTa is not trained on next sentence prediction (NSP). Better results are expected on cased versions of language models as compared to the uncased versions. Uncased versions turn all the sentences to lowercase which might lead to loss of information in some cases. The added weights on the loss function also helped to increase the recall and thereby helped to tackle the class imbalance.

6 Conclusion

We had experimented with various models and compared the relative accuracy on the given dataset. We finally submitted the best results on a given part of the dataset due to computation limitations and obtained an F1 score 0f 0.958. We can conclude that the cased models performed better than uncased models in all scenarios that we encountered.

7 Future Works

The BERT Large Cased model had given relatively good results. However, a domain specific BERT would have provided better results (Gururangan et al., 2020). Also, we had used just a part of the whole dataset due to restricted access to computational power. Including a larger dataset would also help to even improve the scores.

References

D., Mariko and H., Abi Akl and E., Labidurie and S., Durfort and H. de, Mazancourt, and M., El-Haj. 2019. The financial document causality detection shared task (fincausal 2020).

Zihang Dai, Guokun Lai, Yiming Yang, and Quoc V. Le. 2020. Funnel-transformer: Filtering out sequential redundancy for efficient language processing.

Jacob Devlin, Ming-Wei Chang, Kenton Lee, and Kristina Toutanova. 2018. Bert: Pre-training of deep bidirectional transformers for language understanding.

Suchin Gururangan, Ana Marasović, Swabha Swayamdipta, Kyle Lo, Iz Beltagy, Doug Downey, and Noah A. Smith. 2020. Don't stop pretraining: Adapt language models to domains and tasks.

Yaoshiang Ho and Samuel Wookey. 2020. The real-world-weight cross-entropy loss function: Modeling the costs of mislabeling. *IEEE Access*, 8:4806–4813.

Beth Levin and Malka Rappaport Hovav. 1994. A preliminary analysis of causative verbs in english. *Lingua*, 92:35 – 77.

Yinhan Liu, Myle Ott, Naman Goyal, Jingfei Du, Mandar Joshi, Danqi Chen, Omer Levy, Mike Lewis, Luke Zettlemoyer, and Veselin Stoyanov. 2019. Roberta: A robustly optimized bert pretraining approach.

Dominique Mariko, Hanna Abi Akl, Estelle Labidurie, Stephane Durfort, Hugues de Mazancourt, and Mahmoud El-Haj. 2020. The financial document causality detection shared task (fincausal 2020). In *The 1st Joint Workshop on Financial Narrative Processing and MultiLing Financial Summarisation (FNP-FNS 2020*, Barcelona, Spain).

Chi Sun, Xipeng Qiu, Yige Xu, and Xuanjing Huang. 2019. How to fine-tune bert for text classification.

Mingxing Tan and Quoc V. Le. 2019. Efficientnet: Rethinking model scaling for convolutional neural networks.

Zhilin Yang, Zihang Dai, Yiming Yang, Jaime Carbonell, Ruslan Salakhutdinov, and Quoc V. Le. 2019. Xlnet: Generalized autoregressive pretraining for language understanding.

Extractive Financial Narrative Summarisation based on DPPs

Lei Li, Yafei Jiang, Yinan Liu
Beijing University of Posts and Telecommunications (BUPT)
No.10 Xitucheng Road, Haidian District, Beijing, P.R.China
`leili,jiangyafei,lyinan@bupt.edu.cn`

Abstract

We participate in the FNS-Summarisation 2020 shared task to be held at FNP 2020 workshop at COLING 2020. Based on Determinantal Point Processes (DPPs), we build an extractive automatic financial summarisation system for the specific task. In this system, we first analyze the long report data to select the important narrative parts and generate an intermediate document. Next, we build the kernel Matrix L for the intermediate document, which represents the quality of its sentences. On the basis of L, we then can use the DPPs sampling algorithm to choose those sentences with high quality and diversity as the final summary sentences.

1 Introduction

With the development and progress of the economy, the popularity of the financial sector is increasing day by day. There are quite a few new companies gradually emerging and going public, but investors often find it difficult to deal with the long-form annual reports of various companies, because their content may be tedious and redundant, and it is difficult to filter out effective key information by human resources, so an automatic digest system is needed to help investors effectively screen company information.

In this paper, we try to solve the first task contained in FNS (Financial Narrative Summarisation) 2020, the dataset we use is the annual reports in the financial field provided by the organizer. As there is much redundant information in the reports, we plan to select the most useful parts first as the intermediate documents to be summarized. For the shared task of summarisation, we implement a Quality-Diversity model (QD) based on Determinantal Point Processes (DPPs) to represent the intermediate document, and merge three kinds of features to rank the sentences.

2 Related Work

Li L et al. (2018) focused on exploring the sampling process. They used WMD sentence similarity to construct new kernel matrix used in Determinantal Point Processes (DPPs). Ma S et al. (2018) divided all sentences into three categories (motivations, methods, and conclusions), and then extracted sentences from each cluster based on rules and severe features to form a summary. Debnath D et al. (2018) built a summary generation system using the OpenNMT tool. Zhong M et al. (2019) analyzed the relationship between the quality of extractive automatic summarization and the model network, and the influence of network architecture, knowledge transfer and learning mode on the effect of the summary system is verified through a series of experiments. Liu Y and Lapata M (2019) studied the influence of pre-training language models in automatic summarization tasks, and emphasized the importance of document encoding. In the extractive summarization task, they used multiple layers of BERT as the encoder, and obtained good results on three datasets.

3 Data

For the FNS 2020 Shared task we use 3863 UK annual reports for firms listed on The London Stock Exchange (LSE) covering the period between 2002 and 2017. UK annual reports are lengthy documents

Proceedings of the 1st Joint Workshop on Financial Narrative Processing and MultiLing Financial Summarisation, pages 100–104
Barcelona, Spain (Online), December 12, 2020.

with around 80 pages on average, some annual reports could span over more than 250 pages. These UK annual reports are divided into training, testing and validation sets. The training and validation sets include the full text of each annual report along with the gold-standard summaries. On average there are at least 3 gold-standard summaries for each annual report with some reports containing up to 7 gold-standard summaries. For testing dataset, the task participants were given access only to the full texts. Table 1 shows the dataset details.

Data Type	Training	Validation	Testing
Report full text	3000	363	500
Gold summaries	9873	1250	-

Table 1: FNS 2020 Shared Task Dataset

4 System

In our system, we present an original Quality-Diversity model for extractive automatic summarisation based on DPPs sampling algorithm (Kulesza and Taskar, 2012). In this model, a single input document can be regarded as a set of sentences, and the process of extracting abstracts can be regarded as sampling a subset of important sentences from that set. To choose the high-quality and diversity summaries with DPPs, we need to construct the kernel matrix L to represent the document. The main steps of summary generation include pre-processing, feature selection and sentence sampling. Pre-processing, feature selection and sentence sampling are as followed.

4.1 Pre-processing

In this task the summary requires extraction from different key sections found in the annual reports. Those sections are usually referred to as "narrative sections" or "front-end" sections and they usually contain textual information and reviews by the firm's management and board of directors. Sections containing financial statements in terms of tables and numbers are usually referred to as "back-end" sections and are not supposed to be part of the narrative summaries. Therefore, in the data pre-processing part, there are mainly two steps: the first step is to detect and extract the narrative sections of the annual reports; the second step is to organize the format of the dataset, and clean the narrative sections extracted in the previous step. The final processed data represents the important narrative parts and will be used for subsequent summary generation/extraction.More implementation details of pre-processing are given below.

First, we analyze the dataset and try to catch some underlying laws. Comparing the annual reports and gold summaries, we find that each gold summary contains some sentences appearing in the corresponding annual report, and each corresponds to a continuous piece of content. Upon further analysis, we can discover that the gold summary basically corresponds to four sections in the annual report, namely Highlights, At a glance, Chairman's statement and Chief Executive's review. Although not every annual report contains these four sections and the names of the sections may be different, the contents of these sections are similar and are all narrative sections. Therefore, we extract all these sections included in each annual report and use them as a new dataset together with the gold summaries.

Next, we perform further data cleaning and formatting on the new dataset obtained in the previous step. The dataset provided by the organizer is directly converted from pdf files to txt files, thus the data format is confusing and has many useless content such as headers and footers. The reason why they are considered useless is that headers and footers information of each page is basically the same, such as ANNUAL REPORT AND ACCOUNTS XXX, where XXX represents the year. In order to store sentences by lines, we divide the text according to punctuation marks such as periods, exclamation points, etc. In order to delete non-narrative texts such as tables and numbers, we first use regular expressions to filter financial numbers, and then use the open source NLP toolkit to perform dependency syntactic analysis on the data. If a sentence does not contain the subject, predicate and object, We consider the sentence to be unqualified and delete it. Finally, we use the processed data to generate intermediate documents for the subsequent summarisation instead of the original long annual reports.

4.2 Feature Selection

To represent the document, we build a kernel matrix L from statistical feature method. We use Sentence Length (SL), Sentence Position (SP), Sentence Coverage (SC) as features according to the work of (Li L et al., 2017) to construct matrix L. Sentence Length can be calculated by

$$sl_i = \exp\left(-1 * \frac{(len_i - \mu)^2}{\sigma^2}\right) \tag{1}$$

where sl_i is the sentence length feature score, μ and σ are the mean and standard deviation of sentence length respectively. Sentence Position can be calculated by

$$sp_i = 1 - \frac{s_i}{|D|} \tag{2}$$

where s_i represents the position of the $i - th$ sentence in the text, $|D|$ represents the total number of sentences in the text, and sp_i is the score of the sentence position feature. Sentence Coverage can be calculated by

$$SC_i = \frac{\Sigma_{i=1}^{|S|} \frac{num_S(word_i)}{n}}{|S|} \tag{3}$$

where sc_i represents the score of sentence coverage, $word_i$ represents the $i - th$ word in sentence S, $num_s(word_i)$ represents the total number of sentences covered by $word_i$, and $|S|$ represents the total number of words of in the sentence, n represents the total number of sentences in the input sequence. Elements of L can be calculated by

$$L_{ij} = q_i Sim_{ij} q_j \tag{4}$$

where q_i is the quality of a single sentence, Sim_{ij} represents the similarity between sentences. q_i can be calculated by the features of SL, SP and SC. We use the Jaccard similarity between sentences to measure the degree of sentence diversity, so Sim_{ij} can be computed as

$$Sim_{ij} = \frac{|\ \{word|word \in sen_i\ and\ word \in sen_j\}\ |}{|\ \{word|word \in sen_i\ or\ word \in sen_j\}\ |} \tag{5}$$

It can be seen that the matrix L has the function of measuring the quality and diversity of sentences, which is quite important in further sampling process. For the shared task, we select one feature or the sum of multiple features to get the sentence quality q and arrange these methods into three runs.

4.3 Sentence Sampling

In our approach, we use discrete DPPs to select sentences, by constructing matrix L, we can apply the DPPs sampling algorithm to extract summaries. To perform DPPs sampling, we first get the eigenvalue λ_n and the eigenvector v_n of the matrix L, then project all the sentence vectors into a new low-dimensional feature space. In this space, the magnitude of the vector describes the importance and the cosine similarity between two vectors describes the similarity between sentences. When selecting sentences, the number of sentences in the summary is obtained by probability model.

Next, we select a sentence with high quality x_i, then remove a list of feature vectors v_i in the feature space that contributes to its vector modulus length, and perform series of orthogonalization on feature space.

Finally we select new elements according to the new sub-feature space re-projection until the end, which can ensure that the element selected again are both high-quality and low-similar to the previous element, thus choose those high-quality and diversity sentences as summary sentences. the details of DPPs can be referred to the work of Kulesza and Taskar(2012).

5 Results

In the shared task, we submitted a total of three versions of our system. CIST-BUPT-RUN3 uses SC as the feature that represents document, CIST-BUPT-RUN2 uses SL, while CIST-BUPT-RUN1 merges all three features: SC, SL and SP. We tried three versions on the pre-processed training set and table 2 shows the performance from our experiments.

System	ROUGE-1/F	ROUGE-2/F	ROUGE-L/F
CIST-BUPT-RUN1	0.305	0.073	0.166
CIST-BUPT-RUN2	0.293	0.067	0.164
CIST-BUPT-RUN3	**0.313**	**0.079**	**0.167**

Table 2: Results on Official Validation Set

The result shows that the systems using different features have similar performance, while CIST-BUPT-RUN3 performs the best and the performance of others are slightly lower.

System	R-L/R	R-L/P	R-L/F	R-1/R	R-1/P	R-1/F
CIST-BUPT-RUN1	0.294	**0.361**	0.317	0.405	0.423	0.401
CIST-BUPT-RUN2	0.311	0.352	0.324	0.418	0.440	0.416
CIST-BUPT-RUN3	**0.324**	0.348	**0.329**	**0.434**	**0.449**	**0.428**
	R-2/R	R-2/P	R-2/F	R-SU4/R	R-SU4/P	R-SU4/F
CIST-BUPT-RUN1	0.258	0.206	0.220	0.315	0.190	0.228
CIST-BUPT-RUN2	**0.272**	0.224	0.237	0.330	0.204	0.243
CIST-BUPT-RUN3	0.228	**0.233**	**0.248**	**0.346**	**0.209**	**0.251**

Table 3: Evaluation Results on Testing Set

As is shown in table 3, CIST-BUPT-RUN3 still performs the best. We find that the ROUGE score on testing set is higher than that on training set, the reason may be that because for each document in the official training set, there are multiple golden abstracts corresponding to them, we choose to merge these summaries for evaluation, so the ROUGE score is a bit lower. But even so, our experimental results can reflect the pros and cons of the three models. The model of DPPs with SC as feature for the kernel matrix shows the best performance among the three models in our system. We can also infer that SC catches more relations between sentences and thus is superior to the features of sentence's length and position.

6 Conclusion and Future Work

Actually, there are multiple ways to represent the document, one typical way is to train a Sentence2Vec model using neural network, which may improve the performance of the model. But because of the COVID-19, the servers available are limited, we don't have enough computing resources to train the model. In the future, we'll try other feasible methods of document representation, seeing if they can help improve the quality of summaries.

Acknowledgements

This work was supported by Beijing Municipal Commission of Science and Technology [grant number Z181100001018035]; National Social Science Foundation of China [grant number 16ZDA055]; National Natural Science Foundation of China [grant numbers 91546121, 71231002]; Engineering Research Center of Information Networks, Ministry of Education; Beijing BUPT Information Networks Industry Institute Company Limited; the project of Beijing Institute of Science and Technology Information.

References

Li L, Chi J, Chen M, et al. 2018. CIST@ CLSciSumm-18: Methods for Computational Linguistics Scientific Citation Linkage, Facet Classification and Summarization[C]//BIRNDL@ SIGIR. 2018: 84-95.

Ma S, Zhang H, Xu J, et al. 2018. NJUST@ CLSciSumm-18[C]//BIRNDL@ SIGIR. 2018: 114-129.

Debnath D, Achom A, Pakray P. 2018. NLP-NITMZ@ CLScisumm-18 In: Proceedings of the 3nd Joint Workshop on Bibliometric-enhanced Information Retrieval and Natural Language Processing for Digital Libraries[C]//BIRNDL@ SIGIR. 2018: 164- 171.

Zhong M, Liu P, Wang D et al. 2019. Searching for Effective Neural Extractive Summarization: What Works and What's Next. arXiv preprint arXiv:1907.03491.

Liu Y and Lapata M. 2019. Text summarization with pretrained encoders. arXiv preprint arXiv:1908.08345.

Alex Kulesza and Ben Taskar 2012. Determinantal Point Processes for Machine Learning, Foundations and Trends in Machine Learning: Vol. 5: No. 23, pp 123- 286. http://dx.doi.org/10.1561/2200000044.

Li L, Zhang Y, Chi J et al. 2017. UIDS: A Multilingual Document Summarization Frame- work Based on Summary Diversity and Hierarchical Topics [M] // Li L, Zhang Y, Chi J et al. Chinese Computational Linguistics and Natural Language Processing Based on Naturally Annotated Big Data. Springer, 2017: 2017: 343-354.

PoinT-5: Pointer Network and T-5 based Financial Narrative Summarisation

Abhishek Singh
Samsung R&D Bangalore
`abhishek.s.eee15@iitbhu.ac.in`

Abstract

Companies provide annual reports to their shareholders at the end of the financial year that describes their operations and financial conditions. The average length of these reports is 80, and it may extend up to 250 pages long. In this paper, we propose our methodology PoinT-5 (the combination of Pointer Network and T-5 (Test-to-text transfer Transformer) algorithms) that we used in the Financial Narrative Summarisation (FNS) 2020 task. The proposed method uses Pointer networks to extract important narrative sentences from the report, and then T-5 is used to paraphrase extracted sentences into a concise yet informative sentence. We evaluate our method using ROUGE-N (1,2), L,and SU4. The proposed method achieves the highest precision scores in all the metrics and highest F1 scores in ROUGE 1,and LCS and only solution to cross MUSE solution baseline in ROUGE-LCS metrics.

1   Introduction

Annual Reports may extend up to 250 pages long as stated above, which contains different sections General Corporate Information, financial and operating cost, CEOs message, Narrative texts, accounting policies, Financial statement including balance sheet and summary of financial data documents. In the Financial narrative summarisation task, only the narrative section is summarised, which is not explicitly marked in the dataset, making it challenging and interesting. In recent years, previous manual small-scale research in the Accounting and Finance literature has been scaled up with the aid of NLP and ML methods, for example, to examine approaches to retrieving structured content from financial reports, and to study the causes and consequences of corporate disclosure and financial reporting outcomes (El-Haj et al., 2018).

Companies produce glossy brochures of annual reports with a much looser structure, and this makes automatic summarisation of narratives in UK annual reports a challenging task (El-Haj et al., 2020). Hence we summarize the narrative section of annual reports, particular narrative sentences that are spread loosely across the document need to be first identified and summarise those sentences. The summarisation limit is set to 1000 words, where the actual length of the report may go up to 250 pages long. Hence to summarize these long annual reports using a combination of extractive and abstractive summarisation.

The text summary method can be classified into two paradigms: extractive and abstractive. The extractive summarisation method extracts the meaningful sentences or a section of text from the original text and combines them (ranked or unranked) to form a summary (Cheng and Lapata, 2016; Narayan et al., 2018; Yasunaga et al., 2017; See et al., 2017). Whereas abstractive summarisation generates words and sentences that are similar in meaning to the given text to form a summary that may not be in actual text (Nallapati et al., 2016; Rush et al., 2015; Paulus et al., 2017; Li et al., 2018). When summarizing long documents such as in our case up to 250 pages long, extractive summarisation may not produce a coherent and readable summary, and abstractive summarisation cannot cover complete information using encoder-decoder architecture. One problem is that typical seq2seq frameworks often generate unnatural summaries consisting of repeated words or phrases (Li et al., 2018). Hence, we come up with a combination of extractive and abstractive summarisation to first select important narrative sentences and concisely convey them.

Proceedings of the 1st Joint Workshop on Financial Narrative Processing and MultiLing Financial Summarisation, pages 105–111
Barcelona, Spain (Online), December 12, 2020.

Pointer Networks (Vinyals et al., 2015) is used in various combinatorial optimization problems, such as Travelling Salesman Problem (TSP), Convex hull optimization. We used pointer networks in our task of financial narrative summarization to extract relevant narrative sentences in a particular order to have a logical flow in summary. These extracted sentences are paraphrased to summarise these sentences in an abstractive way using the T-5 sequence-to-sequence model. We train the complete model by optimizing the ROUGE-LCS evaluation metric through a reinforcement learning objective.

2   Related Works

In this section and Appendix B, we discuss related works in the fields of abstractive summarisation, extractive summarisation, combinations of these two methods, reinforcement learning applications, and summarisation of Financial Narratives and their methodology. Studies of human summarizers show that it is common to apply various operations while condensing, such as paraphrasing, generalization, sentence-level summarisation and reordering (Jing, 2002). We continue related work in Appendix B.

3   Data Description

The financial narrative summarisation dataset contains 3,863 annual reports for firms listed on LSE covering the period between 2002 and 2017 (El-Haj et al., 2019; El-Haj et al., 2014). Dataset is randomly split into training (75%), testing and validation (25%) Table:2. We use NLTK sentence tokenizer [1] to tokenize sentence in the annual report and summary processing for all our experiments. Data is further described and anayzed in Appendix A.

4   Methodology

4.1   Model Description

Our model is composed of three parts that are first trained or executed individually and then finally brought together using policy gradient algorithm. As stated earlier the model is combination of extractive as well as abtractive methods. Initially dataset is provided in the form $\{x_i, y_i^j\}, 1 <= i <= N, 1 <= j <= 7$. Here i represents number of annual reports, j represents number of summaries for each annual reports and x, y represent report and summary respectively.

In extraction process we assume that for every summary sentence there is matching sentence in the annual report. To train exaction model we need these corresponding sentences in the reports. Since, annual reports are not marked explicitly with sentences we followed ROUGE scores to extract these sentences as done in (Chen and Bansal, 2018; Nallapati et al., 2016).For every summary sentence we calculate ROUGE with every sentence in the report and then choose the sentence with maximum value.

$$j_t = \mathrm{argmax}_i \left(\text{ROUGE-L }_{\text{recall}} \left(d_i, s_t \right) \right) \tag{1}$$

In equation 1 j_t represent sentence with maximum ROUGE score for summary sentence s_t for every sentence in report d_i. For every report in training set there are multiple summaries. We calculate $ROUGE - Lsummary$ for extracted sentences as mentioned in (Lin, 2004).

$$R_{lcs} = \frac{\sum_{i=1}^{n} LCS_U \left(r_i, c_i \right)}{m} \tag{2}$$

In equation 2 R_{lcs} represents ROUGE-L recall, r_i, c_i are report and summary sentences respectively and m is total number of words in extracted report sentences. Once summary level ROUGE-L recall is calculated we choose summary with maximum value for further processing. Once proxy sentences and a summary is selected applying above methods extraction model is trained. In extraction model sentence level representation of report sentences is calculated using hierarchical word to sentence level Bidirectional Long Short Term Memory (Bi-LSTM)(Hochreiter and Schmidhuber, 1997). First Bi-LSTM is

[1] `https://www.nltk.org/api/nltk.tokenize.html`

applied to word sequence of the sentence to get sentence level semantic information. Then Bi-LSTM is applied to sentences representations to get document level information in each sentence representation. We train attention mechanism (Bahdanau et al., 2014) based Pointer Networks (Vinyals et al., 2015) different from copy mechanism used in (See et al., 2017). Given these proxy sentences which we treat as ground truth and sentences extracted using pointer network, we train it to minimize cross-entropy loss.

Once sentences are extracted using above methods we fine-tune T-5 based sequence-to-sequence model for abstraction. T-5 architecture is pretrained on C-4 dataset [2] using denoising method similar to that of Bert (Devlin et al., 2018) produce better result in language modelling. T-5 treats every task classification, summarisation, question answering, and translation as text-to-text format. These extracted sentences are taken as input and ground truth summary sentences are taken as output which is trained using cross-entropy loss. Input and output are prepared using T-5 tokenizer which outputs input_ids and attention masks for input and target. These are then fed to model for training.

Once these individual components are trained individually, final complete model is trained using policy gradient algorithm with similar process as in (Chen and Bansal, 2018). At every extraction step agent samples an action to extract document sentence an receive reward $r(t + 1)$ which is ROUGE-L$_{F_1}$ between output from T-5 after abstraction and ground truth summary sentence.

$$r(t + 1) = \text{ROUGE-L}_{F_1} \left(abstraction \left(d_{j_t} \right), s_t \right) \tag{3}$$

The model is trained using advantage actor-critic model to mitigate bias incurred in REINFORCE (Williams, 1992). Overall idea of our method is that first proxy sentences are extracted using ROUGE score maximisation, then extraction model is trained to extract unique narrative sentences from the report then these sentences are paraphrased using T-5 algorithm for abstraction to give concise yet informative sentence. Reinforcement learning helps to maximise ROUGE score by rewarding good sentences that are extracted and penalising bad sentences.

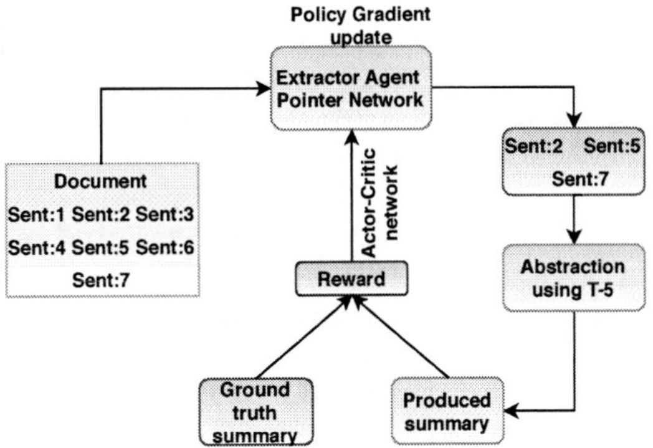

Figure 1: Complete method diagram

4.2 Parameter Tuning

During abstraction we limit maximum number of sentences to 80, since there is limit on word limit of 1000 words and most of the reports' narrative can be summarised in less than 80 sentences as seen in section:3. Word2vec (Mikolov et al., 2013) embedding is used in representation of word in extractor model.. Vocab size is limited to 20000, embedding size is 300, maximum number of words in a sentence 60. Model is trained using Adam optimizer with learning rate of 0.001, decay rate of 0.5. Gradient norm is clipped at 1.0. Beam size if fixed to 2 in T-5 network, repetition penalty of 2.0. Rouge-LCS is used to optimize RL training. Abtractor and extractor networks are trained using cross-entropy loss. Traiing is done on Tesla-K80 12Gb colab GPUs with batch size of 16 and check point frequency of 16 batches.

---

[2]https://www.tensorflow.org/datasets/catalog/c4

5 Results and Analysis

In this section we present results from our experiments and compare with different baselines MUSE (Litvak et al., 2010), Text-rank (Mihalcea and Tarau, 2004), Lex-Rank (Erkan and Radev, 2004), and Polynomial Summarisation (Litvak and Vanetik, 2013). We train three models in our experiments (PoinT-5) Pointer Network with T-5, Pointer Network alone, and Pre-trained Bert for text summarisation. In table

Metrics	Text-Rank	Lex-Rank	Polynomial	MUSE	Pre-trained Bert	Pointer Net	PoinT-5
Prec(R-L)	0.235	0.210	0.260	0.470	0.213	0.603*	**0.605**
Recall(R-L)	0.197	0.263	0.177	0.370	0.254	0.377	0.377
F-1(R-L)	0.206	0.218	0.205	0.407	0.225	0.455*	**0.456**
Prec(R-1)	0.414	0.337	0.324	0.483	0.241	0.611*	**0.612**
Recall (R-1)	0.118	0.269	0.253	0.413	0.378	0.392	0.393
F-1 (R-1)	0.172	0.264	0.274	0.433	0.283	0.465*	**0.466**
Prec (R-2)	0.229	0.193	0.147	0.311	0.114	0.448*	**0.451**
Recall (R-2)	0.044	0.107	0.088	0.198	0.138	0.220	.0.222
F-1 (R-2	0.070	0.120	0.105	0.234	0.118	0.289	0.289
Prec(R-SU4)	0.302	0.253	0.213	0.375	0.165	0.506*	**0.508**
Recall(R-SU4)	0.048	0.117	0.105	0.201	0.149	0.208	0.209
F-1(R-SU4)	0.079	0.140	0.135	0.253	0.149	0.286	0.288

Table 1: ROUGE Evaluation on Financial Narrative Summarisation data (Bold represents highest overall, Prec represents Precision and * represents second-highest overall)

1 bold is marked for highest value amongst all the solutions for the task including baselines. Pre-trained Bert for summarisation is not fine-tuned for this specific task hence its performance is not as good as Pointer Network and PoinT-5 (Pointer Network + T-5). PoinT-5 network gives highest results for precision on all the evaluation metrics ROUGE -1,2,L,SU4. From this it can be inferred that generated summmaries are highly precise in extracting narrative sentences and matches with ground truth summaries. Recall is comparatively much lower than precision in most of the evaluated metrics which means that generated summaries do not cover all the information in ground-truth summaries. This large difference in precision and recall shows that generated summaries do not cover all the sentences possibly due to restriction imposed on the number of sentences during training to follow word limit in summaries. Less recall and high precision value shows that generated summaries provide highly relevant information but does not cover complete information in ground truth summaries. From results it is evident that there is not much difference in performance between pointer net performance and PoinT-5 which extraction played key role in the architecture. PoinT-5 and Pointer Networks are the only system to cross MUSE baseline in ROUGE-L by atleat 5 points. These models give highest F1 results in ROUGE-L and ROUGE_1 metrics and highest precision in ROUGE-L,1,2,SU4.

6 Conclusion and Future work

In this work we present our solution on Financial Narrative Summarisation(FNS2020) dataset using PoinT-5 method explained in 4. It is combination of both extractive and abstractive methods using Pointer Network and T-5. With these methods we are able to achieve highest precision score in every evaluation metric and achieve highest F-1 scores in ROUGE-LCS and ROUGE-1.

In our future work we would like to address several limitation of our method such as factual correctness in summaries which is very important in financial domain as done in (Zhang et al., 2019) in summarizing radiology reports. To improve precision of our generated summaries under 1000 words we would formulate a penalty if system generates more than 1000 words during training of RL algorithm rather than restricting algorithm to fixed number of sentences.

References

Dzmitry Bahdanau, Kyunghyun Cho, and Yoshua Bengio. 2014. Neural machine translation by jointly learning to align and translate. *arXiv preprint arXiv:1409.0473*.

Eddy Cardinaels, Stephan Hollander, and Brian J White. 2018. Automatic summaries of earnings releases: Attributes and effects on investors' judgments. *Available at SSRN 2904384*.

Yen-Chun Chen and Mohit Bansal. 2018. Fast abstractive summarization with reinforce-selected sentence rewriting. *arXiv preprint arXiv:1805.11080*.

Jianpeng Cheng and Mirella Lapata. 2016. Neural summarization by extracting sentences and words. *arXiv preprint arXiv:1603.07252*.

Jacob Devlin, Ming-Wei Chang, Kenton Lee, and Kristina Toutanova. 2018. Bert: Pre-training of deep bidirectional transformers for language understanding. *arXiv preprint arXiv:1810.04805*.

Mahmoud El-Haj, Paul Rayson, Steven Young, and Martin Walker. 2014. Detecting document structure in a very large corpus of uk financial reports.

Mahmoud El-Haj, Paul Rayson, and Andrew Moore. 2018. The first financial narrative processing workshop (fnp 2018). In *Proceedings of the LREC 2018 Workshop*.

Mahmoud El-Haj, Paul Rayson, Paulo Alves, Carlos Herrero-Zorita, and Steven Young. 2019. Multilingual financial narrative processing: Analysing annual reports in english, spanish and portuguese. *Multilingual Text Analysis: Challenges, Models, And Approaches*, page 441.

Mahmoud El-Haj, Ahmed AbuRa'ed, Nikiforos Pittaras, and George Giannakopoulos. 2020. The Financial Narrative Summarisation Shared Task (FNS 2020). In *The 1st Joint Workshop on Financial Narrative Processing and MultiLing Financial Summarisation (FNP-FNS 2020*, Barcelona, Spain.

Günes Erkan and Dragomir R Radev. 2004. Lexrank: Graph-based lexical centrality as salience in text summarization. *Journal of artificial intelligence research*, 22:457–479.

Sepp Hochreiter and Jürgen Schmidhuber. 1997. Long short-term memory. *Neural computation*, 9(8):1735–1780.

Wan-Ting Hsu, Chieh-Kai Lin, Ming-Ying Lee, Kerui Min, Jing Tang, and Min Sun. 2018. A unified model for extractive and abstractive summarization using inconsistency loss. *arXiv preprint arXiv:1805.06266*.

Hongyan Jing. 2002. Using hidden markov modeling to decompose human-written summaries. *Computational linguistics*, 28(4):527–543.

Piji Li, Lidong Bing, and Wai Lam. 2018. Actor-critic based training framework for abstractive summarization. *arXiv preprint arXiv:1803.11070*.

Chin-Yew Lin. 2004. Rouge: A package for automatic evaluation of summaries. In *Text summarization branches out*, pages 74–81.

Marina Litvak and Natalia Vanetik. 2013. Mining the gaps: Towards polynomial summarization. In *Proceedings of the Sixth International Joint Conference on Natural Language Processing*, pages 655–660.

Marina Litvak, Mark Last, and Menahem Friedman. 2010. A new approach to improving multilingual summarization using a genetic algorithm. In *Proceedings of the 48th annual meeting of the association for computational linguistics*, pages 927–936.

Rada Mihalcea and Paul Tarau. 2004. Textrank: Bringing order into text. In *Proceedings of the 2004 conference on empirical methods in natural language processing*, pages 404–411.

Tomas Mikolov, Kai Chen, Greg Corrado, and Jeffrey Dean. 2013. Efficient estimation of word representations in vector space. *arXiv preprint arXiv:1301.3781*.

Ramesh Nallapati, Bowen Zhou, Caglar Gulcehre, Bing Xiang, et al. 2016. Abstractive text summarization using sequence-to-sequence rnns and beyond. *arXiv preprint arXiv:1602.06023*.

Shashi Narayan, Shay B Cohen, and Mirella Lapata. 2018. Ranking sentences for extractive summarization with reinforcement learning. *arXiv preprint arXiv:1802.08636*.

Romain Paulus, Caiming Xiong, and Richard Socher. 2017. A deep reinforced model for abstractive summarization. *arXiv preprint arXiv:1705.04304*.

Colin Raffel, Noam Shazeer, Adam Roberts, Katherine Lee, Sharan Narang, Michael Matena, Yanqi Zhou, Wei Li, and Peter J Liu. 2019. Exploring the limits of transfer learning with a unified text-to-text transformer. *arXiv preprint arXiv:1910.10683*.

Alexander M Rush, Sumit Chopra, and Jason Weston. 2015. A neural attention model for abstractive sentence summarization. *arXiv preprint arXiv:1509.00685*.

Abigail See, Peter J Liu, and Christopher D Manning. 2017. Get to the point: Summarization with pointer-generator networks. *arXiv preprint arXiv:1704.04368*.

Zhaopeng Tu, Zhengdong Lu, Yang Liu, Xiaohua Liu, and Hang Li. 2016. Modeling coverage for neural machine translation. *arXiv preprint arXiv:1601.04811*.

Oriol Vinyals, Meire Fortunato, and Navdeep Jaitly. 2015. Pointer networks. In *Advances in neural information processing systems*, pages 2692–2700.

Qicai Wang, Peiyu Liu, Zhenfang Zhu, Hongxia Yin, Qiuyue Zhang, and Lindong Zhang. 2019. A text abstraction summary model based on bert word embedding and reinforcement learning. *Applied Sciences*, 9(21):4701.

Ronald J Williams. 1992. Simple statistical gradient-following algorithms for connectionist reinforcement learning. *Machine learning*, 8(3-4):229–256.

Michihiro Yasunaga, Rui Zhang, Kshitijh Meelu, Ayush Pareek, Krishnan Srinivasan, and Dragomir Radev. 2017. Graph-based neural multi-document summarization. *arXiv preprint arXiv:1706.06681*.

Yuhao Zhang, Derek Merck, Emily Bao Tsai, Christopher D Manning, and Curtis P Langlotz. 2019. Optimizing the factual correctness of a summary: A study of summarizing radiology reports. *arXiv preprint arXiv:1911.02541*.

Appendices

A   Data Analysis

Table 2 presented total summaries and annual reports in train, validation, and test set. During our analysis, we found that most of the annual reports contain 100-200 sentences. There are 279 summaries with more than 500 sentences, which is large. Whereas in summaries, the average number of sentences is 50. Therefore summaries are one forth on average of annual reports and up to one-tenth in many cases. We present these analysis in Figure 2.

Data Type	Training	Validation	Testing
Report full text	3,000	363	500
Gold Summaries	9,873	1,250	1673

Table 2: FNS 2020 Shared Task Dataset

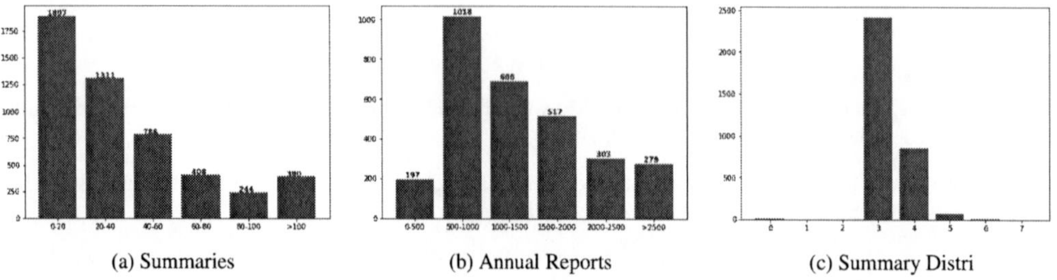

(a) Summaries   (b) Annual Reports   (c) Summary Distri

Figure 2: Sentence wise Distribution (a,b), Number of Summary Distribution (c)

B Extended Related Work

(Li et al., 2018) proposes a training framework based on the actor-critic model. They apply the attention-based sequence-to-sequence model as the actor to conduct summary generation. For the critic, they combine the maximum likelihood estimator with a well designed global summary quality estimator. (Nallapati et al., 2016) propose RNN based encoder-decoder model for abstractive summarisation. They apply bi-directional GRU-RNN at the encoder side and uni-directional GRU in decoder with attention. In their approach, each mini-batch's decoder-vocabulary is restricted to words in the source documents of that batch. (Rush et al., 2015) also propose attention based sequence to sequence model for abstractive summarisation. (Paulus et al., 2017) states that attentional, RNN-based encoder-decoder models for abstractive summarisation have achieved good performance on short input and output sequences. For longer documents and summaries, however, these models often include repetitive and incoherent phrases. Hence they combine standard word prediction with the global sequence prediction training of RL which makes resulting summaries become more readable.

(Narayan et al., 2018) propose a reinforcement learning-based sentence ranking approach in extractive summarisation. (Cheng and Lapata, 2016) use attention architecture for words and sentence level extraction in extractive summarisation method. (Yasunaga et al., 2017) proposes a multi-document summarization system that exploits the representational power of deep neural networks and the sentence relation information encoded in graph representations of document clusters. Specifically, they apply Graph Convolutional Networks on sentence relation graphs.

(See et al., 2017) propose a novel "Pointer Generator" networks for abstractive summarisation. In this model a word is chosen with probability P_{gen} from overall vocabulary and $1 - P_{gen}$ from current sentence using attention weights. They apply coverage mechanism by (Tu et al., 2016) to avoid word repetitions in the summary which is common in large documents.

(Chen and Bansal, 2018) apply combination abstractive and extractive summarisation by join training using reinforcement learning. They apply pointer network for extraction (different from Pointer Generator) and RNN based encoder-decoder for abstraction. (Hsu et al., 2018) propose unified extractive and abstractive with a hierarchical sentence and word level attention model using novel inconsistency loss. (Wang et al., 2019) used T-5 (Raffel et al., 2019) based sentence representation for combined extractive and abstractive training.

Financial Narrative Summarisation has been explored in the past by (Cardinaels et al., 2018). They provide multiple evidence that algorithm-based summaries are less positively biased than management summaries.

Combining financial word embeddings and knowledge-based features for financial text summarization: UC3M-MC System at FNS-2020

Jaime Baldeón[1], Paloma Martínez[1] and Jose L. Martínez[1, 2]
[1]Computer Science Department,
Universidad Carlos III de Madrid, Spain
[2]MeaningCloud LLC, USA
100332810@alumnos.uc3m.es
pmf@inf.uc3m.es
jmartinez@meaningcloud.com

Abstract

This paper describes the systems proposed by HULAT research group from Universidad Carlos III de Madrid (UC3M) and MeaningCloud (MC) company to solve the FNS 2020 Shared Task on summarizing financial reports. We present a narrative extractive approach that implements a statistical model comprised of different features that measure the relevance of the sentences using a combination of statistical and machine learning methods. The key to the model's performance is its accurate representation of the text, since the word embeddings used by the model have been trained with the summaries of the training dataset and therefore capture the most salient information from the reports. The systems' code can be found at https://github.com/jaimebaldeon/FNS-2020.

1.   Introduction

The remarkable extension and diversity of textual and numerical structures in financial reports hinder the summarization process. Therefore, it is paramount to filter the relevant information and represent it accurately to produce high quality summaries. With this objective, we have developed a narrative extractive model with gold standard summaries knowledge.

What makes the proposed approach interesting is its outstanding capacity to capture the relevant information from the gold standard summaries and extract (according to some parameters) the most salient sentences from the reports.

It is the first time the team (HULAT) has participated in the FNS task and our goal was to explore features based on word embeddings that could understand and represent financial reports with higher precision. Therefore, the system implements a combination of statistical and machine learning techniques to determine the salience of the sentences in order to extract the most relevant ones from the original financial report.

2.   Related work

Automatic text summarization can be tackled with two different approaches: extractive and abstractive summarization. The former approach is the most commonly used, since it is less computationally expensive and not as complex as abstractive summarization, furthermore, its performance has shown great results and settled the base to further research and development. However, it still faces some drawbacks, such as lack of cohesion between sentences or balance, and its methodology is still not close enough to human-like text processing, which is more similar to an abstractive approach.

Extractive summarization has implemented multiple different approaches: statistical approaches as purely statistical methods, statistical and linguistic features, and structure representation methods; and machine learning approaches such as Naïve Bayes, Decision Trees, Neural Networks, etc. (Spärck,

Proceedings of the 1st Joint Workshop on Financial Narrative Processing and MultiLing Financial Summarisation, pages 112–117
Barcelona, Spain (Online), December 12, 2020.

2007). As for abstractive summarization, state of the art approaches have been carried out bringing automatic summarization to the cutting edge: Recurrent Neural Networks, Long Short-Term Memory networks (Hochreiter and Schmidhuber, 1997), Sequence to sequence models (Nallapati et al., 2016) and Transformers (Vaswani et al., 2017). From the point of view of evaluation (Ermakova et al, 2019) provides an overview of different international challenges covering summarization tasks in several domains such as DUC (Document Understanding Conference), TAC (Text Analysis Conference) and CLEF (Cross Language Evaluation Forum). A detailed review of evaluation measures (informativeness and readability evaluations) is also given, as well as an automatic framework for evaluating metrics that does not require human annotations to face the problem of laborious and time-consuming generation of annotated corpora.

Depending on the source of the documents, (Xu et al, 2013) and (Li and Zhang, 2020) introduce approaches for tweet summarization, (Cagliero and La Quatra, 2020) describes an extractive supervised approach for scientific articles summarization and (Fabbri et al, 2019) introduces an abstractive approach for news summarization. In the financial domain, however, previous work is almost non-existent; participants in FinTOC-2019 shared task, (Juge et al. 2019), developed systems for title and TOC (table of content) extraction, multi-class text classification and tone detection but not for report summaries extraction. Further research in financial narrative processing with the capacity of analyzing large reports is required, hence the need to explore new approaches to tackle this challenge.

3. Architecture

Aiming to solve the FNS 2020 task, two systems have been developed by the team: HULAT-1 and HULAT-2. The solution proposed is described in Figure 1. Both systems follow the same approach: a statistical model based on different features that measure the relevance of the sentences in different aspects. The main component of the systems is the Summarizer (see Methods section for a detailed description of the component). The difference between HULAT-1 and HULAT-2 lies within this component (Figure 1), where the first system employs sentence position, keyword occurrences and gold standard similarity as features for the model, whereas the second one uses topic extraction instead of keyword occurrences.

4. Methods

The HULAT systems follow a three-stage pipeline: text processing, feature extraction and modelling (Spärck, 2007). However, each system has been divided into different main components: Fin2Vec, Gold Standard Vectorizer and Summarizer.

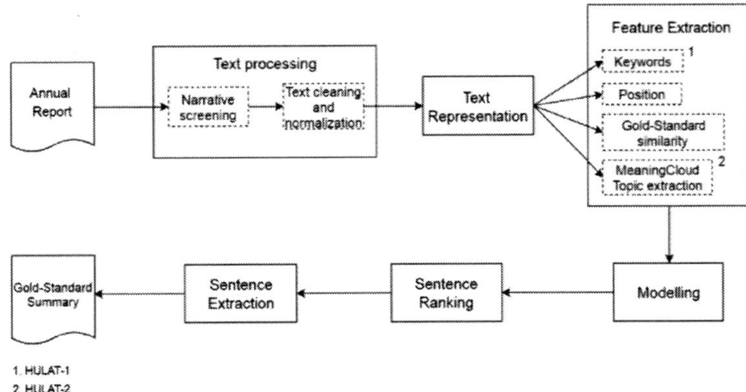

Figure 1. HULAT-1 and HULAT-2 Summarizers overview.

5. HULAT-1

The approach used is a combination of statistical and machine learning methods, since word embeddings generated with a machine learning model are used to produce one of the features that are fed into the statistical model. This approach enables the system to capture insights from the text based on semantic knowledge, which is provided by the representation of the document —using word embeddings— that captures the cohesion and coherence between sentences. Furthermore, the system is able to accurately understand the text since the embeddings have been trained with the specific financial vocabulary of the training dataset summaries. Therefore, sentences are evaluated based on their similarity to this training dataset knowledge captured by the embeddings, thus increasing the precision of the model.

The **Fin2Vec component** analyses financial text and represents it numerically with vectors using a neural network Word2Vec model. Therefore, the embedding model, fed with words from the training dataset summaries, has been trained to learn the correct embedding weights to predict the context of a given word in the corpus text, using the Skip-Gram algorithm. Finally, each word is mapped to its weights from the embedding layer of the model and the word embedding dictionary is stored in a pickle object (i.e a python-specific object) to be accessed by the other components.

The **Gold Standard Vectorizer component** takes the gold standard summaries from the training dataset and produces a final summary vector. First, the gold standard summaries sentences are tokenized and stored as a list for each summary. Sentences are then classified into narrative and non-narrative and only narrative information is processed (punctuation removal, lowercase normalization and stop words cleaning). After cleaning the text, the system transforms the summaries corpus into a vector using the word embeddings generated by the Fin2Vec component. To perform this vectorization of the gold standard summaries the first step is to transform each word into an embedding vector of 300 dimensions and add them up for each sentence to compute the vectors of the sentences. Subsequently, all sentence vectors of each summary are added together to obtain the summary vectors and the same operation is applied again to the latter to compute the final vector, which captures the relevant narrative information from the gold standard summaries. To finish, the final summary vector is stored for its further use by the Summarizer.

The **Summarizer** is the main component of the system, as its objective is to summarize a single report at a time. The Summarizer pipeline is shown in Figure 1. As the system is an extractive summarizer, the initial step is to tokenize the sentences from the original report, since these will be extracted to conform the output summary.

Given the nature of the reports, that is, a combination of numerical and narrative information, in addition to their extended length and the diversity of the information structure, it is paramount to detect narrative sections and discard those that are not, in order to get an insightful representation of the text and produce high quality summaries. The Summarizer applies narrative screening before further processing the text to remove unnecessary sentences and increase efficiency. Therefore, Part-Of-Speech (POS) tagging is applied to each word and a narrative detection analysis is carried out by identifying verb tenses within the sentence. If the sentence is non-narrative it is deleted, otherwise, it is processed for further analyses.

Once the narrative screening has been carried out, some text processing techniques are performed on the sentences: punctuation removal, lowercase normalization and stop words cleaning. After that, the Summarizer loads the word embeddings object generated by the Fin2Vec component and transforms the sentences with it, thus obtaining a word embedding vector for each sentence.

As regards feature extraction, the final system has taken into consideration three different features: (a) keyword score, (b) sentence position and (c) gold standard similarity score.

    (a) To compute the keyword score for each sentence, firstly a keyword list is defined, based on previous analyses conducted manually with the purpose of identifying relevant commonly used words in the gold standard summaries (these analyses were carried out with the use of TfidfVectorizer, using different n-grams range). Then, the final score is calculated by dividing the keyword occurrences in the sentence by its total number of words.

(b) As for the position score, it positively rewards sentences appearing at the beginning of the report, as the correlation between the gold standard summaries and the first sentences from the report is extremely strong.

(c) To compute the gold standard similarity score the system utilizes the final summary vector produced by the Gold Standard Vectorizer. The cosine similarity between each sentence vector in the original report and the summary vector (that contains salient gold standard information) is measured to get the relevance of the sentence. Hence, a high gold standard similarity score demonstrates the sentence contains information relevant to the final summary.

At this point, the feature scores obtained for each sentence in the previous step are transformed into a feature matrix and normalization is applied, thus normalizing the scores between zero and one. To compute the final relevance score of the sentences the values of their three feature scores are added up. Sentences are then ranked in descending order and extracted from the original sentence list prepared at the beginning, until the length of the summary is between 900 and 1000 words.

5.1. HULAT-2

HULAT-2 system approach is identical to HULAT-1, however, it employs distinct features to extract the relevance from the sentences. Therefore, the only different component between this system and the previous one is the Summarizer.

Regarding HULAT-2 Summarizer, as shown in the Figure 1, in the feature extraction step the features used to infer the relevance of the sentences have been: (a) sentence position, (b) named entities occurrences and (c) gold standard similarity score. This approach takes advantage of the Topic Extraction Application Programming Interface (API) provided by MeaningCloud[1], which detects and extracts relevant entities from the text using complex NLP techniques. The Summarizer requests MeaningCloud API to extract the entities given the report text as input, which generates a list of entities ordered by priority.

In order to capture the most relevant information from the report and increase the efficiency of the system, only the first fifty sentences are evaluated by the Topic Extraction API. This decision has been taken after performing multiple analyses on the reports by extracting entities for different ranges of sentences. The results showed that the ten highest priority entities extracted were virtually identical for a sentence range greater than the first fifty sentences, which meant that the first lines already contained the relevant entities, dates and concepts of the entire report.

The advantage of integrating the Topic Extraction API is that it extracts different entities relevant to each report, such as company name, dates, executive names, etc., providing more accurate and important information relative to the report being analyzed, as opposed to the fixed keywords used in HULAT-1.

6. Integrated resources

To create the systems the employed resources have been: NLTK library (Bird et al., 2009) for POS tagging, lemmatization and tokenization of words and sentences (using Wordnet, perceptron and punkt module); spaCy library for the stop words list as it is more complete than other libraries (Honnibal and Montani, 2017); Sklearn library for text vectorization with the TfidfVectorizer module and cosine similarity metrics (Pedregosa et al., 2011; Buitinck et al., 2013); and PyTorch to design and train the model for the word embeddings (Paszke et al., 2019). MeaningCloud Topic Extraction tool has been used to detect entities as features of documents. Google Collab and a GPU Nvidia GeForce RTX 2080, driver version 430.5, CUDA 10.1 in Ubuntu 18.04 provided by the UC3M were used.

7. Results

The FNS results are shown in Figure 2, where the systems highlighted in blue are the HULAT summarizers and the yellow ones are those proposed by the task organizers. As can be appreciated, HULAT-1 is among the eight best systems submitted for the task (from 31 runs), which outperforms the

---

[1] www.meaningcloud.com

topline system proposed by the FNS (SUMM-TL-MUSE) except for the ROUGE-L metric. On the other hand, although HULAT-2 has achieved lower results, it still performs above almost half of all the other systems, what demonstrates its outstanding ability to identify relevant entities from each financial report, thus making it an interesting approach.

The difference in performance between the two systems is due to the list of keywords extracted from the gold standard summaries (using the TfidfVectorizer for different n-grams range), which captures more salience information than the named entities provided by the Topic Extraction API, probably because the dictionaries behind the tool are general purpose resources not adapted to the financial domain.

Figure 2. FNS 2020 results evaluated with the ROUGE 2.0 package (HULAT-1 and HULAT-2 are our summarizers)

8. Conclusion

To conclude, the extractive systems proposed in this paper offer an effective method of summarizing financial reports taking into consideration a set of features that measure the relevance of the sentences based on named entities, gold standard knowledge and sentence position. As for future enhancements, topic clustering could be performed to identify different topic sections within the report and extract the most relevant sentences from each subsection. Furthermore, it is worth noting that the performance of the systems has been limited by the reports' format, as paragraph tokenization has been impossible to perform since sentences were separated by new line characters.

Acknowledgements

This work has been partially supported by DeepEMR project TIN2017-87548-C2-1-R.

References

Adam Paszke et al., 2019. PyTorch: An Imperative Style, High-Performance Deep Learning Library. In H. Wallach et al., eds. *Advances in Neural Information Processing Systems 32*. Curran Associates, Inc., 8024–8035.

Alexander R. Fabbri, Irene Li, Tianwei She, Suyi Li and Dragomir R. Radev, 2019. Multi-news: A large-scale multi-document summarisation dataset and abstractive hierarchical model. *Computing Research Repository*, arXiv:1906.01749.

Ashish Vaswani, et al., 2017. Attention is all you need. *Computing Research Repository*. arXiv:1706.03762.

El-Haj, M., Rayson, P., Bouamor, H., Giannakopoulos, G., Litvak, M., AbuRaed, A., Mariko, D., Valsamou, D., Ferradans, S, Athanasakou, V., El Maarouf, I., Bentabet, N., Juge, R., Pittaras, N., Elhag, A., Gupta, A., Abi-Akl, H., Mazancourt, H., and Salzedo, C., 2020. Proceedings of The 1st Joint Workshop on Financial Narrative Processing and MultiLing Financial Summarisation (FNP-FNS 2020). In *Proceedings of the 28th International Conference on Computational Linguistics (COLING'2020)*, Barcelona, Spain.

Fabian Pedregosa et al., 2011. Scikit-learn: Machine Learning in Python. *Journal of Machine Learning Research*, 12(85):2825–2830.

Karen Spärck Jones, 2007. Automatic summarising: The state of the art. *Information Processing & Management*, 43(6):1449-1481.

Lars Buitinck et al., 2013. API design for machine learning software: experiences from the scikit-learn project. *Workshop: Languages for Data Mining and Machine Learning*, 108–122.

Luca Cagliero and Moreno La Quatra, 2020. Extracting highlights of scientific articles: A supervised summarisation approach. *Expert Systems with Applications*, 113659.

Matthew Honnibal and Ines Montani, 2017. spaCy 2: Natural language understanding with Bloom embeddings, convolutional neural networks and incremental parsing.

Quanzhi Li and Qiong Zhang, 2020. Abstractive Event Summarisation on Twitter. In *Companion Proceedings of the Web Conference 2020*, 22-23.

Ramesh Nallapati, Bowen Zhou, Cicero Nogueira dos santos, Caglar Gulcehre and Bing Xiang, 2016. Abstractive text summarisation using sequence-to-sequence RNNs and beyond. *Computing Research Repository.* arXiv:1602.06023.

Remi Juge, Imane Bentabet and Sira Ferradans, 2019. The fintoc-2019 shared task: Financial document structure extraction. In *Proceedings of the Second Financial Narrative Processing Workshop (FNP 2019)*, 51-57.

Sepp Hochreiter and Jürgen Schmidhuber, 1997. Long Short-Term Memory. *Neural Computation*, 9:1735-1780.

Steven Bird, Ewan Klein and Edward Loper, 2009. *Natural language processing with Python: analyzing text with the natural language toolkit*. Beijing: O'Reilly Media, Inc.

Sukriti Verma and Vagisha Nidhi, 2019. Extractive Summarisation using Deep Learning. *Computing Research Repository*, arXiv:1708.04439. version 2.

Wei Xu, Ralph Grishman, Adam Meyers and Alan Ritter, 2013. A preliminary study of tweet summarisation using information extraction. In *Proceedings of the Workshop on Language Analysis in Social Media*, 20-29.

End-to-end Training For Financial Report Summarization

Moreno La Quatra
Politecnico di Torino
moreno.laquatra@polito.it

Luca Cagliero
Politecnico di Torino
luca.cagliero@polito.it

Abstract

Quoted companies are requested to periodically publish financial reports in textual form. The annual financial reports typically include detailed financial and business information, thus giving relevant insights into company outlooks. However, a manual exploration of these financial reports could be very time consuming since most of the available information can be deemed as non-informative or redundant by expert readers. Hence, an increasing research interest has been devoted to automatically extracting domain-specific summaries, which include only the most relevant information.

This paper describes the *SumTO* system architecture, which addresses the Shared Task of the Financial Narrative Summarisation (FNS) 2020 contest. The main task objective is to automatically extract the most informative, domain-specific textual content from financial, English-written documents. The aim is to create a summary of each company report covering all the business-relevant key points.

To address the above-mentioned goal, we propose an end-to-end training method relying on Deep NLP techniques. The idea behind the system is to exploit the syntactic overlap between input sentences and ground-truth summaries to fine-tune pre-trained BERT embedding models, thus making such models tailored to the specific context. The achieved results confirm the effectiveness of the proposed method, especially when the goal is to select relatively long text snippets.

1 Introduction

Analyzing the annual financial reports is the most established way to assess the health state of business companies. For example, rating agencies, banks, and hedge funds rely on the information extracted from domain-specific reports to assign ratings, grant loans, and drive investment strategies (Piotroski, 2000). Unfortunately, the content of the released financial reports is highly redundant as it typically includes contextual and technical information that is marginally relevant to domain experts. The Shared Task of the Financial Narrative Summarization (FNS) research challenge (El-Haj et al., 2020) aims to address this issue by fostering innovative research on the problem of automatic extraction of domain-specific summaries from the annual financial reports.

The algorithms designed for automatic text summarization can be partitioned into two main classes: *Extractive* approaches and *Abstractive* ones. While extractive approaches pick existing text snippets (e.g., sentences, phrases, keywords) directly from the source text, abstractive methods generate new content based on the analysis of the input documents. The summarization process can be either *supervised*, when a portion of document content already annotated by human experts as relevant or not is available, or *unsupervised* when no a priori knowledge is given. The FNS shared task promotes the study, development, and testing of automated sentence-based summarization techniques tailored to the financial domain. To extract relevant sentences from annual financial reports, it provides researchers with a large set of humanly annotated data (El-Haj, 2019). Therefore, the present work addresses the study of a *supervised, extractive, sentence-based approach* to address the FNS Shared Task.

Proceedings of the 1st Joint Workshop on Financial Narrative Processing and MultiLing Financial Summarisation, pages 118–123
Barcelona, Spain (Online), December 12, 2020.

Extractive summarization methods have found application in several domains, such as the summarization from news articles (e.g., (See et al., 2017; Cagliero et al., 2019; Krishnan et al., 2019)), scientific papers (e.g., (Cagliero and La Quatra, 2020; Cohan and Goharian, 2018; Collins et al., 2017)) and product reviews (i.e., (Ganesan et al., 2010)). Wide-ranging overviews of the state-of-the-art works on text summarization can be found in (Widyassari et al., 2020; Cagliero et al., 2020; El-Kassas et al., 2020). Using Machine Learning techniques to summarize documents entails (i) extracting relevant text features at the sentence level and (ii) feeding the extracted features to a supervised model to produce a sentence rank (El-Kassas et al., 2020). To address the former step, latent text representations based on Deep Learning models have shown to be very effective in generating relevant text features (Chen and Nguyen, 2019; Kobayashi et al., 2015) However, pre-trained deep NLP models need to be tailored to the specific context under analysis (e.g., medical data (Lee et al., 2020; Huang et al., 2019)), patent-related areas (Lee and Hsiang, 2019)). Previous works that use deep language models in the financial domain focused on the sentiment analysis task (Yang et al., 2020). To the best of our knowledge, this is the first attempt to fine-tune pre-trained deep NLP models in order to enhance the quality of the process of financial report summarization.

Section 2 overviews the architecture of the proposed summarizer. Section 3 and 4, 5 separately describe each phase of the summarization process. Section 6 summarizes the outcomes of the evaluation step. Finally, Section 7 draws conclusions and envisions future research steps.

2 The SumTO System

The *Sum*marizer based on end-*TO*-end training (SumTO) consists of a three-phase process, which is depicted in Figure 1. It comprises (i) a *preprocessing phase*, which transforms the raw textual documents and annotates the content at the sentence-level. (ii) a *training step*, which extract relevant concepts and relationships according to two established Deep language models, i.e., BERT (Devlin et al., 2019) and DistilBERT (Sanh et al., 2019). (iii) a *evaluation step*, which rates the sentences of each test document according to the fine-tuned models trained at the previous step and produce a per-document summary consisting of the highly rated sentences.

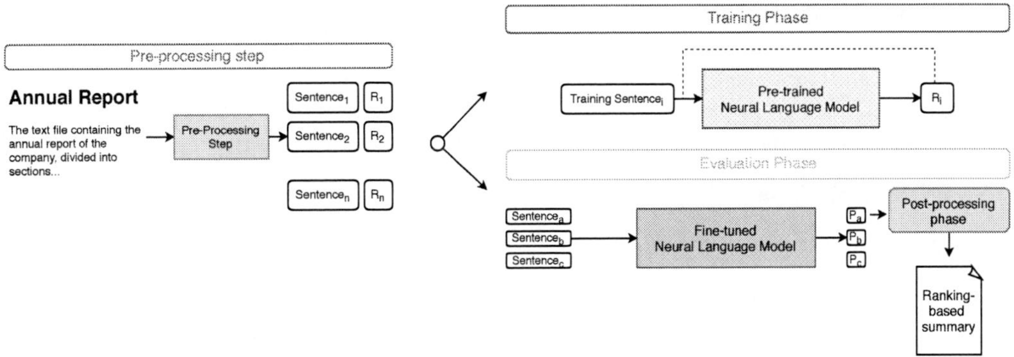

Figure 1: Outline of the proposed method

The fine-tuned model is able to provide better contextual representations for domain-specific vocabulary. The end-to-end process aims at training the model for the identification of relevant topics in the financial domain.

3 Data Collection and preprocessing

The data collection provided by the organizers of the FNS 2020 Shared Task includes the (i) the *training set*, consisting of 3,000 annual reports and 9,873 golden summaries (3.29 summaries per report, on average), (ii) the *evaluation set*, consisting of 363 annual reports and 1,250 golden summaries (3.44 summaries per report, on average), and (iii) the *test set*, consisting of 500 annual reports and 1,673 *blind*

System ID	Pre-Trained Model	Parameters Settings
1pe	`distilbert-base-cased`	N. of epochs: 1, Batch Size: 32, Learning rate: 2e-5
2pe	`distilbert-base-cased`	N. of epochs: 2, Batch Size: 32, Learning rate: 2e-5
3pe	`bert-base-cased`	N. of epochs: 1, Batch Size: 32, Learning rate: 2e-5

Table 1: System configuration settings

golden summaries (3.34 summaries per report, on average). The size of the training data enables the use deep Natural Language Processing models (Kobayashi et al., 2015).

The textual content of the reports in the training, evaluation, and test sets is transformed by applying the following data preparation steps.

1. *Text cleaning*: the source text, parsed from PDF documents, usually contains small errors in text parsing (e.g., a single word that spans over multiple lines is split in two different tokens). By employing ad-hoc regular expressions, the original content of each report is re-assembled as a single textual document.

2. *Sentence splitting:* The text stream is split into sentences by using *PunktSentenceTokenizer* provided by the Natural Language ToolKit (Loper and Bird, 2002) library.

3. *Data Annotation*: The sentence of the reports in the *training* and *evaluation* sets are annotated with the corresponding relevance score. The score indicates the similarity of the sentence with the content of the human-annotated summaries. It is computed by maximizing the syntactic overlap (i.e., Rouge-2 precision values (Lin, 2004)) with respect to all the given summaries[1].

4 Training phase of the Deep language model

A regression model is trained on the sentences of the training documents in order to predict the previously assigned sentence label (i.e., the Rouge-2 precision score). This idea behind to optimize the sentence relevance score according to the provided human annotation by fine-tuning the pre-trained BERT model (Devlin et al., 2019).

The overall architecture is trained using the Mean-Square loss and the *AdamW* optimizer (Loshchilov and Hutter, 2017) for faster convergence. Table 1 reports the settings for each system run. We generated three different fine-tuned models, hereafter denoted as *1pe*, *2pe*, *3pe*. The best performing model (i.e. *3pe*) and the code to apply the summarization algorithm are available on GitHub[2].

5 Evaluation phase

For each test document, the summarizer evaluates and ranks the corresponding sentences according to the fine-tuned model. Specifically, the sentences of the input report are forward-passed through the trained model and sorted in order of decreasing predicted Rouge-2 Precision score. The ranked list is post-processed by removing (i) duplicate sentences, (ii) sentences containing more than 50% of uppercase characters, (iii) sentence containing more than 50% of non alphabetic characters, (iv) sentences shorter than 5 words. The text snippets are selected from the post-processed pool according to their assigned score until the summary length requirement (up to 1000 words) is met. The output summary is generated by concatenating the post-processed sentences in order of decreasing relevance score.

6 Results

The output summaries submitted to the FNS 2020 Shared Task contest were evaluated by the shared task organizers. To evaluate the system outputs provided by the participants, they exploited the JRouge package[3], which is a lightweight, multilingual tool implementing the Rouge metrics (Lin, 2004).

---

[1] Each report may be annotated by multiple summaries provided by different experts.

[2] `https://github.com/MorenoLaQuatra/SumTO_financial_summarization`

[3] `https://bitbucket.org/nocgod/jrouge/wiki/Home`

Evaluation metric	Shared Task Results (3pe)	F1 (3pe)	F1 (2pe)	F1 (1pe)
Rouge 1	7th out of 14	**0.424**	0.422	0.421
Rouge 2	5th out of 14	**0.249**	0.235	0.237
Rouge SU4	5th out of 14	**0.264**	0.252	0.254
Rouge-L	3rd out of 14	**0.394**	0.385	0.387

Table 2: Systems results for the FNS 2020 Shared Task. The results of the best performing system are highlighted in bold.

Summaries were evaluated using the Rouge-1, Rouge-2, Rouge-SU4, and Rouge-L metrics. Beyond the systems proposed by the contest participants, the following baseline methods have been considered: (i) TextRank (Mihalcea and Tarau, 2004), (ii) LexRank (Erkan and Radev, 2004), (iii) POLY (Litvak and Vanetik, 2013), and (iv) a topline algorithm, i.e., MUSE (Litvak et al., 2010). Table 2 summarizes the F1-Score results achieved by our submitted runs. The scores of the best performing model (*3pe*) are reported in bold.

The SumTO system achieved fairly good results in terms of Rouge-L (i.e., finding the longest N-gram match with the ground truth), because our system tends to prefer relatively longer sentences. For the same reason, ROUGE-1 performance is on average worse than that achieved for Rouge-2 and rouge-SU4.

6.1 Computational requirements and execution times

The models were trained on a machine equipped with Intel® Xeon® Gold 5115 CPU, NVIDIA® Tesla® V100 16GB GPU and 512GB of RAM. Using this configuration the fine-tuning of the BERT model (on the full training set) took on average 36 hours per epoch, wheras for DistilBERT each epoch took less than 20 hours. During the evaluation phase, the summarization of a single annual report took around 30 seconds.

7 Conclusions and future research steps

The paper described an extractive summarization approach to summarizing textual financial reports. The proposed approach relies on the fine-tuning of a BERT deep language model. The goal is to deeply tailor the Deep NLP model to the specific context under analysis. The system runs were submitted to the FNS 2020 Shared Task, achieving fairly high performance in terms of Rouge-L score.

Our future research agenda will cover the following aspects:

Pruning of redundant information: The current summarization architecture is not able to prune redundant content, with respect to the previously selected sentences, during the sentence evaluation phase. We plan to extend system by embedding ad hoc redundancy penalty score.

Deeper model contextualization: The results have confirmed the effectiveness of the BERT architecture to support text summarization. We aim to explore the applicability of larger and deeper neural language models in order to better capture the semantic meaning of the analyzed sentences.

Acknowledgements

The research leading to these results is supported by the SmartData@PoliTO center for Big Data technologies.

References

Luca Cagliero and Moreno La Quatra. 2020. Extracting highlights of scientific articles: A supervised summarization approach. *Expert Systems with Applications*, 160:113659.

Luca Cagliero, Paolo Garza, and Elena Baralis. 2019. Elsa: A multilingual document summarization algorithm based on frequent itemsets and latent semantic analysis. *ACM Trans. Inf. Syst.*, 37(2), January.

Luca Cagliero, Paolo Garza, and Moreno La Quatra. 2020. Combining machine learning and natural language processing for language-specific, multi-lingual, and cross-lingual text summarization: A wide-ranging overview. In *Trends and Applications of Text Summarization Techniques*, pages 1–31. IGI Global.

L. Chen and M. L. Nguyen. 2019. Sentence selective neural extractive summarization with reinforcement learning. In *2019 11th International Conference on Knowledge and Systems Engineering (KSE)*, pages 1–5.

Arman Cohan and Nazli Goharian. 2018. Scientific document summarization via citation contextualization and scientific discourse. *International Journal on Digital Libraries*, 19(2-3):287–303.

Ed Collins, Isabelle Augenstein, and Sebastian Riedel. 2017. A supervised approach to extractive summarisation of scientific papers. In *Proceedings of the 21st Conference on Computational Natural Language Learning (CoNLL 2017)*, pages 195–205, Vancouver, Canada, August. Association for Computational Linguistics.

Jacob Devlin, Ming-Wei Chang, Kenton Lee, and Kristina Toutanova. 2019. Bert: Pre-training of deep bidirectional transformers for language understanding. In *Proceedings of the 2019 Conference of the North American Chapter of the Association for Computational Linguistics: Human Language Technologies, Volume 1 (Long and Short Papers)*, pages 4171–4186.

Mahmoud El-Haj, Ahmed AbuRa'ed, Nikiforos Pittaras, and George Giannakopoulos. 2020. The Financial Narrative Summarisation Shared Task (FNS 2020). In *The 1st Joint Workshop on Financial Narrative Processing and MultiLing Financial Summarisation (FNP-FNS 2020*, Barcelona, Spain.

Mahmoud El-Haj. 2019. Multiling 2019: Financial narrative summarisation. In *Proceedings of the Workshop MultiLing 2019: Summarization Across Languages, Genres and Sources*, pages 6–10.

Wafaa S El-Kassas, Cherif R Salama, Ahmed A Rafea, and Hoda K Mohamed. 2020. Automatic text summarization: A comprehensive survey. *Expert Systems with Applications*, page 113679.

Günes Erkan and Dragomir R Radev. 2004. Lexrank: Graph-based lexical centrality as salience in text summarization. *Journal of artificial intelligence research*, 22:457–479.

Kavita Ganesan, ChengXiang Zhai, and Jiawei Han. 2010. Opinosis: a graph-based approach to abstractive summarization of highly redundant opinions. In *Proceedings of the 23rd international conference on computational linguistics*, pages 340–348. Association for Computational Linguistics.

Kexin Huang, Jaan Altosaar, and Rajesh Ranganath. 2019. Clinicalbert: Modeling clinical notes and predicting hospital readmission. *arXiv preprint arXiv:1904.05342*.

Hayato Kobayashi, Masaki Noguchi, and Taichi Yatsuka. 2015. Summarization based on embedding distributions. In *Proceedings of the 2015 Conference on Empirical Methods in Natural Language Processing*, pages 1984–1989, Lisbon, Portugal, September. Association for Computational Linguistics.

D. Krishnan, P. Bharathy, Anagha, and M. Venugopalan. 2019. A supervised approach for extractive text summarization using minimal robust features. In *2019 International Conference on Intelligent Computing and Control Systems (ICCS)*, pages 521–527.

Jieh-Sheng Lee and Jieh Hsiang. 2019. Patentbert: Patent classification with fine-tuning a pre-trained bert model. *arXiv preprint arXiv:1906.02124*.

Jinhyuk Lee, Wonjin Yoon, Sungdong Kim, Donghyeon Kim, Sunkyu Kim, Chan So, and Jaewoo Kang. 2020. Biobert: a pre-trained biomedical language representation model for biomedical text mining. *Bioinformatics*, 36(4):1234–1240.

Chin-Yew Lin. 2004. Rouge: A package for automatic evaluation of summaries. In *Text summarization branches out*, pages 74–81.

Marina Litvak and Natalia Vanetik. 2013. Mining the gaps: Towards polynomial summarization. In *Proceedings of the Sixth International Joint Conference on Natural Language Processing*, pages 655–660.

Marina Litvak, Mark Last, and Menahem Friedman. 2010. A new approach to improving multilingual summarization using a genetic algorithm. In *Proceedings of the 48th annual meeting of the association for computational linguistics*, pages 927–936.

Edward Loper and Steven Bird. 2002. Nltk: The natural language toolkit. In *In Proceedings of the ACL Workshop on Effective Tools and Methodologies for Teaching Natural Language Processing and Computational Linguistics. Philadelphia: Association for Computational Linguistics*.

Ilya Loshchilov and Frank Hutter. 2017. Decoupled weight decay regularization. *arXiv preprint arXiv:1711.05101*.

Rada Mihalcea and Paul Tarau. 2004. Textrank: Bringing order into text. In *Proceedings of the 2004 conference on empirical methods in natural language processing*, pages 404–411.

Joseph D. Piotroski. 2000. Value investing: The use of historical financial statement information to separate winners from losers. *Journal of Accounting Research*, 38:1–41.

Victor Sanh, Lysandre Debut, Julien Chaumond, and Thomas Wolf. 2019. Distilbert, a distilled version of bert: smaller, faster, cheaper and lighter. *arXiv preprint arXiv:1910.01108*.

Abigail See, Peter J. Liu, and Christopher D. Manning. 2017. Get to the point: Summarization with pointer-generator networks. *CoRR*, abs/1704.04368.

Adhika Pramita Widyassari, Supriadi Rustad, Guruh Fajar Shidik, Edi Noersasongko, Abdul Syukur, Affandy Affandy, and De Rosal Ignatius Moses Setiadi. 2020. Review of automatic text summarization techniques & methods. *Journal of King Saud University - Computer and Information Sciences*.

Yi Yang, Mark Christopher Siy UY, and Allen Huang. 2020. Finbert: A pretrained language model for financial communications.

SCE-SUMMARY at the FNS 2020 shared task

Marina Litvak
Shamoon College of
Engineering (SCE)
Beer-Sheva
Israel
marinal@ac.sce.ac.il

Natalia Vanetik
Shamoon College of
Engineering (SCE)
Beer-Sheva
Israel
natalyav@sce.ac.il

Tzvi Puchinsky
Shamoon College of
Engineering (SCE)
Beer-Sheva
Israel
tzvipu@ac.sce.ac.il

Abstract

With the constantly growing amount of information, the need arises to automatically summarize this written information. One of the challenges in the summary is that it's difficult to generalize. For example, summarizing a news article is very different from summarizing a financial earnings report. This paper reports an approach for summarizing financial texts, which are different from the documents from other domains at least in three parameters: length, structure, and format. Our approach considers these parameters, it is adapted to hierarchical structure of sections, document length, and special "language". The approach builds an hierarchical summary, visualized as a tree with summaries under different discourse topics. The approach was evaluated using extrinsic and intrinsic automated evaluations, which are reported in this paper. As all participants of the Financial Narrative Summarisation (FNS 2020) shared task, we used FNS2020 dataset for evaluations.

1 Introduction

The area of text summarization exists for several decades, since the first work of Luhn (Luhn, 1958). The summarization approaches developed from extractive unsupervised statistical approaches to abstractive supervised methods, using deep learning models (Liu, 2019). However, the most advanced seq2seq models (transformers) are very limited in input size and, therefore, are inapplicable to long texts. Also, only few of state-of-the-art summarizers consider hierarchical structure of the input documents (Yang and Wang, 2008; Zhang et al., 2019), their key concepts (Ouyang et al., 2009; Plaza et al., 2011) or topics (Wang et al., 2013; Akhtar, 2017) and build a hierarchical summary (Christensen et al., 2014; Akhtar et al., 2019). Usually, hierarchical summary is built per document collection. The top level of hierarchy provides a general overview and users can navigate the hierarchy to drill down for more details on topics of interest.

There is a growing interest in the application of automatic and computer-aided approaches for extracting, summarising, and analysing both qualitative and quantitative financial data, as a series of FNP and related workshops (El-Haj, 2019; El-Haj et al., 2018) recently demonstrates. However, summarization of documents in financial domain is usually limited to summarization of financial news (Filippova et al., 2009; Yang and Wang, 2003; de Oliveira et al., 2002; Baralis et al., 2016; Zhang et al., 2018) which are not very different from the general news in length and format. Only few attempts were made to summarize financial reports (Isonuma et al., 2017), which are different from the news articles in at least four parameters: length, structure, format, and lexicon.

This paper reports an approach for hierarchical summarization of financial reports. Financial annual reports in the data of Financial Narrative Summarisation (FNS 2020) shared task[1] (El-Haj et al., 2020) are long, have many sections, and are written in "financial" language using many special terms, numerical data, and tables. Our system for summarization and hierarchical visualization financial reports (named by SCE-SUMM) considers discourse and topic hierarchical structure and builds an hierarchical view of the summarized report with interactive user interface.

[1] http://wp.lancs.ac.uk/cfie/fns2020/

Proceedings of the 1st Joint Workshop on Financial Narrative Processing and MultiLing Financial Summarisation, pages 124–129
Barcelona, Spain (Online), December 12, 2020.

2 The SCE-SUMM System

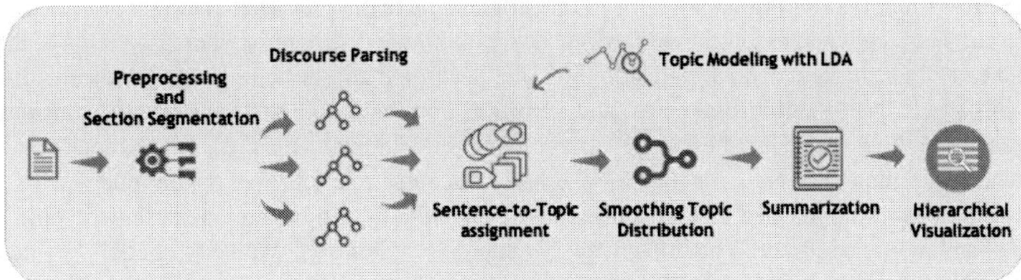

Figure 1: SCE-SUMM pipeline

SCE-SUMM utilizes two main methods: topic modeling (TM) and discourse parsing (DP). The pipeline of the proposed methodology is depicted in Figure 1 and includes the following steps:

Text preprocessing, that includes text cleaning, sentence splitting and tokenization. We developed our own tool that cleaned text before segmenting it to sentences and tokens. Financial reports usually contain a lot of sections, figures, and tables. Because the text files in the FNS-2020 dataset were obtained by converting pdf files to plain texts, these texts contain a lot of "noise" left from broken tables and meta-data such as section and page numbers. We cleaned the noise by measuring the ratio between text and numbers and ratio between number of words and whitespaces. Lines with ratio less than 0.4 were removed. Then, regular expressions were applied to find and mark such entities as URL, phone number, date, time, email. Finally, non-Unicode characters were filtered out.

Section segmentation, where section headers are identified and a document is segmented into sections. The section titles were extracted following the heuristic rules saying that (1) each title appears in a separate line, (2) does not end with period mark, and (3) contains only few (up to 5) words with (4) each word either starting with capital case letter or containing only upper case letters. The extracted candidates were then compared against the list of 13 manually edited titles[2]. The candidate that obtained Jaccard similarity above 0.4 to one of the titles from the list was extracted as a title. The text body between two consequent titles was marked as a section.

Discourse parsing of each section. For discourse parsing we used the CODRA parser (Joty et al., 2015). CODRA parser performs two-part process: (1) a discourse segmenter creates a segmentation analysis on the sentence level and EDU's for the discourse parsing process and (2) a discourse parser parses the text on sentence level and document level to identify relations between parts of sentences and sentences in the document. The rhetorical analysis of the parser starts from a breaking a text into Elementary Discourse Units (EDUs). Because EDUs do not span across multiple sentences, this segmentation task finds EDUs inside the sentence boundaries. As a result, some sentences (actually, most, according to our observations) are split into EDUs. Every EDU is marked as a *nucleus* (an essence part) or a *satellite* (a complementary part of the related nucleus), based on the relation that they are connected to. Internal (relation) nodes represent different inter-sentence relations: elaboration, same-unit, etc.

Topic modeling. For topic modeling we applied Latent Dirichlet Allocation (LDA) model (Blei et al., 2003). It was applied on all files in the FNS-2020 dataset with predefined number of topics[3].

Topic-to-text assignment, where each sentence (or sentence part) represented by a leaf node of the discourse tree, is assigned to one of the topics obtained by LDA. We refer topic probabilities $p(t|w)$ for all sentence S words $w \in S$ as their topic-related importance scores. Therefore, we extract a dominant

---

[2]Titles that appear in almost every report in FNS-2020 dataset, such as: 'chairman statement', 'chief executive officer CEO review', 'chief executive officer CEO report', 'governance statement', 'remuneration report', 'business review', 'financial review', 'operating review', 'highlights', 'auditors report', 'risk management', 'chairman governance introduction', 'corporate social responsibility CSR disclosures'.

[3]We experimented with 4, 6, and 10 topics, and finally decided to keep 10 topics as best performing value.

topic ($t \in T$) for each sentence S, as a topic with the maximal normalized sum of topic probabilities for all sentence words $w \in S$: $\max_{t \in T} \frac{\sum_{w \in S} p(t|w)}{\sum_{w \in S} 1}$.

Topic distribution smoothing. We noticed that after single text nodes (that stand for sentences or sentence parts) are assigned to topics, we can get unexpected topic distribution where two parts of the same sentence or two adjacent sentences inside the same paragraph and/or belonging to the same discourse relation are assigned to different topics, and transition from one topic to another is not coherent.[4] We decided to smooth topic distribution by extrapolating one dominant topic on entire block of adjacent sentences and sentence parts, connected by a direct discourse relation. We denote nodes with at least one leaf node as "simple" and all leaves in its sub-tree are finally assigned to one dominant topic, so that a "random" noise is left out. The implement this approach as follows. We know that all leaf nodes are arranged in the natural sequential order of their texts from right-to-left (top-down) in a discourse tree. We assume that the important information usually comes first (important part of a sentence usually precedes its complementary part, and a sentence stating some fact usually precedes a sentence that elaborates more about this fact) and, therefore, upper right nodes and nucleuses should propagate their topics on their siblings. According to this assumption and our empirical observations on each parameter's influence, the final impact factor NI of node n is calculated as follows. $NI(n) = \sum_{i=1}^{3} w_i \times f_i(n)$, where:

f_1 is a relative depth feature $rd(n) = \frac{h(t)+1-d(n)}{h(t)+1}$, $h(t)$ is a tree height, $d(n)$ is n's depth

f_2 is a position feature $pos(n) = \begin{cases} 1, \text{if } n \text{ is on right} \\ 0, \text{else} \end{cases}$

f_3 is a discourse label feature $l(n) = \begin{cases} 1, \text{if } n \text{ is nucleus} \\ 0, \text{else} \end{cases}$

$w_1 = 0.5$, $w_2 = 0.3$, and $w_3 = 0.2$.

Then, the final dominant topic for a "simple" sub-tree is calculated as follows: $\max_{t \in T} \left\{ \sum_{n \in leaves} NI(n) * score_{t,n} \right\}$. After topic-to-sentence assignment (at previous stage), every leaf node has non-zero value for only one dominant topic, other topics have $score_{t,n} = 0$.

Summarization of entire report (regardless visualization) and of each section (for visualization needs) was performed as follows. All topics t are ranked by their importance $TI(t)$ (normalized sum of their probabilities for all document/section words). Then, summaries are created by extraction of nucleuses from each topic, in the topics' importance order, until the maximum length limit is reached. As for entire report a summary should not exceed 1000 words according to the shared task instructions, we limit a section summary to 100 words.

Hierarchical visualization. At this stage SCE-SUMM creates an interactive html file with the data from all the stages for a user to browse. The file contains the following sections: (1) original text; (2) processed XML text after cleaning and section segmentation; (3) discourse trees for all the sections; (4) sentences (nodes) with assigned topics after smoothing; (5) the final hierarchical tree with the section summaries, and (6) a general report summary. For visualization and interactive user's navigation, the following tree structure of a document is built and present to a user: root represents an entire document and points to its sections, each section is split to major topics inside this section after smoothing, and each topic points to a summary of this particular section focused on the chosen topic. Visualization is performed in interactive manner, upon a user's request. Demo video[5] demonstrates all interactive options provided by the system.

3 Experiments

3.1 Dataset

The Financial Narrative Summarisation (FNS 2020) shared task aims to demonstrate the value and challenges of applying automatic text summarisation to financial text written in English, usually referred to

---

[4]We assume that in a natural topic distribution, that is usually observed in general domains, topics must flow from one paragraph (or sections or cluster of sentences) to another, without mix of topics inside clusters.

[5]https://drive.google.com/file/d/14qMRUhZIwaVoSltaLPSiH6NZx13M_9ue/view

as financial narrative disclosures. The task dataset has been extracted from UK annual reports published in PDF file format. UK annual reports are lengthy documents with around 80 pages on average, some annual reports could span over more than 250 pages, while the summary length should not exceed 1000 words. The training set includes 3,000 annual reports, with 3-4 human-generated summaries as gold standard. For the evaluation process the test set of 500 files were provided. To address the time limitations and processing long files[6] the project reduced the length of the original files (to 15000 characters) to be able to process in feasible time limit (20 minutes per file at most).

3.2 Tools and runtime environment

For LDA, we used the Python gensim4 package. Corpus tf-idf vectorization and K-means clustering were performed by the Python sklearn package. For running Rouge, we used ROUGE 2.05 java package (Ganesan, 2018). Our approach was implemented in Python and run on Intel Pentium Gold G5400 with 16GB memory server with 40GB swap file configured.

3.3 Results

Automatic evaluation was performed using ROUGE metrics (Lin, 2004) which work by comparing an automatically produced summary against a set of reference summaries (typically human-produced). We applied three ROUGE metrics—ROUGE-1, ROUGE-2, and ROUGE-L. We compared our approach with two baseline methods—MUSE (Litvak et al., 2010) and POLY (Litvak and Vanetik, 2013). MUSE is a supervised approach based on a genetic algorithm, it was trained on 30 randomly selected gold standard summaries provided with FNS-2020 dataset. POLY is unsupervised approach based on linear programming, it was applied with Maximal Weighted Term Sum (OBJ1 in (Litvak and Vanetik, 2013)) objective function. Table 1 show the results, with recall, precision, and F-measure for each metric. The best scores are marked in bold and the second best are marked by grey background. It can be seen that SCE-SUMM performs better than POLY (both are unsupervised), and even outperforms MUSE (which is supervised) in one metric (ROUGE-L, Precision), meaning that its summaries are less "scattered" and more coherent (and therefore probably more readable) then other summaries. The comparative results with other systems participating in the FNS 2020 shared task can be seen in (El-Haj et al., 2020).[7]

system	R-1 R	R-1 P	R-1 F	R-2 R	R-2 P	R-2 F	R-L R	R-L P	R-L F
MUSE	0.483	0.413	0.433	0.311	0.198	0.234	0.486	0.381	0.419
POLY	0.324	0.253	0.274	0.147	0.088	0.105	0.270	0.182	0.212
SCE-SUMM	0.290	0.396	0.324	0.150	0.153	0.144	0.290	0.396	0.324

Table 1: Rouge results.

4 Conclusions and Future Work

This paper describes a new method for hierarchical summarization of financial reports, based on integrating the discourse structure and topic modeling. Our approach is mainly based on heuristic assumptions. In future, we intend to develop a new supervised method utilizing the discourse and topics knowledge. Also, we would like to apply this method and its extension to educational materials, which also have highly hierarchical structure and an evolving flow of topics in a discourse. Hierarchical summarization can help to organize those materials in a hierarchical structure and provide users with interactive navigation to the topics of interest. SCE-SUMM's source code is available[8] and can be run using the provided instructions[9].

---

[6]mostly, due to a very time-consuming discourse parsing
[7]Due to significant updates in the SCE-SUMM's code since the task submission the scores might differ.
[8]https://github.com/Tzvi23/Hierarchical-Summarization-Part1
[9]https://drive.google.com/drive/folders/1YxnNQ-9ebPX1Gtd6Dmr0to6UIBgudflC

References

Nadeem Akhtar, Hira Javed, and Tameem Ahmad. 2019. Hierarchical summarization of text documents using topic modeling and formal concept analysis. In *Data Management, Analytics and Innovation*, pages 21–33. Springer.

Nadeem Akhtar. 2017. Hierarchical summarization of news tweets with twitter-lda. In *Applications of Soft Computing for the Web*, pages 83–98. Springer.

Elena Baralis, Luca Cagliero, and Tania Cerquitelli. 2016. Supporting stock trading in multiple foreign markets: a multilingual news summarization approach. In *Proceedings of the Second International Workshop on Data Science for Macro-Modeling*, pages 1–6.

David M Blei, Andrew Y Ng, and Michael I Jordan. 2003. Latent dirichlet allocation. *Journal of machine Learning research*, 3(Jan):993–1022.

Janara Christensen, Stephen Soderland, Gagan Bansal, et al. 2014. Hierarchical summarization: Scaling up multi-document summarization. In *Proceedings of the 52nd annual meeting of the association for computational linguistics (volume 1: Long papers)*, pages 902–912.

Paulo Cesar Fernandes de Oliveira, Khurshid Ahmad, and Lee Gillam. 2002. A financial news summarization system based on lexical cohesion. In *Proceedings of the International Conference on Terminology and Knowledge Engineering, Nancy, France*.

Mahmoud El-Haj, Paul Rayson, and Andrew Moore. 2018. The first financial narrative processing workshop (fnp 2018). In *Proceedings of the LREC 2018 Workshop*.

Mahmoud El-Haj, Ahmed AbuRa'ed, Nikiforos Pittaras, and George Giannakopoulos. 2020. The Financial Narrative Summarisation Shared Task (FNS 2020). In *The 1st Joint Workshop on Financial Narrative Processing and MultiLing Financial Summarisation (FNP-FNS 2020, Barcelona, Spain.*

Mahmoud El-Haj. 2019. Multiling 2019: Financial narrative summarisation. In *Proceedings of the Workshop MultiLing 2019: Summarization Across Languages, Genres and Sources*, pages 6–10.

Katja Filippova, Mihai Surdeanu, Massimiliano Ciaramita, and Hugo Zaragoza. 2009. Company-oriented extractive summarization of financial news. In *Proceedings of the 12th Conference of the European Chapter of the ACL (EACL 2009)*, pages 246–254.

Kavita Ganesan. 2018. Rouge 2.0: Updated and improved measures for evaluation of summarization tasks. *arXiv preprint arXiv:1803.01937*.

Masaru Isonuma, Toru Fujino, Junichiro Mori, Yutaka Matsuo, and Ichiro Sakata. 2017. Extractive summarization using multi-task learning with document classification. In *Proceedings of the 2017 Conference on Empirical Methods in Natural Language Processing*, pages 2101–2110.

Shafiq Joty, Giuseppe Carenini, and Raymond T Ng. 2015. Codra: A novel discriminative framework for rhetorical analysis. *Computational Linguistics*, 41(3):385–435.

Chin-Yew Lin. 2004. Rouge: A package for automatic evaluation of summaries. In *Text summarization branches out*, pages 74–81.

Marina Litvak and Natalia Vanetik. 2013. Mining the gaps: Towards polynomial summarization. In *Proceedings of the Sixth International Joint Conference on Natural Language Processing*, pages 655–660.

Marina Litvak, Mark Last, and Menahem Friedman. 2010. A new approach to improving multilingual summarization using a genetic algorithm. In *Proceedings of the 48th annual meeting of the association for computational linguistics*, pages 927–936.

Yang Liu. 2019. Fine-tune bert for extractive summarization. *arXiv preprint arXiv:1903.10318*.

Hans Peter Luhn. 1958. The automatic creation of literature abstracts. *IBM Journal of research and development*, 2(2):159–165.

You Ouyang, Wenjie Li, and Qin Lu. 2009. An integrated multi-document summarization approach based on word hierarchical representation. In *Proceedings of the ACL-IJCNLP 2009 Conference Short Papers*, pages 113–116.

Laura Plaza, Alberto Díaz, and Pablo Gervás. 2011. A semantic graph-based approach to biomedical summarisation. *Artificial intelligence in medicine*, 53(1):1–14.

Chi Wang, Xiao Yu, Yanen Li, Chengxiang Zhai, and Jiawei Han. 2013. Content coverage maximization on word networks for hierarchical topic summarization. In *Proceedings of the 22nd ACM international conference on Information & Knowledge Management*, pages 249–258.

Christopher C Yang and Fu Lee Wang. 2003. Automatic summarization for financial news delivery on mobile devices. In *WWW (Posters)*.

Christopher C Yang and Fu Lee Wang. 2008. Hierarchical summarization of large documents. *Journal of the American Society for Information Science and Technology*, 59(6):887–902.

Yong Zhang, Erdan Chen, and Weidong Xiao. 2018. Extractive-abstractive summarization with pointer and coverage mechanism. In *Proceedings of 2018 International Conference on Big Data Technologies*, pages 69–74.

Xingxing Zhang, Furu Wei, and Ming Zhou. 2019. Hibert: Document level pre-training of hierarchical bidirectional transformers for document summarization. *arXiv preprint arXiv:1905.06566*.

Knowledge Graph and Deep Neural Network for Extractive Text Summarization by Utilizing Triples

Amit Vhatkar
Student / IIT Bomaby, India
asvhatkar@iitb.ac.in

Pushpak Bhattacharyya
Professor / IIT Bomaby, India
pb@iitb.ac.in

Kavi Arya
Professor / IIT Bombay, India
kavi@iitb.ac.in

Abstract

In our research work, we represent the content of the sentence in graphical form after extracting triples from the sentences. In this paper, we will discuss novel methods to generate an extractive summary by scoring the triples. Our work has also touched upon sequence-to-sequence encoding of the content of the sentence, to classify it as a summary or a non-summary sentence. Our findings help to decide the nature of the sentences forming the summary and the length of the system generated summary as compared to the length of the reference summary.

1 Introduction

Extractive summaries contain the most informative sentences from the input text. The ordered pair of Subject(S), Verb(V) and Object(O) i.e. [1]$< S, V, O>$ represent the content of the sentence. We form a knowledge-graph(KG) by considering words in the triples. Our novel methods choose the informative sentences based on the count of frequencies calculated using generated KG. We also have implemented machine Learning(ML) and Deep Neural Network(DNN) based models. These models make use of the KG based features which try to capture information available. We are making use of dataset made available for FNS-2020 shared task by El-Haj et al. (2020). [2]We have used SpaCy library for extracting triples. We have used python implementation of Rouge package made available by [3]PyPI, which implements ROUGE described by Lin (2004).

2 Implemented Approaches

In general, we pose extractive summarization as a sentence classification and a triple classification task. We perform this classification using algorithms like SVM, SVR, Neural Network(NN) and Long Short-Term Memory(LSTM/DNN). This section describes our implemented approaches in details.

2.1 Labelling and Feature Extraction

	Summary Sentences	Non Summary Sentences	Total Sentences
Train Set	0.3M	2.6M	2.9M
Validation Set	0.051M	0.663M	0.714M

Table 1: Distribution of Summary, Non-Summary Sentences Extracted from Training and Validation Set

FNS-2020 Shared task training and validation dataset comes with up to seven gold summaries. All the sentences present in the gold summary are extractive in nature. All available gold summaries of the specific document are used for labelling the sentences in the given text.

[1]Referred to as triple
[2]https://spacy.io/
[3]https://pypi.org/project/rouge/

Proceedings of the 1st Joint Workshop on Financial Narrative Processing and MultiLing Financial Summarisation, pages 130–136
Barcelona, Spain (Online), December 12, 2020.

We have considered features as, *Position of the sentence*- each sentence is marked according to its position (i.e. 1-Introductory, 2-Concluding and 3-Explanatory), *Length*- number of words present in the sentence, *Thematic Words*- number of most [4]frequent words present in the sentence, *Indicator Words*- Count of words present in the available [5]synset(i.e. the group of synonymous words) of words 'conclusion' and 'summary', *Uppercase*- number of uppercase words present in the [6]sentence, *Important Word Feature*- It represents quotient of the available triple in the sentence to the total triples in the text file, and *KG File Feature*- It represents quotient of the available triples in the sentence represented in terms of [7]lookup frequencies to the number of total triples in the text file. We also have used pre-trained 100-dimensional GloVe(Pennington et al., 2014) embedding for DNN based approaches.

2.2 Triple Frequency-based Models(TFM)

Subject, verb and object($<$S, V, O$>$ i.e. triple) are main content words available in any sentence. Individual count of S, V and O present in the document fails to represent content available the sentence. To generate a content-aware extractive summary, TFM chooses sentences containing the highest scoring triples. Based on score computation, we have defined three different models.

2.2.1 Plain Frequency Model(PKG)

This is the simplistic approach to generate extractive summaries by making use of Triple Frequencies. This method fails to identify important sentences in the case of equal distribution of triples.

1. Extract all triples available in the text document and maintain it's count

2. Generate the score of the triple by considering its count

3. Generate extractive summary by selecting the sentences containing top-K triples

2.2.2 Updated Frequency Model(UKG)

PFM fails when the majority of the extracted triples gets an equal score. We tried to remove the equal scoring by considering frequencies of the subject and object present in the triples for scoring the triples.

1. Extract all triples available in the text document

2. Generate the score of the triple using the following formula,

$$triple\,score = Frequency\,of\,triple + frequency\,of\,subject + frequency\,of\,object \quad (1)$$

3. Generate extractive summary by selecting the sentences containing top-K triples

The formula 1, helps to break the uniformity of the scores occurring in the PFM by giving importance to the subjects and the objects available in the sentence.

2.2.3 Five Fold Cross Validation Model(FKG)

This approach considers two disjoint sets of documents to generate a score of the triples, 1- Train fold: used to extract and score the triple, 2- Test fold: used to generate the summaries and check the performance.

1. Extract and pre-compute frequencies of triples based on all documents present in the training folds and extract triples from the document present in test fold

2. Generate the score of the triple extracted from test document by considering its count which is computed (after considering all documents in remaining folds) in Step-1.

---

[4]Based on occurrence in the document
[5]We have used wordnet made available in nltk library for getting synset
[6]Excluding word 'I'(most commonly occurring uppercase word)
[7]Entire dataset is divided in five disjoint folds of which four-fold forms training set i.e. lookup

3. Generate extractive summary by selecting the sentences containing top-K triples

This method helps us to gain an insight over the presence of general sentences related to the topic or domain and the presence of the sentences specific to the document. Table 2 represents the extraction statistics of FNS-2020 training set. We have considered 2580 training documents for extraction.

	Fold 1	Fold 2	Fold 3	Fold 4	Fold 5	Average
# Important Words	186505	186526	186249	188363	186631	186854
# Triples	758701	758657	760248	767476	761487	761313

Table 2: Fold wise Extraction Statistics of FNS-2020 Shared Task Training Set

2.3 Machine Learning based Summarization

We have implemented two machine learning-based approaches, 1-SVM, 2-SVR. Implementation of SVM for extractive summarization roughly follows the method used by Chali et al. (2009); where the task of extractive summarization is posed as a binary classification task. SVR for extractive summarization is based on the discussion by Li et al. (2007). SVR for extractive summarization assigns the score to the sentence. Summary sentences are scored as 1 and non-summary as 0. SVR approach predicts the score for sentences in the document and we select top-k scoring sentences as a summary sentences. SVM and SVR make use to the features mentioned in section 2.1. Both of the models are trained on 0.6M sentences with an equal mix of the classes.

2.4 Deep Neural Network based Approaches

Along with KG and ML-based approaches, we have implement DNN based approaches to generate extractive summaries by performing binary class classification.

2.4.1 Neural Network Model

We have trained a feed-forward neural network to classify a given sentence. Input layer consumes the features mentioned in the section 2.1. The model's architecture is the input layer followed by a dense layer with eight neurons followed by an output layer. *ReLU* and *Sigmoid* activation functions were used with *Binary Cross Entropy* as a loss function and *Adam* as an optimizer. Model Performs best when we set batch size as 32, Train-Validation split as 70-30% and train for 150 epochs.

2.4.2 S-LSTM for Extractive Summarization

We have trained LSTM models to classify the **sentence** as a summary and non-summary sentence. The encoder uses the entire sequence of the words present in the sentence to capture content information, for that we have used pre-trained 100-dimensional GloVe embedding which does not evolve during the training phase. The architecture is made up of an embedding layer followed by LSTM layer (with 2% dropout) followed by a softmax layer. Categorical cross-entropy(a generalized form of binary-cross entropy) with Adam optimization technique is used for training.

Models	Training Instances	Validation Instances	[8]LR in %	Epoch	Batch Size	[9]MSL
S-LSTM	0.48M Sentences	0.12M Sentences	1	5	32	35
T-LSTM	0.8M Triples	0.2M Triples	1	15	65	5

Table 3: Training Parameters Used to Train S-LSTM and T-LSTM Model

---

[8]Learning Rate
[9]Maximum Sequence Length

2.4.3 T-LSTM for Extractive Summarization

In this approach, words present in the **triples** were passed to the LSTM encoder, unlike S-LSTM where all the words in the sentence get passed. Based on the presence in the summary sentences, triples are marked as a summary or a non-summary triples. We have trained this model on positional embedding. All words in all triples are used to generate positional embedding. Embedding of the words presented in the triples are concatenated and is passed as input to the encoder of LSTM. The total number of words in the triples are less than the total number of words in all of the documents. Positional embedding tries to get an exact representation of the content of the sentence represented by the triple. Architecture details of this model remain the same as S-LSTM. Table 3 represents parameters used for S-LSTM and T-LSTM and table 4 represents extraction statistics related to T-LSTM model.

	Total Triples	Non Summary Triples	Summary Triples
Training Set	1389758	1158854	230904
Validation Set	352435	315418	37017

Table 4: Extraction Statistics of Triples from Sentences from FNS-2020 Shared Task Dataset

3 Results and Analysis

We have implemented eight different approaches while considering TextRank (Mihalcea and Tarau, 2004) as the baseline approach. In this section, we discuss the performance of the implemented models on the validation set followed by a performance on the test set.

3.1 Validation Set

The validation set of FNS-2020 Shared Task consists of 363 documents each having up to seven gold summaries. We are comparing results obtained over *single* gold summary of the specific document. System generated summaries were constrained to have 1000 words and our approaches select *first* 1000 words because, After segmenting given text in three parts each containing equal portions of the text we have found that in the training set 96%(i.e. 0.28M out of 0.29M) and in the validation set 95%(i.e. 49K out of 51K) of the summary sentences of the gold summaries are present in the first part of the text.

Model Name	ROUGE-1 with respect to Single Full Length Gold Summary			ROUGE-1 with respect to Single Limited Length Gold Summary		
	F	P	R	F	P	R
T-LSTM	0.3815	0.528	0.3162	*0.4888*	*0.4829*	*0.5013*
S-LSTM	*0.3911*	*0.5898*	*0.3238*	0.4288	0.4205	0.4434
NN	0.362	0.5527	0.3009	0.4471	0.4404	0.4604
SVM	*0.3114*	*0.435*	*0.2615*	*0.4368*	*0.4292*	*0.451*
SVR	0.2883	0.4045	0.2423	0.3665	0.3532	0.3875
PKG	*0.2891*	0.2546	*0.3768*	*0.426*	*0.4489*	*0.4126*
UKG	0.2689	*0.3837*	0.2213	0.3891	0.3848	0.3975
FKG	0.1933	0.3049	0.151	0.3413	0.3364	0.3498
[10]TextRank	0.2886	0.2535	**0.3778**	0.4244	0.4122	0.4438

Table 5: ROUGE-1 Score Comparison of All Implemented Models concerning Single Full Length Gold Summary and Single Limited Length Gold Summary

Table 5 represents ROUGE-1 score of all implemented models when reference gold summary is allowed to contain all of its text(i.e. Full Length) and when it is allowed to contain first 1000 words(i.e.

---

[10]Our Baseline Model

Limited Length) of its text. The ROUGE score values in the table are averaged over the averaged(over 3 runs) ROUGE score of all documents in the validation set. In the result table, overall highest score are **bold-faced** while highest score among specific category is *italicized*.

Considering the full-length gold summary S-LSTM performs the best amongst all approaches. In the setting of limited length gold summary T-LSTM approach performs best. All approaches perform best in the limited length gold summary setting. Therefore, to obtain better results, length of system generated summary should be equal to the length of the reference summary.

Even after being rule-based models, TFM models have performed comparably well. Nature of text causes UKG to give an equal score to the triples affecting its performance. In the FKG model, generic triples get a higher score as the effect of considering all documents in training fold. This leads to a summary containing generic sentences. However, as PKG and UKG performance better than FKG, the summary should contain sentences specific to the document

3.2 Test Set

We have generated summaries of the 500 documents present in the test set using our [11]NN, S-LSTM and an SVM approach. Gold summaries of the documents in the test set are used by the organizers as a reference summaries to compute the results. The ROUGE values in the table 6 are published by the organizers of the shared task. Organizers also had computed the ROUGE scores of their baseline approaches(as mentioned in table 6) employing SUMM-TL-MUSE, LEXRANK-SUMMARY, SUMM-BL-POLY, TEXTRANK-SUMMARY.

Model Name	ROUGE-1 F	ROUGE-2 F	ROUGE-L F	ROUGE-SU F
[12]Best Performing	0.466	0.306	0.456	0.318
NN	0.445	0.246	0.318	0.242
S-LSTM	0.438	0.243	0.317	0.245
SVM	0.438	0.247	0.312	0.248
SUMM-TL-MUSE	0.433	0.234	0.407	0.253
LEXRANK-SUMMARY	0.264	0.12	0.218	0.14
SUMM-BL-POLY	0.274	0.105	0.205	0.135
TEXTRANK-SUMMARY	0.172	0.07	0.206	0.079

Table 6: ROUGE Score Comparison of KG-based Approaches with Top Scoring Approaches and Baseline Approaches, on Test Set, Computed by the Organizers using the Gold Summary

When compared on ROUGE-1, our NN based approach is among top-5 while SVM and S-LSTM approaches have secured 9th and 10th position respectively. SVM, NN and S-LSTM ranked 10th, 11th and 12th respectively on ROUGE-2 metric. Our approaches perform quite well as compare to the baseline approaches. No one approach outperformed the others in all ROUGE metrics.

4 Conclusion

We have successfully generated extractive summaries using our novel methods of triple scoring which are based on KG generated by the words in the triples. We have also proposed novel DNN based approaches for extractive summarization, where summarization is carried by performing binary classification after sequence-to-sequence encoding(either sentence or triples) content present in the input text. From our discussion in section 3.1, we can conclude that the summary should contain sentences specific to the document. We have seen that, in order to get better results, length of system generated summary should be equal to the length of the reference summary. We also have seen that KG-based Triple Frequency models perform comparably well than baseline models and possess scope of the improvement.

---

[11]Only up to 3 summaries per document are allowed by organizers of FNS-Shared Task
[12]Different systems performed well on different ROUGE metric

References

Yllias Chali, Sadid A Hasan, and Shafiq R Joty. 2009. A svm-based ensemble approach to multi-document summarization. In *Canadian Conference on Artificial Intelligence*, pages 199–202. Springer.

Mahmoud El-Haj, Ahmed AbuRa'ed, Nikiforos Pittaras, and George Giannakopoulos. 2020. The Financial Narrative Summarisation Shared Task (FNS 2020). In *The 1st Joint Workshop on Financial Narrative Processing and MultiLing Financial Summarisation (FNP-FNS 2020*, Barcelona, Spain.

Sujian Li, You Ouyang, Wei Wang, and Bin Sun. 2007. Multi-document summarization using support vector regression. In *Proceedings of DUC*. Citeseer.

Chin-Yew Lin. 2004. ROUGE: A package for automatic evaluation of summaries. In *Text Summarization Branches Out*, pages 74–81, Barcelona, Spain, July. Association for Computational Linguistics.

Rada Mihalcea and Paul Tarau. 2004. Textrank: Bringing order into text. In *Proceedings of the 2004 conference on empirical methods in natural language processing*, pages 404–411.

Jeffrey Pennington, Richard Socher, and Christopher D Manning. 2014. Glove: Global vectors for word representation. In *Proceedings of the 2014 conference on empirical methods in natural language processing (EMNLP)*, pages 1532–1543.

A   Web Service

We have created web service for end-users to summarize their text either by uploading a file or by type-in text functionality. Figure 1 depicts the landing page of web service where users can see the summarized text along with the [13]KG that gets generated and used for summarizing the input text. The web portal also mentions the percentage reduction in terms of the number of words and ROUGE score calculated using TextRank as a reference summary. Web service displays PKG, UKG summaries along with TextRank summary. It also has provision to host a dataset and it currently hosts part of CNN-Daily mail dataset. Currently, the web service is running in a private domain.

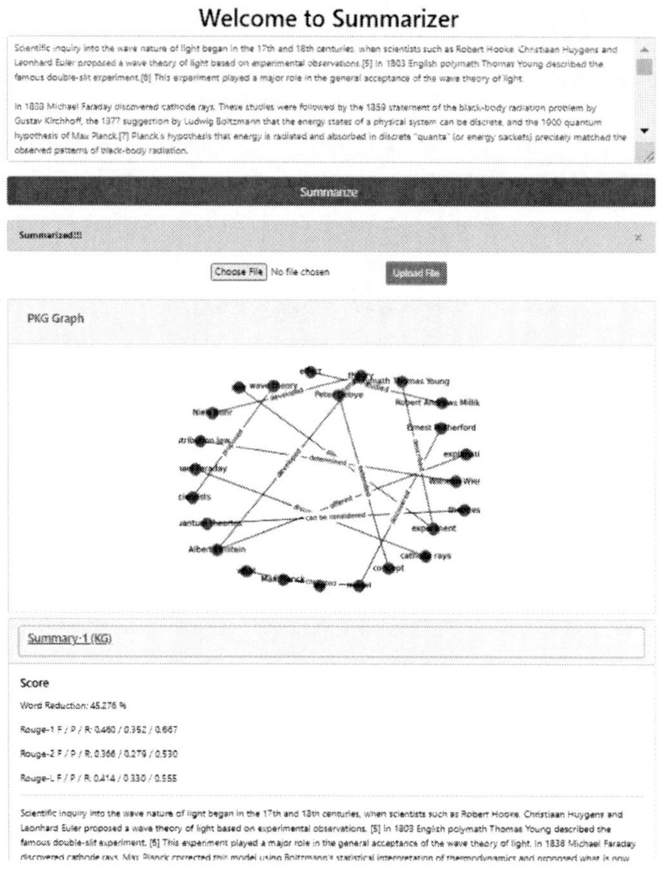

Figure 1: Web Service for Extractive Text Summarization by Triple Frequency-based Approaches

---

[13]Graph shown does not capture the notion of frequency

AMEX AI-Labs: An Investigative Study on Extractive Summarization of Financial Documents

Piyush Arora and Priya Radhakrishnan
American Express AI Labs
Bangalore, India
{piyush.arora1,priya.radhakrishnan}@aexp.com

Abstract

We describe the work carried out by AMEX AI-LABS on an extractive summarization benchmark task focused on Financial Narratives Summarization (FNS). This task focuses on summarizing annual financial reports which pose two main challenges as compared to typical news document summarization tasks : i) annual reports are lengthier (average length about 80 pages) as compared to typical news documents, and ii) annual reports are more loosely structured e.g. comprising of tables, charts, textual data and images, which makes it challenging to effectively summarize. To address this summarization task we investigate a range of *unsupervised, supervised* and *ensemble* based techniques. We find that ensemble based techniques perform relatively better as compared to using only the unsupervised and supervised based techniques. Our ensemble based model achieved the highest rank of 9 out of 31 systems submitted for the benchmark task based on Rouge-L evaluation metric.

1 Introduction

The publicly available financial information has been rising rapidly with periodic updates, earnings reports etc. from companies and institutions. These financial reports not only increase in volume but also in terms of the diversity, comprising different structure and format, depending on the location of the respective institutes and companies (El-Haj et al., 2014). The rise in quantity and diversity of financial information, needs to be adequately processed, analyzed and summarized to make it easy to disseminate and consume by the end-users (El-Haj et al., 2019).

The financial narrative summarization task focuses on summarizing publicly available annual financial reports produced by UK firms listed on the London Stock Exchange (El-Haj et al., 2020). These reports are quite lengthy (average length about 80 pages), with some reports spanning more than 250 pages, which makes this task quite challenging. These reports broadly consist of two main sections :i) "*narrative sections*" also known as "*front-end sections*": part of the report which contain textual information and reviews by the firm's management and board of directors and ii) "*back-end sections*": sections containing financial statements in terms of tables and numbers. This task focuses on finding effective narratives sections and then performing the summarization over these narrative sections to generate a summary of about 1000 words. For more details about the task kindly refer (El-Haj et al., 2020).

We address this task by exploring the approaches which have shown to perform well for document summarization. We investigate page-rank based techniques to find effective summaries in an unsupervised fashion, which have shown to perform well in past (Mihalcea and Tarau, 2004; Erkan and Radev, 2004; Zheng and Lapata, 2019). Given the recent advancement in exploring deep learning techniques to extract effective summaries we explore a Bi-directional LSTM (Graves and Schmidhuber, 2005) based approach for extracting top sentence for a given document and generate summaries using the top-k ranked sentences. We combine complementary information captured using unsupervised and Bi-LSTM based supervised models along with Lead-k sentences approach (Lin and Hovy, 2002), to generate effective summaries (more details provided in Section 3).

Proceedings of the 1st Joint Workshop on Financial Narrative Processing and MultiLing Financial Summarisation, pages 137–142
Barcelona, Spain (Online), December 12, 2020.

The paper is organized as follows: Section 2 describes the dataset details and the evaluation mechanism used, Section 3 discusses the approaches explored in this work, Section 4 presents the result of our experiments, we describe our main findings and conclude in Section 5.

2 Dataset & Evaluation mechanism

The dataset provided by the task organizers consist of a training and a validation set consisting of 3000 and 363 financial documents respectively, as shown in Table 1. For each document we are provided with gold summaries which varies between two to seven for the training and validation set. The test set consists of 500 documents, we have to generate a document summary consisting of **1000** words for each of the documents in a test set. At most three different submissions were allowed for the task. Table 1 presents more detail such as number of sentences, average length etc., across training, validation and test set.

Dataset	Documents	Gold Summaries	Average length of Documents	Average length of Summaries
Training Set	3000	9873	1394 sentences	39 sentences
Validation Set	363	1250	1970 sentences	43 sentences
Test Set	500	-	2055 sentences	-

Table 1: Dataset statistics

The automatically generated summaries are evaluated against the gold summaries using the evaluation metric ROUGE (Lin, 2004), commonly used for summarization tasks. Rouge-1, Rouge-2, Rouge-L, Rouge-SU4 are the four variants of rouge which are used for evaluating the submitted systems on the test set. Rouge-L indicates longest common subsequence statistics, Rouge-1 indicates overlap of unigram, Rouge-2 indicates overlap of bigram and Rouge-SU indicates overlap of skip-bigram plus unigram statistics between the generated and the gold summary.

3 Methodology

We describe three types of approaches that we explored for addressing the financial narrative summarization task.

Unsupervised approach: Within the unsupervised approach we explored three methods namely Lead-k (Lin and Hovy, 2002), TextRank (Mihalcea and Tarau, 2004), and LexRank (Erkan and Radev, 2004) for performing extractive summarization.

Lead-k: In general, news documents tend to contain the most informative content at the top and are further detailed. In this method the top k sentences from a document, based on the order of their occurrence are extracted and combined to form a summary. This method has proved to be quite robust and have been used as a good baseline for the task of extractive summarization (Lin and Hovy, 2002; Lewis et al., 2019; Zheng and Lapata, 2019).

TextRank and *LexRank*: The initial work on PageRank (Page et al., 1999) for crawling web pages, motivated the idea of TextRank and LexRank, which are graph based approaches for performing extractive summarization of documents. In graph based approaches all the sentences in a document are represented as the vertices of a graph where the edges are vertex (sentence) to vertex (sentence) similarity, and hence weighted. The weights of the edges are calculated using the textual similarity between the sentences. Top k salient sentences are combined to form a summary. For a given document, a connected graph of the sentences in constructed and then the salient sentences from the graph are extracted as shown in Equation 1 and Equation 2. S_i and S_j are two sentences comprising of words $w_i, w_{i+1}.., w_n$ in Equation 1. In Equation 2, $WS(V_i)$ represent a weighted score for a Vertex i, $In(V_i)$ and $Out(V_i)$ indicates in-degree and out-degree scores respectively, and d is a damping factor having a value between 0 and 1.

TextRank approach looks at the absolute number of words two sentences have in common, which are then normalized by the sentences length. Whereas, LexRank calculates cosine similarity of the word vectors for both the sentences as shown in Equation 3. Each sentence is represented as a N dimensional vector using a bag-of-words based model, where N represents the number of unique words in the document. In Equation 3, x and y represents the N dimensional sentence vector for Sentences S_i and S_j respectively, and tf indicates the term frequency and idf indicates the inverse document frequency for a word w.

$$Similarity(S_i, S_j) = \frac{|\{w_k | w_k \in S_i \& w_k \in S_j\}|}{log(|S_i|) + log(|S_j|)} \tag{1}$$

$$WS(V_i) = (1 - d) + d * \sum_{V_j \in In(V_i)} \frac{w_{ji}}{\sum_{V_k \in Out(V_j)} w_{jk}} WS(V_j) \tag{2}$$

$$Idf - modified - cosine(x, y) = \frac{\sum_{w \in x,y} tf_{w,x} tf_{w,y} (idf_w)^2}{\sqrt{\sum_{x_i \in x} (tf_{x_i,x} idf_{x_i})^2} \times \sqrt{\sum_{y_i \in y} (tf_{y_i,y} idf_{y_i})^2}} \tag{3}$$

We used the sumy tool[1] for performing LexRank based summarization. We used the gensim (Řehřek and Sojka, 2011) implementation of TextRank algorithm from (Barrios et al., 2015). This revised version of TextRank performs better as compared to the original version proposed in (Mihalcea and Tarau, 2004). For more details on these models, we advise readers to refer (Barrios et al., 2015; Mihalcea and Tarau, 2004; Erkan and Radev, 2004).

Supervised approach: Extractive summarization focuses on finding good representative sentences from a document to represent document summaries. Thus the summarization task can be approached as a binary level sentence classification task where sentences which form a part of document summaries are positive samples and rest being categorized as negative samples. Thus given a new document we have to classify sentences as positive and negative instances. Top k positive sentences in their chronological occurrence are considered as document summaries. We experimented with a Bi-directional LSTM (Bi-LSTM) based approach for sentence extraction for generating document summaries by combining top-k ranked sentences. We used the training dataset which has about 350k positive samples and we randomly sample a similar number of negative samples from the training set. Similarly a validation dataset was created which has about 100k sentences. Both the training and validation set have equal numbers of positive and negative samples.

We use the PyTorch library (Paszke et al., 2017) for Bi-LSTM based method, with following parameters: number of hidden units set to 48, loss function used is binary cross entropy loss, we used fasttext textual embeddings (Joulin et al., 2016), dimensionality = 300 to represent the textual input. We perform dropout to avoid overfitting of the model.

Ensemble approach: We find quite promising results using Lead-k, TextRank and LexRank based unsupervised approaches and a Bi-LSTM based supervised approach on the training and validation set (described later in Section 4). As described above that the Lead-k sentences based summaries has been used as a strong baseline for the summarization task so we performed an ensemble approach where we combine the output of i) TextRank, ii) LexRank, iii) Lead-k and iv) Bi-LSTM approaches. For a given document we sort and rank the sentences using these four approaches in descending order, we take the top 20 sentences from each of these approaches and combine the output using an ensemble technique. We chose 20 sentences empirically, as the length of summary is constrained to 1000 words only, so all the sentences occurring lower in the order do not impact the Rouge scores. This ensemble model is a linear combination of the output of multiple approaches, where the sentences that have occurred in the output of most approaches are ranked higher. In case of the same frequency of the sentences, preferences are given to the following models' output: Bi-LSTM > TextRank > LexRank > Lead-k, determined empirically based on the training set. A detailed worked out example of the ensemble approach is shown in Figure 1.

We used Stanford CoreNLP pipeline (Manning et al., 2014) to perform sentence splitting for each document before applying all three approaches described above. A post-processing step is performed after

---

[1] https://pypi.org/project/sumy/

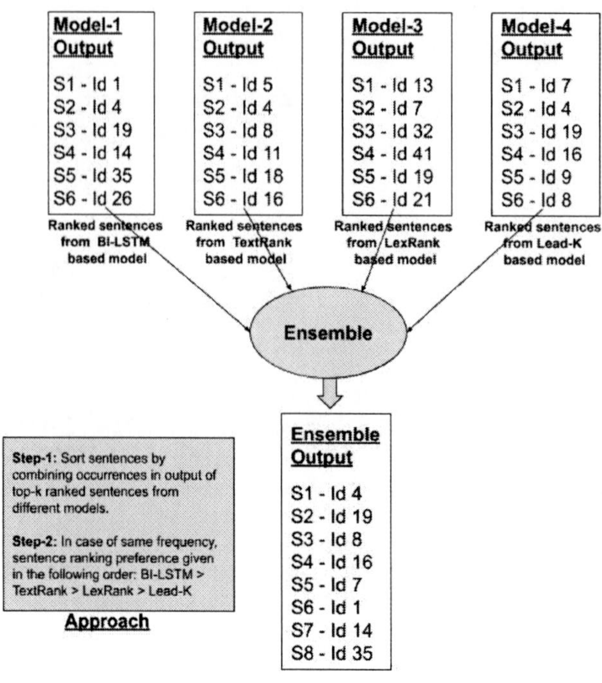

Figure 1: Ensemble Approach

generating document summaries from these three methods (Unsupervised, Supervised and Ensemble), where all the textual information beyond 1000 words is removed, as per the task requirement.

4 Results & Analysis

Results of different unsupervised approaches such as TextRank, Lead-k are shown in Table 2. We found that the TextRank based approach performs relatively better than LexRank and Lead-5 approach for both training as well as the validation set. We compare TextRank with Lead-5 as the average length of sentences for the output of TextRank is 4.6. We select TextRank as one of our system submissions on the test set which is referred to as $AMEX - TextRank$.

	ROUGE-1			ROUGE-2		
Training set	Recall	Precis	F-Meas	Recall	Precis	F-Meas
Lead-5	0.156	0.474	0.213	0.073	0.203	0.097
LexRank	0.310	0.269	0.259	0.098	0.088	0.083
TextRank	0.303	0.282	**0.277**	0.100	0.094	**0.092**
Validation set	Recall	Precis	F-Meas	Recall	Precis	F-Meas
Lead-5	0.148	0.516	0.211	0.065	0.219	0.092
LexRank	0.436	0.247	0.293	0.141	0.08	0.094
TextRank	0.308	0.330	**0.304**	0.099	0.107	**0.098**

Table 2: Results of unsupervised models on training and validation set, the best scores are in bold face

Our second system submission is a Bi-LSTM based binary classification model referred to as $AMEX - BILSTM$. Our final submission is an ensemble model referred to as $AMEX - Ensemble$. Table 3 presents the result of our three submissions on the test set. We find that the ensemble approach

Description	R-L / R	R-L / P	R-L / F	Rank	R-1 / R	R-1 / P	R-1 / F	Rank
Top System	0.6050	0.3764	0.4556	1	0.6123	0.3934	0.4663	1
Top Baseline	0.4696	0.3704	0.4067	3	0.4827	0.4135	0.4329	10
AMEX-Ensemble	**0.4077**	**0.3652**	**0.3778**	**9**	**0.4417**	**0.4080**	**0.4125**	**16**
AMEX-BILSTM	0.4017	0.3601	0.3718	10	0.4361	0.4063	0.4088	17
AMEX-TextRank	0.2461	0.2448	0.2370	23	0.3533	0.2715	0.2950	26
Description	R-2 / R	R-2 / P	R-2 / F	Rank	R-SU4 / R	R-SU4 / P	R-SU4 / F	Rank
Top System	0.3655	0.2951	0.3060	1	0.3440	0.3324	0.3184	1
Top Baseline	0.3108	0.1978	0.2338	17	0.3748	0.2008	0.2530	11
AMEX-Ensemble	**0.2639**	**0.1919**	**0.2142**	**20**	**0.3285**	**0.1941**	**0.2352**	**20**
AMEX-BILSTM	0.2603	0.1897	0.2111	21	0.3247	0.1921	0.2323	21
AMEX-TextRank	0.1838	0.0967	0.1200	26	0.2499	0.1079	0.1438	28

Table 3: Results of our three submitted models, our best scoring system is in boldface. R-1, R-2, R-L, R-SU4 indicates rouge scores at unigram, bigram, longest common subsequence and skip-gram based metrics respectively, and P,R,F indicates precision, recall and f-scores respectively. Top baseline model is a genetic algorithm based approach for summarization (Litvak et al., 2010)

performs relatively better than the TextRank and Bi-LSTM based approach. Our ensemble based model achieved the highest rank of 9 out of 31 systems submitted for the benchmark task based on Rouge-L evaluation metric.

Overall ranking of the systems varies depending on the evaluation metric being considered. Based on Rouge-L and Rouge-1 metrics our system submissions achieved quite high precision but scored lower on recall values hence the F-score are relatively averaged. In our ensemble based approach, we combined the output of multiple approaches by a linear combination, in future we will like to explore learning effective weights while combining the output of multiple models, to generate effective summaries which can possibly address the problem of low recall, by including potential good candidates occurring lower in the order.

5   Conclusion & Future work

We present our work on an initial investigation of extractive summarization for annual financial reports. We explored alternative approaches using unsupervised, supervised and an ensemble based method. We find that Bi-LSTM based supervised approaches perform relatively better than using unsupervised based approaches such as TextRank. The ensemble based model performs best as compared to supervised and unsupervised models and obtained a rank of 9/31 on the test set using $Rouge - L$ evaluation metric.

We used a Bi-LSTM based model for extracting good representative sentences to be included in the document summary. However we lose the document level information while treating the problem of extracting good representative sentences as a binary class classification problem while training the model. In future we will like to explore recent models (Lewis et al., 2019; Zheng and Lapata, 2019) for performing extractive summarization. These models leverage BERT based distributed representation (Devlin et al., 2019) and train summarization models by optimizing the Rouge scores, to generate effective document summaries.

Acknowledgements

We would like to thank the task organizers for organizing this interesting benchmark task and the reviewers for their valuable feedback. We would like to thank our colleague Arpan Somani for helping in running initial experiments using the Bi-LSTM based model, and Salil Rajeev Joshi, Himanshu Sharad Bhatt & Shourya Roy for their guidance and suggestions.

References

Federico Barrios, Federico López, Luis Argerich, and Rosita Wachenchauzer. 2015. Variations of the similarity function of textrank for automated summarization. In *Argentine Symposium on Artificial Intelligence (ASAI 2015)-JAIIO 44 (Rosario, 2015)*.

Jacob Devlin, Ming-Wei Chang, Kenton Lee, and Kristina Toutanova. 2019. Bert: Pre-training of deep bidirectional transformers for language understanding. In *Proceedings of the 2019 Conference of the North American Chapter of the Association for Computational Linguistics: Human Language Technologies, Volume 1 (Long and Short Papers)*, pages 4171–4186.

Mahmoud El-Haj, Paul Rayson, Steve Young, and Martin Walker. 2014. Detecting document structure in a very large corpus of uk financial reports. In *Proceedings of the Ninth International Conference on Language Resources and Evaluation (LREC'14)*, pages 1335–1338.

Mahmoud El-Haj, Paul Rayson, Paulo Alves, Carlos Herrero-Zorita, and Steven Young. 2019. Multilingual financial narrative processing: Analysing annual reports in english, spanish and portuguese. *Multilingual Text Analysis: Challenges, Models, And Approaches*, page 441.

Mahmoud El-Haj, Ahmed AbuRa'ed, Marina Litvak, Nikiforos Pittaras, and George Giannakopoulos. 2020. The Financial Narrative Summarisation Shared Task (FNS 2020). In *The 1st Joint Workshop on Financial Narrative Processing and MultiLing Financial Summarisation (FNP-FNS 2020)*, Barcelona, Spain.

Günes Erkan and Dragomir R Radev. 2004. Lexrank: Graph-based lexical centrality as salience in text summarization. *Journal of Artificial Intelligence Research*, 22:457–479.

Alex Graves and Jürgen Schmidhuber. 2005. Framewise phoneme classification with bidirectional lstm networks. In *Proceedings. 2005 IEEE International Joint Conference on Neural Networks, 2005.*, volume 4, pages 2047–2052. IEEE.

Armand Joulin, Edouard Grave, Piotr Bojanowski, Matthijs Douze, Hérve Jégou, and Tomas Mikolov. 2016. Fasttext. zip: Compressing text classification models. *arXiv preprint arXiv:1612.03651*.

Mike Lewis, Yinhan Liu, Naman Goyal, Marjan Ghazvininejad, Abdelrahman Mohamed, Omer Levy, Ves Stoyanov, and Luke Zettlemoyer. 2019. Bart: Denoising sequence-to-sequence pre-training for natural language generation, translation, and comprehension. *arXiv preprint arXiv:1910.13461*.

Chin-Yew Lin and Eduard Hovy. 2002. From single to multi-document summarization. In *Proceedings of the 40th Annual Meeting of the Association for Computational Linguistics*, pages 457–464.

Chin-Yew Lin. 2004. Rouge: A package for automatic evaluation of summaries. In *Text Summarization Branches Out*, pages 74–81.

Marina Litvak, Mark Last, and Menahem Friedman. 2010. A new approach to improving multilingual summarization using a genetic algorithm. In *Proceedings of the 48th Annual Meeting of the Association for Computational Linguistics*, pages 927–936.

Christopher D Manning, Mihai Surdeanu, John Bauer, Jenny Rose Finkel, Steven Bethard, and David McClosky. 2014. The stanford corenlp natural language processing toolkit. In *Proceedings of 52nd Annual Meeting of the Association for Computational Linguistics: System Demonstrations*, pages 55–60.

Rada Mihalcea and Paul Tarau. 2004. Textrank: Bringing order into text. In *Proceedings of the 2004 Conference on Empirical Methods in Natural Language Processing*, pages 404–411.

Lawrence Page, Sergey Brin, Rajeev Motwani, and Terry Winograd. 1999. The pagerank citation ranking: Bringing order to the web. Technical report, Stanford InfoLab.

Adam Paszke, Sam Gross, Soumith Chintala, Gregory Chanan, Edward Yang, Zachary DeVito, Zeming Lin, Alban Desmaison, Luca Antiga, and Adam Lerer. 2017. Automatic differentiation in pytorch.

Radim Řehřek and Petr Sojka. 2011. Gensim—statistical semantics in python. *Retrieved from genism. org*.

Hao Zheng and Mirella Lapata. 2019. Sentence centrality revisited for unsupervised summarization. In *Proceedings of the 57th Annual Meeting of the Association for Computational Linguistics*, pages 6236–6247.

FNS-Summarisation 2020 shared task: system description paper
Extractive Summarization System for Annual Reports

Abderrahim Ait Azzi
Fortia Financial Solutions
17 av. George V, 75008
Paris, France
`abderrahim.aitazzi@fortia.fr`

Juyeon Kang
Fortia Financial Solutions
17 av. George V, 75008
Paris, France
`juyeon.kang@fortia.fr`

Abstract

In this paper, we report on our experiments in building a summarization system for generating summaries from annual reports. We adopt an "extractive" summarization approach in our hybrid system combining neural networks and rules-based algorithms with the expectation that such a system may capture key sentences or paragraphs from the data. A rules-based TOC (Table Of Contents) extraction and a binary classifier of narrative section titles are main components of our system allowing to identify narrative sections and best candidates for extracting final summaries. As result, we propose one to three summaries per document according to the classification score of narrative section titles.

1 Introduction

The Financial Narrative Summarization (FNS) aims to generate textual summaries from annual reports where financial overview of a company over a year stated. In this FNS shared task 2020 (El-Haj et al., 2020), we focus on "narrative" parts of those documents, all textual parts except tables, figures and diagrams. The provided dataset contains the narrative summaries as the gold standard and the expected summaries should be formed only from the narrative parts of the documents. These documents often contain more than 100 pages of texts, tables, figures, diagrams, etc. Summarizing an annual report of a company into a short text allows to get insights on annual financial status of the company.

The summarization approaches can be extractive or abstractive not only according to the techniques we adopt but also depending on the dataset on which we build the system. Our experiments are designed based on the extractive approach where we develop a pipeline in order to extract the most informative sections. We suppose that each narrative section is already a summary as the author of annual reports aim to resume key financial overview in each section. This is why we adopt the extractive summarization approach and the results of our system largely depend on the narrative sections prediction.

First, we create a binary classification dataset and implement Machine Learning algorithms to identify the narrative sections with its sections titles, then analyze which sections contain key information on annual financial status. Second, we select the summaries which capture the most informative parts of texts from the previously selected sections.

For this shared task, we experiment hybrid methods combining neural networks and rules-based systems in our summaries extraction algorithms, according to the results of the narrative sections prediction, a document can be assigned one to three summaries as described in the section 4. In the section 5, we shows that our system obtains encouraging ROUGE scores and discuss on the major errors that we could observe in our final summaries. We conclude the paper by proposing some future works.

2 Related work

Text summarization is one of the most challenging tasks in NLP. In general, two methods are used to handle this task, extractive and abstractive methods.

Extractive summarization methods produce summaries by selecting the most relevant sentences directly from the source text. Many approaches proposed for this type of summarization, some studies address the problem as a sentence-level sequence labeling task where each label indicates if the sentence

Proceedings of the 1st Joint Workshop on Financial Narrative Processing and MultiLing Financial Summarisation, pages 143–147
Barcelona, Spain (Online), December 12, 2020.

should be included in the summary or not, using either a CRF model (Nguyen MT., 2017) or using attention RNN-based Seq2seq Models as in (Cheng and Lapata, 2016; Nallapati et al., 2016). These models require generally a large and high-quality training sets. There are also some unsupervised methods in the extractive approach using statistical methods as a simple tf-idf (Saggion et al., 2016) or graph-based approaches as (Barrios et al., 2016) that represent text as a network linking sentences and use graph-based ranking methods to generate a summary.

Abstractive summarization, on the other hand, is a technique in which the summary is generated by generating novel sentences. This method requires then a deeper interpretation and understanding of the text and a text generation system. Most researches are based on a sequence to sequence attention based models and more recently transformers to handle this challenge (Zhang et al., 2020).

3 Data

The financial annual reports are publicly available documents on which firms publish a year-end summary of their operations and financial conditions. An annual report covers a broad scope of contents in different sections. The main data sets of the FNS shared task (see Table 1) have been taken from the UK firms annual reports, and previously converted into text file format.

Dataset	Train	Valid	Test
Annual report full text	3000	363	500
Gold Summaries	9873	1250	1673 (not released)

Table 1: Dataset.

The key narrative sections we have identified from the given train set are *Financial and Operational Highlights, Chief Executive's Review, Financial Review*, etc., it means that those sections typically contain summarized financial issues. As those documents include a lot of statistical informations over a year, tables, graphs, diagrams and figures are often used for key informations along with textual statements, called *narrative* sections. We only focus on the *narrative* sections for building our summarization system.

4 System overview

As shown in Figure 1, We first identify narrative sections from the reports, then extract summaries from those sections. To do that, we extract the TOC from each document and train a binary classification model with Keras using the list of narrative sections found in the gold summaries as train set.

4.1 TOC extraction

In this first step, we design a rules-based algorithm extracting the table of contents (TOC) from a document. For that purpose, we segment a document into sentences, then each sentence is matched with a rules set in order to verify if it is a title of the TOC. We consider a sentence as title if it satisfies predefined conditions, some examples are given as follows : 1) a sentence starts with a digit, 2) it does not contain any of the predefined noisy words and special characters and 3) the word length in a sentence is less than 10. We applied this approach to all the documents in the training set.

4.2 Narrative sections prediction

The second step is to identify from the titles of the extracted TOC, the ones that correspond to narrative sections. For this purpose, we concatenated all the TOCs extracted from the training set and built a binary classification dataset with the labels: 1 if the title is narrative (a title is considered as narrative if it is seen in the gold summary), 0 otherwise. The labels attribution was not obvious, because some titles can be narrative in reports and non narrative in others. Therefore, we use the most frequently occurring label of each unique title as its ground truth label. Once we prepared the data set, we designed a binary classifier to predict if a section is narrative or non narrative. We implemented a Convolutional Neural

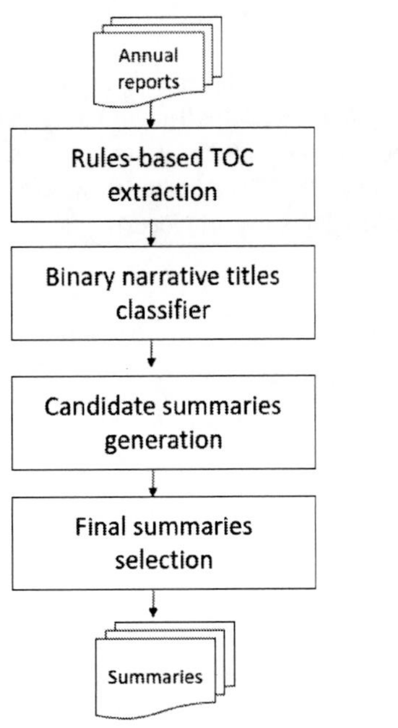

Figure 1: System overview

Figure 2: Binary classifier architecture

Network (CNN) classifier using Keras. Figure 2 (Mansar and Ferradans, 2018) shows the architecture of the model that contains: a word embeddings layer to give a dense representation of each token of a title. This representation passes through a convolutional network and pooling layer to encode the title. Finally, a linear layer with a sigmoid activation to predict the output. We split the dataset into a train set (80 %) and test set (20%). For the TOCs given in the test set, the classifier predicts if a title is a narrative section title or not with a score for each title and results the titles of narrative sections for each document. The trained model reaches a classification accuracy of around 70% on the test set.

4.3   Candidate summaries extraction

We identified the titles of narrative sections from the test set using our narrative sections titles classifier. For a report, the classification results show that we have in average 5∼6 narrative sections knowing that the average sections number in a report is 29.5. We now generate "*candidate*" summaries by the way that we first select the top 3 predictions having the top classification scores among the narrative section titles of a report. Then, for each narrative title, we search of its first occurrence in the report in such a way that it is not a part of the TOC but a title of a section. Finally, we extract the first 1000 words of the report starting from thie occurrence title . The extracted content of each of the top 3 titles corresponds to the system 1, 2 and 3, respectively.

4.4   Final summaries generation

In this last step, we focus on post-processing the "*candidate*" summaries extracted in section 4.3. The post-processing is mainly to check if the candidate summaries are not overlapping. This overlapping can occur due to the strategy of taking the first 1000 words starting from the narrative title. Therefore, for a candidate summary, if the range of the 1000 words contains contents from the next narrative section (hence the next candidate summary), we delete the overlapped contents from the first summary.

5   Results and Discussion

At the time of the deadline, the best summaries we had were the summaries gathered from the sections with the top 3 classification score, which are corresponding to the systems 1, 2 and 3, respectively. We also randomly selected all the final summaries of 100 reports and read the summaries focusing on the contents of each summary if it provides firm's financial overview of the business over the year. This defined which system's summary we should submit, whose results (as provided by the organizers) are reported in Table 2.

Metrics	System 1	System 2	System 3
R.L-R/R.L-P/**R.L-F**	0.40/0.40/**0.38**	0.37/0.34/0.33	0.34/0.34/0.33
R.1-R/R.1-P/**R.1-F**	0.43/0.43/**0.41**	0.39/0.41/0.38	0.37/0.37/0.35
R.2-R/R.2-P/**R.2-F**	0.30/0.28/**0.27**	0.25/0.26/0.24	0.21/0.22/0.20
R.SU4-R/R.SU4-P/**R.SU4-F**	0.34/0.33/**0.32**	0.30/0.31/0.29	0.26/0.27/0.25

Table 2: Results measured by the organizers for the test set.

The multiple variants of ROUGE measures, ROUGE-L, ROUGE-1, ROUGE-2 and ROUGE-SU4 are used for automatic evaluation. ROUGE (Lin, 2004) compares any summary to any other (normally human generated) summary. ROUGE -1 and ROUGE-2 are based on unigrams and bigrams, respectively, and ROUGE-SU4 uses bigrams with a maximum skip distance of 4 between bigrams.

With the information given in the evaluation results, we carried out an error analysis on the final summaries that we have submitted. We sum up the main elements which can be improved in the future works. First, noisy texts can be cleaned. We observed that many of the final summaries still contain pages number (see Figure 3) and tables (see Figure 4). Tables contain statistical informations which are not considered as narrative statement.

Figure 3: Noisy text: pages numbers   Figure 4: Noisy texts: tables

Second, some titles predicted as narrative section are false positives. They are often mentioned in sections contents, for example, a narrative section title, *Chairman's statement* can be seen as a part of a sentence like *Chairman's statement on pages 2 and 3*. In both cases, *Chairman's statement* is considered as positive title and its content is extracted as a part of a summary. We also observe that a section title can be seen as narrative in a report and non narrative in other report. This needs taking into account contextual information in building the classifier. The other issue related to narrative titles prediction is seen in some section titles which are too general like *Introduction* and *At a glance*. Those sections are normally narrative sections but rarely give an interesting overview on the financial status and limited to mention general presentation of the firm's activities.

6 Future work

For future works, we plan to improve the TOC extraction algorithm by adding POS (Part-Of-Speech) tagging step before applying rules set to the dataset, this will help to implement new rules which discriminates some unusually used syntactic categories like verbs and modals in the TOC. TOC extraction results are used as the dataset for training our binary classifier of narrative titles, consequently, we expect that the best narrative sections prediction would be improved.

We also believe that giving a weight to some narrative sections titles may help selecting the more relevant summaries. An idea is to use the number of occurrences of each unique narrative title as a weight of its importance.

References

F Barrios, F Lopez, L Argerich, and R Wachenchauzer. 2016. Variations of the Similarity Function of TextRank for Automated Summarization.

J. Cheng and M. Lapata. 2016. Neural summarization by extracting sentences and words. arXiv preprint arXiv:1603.07252.

Mahmoud El-Haj, Ahmed AbuRa'ed, Nikiforos Pittaras, and George Giannakopoulos. 2020. The Financial Narrative Summarisation Shared Task (FNS 2020). In *The 1st Joint Workshop on Financial Narrative Processing and MultiLing Financial Summarisation (FNP-FNS 2020)*, Barcelona, Spain.

Chin-Yew Lin. 2004. ROUGE: A Package for Automatic Evaluation of Summaries. In *Text Summarization Branches Out*, pages 74–81, Barcelona, Spain. Association for Computational Linguistics.

Y Mansar and S Ferradans. 2018. Sentence Classification for Investment Rules Detection. In *Proceedings of the First Workshop on Economics and Natural Language*.

Ramesh Nallapati, Feifei Zhai, and Bowen Zhou. 2016. SummaRuNNer: A Recurrent Neural Network based Sequence Model for Extractive Summarization of Documents. 1611.04230.

Tran CX. Nguyen ML. Nguyen MT., Tran DV. 2017. Summarizing Web Documents Using Sequence Labeling with User-Generated Content and Third-Party Sources.

Horacio Saggion, Thierry Poibeau, J. Piskorski, and R. Yangarber. 2016. Automatic Text Summarization: Past, Present and Future.

Jingqing Zhang, Yao Zhao, Mohammad Saleh, and Peter J. Liu. 2020. PEGASUS: Pre-training with Extracted Gap-sentences for Abstractive Summarization.

SUMSUM@FNS-2020 Shared Task

Siyan Zheng, Anneliese Lu, Claire Cardie
Department of Computer Science, Cornell University, Ithaca, NY 14853
{sz488, yl668}@cornell.edu
cardie@cs.cornell.edu

Abstract

This paper describes the SUMSUM systems submitted to the Financial Narrative Summarization Shared Task (FNS-2020). We explore a section-based extractive summarization method tailored to the structure of financial reports: our best system parses the report Table of Contents (ToC), splits the report into narrative sections based on the ToC, and applies a BERT-based classifier to each section to determine whether it should be included in the summary. Our best system ranks 4th, 1st, 2nd and 17th on the Rouge-1, Rouge-2, Rouge-SU4, and Rouge-L official metrics, respectively. We also report results on the validation set using an alternative set of Rouge-based metrics that measure performance with respect to the best-matching of the available gold summaries.

1 Introduction

The number of financial reports available each year is increasing rapidly. Consequently, exhaustive reading of such documents has become unreasonably laborious. Automatic summarization methods could greatly simplify this task. The Financial Narrative Summarization Shared Task for 2020 (FNS-2020) aims to study the application of automatic summarization methods to annual reports from UK firms listed on The London Stock Exchange (LSE) (El-Haj et al., 2020). These reports, compared to those written by U.S. firms, exhibit a much less rigid structure, which makes summarization a challenging task.

In recent years, recurrent neural networks (RNNs) (e.g. (Nallapati et al., 2016)) and transformer-based neural networks (e.g. BERT (Devlin et al., 2019)) have been widely and successfully employed for extractive summarization in numerous text genres. We had hoped to employ such models for the FNS-2020 shared task. Unfortunately, the length of documents is beyond the models' limits: with an average training document length of 6086 tokens, RNNs and transformers struggle to encode useful hidden representations in an end-to-end fashion. As a result, we hypothesized that some pre-selection over the input text is mandatory to obtain reasonable performance. In particular, we determined (see Section 3) that *most sentences in the gold-standard report summaries come from a single narrative section of the report*. Therefore, we ultimately built our system based on a classification-based extractive summarization approach that uses BERT-based models (Devlin et al., 2019) simply to determine the section(s) to extract as the summary subject to truncation constraints (as described in Section 3).

2 Data Preprocessing

Data Type	Training Set	Validation Set	Testing Set	Total
full reports	3000	363	500	3863
gold summaries	9873	1250	1673	12796

Table 1: Dataset statistics. (El-Haj et al., 2020)

As shown in Table 1, on average there are no fewer than 3 gold-standard summaries provided for each annual report, with some reports containing up to 7 gold-standard summaries (El-Haj et al., 2020). In

Proceedings of the 1st Joint Workshop on Financial Narrative Processing and MultiLing Financial Summarisation, pages 148–152
Barcelona, Spain (Online), December 12, 2020.

addition, summaries in the training set are highly extractive: there is a $>99\%$ unigram overlap between each summary and corresponding report. That is to say, except for an extremely small number of gold summaries, all other summaries are comprised of phrases and sentences of its respective full report — even given the spelling and formatting errors that arise in the PDF to plain text conversion. As a result, our preprocessing of the data is relatively straightforward: other than a few recurring encoding errors, we focused primarily on making sure that sentences remain intact to allow high-quality matching of gold-standard summary sentences to a candidate summary section during training. For example, we remove blank spaces within a sentence; and concatenate lines of the same sentence that might be mistakenly split due to punctuation or lack of punctuation.

3 System Description

Our approach to FNS summarization requires first that we split the document into coherent narrative sections (Section 3.2), which is accomplished by the heuristic parsing of the Table of Contents (ToC) (Section 3.1). We then train neural network models (Section 3.3) to identify which section(s) of a report to extract to comprise the summary.

3.1 Parsing the Table of Contents

Through observation, most ToCs contain titles and page numbers for each listed section of the report. However, some page numbers are left aligned while the others are right aligned. Some ToCs include both the start and the end page numbers for each section; others contain only the start page numbers. Our ToC parser attempts to consider all possible formatting situations with the goal of identifying a title and start page for each section. We clean the data by deleting the end page numbers from all ToCs. Special characters such as dots which are ornaments between page numbers and titles are also deleted. We search for continuous numbers and string combinations only if there exists the same alignment within one ToC, The search starts from the head of a document as we assume ToCs appear in the first few pages. Some exceptions are allowed since a few ToCs have subtitles.

3.2 Split Narrative Section

Because the given data is partially damaged when converted from PDF format to TXT format — even sometimes including the loss of page numbers and section titles — we experimented with both title-based and page-number-based heuristics to split each report into narrative sections according to the TOC. *Title-based search* is the process of scanning the report for titles in the order extracted from the ToC; we assume that these delimit one section from the next. Some spelling error tolerance is employed. If a title is not found, it is temporarily skipped. For *page-based search*, we look for the presence of a single, isolated number associated with the start of each section, and assume that these delimit the sections.

For a given report, we estimate which of the above approaches is more accurately identifying the sections. We consider both the number of sections found and the number of lines on each page. For example, we assume that the number of lines on each page should be similar; that identification of earlier sections from the TOC is important (since sentences extracted for the summary usually appear in the first few sections of the report); and reject the section that has an extreme number of lines to a number of page proportions. We prioritize the title-search method as it returns better results. If some sections cannot be found, we split the number of unassigned lines evenly into those missing sections bounded by neighboring found sections.

3.3 Models

SUMSUM-BASE: the Baseline Model

Our baseline summarization model extracts as the summary the concatenation of the first and second sections (referred as Section 0 and 1) from the full report, truncating extracted text to 1000 tokens.

SUMSUM-BERT

Our BERT-based summarization model is trained to make a binary classification for a given section — INCLUDE or DO NOT INCLUDE it in the summary. To do this, we require a training set that pairs individual sections of a report with a positive (include) or negative (don't include) label depending on whether or not the gold-standard summary is derived from it. Given the existing FNS training data, there are a number of options for doing this, none of which is guaranteed to produce noise-free labels. But examination of the training and validation sets indicated that 2761 out of 3000 (training), and 351 out of 363 (validation) financial reports have more than $\frac{2}{3}$ of their summary sentences originating from the same section. As a result, we employ a sentence-overlap method to identify a single section as the "summary section" section, and label all other sections as negative. Specifically, we regard one sentence as overlapping a report section if most of its words appear in that section. When there are multiple gold-standard summaries for a financial report, we choose the summary with the highest sentence overlap rate as the gold standard. Finally, to prevent extremely unbalanced data, we only consider the first five sections, as the gold-standard summary for 2893 of out 3000 number of financial reports in the training set overlaps with text from the first five sections.

We considered the following BERT-based models:

Model 1: Truncate sections to 512 tokens. Apply BERT to get the embedding for the section input, and add a linear layer to produce a Boolean output[1] .

Model 2: Truncate each sentence to 100 tokens. Apply BERT[1] to obtain sentence embeddings, take the average of all sentence embeddings, and add a linear layer to produce a Boolean output.

Model 3: Apply Hierarchical BERT[2] (Zhang et al., 2019) as above with a maximum of 50 words per sentence and a maximum of 100 sentences.

Model	Precision	Recall	F1
Model 1	0.869	0.869	0.869
Model 2	0.847	0.847	0.847
Model 3	0.855	0.855	0.855

Table 2: Selecting sections using Bert models.

As shown in Table 2, the first model performs best at selecting summary sections (on the validation set). Therefore, SUMSUM-BERT uses sections predicted by Model 1 as the summary, truncating it to 1000 words. If more than one section is selected, their truncated versions are concatenated to produce the summary.

SUMSUM-01: BERT-based Model with Section 0 & 1 as Candidates:

These models use Section 0, Section 1, and both Section 0 & 1 as candidate summary sections for classification. For training, we labeled the one with the highest Rouge-2 F-1 score as the gold summary, and truncate each input to 512 tokens. (For input concatenated from section 0 & 1, we limit each section to 256 tokens.) At test time, we apply BERT with a maximum input length of 512 tokens to determine section(s) selected for summary.

4   Results

For the evaluation, we employed the three systems described above. We show our results using two different evaluation metrics: the *official* metrics, which take the average of the Rouge scores of the produced summary against all available gold summaries; and *alternative* metrics, which use the Rouge scores of the single gold summary that best matches the system-generated summary. The latter is the metric proposed in the FNS-2020 workshop call, and the metric that we optimized for when training the SUMSUM models.

4.1   Official Results: Average

The official results of the SUMSUM systems are given in Table 3. The rows in light gray are the official baselines, provided for comparison. The highest scores among the SUMSUM systems and the given baselines are in bold. We see that SUMSUM-BASE and SUMSUM-BERT perform similarly, and

---

[1]Scripts available at https://github.com/castorini/hedwig/tree/master/models/bert.

[2]Scripts available at https://github.com/castorini/hedwig/tree/master/models/hbert.

Model	Rouge-1			Rouge-2			Rouge-SU4			Rouge-L		
	F	P	R	F	P	R	F	P	R	F	P	R
SUMSUM-BASE	**.462**	.481	**.494**	.294	.259	**.398**	.288	.236	**.442**	.324	.350	.332
SUMSUM-BERT	.460	**.530**	.450	**.306**	**.295**	.365	**.302**	**.268**	.406	.322	**.389**	.304
SUMSUM-01	.442	.511	.447	.286	.277	.358	.282	.253	.398	.313	.375	.304
SUMM-TL-MUSE	.433	.413	.483	.234	.198	.311	.253	.201	.375	**.407**	.370	**.470**
LEXRANK-SUMMARY	.264	.269	.337	.120	.107	.193	.140	.117	.253	.218	.263	.210
TEXTRANK-SUMMARY	.172	.118	.414	.070	.044	.229	.079	.048	.302	.206	.197	.235
SUMM-BL-POLY	.274	.253	.324	.105	.088	.147	.135	.105	.213	.205	.177	.260

Table 3: Official scores: averages scores over all gold summaries corresponding to each annual report.

outperform the official baselines when measured by Rouge-1, Rouge-2 and Rouge-SU4. The official baseline SUMM-TL-MUSE beats the SUMSUM systems when measured by Rouge-L due to its much higher recall.

4.2 Alternative Results: Best Match

Model	Rouge-1			Rouge-2			Rouge-SU4			Rouge-L		
	F	P	R	F	P	R	F	P	R	F	P	R
SUMSUM-BASE	.674	.647	**.823**	.630	.562	**.778**	.635	.599	**.783**	.670	.684	.738
SUMSUM-BERT	**.727**	**.750**	.794	**.681**	**.691**	.748	**.686**	**.699**	.752	**.698**	.704	**.754**
SUMSUM-01	.691	.723	.775	.647	.662	.731	.652	.672	.736	.661	**.735**	.676

Table 4: Alternative metric scores: uses the highest-scoring gold summary corresponding to each annual report. Scores are computed for the FNS-2020 validation set.

Results on the validation set according to the alternative metric are shown in Table 4. With this metric, all scores are substantially higher, and SUMSUM-BERT is the best system among the three models.

5 Discussion of Results

As mentioned above, we relied on the alternative evaluation metric (that takes the highest score among all gold summaries of one financial report) for model selection. And as shown in Table 4, the SUMSUM-BERT system, which uses BERT to select the summary sections from among the first five sections as candidates for the summary, returns the best results under this metric by far. It reaches a 86.9% F1 score in selecting the correct summary section. Occasionally, the system does not return the correct section, but the alternative section chosen still seems to perform well. Presumably, this is the case because there are multiple summaries corresponding to one financial report.

However, when measured according to the official metrics, the results of the BASE and BERT model are quite close to one another (Table 3). We believe this is because the different gold summaries for each report have varying characteristics. Most of the time, there is one gold summary that is primarily constructed of extracted snippets from one section and another summary that is constructed of sentences taken from a few sections. This causes SUMSUM-BERT to outperform the other models when using the alternative metrics that use the gold summary with the highest Rouge score. Finally, almost all gold summaries are comprised of some sentences extracted from the first two sections. This makes the BASE method perform well according to the average-based official metrics.

As described in the Introduction, we initially hoped to employ neural network-based summarization methods directly for the FNS-2020 Shared Task. In particular, we experimented with neural network NLP models such as PreSumm (Liu and Lapata, 2019) and Transformer-XL (Dai et al., 2019), using them to generate summaries given the chosen sections as input (instead of outputting the first 1000 tokens). All, however, led to worse results. Specifically, the models performed poorly on Recall though the Precision scores were close to those of our submitted SUMSUM-BERT systems: the methods failed to select enough sentences compared to the gold summaries. A future direction of work could be improving sentence extraction from sections of different report components.

6 Conclusion

In this paper, we describe the SUMSUM systems for the Financial Narrative Summarisation Shared Task (FNS-2020.) Our best system parses the report Table of Contents (ToC), splits the report into narrative sections based on the ToC, and applies BERT to each section to determine which section(s) to include for the summary. The best system achieves F1 scores of 72.66%, 68.12%, 68.58%, 69.75% with Rouge-1, Rouge-2, Rouge-SU4, and Rouge-L on the validation set using our alternative evaluation metric that the systems were optimized for. The F1 scores are 46.0%, 30.6%, 30.2%, 32.2% according to the official metrics.

Acknowledgments. We thank the reviewers for their comments and suggestions; and thank the organizers for their work to create this Shared Task.

References

Zihang Dai, Zhilin Yang, Yiming Yang, Jaime Carbonell, Quoc Le, and Ruslan Salakhutdinov. 2019. Transformer-XL: Attentive language models beyond a fixed-length context. In *Proceedings of the 57th Annual Meeting of the Association for Computational Linguistics*, pages 2978–2988, Florence, Italy, July. Association for Computational Linguistics.

Jacob Devlin, Ming-Wei Chang, Kenton Lee, and Kristina Toutanova. 2019. BERT: Pre-training of deep bidirectional transformers for language understanding. In *Proceedings of the 2019 Conference of the North American Chapter of the Association for Computational Linguistics: Human Language Technologies, Volume 1 (Long and Short Papers)*, pages 4171–4186, Minneapolis, Minnesota, June. Association for Computational Linguistics.

Mahmoud El-Haj, Ahmed AbuRa'ed, Nikiforos Pittaras, and George Giannakopoulos. 2020. The Financial Narrative Summarisation Shared Task (FNS 2020). In *The 1st Joint Workshop on Financial Narrative Processing and MultiLing Financial Summarisation (FNP-FNS 2020)*, Barcelona, Spain.

Yang Liu and Mirella Lapata. 2019. Text summarization with pretrained encoders. In *Proceedings of the 2019 Conference on Empirical Methods in Natural Language Processing and the 9th International Joint Conference on Natural Language Processing (EMNLP-IJCNLP)*, pages 3730–3740, Hong Kong, China, November. Association for Computational Linguistics.

Ramesh Nallapati, Bowen Zhou, Cicero dos Santos, Çağlar GuÌ‡lçehre, and Bing Xiang. 2016. Abstractive text summarization using sequence-to-sequence RNNs and beyond. In *Proceedings of The 20th SIGNLL Conference on Computational Natural Language Learning*, pages 280–290, Berlin, Germany, August. Association for Computational Linguistics.

Xingxing Zhang, Furu Wei, and Ming Zhou. 2019. HIBERT: Document level pre-training of hierarchical bidirectional transformers for document summarization. In *Proceedings of the 57th Annual Meeting of the Association for Computational Linguistics*, pages 5059–5069, Florence, Italy, July. Association for Computational Linguistics.

Investigating Transfer Learning for Title Detection in Table of Contents Generation

Dhruv Premi, Amogh Badugu and Himanshu Sharad Bhatt
{Dhruv.Premi, Amogh.Badugu, Himanshu.S.Bhatt}@Aexp.com

Abstract

We present a transfer learning approach for Title Detection in FinToC 2020 challenge. Our proposed approach relies on the premise that the geometric layout and character features of the titles and non-titles can be learnt separately from a large corpus, and their learning can then be transferred to a domain-specific dataset. On a domain-specific dataset, we train a Deep Neural Net on the text of the document along with a pre-trained model for geometric and character features. We achieved an F-Score of 83.25 on the test set and secured top rank in the title detection task in FinToC 2020 (Bentabet et al., 2020)

1 Introduction

Title detection and table of contents generation are important sub-parts of the bigger problem, known as, document structure analysis. Understating the inherent document layout and structure benefits several downstream document AI tasks such as search, summarizing, entity extraction and table detection etc. from a document. Humans glance at a document and comprehend the document structure including the titles vs non-titles as well as the overall hierarchy of the titles. Many reasons can be attributed to it, like the sequential nature of the document, geometrical features or the semantic meaning of the sentences. We have tried to incorporate these basic human instincts into our model.

Humans have intuitive notions of how a document is structured and the assumption is confirmed after reading a text block. Transfer learning can be used to model the structural properties of a general document. We use Arxiv documents[1] available in the open-domain to learn the structural model of a general document. Semantic properties are learned using LSTM (Hochreiter and Schmidhuber, 1997) at title level for a domain specific document. The final model is trained on a domain-specific dataset with structural weights pre-trained from Arxiv documents. We see considerable improvements by applying transfer learning to the title detection task. Combining Deep neural networks based on manual features and Character CNN(Zhang et al., 2015) on the starting eight characters helps us model the structural signature of a general document.

2 Related Work

The literature on title detection can be classified broadly into three categories: works that deal with ToC page of documents, works that use images of document pages and works which use the geometrical and textual features of the text blocks.

In the approaches dealing with ToC pages of documents, after the ToC pages are detected, the title entries are extracted and mapped to the pages by finding links between title and corresponding pages. El Haj et al.(2014) used this approach in detecting titles in UK Financial Reports. As they rely on ToC pages, they cannot be applied to documents that do not have ToC pages.

Other approaches use computer vision to fragment the page image into entities such as text, title and table. Yang et al.(2017) used Multimodal Fully Convolutional Neural Networks for this task. Li et

---

[1]https://arxiv.org/help/bulk_data

Proceedings of the 1st Joint Workshop on Financial Narrative Processing and MultiLing Financial Summarisation, pages 153–157
Barcelona, Spain (Online), December 12, 2020.

al.(2020b) used Convolutional neural networks combined with graphical models to identify the entities in a document page. Few datasets for these tasks are publicly available.(Zhong et al., 2019; Li et al., 2020a)

Finally, some approaches use learning or rule-based methods to detect headers based on textual and geometrical features(Bentabet et al., 2019; Gopinath et al., 2018; Liu et al., 2011; Budhiraja and Mago, 2018; Klampfl and Kern, 2013). These methods are usually used in digitally generated documents like webpages and native PDF documents.

3 Methodology

We pre-process the PDF files by converting them to XML documents by Poppler[2] library. These files are then parsed to merge elements similar in styling and located in close proximity. Headers and Footers are identified and removed by page association (Lin, 2003) as they would hinder the process of title detection.

Our proposed title detection method has three components; Pre-trained neural network to model general structural information, Sequential Network to learn domain-specific text and training of both the networks combined.

3.1 Pre-trained Neural Network to Model Structural Information on Arxiv Documents

The network composes of two key components geometrical and a character network.

3.1.1 Geometrical Network

The network comprises 22 manual features as depicted in Table 1. Model is trained by multi-layer neural network as described by the architecture in Table 2.

Alignment	Distance
-Center Alignment with parent text block	-Normalized vertical distance to the Child text Block
-Left Alignment with parent text block	-Normalized vertical distance to the Parent text Block
-Right Alignment with parent text block	
-Center Alignment with child text block	
-Left Alignment with child text block	
-Right Alignment with child text block	
Font	**Extra**
-Font Difference between current and child	-Number of New Lines
-Font Difference between current and parent	-Number of Poppler blocks
-Font Size	-Number of words
-All first word in caps	-Majority of the characters in the start are in Bold
-Is Bold	-Has Verb
-Is Italic	
-Number of Fonts	
-Font Change	
-Begins with numbering	

Table 1: Features for Geometric Model

3.1.2 Character Network

Input to the Character CNN is the first eight characters. The aim is to extract patterns that denote start of a title like 1.1, a.1, (a). Architecture is mentioned in Table 3. The trained module did not achieve as high F Score as expected. However, our focus was to capture patterns for a general document. Network benefits can be utilized in steps further.

---

[2]https://poppler.freedesktop.org/

Hyper-parameters	Value (After Validation)
Input Layer	22
First Hidden Layer	15
Second Hidden Layer	4
Epochs	10
Batch Size	100
Dropout (Between 1st and 2nd Layer)	0.2
Activation	ReLU
Loss Function	binary cross entropy
optimizer	Adam*

Table 2: Hyper Parameters for Geometrical Model

Hyper-parameters	Value (After Validation)
Vocabulary length	71
sequence of characters length	8
convolutions (number of kernels, kernel size, pool size)	[256, 3, 2] , [256, 2, 2]
Dense 1	50
Dense 2	10
Loss Function	binary cross entropy
Dropout (Between 1st and 2nd Dense)	0.5
Activation	ReLU
optimizer	Adam

Table 3: Hyper Parameters for Character Model

3.1.3 Dataset and Training

We take around 6000 Arxiv documents from the annotated documents provided by Muhammad Mahbubur Rahman and Tim Finin (2017). The data split is shown in Table 4. The training was done for three models, namely, geometric, character and character plus geometric. Character plus geometric model performed the best as expected. Intuition being features from geometric and character will complement each other when trained together. We got a significant rise of 5% as compared to the geometric model. Training metrics are depicted in Table 6.

	Train		Validate		Test	
	Title	**Non-Title**	**Title**	**Non-Title**	**Title**	**Non-Title**
Arxiv	59656	536910	3314	29828	3314	29828
FinToC	6666	64719	952	12341	694	6609

Table 4: Train,Test and Validate sizes for Arxiv and FinToC datasets

3.2 Sequence network to learn domain-dependent semantics

We use LSTM as a sequence classification model. Intuition being common phrases that are part of financial titles can be learnt by a sequence network such as LSTM. We use Glove word vector embedding. Last word cell state is passed as input to two dense layers. Final layer after the dense layer performs title detection Table 5. Out Best F Score on the test dataset was at 73.

3.2.1 Dataset and Training

The architecture is mentioned in Table 5. Dataset Split can be seen in Table 4. Our best performing model on validation set gave 73% F-Score on test set. Due to time constraints, we could not explore bidirectional and attention mechanisms (Abi Akl et al., 2019) .

Hyper-parameters	Value (After Validation)
Embedding Size	300
Number of words (From Start)	12
cell state size	13
Dense 1	10
Dense 2	5
optimizer	Adam
Epochs	30
Batch Size	500

Table 5: Hyper Parameters of Sequential Model

3.3 Joint Trained combination of both of the above networks

Full network comprises of pre-trained weights from Character plus Geometric Model trained on Arxiv PDF and Sequence Model trained on FinToC dataset. Last dense layer from Sequence Model and Character Plus Geometric Model are concatenated. One more and last dense Layer of 10 units is added after that. Loss function is binary cross entropy. Total trainable parameters are $2, 26, 335$. No layers is freezed for subsequent training.

3.3.1 Dataset and Training

FinToC Dataset as mentioned in Table 4 was used. Adam optimizer, epochs equal to 30 and batch size of 500 were used as hyperparameters in the model. The code was written in Tensorflow v1.15 (Abadi et al., 2015) Jointly trained final architecture got the F-Score of 83.25 on the test set.

		Fscore (Test)	
Models		**Arxiv**	**FinToC**
Geometric		87.38	-
CharCNN		58.56	-
Geometric+CharCNN		91.5	-
XGBoost		-	73.01
LSTM		-	73.02
Joint Trained LSTM and Geometric+CharCNN		-	83.25

Table 6: F-Scores of models on Arxiv and FinToC datasets

4 Results & Conclusion

4.1 Investigations

Final results are shown in Table 6. Two highlights of the final model are

- Pre-trained weights captured the generic structure of documents, giving a boost to accuracy. This transfer learning approach can be improved further by using better architectures and features which are domain-independent.This procedure achieved a 10% increase in F Score.

- Combination of geometric and character-based features complemented each other to attain higher accuracy compared to either of them separately.

4.2 Submitted system

We submitted two systems for the final evaluation.

- First one is the Joint Trained LSTM and Geometric+CharCNN network.

- Second one was the ensemble of the first one and an XGBoost(Chen and Guestrin, 2016) model as shown in Table 6.

References

Martín Abadi, Ashish Agarwal, Paul Barham, Eugene Brevdo, Zhifeng Chen, Craig Citro, Greg S. Corrado, Andy Davis, Jeffrey Dean, Matthieu Devin, Sanjay Ghemawat, Ian Goodfellow, Andrew Harp, Geoffrey Irving, Michael Isard, Yangqing Jia, Rafal Jozefowicz, Lukasz Kaiser, Manjunath Kudlur, Josh Levenberg, Dandelion Mané, Rajat Monga, Sherry Moore, Derek Murray, Chris Olah, Mike Schuster, Jonathon Shlens, Benoit Steiner, Ilya Sutskever, Kunal Talwar, Paul Tucker, Vincent Vanhoucke, Vijay Vasudevan, Fernanda Viégas, Oriol Vinyals, Pete Warden, Martin Wattenberg, Martin Wicke, Yuan Yu, and Xiaoqiang Zheng. 2015. TensorFlow: Large-scale machine learning on heterogeneous systems. Software available from tensorflow.org.

Hanna Abi Akl, Anubhav Gupta, and Dominique Mariko. 2019. Fintoc-2019 shared task: Finding title in text blocks. In *Proceedings of the Second Financial Narrative Processing Workshop (FNP 2019)*, pages 58–62.

Najah-Imane Bentabet, Rémi Juge, and Sira Ferradans. 2019. Table-of-contents generation on contemporary documents. *arXiv preprint arXiv:1911.08836*.

Najah-Imane Bentabet, Rémi Juge, Ismail El Maarouf, Virginie Mouilleron, Dialekti Valsamou-Stanislawski, and Mahmoud El-Haj. 2020. The Financial Document Structure Extraction Shared task (FinToc 2020). In *The 1st Joint Workshop on Financial Narrative Processing and MultiLing Financial Summarisation (FNP-FNS 2020, Barcelona, Spain*.

Sahib Singh Budhiraja and Vijay Mago. 2018. A supervised learning approach for heading detection. *Expert Systems*, page e12520.

Tianqi Chen and Carlos Guestrin. 2016. Xgboost: A scalable tree boosting system. In *Proceedings of the 22nd acm sigkdd international conference on knowledge discovery and data mining*, pages 785–794.

Mahmoud El-Haj, Paul Rayson, Steven Young, and Martin Walker. 2014. Detecting document structure in a very large corpus of uk financial reports.

Abhijith Athreya Mysore Gopinath, Shomir Wilson, and Norman Sadeh. 2018. Supervised and unsupervised methods for robust separation of section titles and prose text in web documents. In *Proceedings of the 2018 Conference on Empirical Methods in Natural Language Processing*, pages 850–855.

Sepp Hochreiter and Jürgen Schmidhuber. 1997. Long short-term memory. *Neural computation*, 9(8):1735–1780.

Stefan Klampfl and Roman Kern. 2013. An unsupervised machine learning approach to body text and table of contents extraction from digital scientific articles. In *International Conference on Theory and Practice of Digital Libraries*, pages 144–155. Springer.

Minghao Li, Yiheng Xu, Lei Cui, Shaohan Huang, Furu Wei, Zhoujun Li, and Ming Zhou. 2020a. Docbank: A benchmark dataset for document layout analysis. *arXiv preprint arXiv:2006.01038*.

Xiao-Hui Li, Fei Yin, and Cheng-Lin Liu. 2020b. Page segmentation using convolutional neural network and graphical model. In *International Workshop on Document Analysis Systems*, pages 231–245. Springer.

Xiaofan Lin. 2003. Header and footer extraction by page association. In *Document Recognition and Retrieval X*, volume 5010, pages 164–171. International Society for Optics and Photonics.

Caihua Liu, Jiajun Chen, Xiaofeng Zhang, Jie Liu, and Yalou Huang. 2011. Toc structure extraction from ocr-ed books. In *International Workshop of the Initiative for the Evaluation of XML Retrieval*, pages 98–108. Springer.

Muhammad Mahbubur Rahman and Tim Finin. 2017. Understanding the logical and semantic structure of large documents. *CoRR*, abs/1709.00770.

Xiao Yang, Ersin Yumer, Paul Asente, Mike Kraley, Daniel Kifer, and C Lee Giles. 2017. Learning to extract semantic structure from documents using multimodal fully convolutional neural networks. In *Proceedings of the IEEE Conference on Computer Vision and Pattern Recognition*, pages 5315–5324.

Xiang Zhang, Junbo Zhao, and Yann LeCun. 2015. Character-level convolutional networks for text classification. In *Advances in neural information processing systems*, pages 649–657.

Xu Zhong, Jianbin Tang, and Antonio Jimeno Yepes. 2019. Publaynet: largest dataset ever for document layout analysis. In *2019 International Conference on Document Analysis and Recognition (ICDAR)*, pages 1015–1022. IEEE.

UWB@FinTOC-2020 Shared Task: Financial Document Title Detection

Tomáš Hercig
NTIS – New Technologies
for the Information Society,
Faculty of Applied Sciences,
University of West Bohemia,
Technická 8, 306 14 Plzeň
Czech Republic
tigi@kiv.zcu.cz

Pavel Král
Department of Computer
Science and Engineering,
Faculty of Applied Sciences
University of West Bohemia,
Univerzitní 8, 306 14 Plzeň
Czech Republic
pkral@kiv.zcu.cz

Abstract

This paper describes our system created for the Financial Document Structure Extraction Shared Task (FinTOC-2020): Title Detection. We rely on the Apache PDFBox library to extract text and all additional information e.g. font type and font size from the financial prospectuses. Our constrained system uses only the provided training data without any additional external resources. Our system is based on the Maximum Entropy classifier and various features including font type and font size. Our system achieves F1 score 81% and #1 place in the French track and F1 score 77% and #2 place among 5 participating teams in the English track.

1 Introduction

Financial documents are used to report activities, financial situation, investment plans, and operational information to shareholders, investors, and financial markets. These reports are usually created on an annual basis in machine-readable formats often only with minimal structure information. The majority of these prospectuses are published without a table of content (TOC), which is usually needed to help readers navigate within the document.

The goal of the First Financial Document Structure Extraction Shared Task (FinTOC-2019) (Juge et al., 2019) was to analyse the financial prospectuses and automatically extract their structure similarly to Doucet et al. (2013). The Second Financial Document Structure Extraction Shared Task (FinTOC-2020) (Bentabet et al., 2020) adds French documents and greatly simplifies the data formats at the cost of not providing any text representation of the PDF files.

2 Task

The goal of FinTOC-2020 shared task is to extract the table of content from the financial prospectuses. Systems participating in this shared task were given a sample collection of financial prospectuses with different levels of structure and different lengths as training data. Data statistics for the title detection subtask are shown in Table 1.

The shared task can be divided into two steps: **1) Title detection** classifies given text blocks as titles or non-titles. **2) TOC generation** organizes provided headers into a hierarchical table of content.

We participated only in the Title detection subtask for both languages. For additional information (e.g. about TOC generation subtask) see the task description paper (Bentabet et al., 2020).

Label	French	English
Non-title	65.8k (90.8%)	186.3k (94.9%)
Title	6.6k (9.2%)	10.1k (5.1%)
PDF	47	52

Table 1: Data statistics for Title detection.

Proceedings of the 1st Joint Workshop on Financial Narrative Processing and MultiLing Financial Summarisation, pages 158–162
Barcelona, Spain (Online), December 12, 2020.

We approached the title detection subtask as a binary classification task. For all experiments, we use Maximum Entropy classifier with default settings from Brainy machine learning library (Konkol, 2014).

3   Dataset

The provided training collection of documents contains the original documents in **PDF** format and annotations **JSON** file with gold labels. The JSON file consists of an array of TOC items representing each title with the following properties: **text** - text of the title, **id** - order of occurrence the title, **depth** - depth level of the title, and **page** - page of title occurrence.

In Table 1 we can see that title distribution among French and English data differs greatly, however, we don't know if the reason for this is that the documents have a different structure or a different approach to annotation was used.

4   Extraction

We decided to use the Apache PDFBox `https://pdfbox.apache.org/` version 2.0.20 to extract text and other metadata from the PDF files and then we use our own algorithm to link the annotations to the extracted text representation.

We consider each line of text a separate text segment and classify each segment as title or non-title. If there is a change in the font size or type we split the text into two lines. Additional metadata are extracted from the first occurring word of the given line. The metadata include the following features: Is_bold, Is_italic, Is_all_caps, Begins_with_cap, Begins_with_numbering, Left_position, Font_size, and Font_type. Note that some of these features were difficult to extract as there are more ways to create e.g. bold text in PDF format and the library does not provide a convenient interface to access e.g. vector elements.

5   Issues

The first shared task (FinTOC-2019) had some issues with the mapping of the XML text representation to the annotated CSV gold labels representation as reported by (Hercig and Král, 2019).

The second shared task (FinTOC-2020) removed the XML text representation and simplified the gold labels representation to JSON format, however, some of the problems still remained.

We did not get any annotation guidelines or explanation of some labels. It seems that the annotation process was incoherent - leaving us with different levels of depth and various parts of the title included or left out depending probably on the annotator of the current file or title.

We wrote an algorithm that tries to find the best mapping on a given page assuming the annotated text from the JSON training file appears in the same order of occurrence as the text extracted from the PDF file. Unfortunately, that is not always true, thus we decided to modify the training JSON files and fix the issues, described in the following sections, which caused our algorithm to fail. We manually fixed only the necessary part of the dataset in order for our algorithm to work.

5.1   Wrong Parameter

When we found a typo in the **id** or the **page** parameters in the JSON file we corrected the value according to the original PDF.

5.2   Missing Text Beginning

In some cases, the beginning of annotated text from the JSON file was missing. We fixed the occurrences our algorithm discovered. See the example below.

```
original:SUBSCRIPTIONS ...
fixed:(5) SUBSCRIPTIONS ...
```

5.3   Wrong Text Transcription

The JSON file contained wrong text transcription (e.g. additional spaces) that caused our mapping algorithm to fail on the given page because no match for the text was found. We corrected the text according to the original PDF.

6 Features

We tried to create the best feature set using all the extracted meta-information. The following features proved useful and were used in our submissions.

- **Character n-grams (ChN$_n$):** Separate feature for each n-gram representing the n-gram presence in the text. We do it separately for different orders $n \in \{1, 2\}$ and remove n-gram with frequency $f \leq 2$.

- **Binary Features (B):** We use separate binary feature for the following text characteristics (Is_bold, Is_italic, Is_all_caps, Begins_with_cap, Begins_with_numbering, Is_next_line_empty, Is_prev_line_empty).

- **Position Features (P):** We use four separate binary features to represent the difference in the left position of the text for two sentences. The positions can be equal, lower, greater, and missing. We compare sentence at position p with sentence at position $p - 2$, $p - 1$, and $p + 1$.

- **First Orto-characters (FO):** Bag of first three orthographic[1] characters with at least 2 occurrences.

- **Last Orto-characters (LO):** Bag of last three orthographic[1] characters with at least 2 occurrences.

- **Font Size (FS):** We map the font size of text into a one-hot vector with length twelve and use this vector as features for the classifier. The frequency belongs to one of twelve equal-frequency bins[2]. Each bin corresponds to a position in the vector. We remove font sizes with frequency ≤ 2.

- **Font Size Diff (FSD):** We use four separate binary features to represent the difference in font size (FS) of the text for two sentences. The positions can be equal, lower, greater, and missing. We compare sentence at position p with sentence at position $p - 1$ and $p + 1$.

- **Font Type Diff (FTD):** We use three separate binary features to represent the difference in font type for two sentences. The font type can be equal, different, and missing. We compare sentence at position p with sentence at position $p - 1$ and $p + 1$.

- **Font Type Unigrams (FTU):** We tokenize font type name and use the presence of unigrams as a feature we remove unigrams with frequency $f \leq 1000$.

7 Results

The results in Table 4 show our ranking in the FinTOC-2020 shared task using the original test dataset. Our submissions and the fixed train datasets for both English and French are available for research purposes at `https://gitlab.com/tigi.cz/fintoc-2020`.

We performed ablation experiments to illustrate which features are the most beneficial (see Table 3). Numbers represent the performance change when the given feature is removed (i.e. lower number means better feature). We used approximately 30% of the fixed training dataset[3] for evaluation *(test)* and we used the rest of the dataset for training the features (see Table 2). We also repeated the experiment using *leave-one-out* cross-validation as the previous experiment seemed inaccurate. Our evaluation measure is macro-averaged F1-score.

We can see that the experiments are inconclusive as some of the findings are in contradiction. The most helpful features in terms of *leave-one-out* cross-validation apart from character bi-grams include both first and last orto-characters and font type unigrams. Last orto-characters, *FSD* and *FTD* were always beneficial. On the contrary position features and font size features were the least helpful features.

We believe that the reason that binary features were not very successful (except in French *test* setting) is that the extraction of these features was not accurate as mentioned in Section 4.

---

[1] All lower cased letters were replaced by "a", upper cased letters by "A" and digits by "1" (e.g. `"Char3"` = `"Aaaa1"`).

[2] The frequencies from the training data are split into twelve equal-size bins according to corresponding quantile.

[3] We used all annotations for ten and twelve JSON files for French and English respectively.

Language	French		English	
Label	Test*	Train*	Test*	Train*
Non-title	21.0k (31.9%)	44.8k (68.1%)	57.2k (30.7%)	129.0k (69.3%)
Title	1.7k (25.5%)	5.0k (74.5%)	3.4k (33.6%)	6.7k (66.4%)
Sum	22.7k (31.3%)	49.8k (68.7%)	60.6k (30.9%)	135.7k (69.1%)
PDF	10 (21.3%)	37 (78.7%)	12 (23.1%)	40 (76.9%)

Table 2: Dataset split for experiments.

Detailed statistical analysis into the datasets and gold labels for the test set would be needed in order to infer further, more accurate, insides.

Feature	F1-*test*	F1-*leave-one-out*
ALL*	89.15%	96.19%
ChN_1	-1.11%	-0.08%
ChN_2	0.54%	-3.54%
B	-1.67%	0.00%
P	-0.19%	0.02%
FO	-1.18%	-1.18%
LO	-1.50%	-0.90%
FS	0.14%	-0.24%
FSD	-0.61%	-0.11%
FTD	-0.64%	-0.24%
FTU	1.03%	-0.47%

* Using all features in the ablation study.

(a) French

Feature	F1-*test*	F1-*leave-one-out*
ALL*	87.74%	95.88%
ChN_1	0.70%	-0.09%
ChN_2	0.69%	-2.59%
B	1.51%	0.00%
P	0.38%	0.06%
FO	0.84%	-0.67%
LO	-0.78%	-0.97%
FS	1.68%	0.00%
FSD	-1.11%	-0.19%
FTD	-0.60%	-0.03%
FTU	-3.29%	-0.60%

* Using all features in the ablation study.

(b) English

Table 3: Feature ablation study.

Team	Submission	F1
UWB	1	81%
taxy.io	1	69%
Daniel	1	66%
DNLP	1	64%
Daniel	2	64%
Daniel	3	64%

(a) French

Team	Submission	F1
Amex	1	79%
Amex	2	79%
UWB	1	77%
Daniel	1	69%
Daniel	3	63%
Daniel	2	62%
DNLP	1	59%
taxy.io	1	55%

(b) English

Table 4: Results for Title detection.

8 Conclusion

In this paper, we described our UWB system participating in the FinTOC 2020 shared task.

Our best results have been achieved by the Maximum Entropy classifier combining available metadata, such as font type and font size, by careful feature engineering. Our system is ranked #1 in the French track and #2 among 5 participating teams in the English track.

Acknowledgements

This work has been partly supported by Cross-border Cooperation Program Czech Republic - Free State of Bavaria ETS Objective 2014-2020 (project no. 211).

References

Najah-Imane Bentabet, Rémi Juge, Ismail El Maarouf, Virginie Mouilleron, Dialekti Valsamou-Stanislawski, and Mahmoud El-Haj. 2020. The Financial Document Structure Extraction Shared task (FinToc 2020). In *The 1st Joint Workshop on Financial Narrative Processing and MultiLing Financial Summarisation (FNP-FNS 2020*, Barcelona, Spain.

A. Doucet, G. Kazai, S. Colutto, and G. Mhlberger. 2013. ICDAR 2013 Competition on Book Structure Extraction. In *2013 12th International Conference on Document Analysis and Recognition*, pages 1438–1443, Aug.

Tomáš Hercig and Pavel Král. 2019. UWB@FinTOC-2019 shared task: Financial document title detection. In *Proceedings of the Second Financial Narrative Processing Workshop (FNP 2019)*, pages 74–78, Turku, Finland, September. Linköping University Electronic Press.

Rémi Juge, Najah-Imane Bentabet, and Sira Ferradans. 2019. The FinTOC-2019 Shared Task: Financial Document Structure Extraction. In *The Second Workshop on Financial Narrative Processing of NoDalida 2019*.

Michal Konkol. 2014. Brainy: A Machine Learning Library. In Leszek Rutkowski, Marcin Korytkowski, Rafal Scherer, Ryszard Tadeusiewicz, Lotfi Zadeh, and Jacek Zurada, editors, *Artificial Intelligence and Soft Computing*, volume 8468 of *Lecture Notes in Computer Science*, pages 490–499. Springer International Publishing.

Taxy.io@FinTOC-2020: Multilingual Document Structure Extraction using Transfer Learning

Frederic Haase
Taxy.io GmbH
Aachen, Germany
`haase@taxy.io`

Steffen Kirchhoff
Taxy.io GmbH
Aachen, Germany
`kirchhoff@taxy.io`

Abstract

In this paper we describe our system submitted to the FinTOC-2020 shared task on financial document structure extraction. We propose a two-step approach to identify titles in financial documents and to extract their table of contents (TOC). First, we identify text blocks as candidates for titles using unsupervised learning based on character-level information of each document. Then, we apply supervised learning on a self-constructed regression task to predict the depth of each text block in the document structure hierarchy using transfer learning combined with document features and layout features. It is noteworthy that our single multilingual model performs well on both tasks and on different languages, which indicates the usefulness of transfer learning for title detection and TOC generation. Moreover, our approach is independent of the presence of actual TOC pages in the documents. It is also one of the few submissions to the FinTOC-2020 shared task addressing both subtasks in both languages, English and French, with one single model.

1 Introduction

While large amounts of documents are created and published in machine-readable file formats such as PDF, only a small fraction come with structural information, e.g. on their table of contents (TOC). This is especially true in the financial domain where a table of contents, e.g. for annual reports or shareholder reports, would be particularly helpful. Even though it is often regulated which content these documents must include (Juge et al., 2019), an automated analysis of their structure remains difficult for several reasons. One is that financial documents usually come with a complicated layout consisting of text blocks, tables and figures of various kinds. Also, such documents typically come with a highly nested hierarchy of subsections. Additionally, most of these documents are published as PDF, which is the defacto standard for the creation of electronic documents, even though this file format comes with several inherent drawbacks (Hu and Liu, 2014). PDF files contain little structural information about the contents, such as words, lines or paragraphs, which would be helpful for automatic structure analysis. Moreover, there exist various different ways to generate a PDF, which further complicates the automatic analysis of the structure of such documents, especially in multicolumn settings.

Despite the importance and diverse use cases of automatic structure analysis of documents, there is only a small research stream focusing on this topic. The FinTOC-2020 shared task about Financial Document Structure Extraction (Bentabet et al., 2020) promotes research in this field by proposing two language tracks for English and French together with a benchmark data set of financial documents. The goal of the shared task is to design systems that solve the following two subtasks:

- Title detection: Given a document, extract text blocks and identify which ones are titles.
- Table of contents (TOC) generation: Given a document, identify titles and their nesting depths.

In this paper we describe our solution to the shared task, a multilingual approach based on transfer learning that jointly solves both problems title detection and TOC generation for both languages.

Proceedings of the 1st Joint Workshop on Financial Narrative Processing and MultiLing Financial Summarisation, pages 163–168
Barcelona, Spain (Online), December 12, 2020.

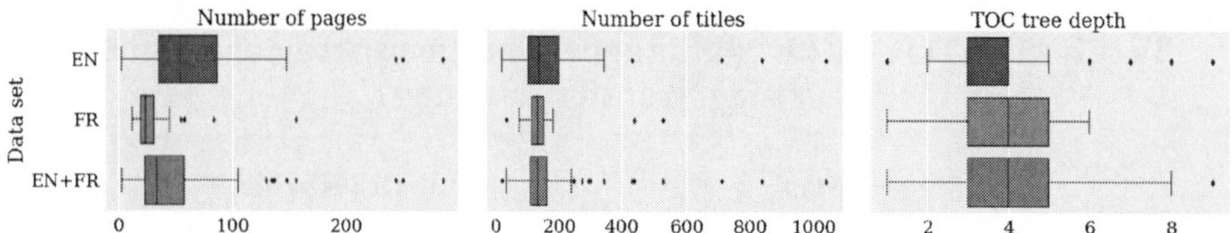

Figure 1: The financial documents of the FinTOC-2020 shared task vary greatly with respect to their number of pages, number of titles and the depth of their TOC tree. On the entire set across both languages, the number of pages ranges from 3 to 285, the number of titles ranges from 20 to 1039 and the TOC tree depth from 1 to 9.

The paper is organized as follows. We first review previous work in Section 2 and describe the data that was provided for the FinTOC-2020 shared task in Section 3. We then present our system in Section 4 before we report and discuss our results in Section 5. The paper ends with a conclusion in Section 6.

2   Previous Work

The first approaches to TOC generation are based on physical layout analysis, e.g. (Conway, 1993). Here, physical entities of a document, such as pages, paragraphs, and figures are extracted and mapped onto a hierarchy of logical entities such as titles, authors and sections from which the TOC is then derived. These approaches are often based on heuristic rules and grammars (Mao et al., 2003). As these predefined rules are mostly domain-specific, these approaches fail to generalize to a diverse set of documents from different domains (Najah-Imane et al., 2019).

Other approaches explicitly parse the title hierarchy from embedded TOC pages (Dresevic et al., 2009; Nguyen et al., 2017). While these approaches generalize across different domains, they fail on documents without TOC pages or whenever the TOC page does not reflect the entire document structure, e.g. in cases of deeply nested subtitles not mentioned on the TOC page (Giguet and Lejeune, 2019).

Yet another set of approaches leverage learning-based methods to predict the TOC, e.g. based on both layout and text features of the document. In (Najah-Imane et al., 2019), for example, titles are first detected using a convolutional neural network (CNN) (Kim, 2014); then the corresponding depth of each title is predicted using a combination of a bidirectional long short term memory (BiLSTM) network and a conditional random field (CRF) model, as suggested by (Huang et al., 2015) for sequence tagging.

The approaches from the FinTOC-2019 challenge (Juge et al., 2019) mostly fall into the latter two categories: explicit TOC parsing and learning-based methods.

3   Data

The training data of the FinTOC-2020 shared task consists of 52 English and 47 French financial PDF documents. Every document page comes along with a set of annotations, which include both the text and the depth for each title. The box plots in Figure 1 show the heterogeneity of the financial documents from this data set. In the median, a financial document from this data set has 34 pages, 132 titles and a TOC tree depth of 4. However, the number of pages ranges from 3 to 285, so some documents are very small while others are rather large. Also, the number of titles varies from 20 to 1039 across the different documents. While some TOC trees are flat with a depth of only 1, some are very nested with a depth of 9. This heterogeneity of the financial documents in the data set underlines their complex layout and hence the difficulty of the task to detect titles and extract the TOC.

4   System

Our system works directly on the entire content of a document and is trained for both English and French documents jointly. We apply a two-step approach, where we first detect candidate text blocks and predict their TOC depth in a subsequent step as a regression task. The system is described in Figure 2.

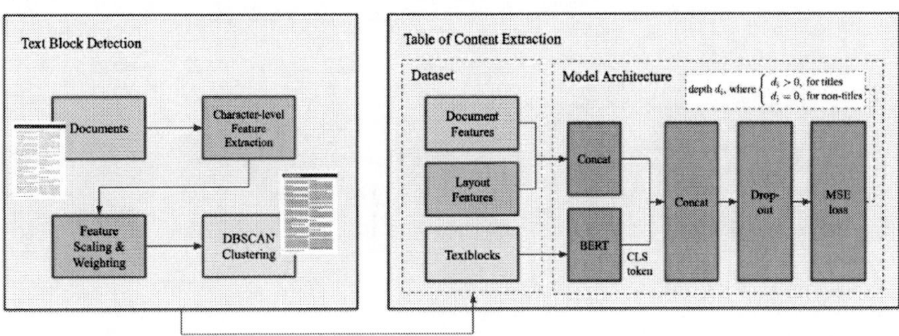

Figure 2: Text blocks are detected (left side) by extracting, scaling and weighting character-level features on which a DBSCAN clustering is applied. For TOC generation (right side), document features, layout features and text blocks are combined to train a neural network to predict the depth of each text block.

4.1 Text Block Detection

Previous work on text block detection applies spatial layout processing in combination with a defined set of rules, e.g. (Ramakrishnan et al., 2012). Other works leverage learning-based approaches, e.g. the work of (Klampfl et al., 2014), where text blocks are detected using the unsupervised learning approach of hierarchical agglomerative clustering (HAC). Their clustering mechanism joins characters into groups that represent words, and groups of words into contiguous blocks of text.

Similarly, we apply DBSCAN clustering (Ester et al., 1996) and combine layout features (character coordinates) as well as font features (font size, font color and font type). We find DBSCAN clustering to outperform HAC on this given data set. For each character on a page of a document, we extract the bounding box coordinates and label-encode font color, font size and font type. After extraction, these features are scaled using min-max normalization. Then, we apply the DBSCAN clustering with Minkowski distance of order 1 on the character-level data set per page.

To find appropriate hyperparameters for the DBSCAN clustering and appropriate scaling weights for our layout features and font features, we use Bayesian optimization as suggested in (Snoek et al., 2012). As objective we maximize the amount of titles that can be mapped correctly to the training data annotations. To map candidate titles to ground truth titles we use the same customized Levenshtein distance from the evaluation metric of the FinTOC-2020 shared task (Bentabet et al., 2020). While we optimize the Eps hyperparameter of DBSCAN, we fix the $MinPts$ parameter to 1. This hyperparameter optimization process has revealed the following: The vertical position, font type, font color and font size are important features when applying clustering on character-level. After optimization, our approach was able to extract text blocks that could be matched to 95.7% of the titles from the training data annotations.

4.2 Table of Contents Extraction

To estimate the depth of the text blocks extracted in the previous step, we construct a data set that can be used for supervised learning. For each text block t_i that can be mapped to a ground truth title, we set its label to the ground truth depth d_i. We assume that text blocks that cannot be mapped to a ground truth title to be in fact not a title. For such text blocks we define their TOC depth to be $d_i = 0$. That is, we treat depth 0 as a placeholder for everything that is not a title. This notation allows to train one model that can be applied to both the title detection subtask and the TOC generation subtask. Now, we have an annotated set of text blocks together with their depth in the TOC tree. We aim to train a model that we can use to predict the TOC tree depth of a given text block. For every text block we compute the following features: First, we represent a text block by the features used for the DBSCAN clustering as described in section 4.1. Then, we add layout features to describe the majority font color, font size and font type of all characters in the text block. To also capture information that puts the text block in relation to the document, we further compute the following features: `is_most_frequent_font`, `is_most_frequent_color` and `is_most_frequent_size`. Additionally, we add document features to the data set, comprising min, max and mean font size of the entire document.

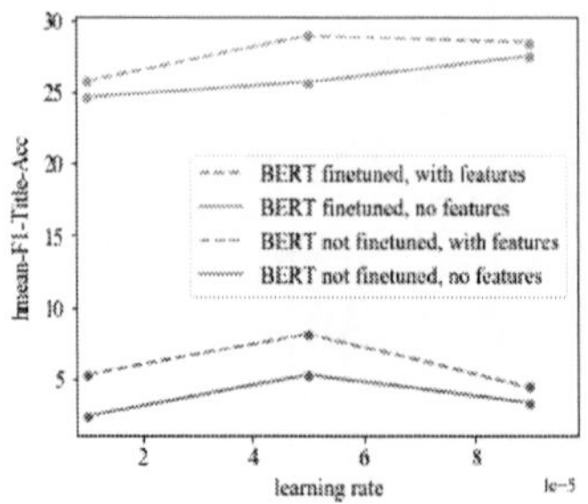

| Title detection task | | | | TOC generation task | | | |
| FR | | EN | | FR | | EN | |
Team	F1	Team	F1	Team	hmean-F1-Title-Acc	Team	hmean-F1-Title-Acc
UWB	0.81	Amex 1	0.79	DNLP	0.37	DNLP	0.34
Taxy.io	0.69	Amex 2	0.79	Taxy.io	0.32	Daniel 3	0.28
Daniel 1	0.66	UWB	0.77	Daniel 1	0.22	Daniel 2	0.28
DNLP	0.64	Daniel 1	0.69	Daniel 2	0.22	Daniel 1	0.26
Daniel 2	0.64	Daniel 3	0.63	Daniel 3	0.20	Taxy.io	0.24
Daniel 3	0.64	Daniel 2	0.62			Amex 1	0.23
		DNLP	0.59			Amex 2	0.23
		Taxy.io	0.55				

Figure 3: In our experiments we observed a positive impact of both fine-tuning the pretrained layers of the BERT model (orange vs blue lines) and of additionally incorporating document and layout features (dashed vs solid lines).

Table 1: In comparison to the other approaches submitted to the shared task, our approach ranks 2nd on the title detection task and 2nd on the TOC generation task for French, while we rank 8th and 5th on the respective tasks for English.

Using this data set, we train a model that combines the text blocks with the document features and the layout features to predict the depth d_i. To encode the text block t_i, we use the pre-trained multilingual cased BERT-Base model[1] (Devlin et al., 2019). The classification token (CLS) output of BERT, which serves as aggregate sequence representation, is concatenated with the document and layout features and put through a dropout layer. The training objective of the model is to optimize the mean squared error (MSE) loss to predict the depth of each text block according to our data set as a regression task.

5   Results and Discussion

In our experiments, we optimized our model for different hyperparameters using a 20% dev set and the evaluation metric from the FinTOC-2020 shared task (Bentabet et al., 2020). More specifically, we evaluated 1) the impact of fine-tuning the pretrained layers of the BERT model, 2) the impact of additionally incorporating document and layout features, and 3) the impact of different learning rates. Figure 3 shows a positive impact of both fine-tuning the pretrained layers of the BERT model (orange vs blue lines) and of additionally incorporating document and layout features (dashed vs solid lines). The inverted U-shape of the curve indicates that 5e-5 is a good choice for the learning rate. Across all experiments we trained our models for 2 epochs using a fixed 0.25 dropout ratio in the dropout layer. We trained the model 3 times with different seeds and averaged the outcomes for the final depth prediction, which we rounded to get an integer depth. We discarded text blocks with depth 0 to only submit titles.

Table 1 shows the final results on the test set in comparison to the other approaches that were submitted to the challenge. Our approach ranks 2nd on the title detection task and 2nd on the TOC generation task for French, while we rank 8th and 5th on the respective tasks for English. It is noteworthy that our single multilingual model performs well on both tasks and on both languages, which indicates the usefulness of transfer learning for both title detection and TOC generation. The advantage of jointly training a model for both languages is that we can leverage the small amount of training data, which is particularly useful for the language independent layout features. Moreover, our approach is independent of the presence of actual TOC pages in the documents. It is furthermore one of the few submissions addressing both subtasks in both languages with one single model. The constructed data set for supervised learning allowed us to train one model for both subtasks, which we find to be advantageous on the small amount of labeled training documents.

However, our approach also comes with limitations. Selecting fixed clustering hyperparameters assumes that all documents share a similar layout. While we optimized the text block detection hyperparameters for the given set of financial documents, this does not generalize well for other documents, which is mainly due to the limited size of the training set with only 99 documents. Moreover, our text block detection is based on DBSCAN, which requires label encoding where categorical features, e.g. font type, are artificially transformed into numerical ones. Using clustering algorithms such as (Ahmad and Khan, 2019), which handle numerical and categorical attributes directly, is promising future work.

---

[1] `https://github.com/google-research/bert/blob/master/multilingual.md`

6 Conclusion

We proposed a multilingual two-step approach for both title detection and TOC generation. First, we identified title candidates by clustering a document into text blocks using DBSCAN. Then, we trained a neural network to predict the depth of each text block in the document structure hierarchy. The architecture of the network combines a pre-trained multilingual BERT model with a carefully selected set of document and layout features. We have learned that fine-tuning BERT and adding document and layout features improves the TOC generation accuracy. The approach presented in this paper can be used for both English and French financial documents, even in cases where a TOC page is not present.

References

A. Ahmad and S. S. Khan. 2019. Survey of state-of-the-art mixed data clustering algorithms. *IEEE Access*, 7:31883–31902.

Najah-Imane Bentabet, Rémi Juge, Ismail El Maarouf, Virginie Mouilleron, Dialekti Valsamou-Stanislawski, and Mahmoud El-Haj. 2020. The Financial Document Structure Extraction Shared task (FinToc 2020). In *The 1st Joint Workshop on Financial Narrative Processing and MultiLing Financial Summarisation (FNP-FNS 2020,* Barcelona, Spain.

A. Conway. 1993. Page grammars and page parsing. a syntactic approach to document layout recognition. In *Proceedings of 2nd International Conference on Document Analysis and Recognition (ICDAR '93)*, pages 761–764.

Jacob Devlin, Ming-Wei Chang, Kenton Lee, and Kristina Toutanova. 2019. BERT: Pre-training of deep bidirectional transformers for language understanding. In *Proceedings of the 2019 Conference of the North American Chapter of the Association for Computational Linguistics: Human Language Technologies, Volume 1 (Long and Short Papers)*, pages 4171–4186, Minneapolis, Minnesota, June. Association for Computational Linguistics.

Bodin Dresevic, Aleksandar Uzelac, Bogdan Radakovic, and Nikola Todic. 2009. Book layout analysis: Toc structure extraction engine. volume 5631, pages 164–171, 09.

Martin Ester, Hans-Peter Kriegel, Jörg Sander, Xiaowei Xu, et al. 1996. A density-based algorithm for discovering clusters in large spatial databases with noise. In *Kdd*, volume 96, pages 226–231.

Emmanuel Giguet and Gaël Lejeune. 2019. Daniel@FinTOC-2019 shared task : TOC extraction and title detection. In *Proceedings of the Second Financial Narrative Processing Workshop (FNP 2019)*, pages 63–68, Turku, Finland, September. Linköping University Electronic Press.

Jianying Hu and Ying Liu, 2014. *Analysis of Documents Born Digital*, pages 775–804. Springer London, London.

Zhiheng Huang, Wei Xu, and Kai Yu. 2015. Bidirectional LSTM-CRF models for sequence tagging. *CoRR*, abs/1508.01991.

Remi Juge, Imane Bentabet, and Sira Ferradans. 2019. The FinTOC-2019 shared task: Financial document structure extraction. In *Proceedings of the Second Financial Narrative Processing Workshop (FNP 2019)*, pages 51–57, Turku, Finland, September. Linköping University Electronic Press.

Yoon Kim. 2014. Convolutional neural networks for sentence classification. *CoRR*, abs/1408.5882.

Stefan Klampfl, Michael Granitzer, Kris Jack, and Roman Kern. 2014. Unsupervised document structure analysis of digital scientific articles. *International journal on digital libraries*, 14(3-4):83–99.

Song Mao, Azriel Rosenfeld, and Tapas Kanungo. 2003. Document structure analysis algorithms: a literature survey. In Tapas Kanungo, Elisa H. Barney Smith, Jianying Hu, and Paul B. Kantor, editors, *Document Recognition and Retrieval X*, volume 5010, pages 197 – 207. International Society for Optics and Photonics, SPIE.

Bentabet Najah-Imane, Juge Rémi, and Ferradans Sira. 2019. Table-of-contents generation on contemporary documents. In *2019 International Conference on Document Analysis and Recognition (ICDAR)*, pages 100–107. IEEE.

Thi-Tuyet-Hai Nguyen, Antoine Doucet, and Mickaël Coustaty. 2017. Enhancing table of contents extraction by system aggregation. pages 242–247, 11.

Cartic Ramakrishnan, Abhishek Patnia, Eduard Hovy, and Gully APC Burns. 2012. Layout-aware text extraction from full-text pdf of scientific articles. *Source code for biology and medicine*, 7(1):7.

Jasper Snoek, Hugo Larochelle, and Ryan P. Adams. 2012. Practical bayesian optimization of machine learning algorithms. In *Proceedings of the 25th International Conference on Neural Information Processing Systems - Volume 2*, NIPS'12, page 2951–2959, Red Hook, NY, USA. Curran Associates Inc.

DNLP@FinTOC'20: Table of Contents Detection in Financial Documents

Dijana Kosmajac   **Mozhgan Saeidi**   **Stacey Taylor**
Faculty of Computer Science
Dalhousie University, Halifax, Canada
`{dijana.kosmajac,mozhgan.saeidi,stacey.taylor}@dal.ca`

Abstract

Title Detection and Table of Contents Generation are important components in detecting document structure. In particular, these two elements serve to provide the *skeleton* of the document, providing users with an understanding of organization, as well as the relevance of information, and where to find information within the document. Here, we show that using *tesseract* with Levenstein distance, a feature set inspired by Alk *et al.*, we were able to correctly classify the title to an F1 measure 0.73 and 0.87, and the table-of-contents to a harmonic mean of 0.36 and 0.39, in English and French respectively. Our methodology works with both PDF and scanned documents, giving it a wide range of applicability within the document engineering and storage domains.

1 Introduction

In recent years, there has been increasing interest in applying Natural Language Processing (NLP) techniques to financial documents. One of the main publishing formats for these documents is portable document format (PDF), which are usually available on stock exchange websites, company websites, or linked to as part of regulatory filings. Generally, financial documents are professionally created (which reduces spelling and grammatical noise), are relatively commonly structured (from a reader's point of view), and provide very similar end-user information. There are, however, variations in the organization and naming conventions, which present challenges in extracting information from documents. The main focus of the FinTOC task (Bentabet et al., 2020) is to analyze the the structure of financial documents to detect elements such as headings, sub-headings, and titles. The task is split into two parts: title detection and table-of-contents generation, for both English and French documents.

Our team participated in both tasks, but found more success in the table-of-contents generation (TOC), placing first in the standings. Using the Python implementation of *tesseract*, we identified the text regions, and then used Levenstein distance to match the provided labels to the detected regions. We then selected features, inspired by the work of Akl *et al.* to be used in classification for both the title detection and the table of contents generation (Abi Akl et al., 2019). For the classification, we used Logistic Regression (LR), Random Forest (RF), and Support Vector Machines (SVM).

The rest of the paper is organized as follows: we first begin with Background and Related Works, then outline our Method, Dataset, and finally present our Results, for each task, starting with Title Detection.

2 Background

Title detection and table-of-contents generation are highly related tasks, as they both depend on being able to successfully first detect document structure. A better computational understanding of the structure of annual financial reports will provide opportunities for a much more fine-grained analysis of the narratives, temporal comparison, and provide a basis of comparability between companies and sectors.

The United States (U.S.) is often seen as a benchmark for financial reporting layout as the U.S. Securities and Exchange Commission (SEC) mandates a particular structure for regulatory filing. Another

Proceedings of the 1st Joint Workshop on Financial Narrative Processing and MultiLing Financial Summarisation, pages 169–173
Barcelona, Spain (Online), December 12, 2020.

aspect of the U.S. standard is that the SEC publishes its regulatory filings in HTML format on its on-line repository, *Edgar*; companies will then simultaneously make the same information available in PDF format, most often on its corporate website. (El-Haj et al., 2019) This rigorous structure is not found in other countries, making multi-jurisdictional information extraction a significant challenge. To address this, el-Haj *et al.* used 10,000 annual reports during the period of 2003-2014 in Spanish and Portuguese from the London Stock Exchange, and created a tool called FRIE-FRSE (Corporate Financial Information Environment - Final Report Structure Extractor) to detect the annual report structure (El-Haj et al., 2019).

A variety of approaches have been taken in previous work to detect titles. Gopinath *et al.* (Gopinath et al., 2018) used two main approaches for extraction of title and prose: a domain-independent approach (DI) and a domain-dependent approach (DD). The data is mutually exclusively grouped into two subgroups using *k-means* clustering. An overlap score is then generated for potential titles, and those which exceed the 75% overlap threshold are added as candidate titles. The approaches only differ in the feature selection in that a neural network is used to classify examples previously labelled during DI. Hercig and Kral used the *Brainy Maximum Entropy* classifier to detect titles, using 7 key features: character n-grams, binary features, first and last orto-characters, font size and type, as well as text length (Hercig, 2019). At the 2019 FinToc workshop, Daniel also proposed using various features such as visual characteristics, punctuation density and character n-grams, achieving an F1-measure score of 94.88% (Giguet and Lejeune, 2019). The FinDSE team used a supervised learning approach that used linguistic, semantic, and morphological features to classify a block of text as either *title* or *non-title*, resulting in an F1-measure of 97.01% (Abreu et al., 2019).

A table-of-contents is a document's *roadmap*; it shows the hierarchy and organization of a document, helps users quickly access relevant information according to their query, and provides additional information such as the length of the document. Yet, while there is a commonly accepted idea of what information the table-of-contents should contain, there is no actual imposed or required standard that corporate entities must use. In fact, it can be seen that some companies provide a sparse table-of-contents with only the major sections included, whereas others provide much more fine-grained detail. Therefore, being able to independently generate a table-of-contents can significantly enrich the search of electronic documents.

Tian and Peng augmented their training and testing data provided in the task by adding additional fields to the data (Tian and Peng, 2019). From the augmented data, they retrieved unique tokens for training the word embedding. The vectors were then in attention based long-short term memory (LSTM) and bidirectional LSTM models, using 10-fold cross-validation. Their method performed very well, and they ranked 1st in the 2019 competition. Najah-Imane et al. proposed a TOC-generation pipeline based on binary classification and sequence label modelling (Bentabet et al., 2019). Classification is done to separate titles from non-titles, and sequence labelling provides a hierarchical structure to the detected titles. Tuyet et al. (2017) introduced an aggregation-based method to enhance ToC extraction using system submissions from the International Conference on Document Analysis and Recognition (ICDAR) *Book Structure Extraction* competitions (2009, 2011, and 2013). Their results show that using both methods together outperforms existing approaches using both the title-based and link-based evaluation measures on a dataset of more than 2,000 books. By efficiently combining the results of existing systems in an unsupervised way, they consistently beat the state-of-the-art in book structure extraction, with performance improvements that are statistically significant. Akl et al. (2019) used DNN-based approach which it scored a weighted F1 of 97.16% on the test data. They evaluated a SVM classifier. It was trained on a combination of features, compiled from the existing features presented within the original csv file as well as additional features extracted from pre-processing work on the xml files. Their second model is a BiLSTM–Attention model relying on word embedding, to make use of the attention mechanism. The third model is a CNN classifier. The purpose of this method is to evaluate the combinatorics of characters at word level (as predictors) and how relevant they are for the task.

3   Methodology

In the following sections we describe the methodology used to build the prediction models. The processing pipeline consists of two general steps: feature extraction and classification.

3.1   Feature Extraction

First, we used *tesseract* (Kay, 2007), an open-source OCR tool to extract the text regions. For the training set, the matching between the provided labelled titles and the extracted text regions is done using Levenstein distance (with the threshold of maximum allowed distance of 3). The choice for Levenstein distance threshold was done empirically by observing the optimal match between gold standard titles and detected ones (by optimal match we consider the highest number of matched pairs). Although the dataset provided by the organizers contains only searchable PDFs, we opted for using OCR scanning instead of PDF-specific mining libraries to make our approach applicable to the documents that are scanned. Inspired by Akl et al. (2019) we used a similar feature set. The features considered are enlisted below:

- **top distance:** integer indicating the distance of the text with respect to the previous text block of the document page;

- **bottom distance:** integer indicating the distance of the text with respect to the next text block of the document page;

- **indent:** integer indicating the placement of the text with respect to the left of the document page;

- **boldness:** float indicating approximation if the text is bold. This is done by counting the average value of all pixels in the bounding box;

- **height:** integer indicating the vertical space occupied by the text;

- **width:** integer indicating the number of characters in the bounding box;

- **PoS tags:** part of speech tags appearing in the text;

- **is title case:** flag true/false indicating if the text is in title case;

- **is upper case:** flag true/false indicating if the text is in upper case;

- **is lower case:** flag true/false indicating if the text is in lower case;

- **is numbered:** flag true/false indicating if the text starts with numbers;

- **is numbered with letters:** flag true/false indicating if the text starts with enumeration letters (roman numerals or a, b, c,...)

- **enumeration level:** integer indicating the level of numbering (for example 1. is 1, 1.1. is 2, 1.1.1. is 3 etc.). text

3.2   Classifiers

For both tasks we experimented with the same features and three classifiers: Logistic Regression (LR), Random Forests (RF) and linear kernel SVM. The library used is *scikit learn* in Python. For all classifiers hyperparameters used are the ones provided as default by the library.

Language	Classifier	Title detection	TOC
English	SVM	0.67 ($\pm$0.06)	0.24 ($\pm$0.05)
	LR	0.70 ($\pm$0.06)	0.25 ($\pm$0.06)
	RF	**0.73 ($\pm$0.04)**	**0.36 ($\pm$0.06)**
French	SVM	0.76 ($\pm$0.05)	0.28 ($\pm$0.04)
	LR	0.77 ($\pm$0.04)	0.28 ($\pm$0.05)
	RF	**0.87 ($\pm$0.07)**	**0.39 ($\pm$0.05)**

Table 1: Development results.

3.2.1 Results

The results are presented in Tables 1 and 2, for the development and the official test phase, respectively. The development tests are conducted using 10-fold cross validation for each classifier. The results for title detection are reported using F1 measure. The results for TOC generation are reported using *harmonic mean (Inex F1, Inex Lvl Acc)*. The evaluation script is provided by the organizers.

In the official evaluation for the title detection task, our team was placed 7th for the English subset and 4th for the French subset respectively. In the TOC generation task we were placed 1st for both subsets (Table 2).

Language	Title detection*	Placement	TOC	Placement
English	0.59	7	0.34	1
French	0.64	4	0.37	1

Table 2: Official results.

Because our best model in all cases was Random Forest, we used feature permutation importance technique (Breiman, 2001) to explore the most important features. For the title detection task, for both languages we found that the top three features are:

1. **top distance:** 0.0295 ($\pm$0.0003)

2. **boldness:** 0.0247 ($\pm$0.0002)

3. **width:** 0.0162 ($\pm$0.0003)

The general idea behind this technique is to see how much the performance of the classifier decreases when a feature of interest in not available (that is, contains a random noise instead of a true sample value). The most influential features in the title detection task are very intuitive: the distance of the text from the closest upper neighbouring text, estimation of the boldness and width of the bounding box.

The results show a significant difference in the performance between English and French subsets. The choice of feature set is the main source of it. Namely, English language subset had only 64 features in total, while French had 200. Note that the *PoS tag* features are language specific. The French language, besides general labels for part-of-speech tags, has gender, number, verb form that are absent in English language. Additionally, the PoS tagging tool itself did not have more granular labels for English. To validate this claim, we run title detection on French subset and removed gender, number, verb form and other additional information and kept only the PoS tag labels. 10-fold cross validation in this case was 0.74 (+/- 0.04), which is in the same range as the English, and we observe a significant drop in performance from the original experiment for French.

4   Conclusion

In this paper, we presented our work as part of the 2020 FinToc task for title detection and table-of-contents generation. We also demonstrated that using *tesseract* in conjunction with Levenstein distance and a set of key features returned a harmonic mean of 0.34 and 0.37 for English and French, respectively, earning us 1st place for table-of-contents generation. Our method also returned F1 measures of 0.59 and 0.64 for English and French, respectively. While previous researchers have used methods primarily focused on PDF documents, our approach used OCR scanning in order to include scanned documents in addition to PDFs. While document storage practices have evolved over time with PDF being the *standard*, this has not always been the case. Many older documents were scanned and are archived in that format. Employing an approach that considers this evolution, as we did, makes our method more widely applicable to electronic documents.

In the future, we would like to apply deep learning methods to both title detection and table-of-contents generation, as this approach is currently not widely researched. Another area of interest would be in embedding information pointers in documents to help better identify titles, sections, headers, and sub-headers. Finally, we would like to experiment using computer vision for title detection and use it to guide better generation of tables-of-contents.

References

Hanna Abi Akl, Anubhav Gupta, and Dominique Mariko. 2019. Fintoc-2019 shared task: Finding title in text blocks. In *Proceedings of the Second Financial Narrative Processing Workshop (FNP 2019)*, pages 58–62.

Carla Abreu, Henrique Cardoso, and Eugénio Oliveira. 2019. FinDSE@ FinTOC-2019 shared task. In *Proceedings of the Second Financial Narrative Processing Workshop (FNP 2019)*, pages 69–73.

Najah-Imane Bentabet, Rémi Juge, and Sira Ferradans. 2019. Table-of-contents generation on contemporary documents. *arXiv preprint arXiv:1911.08836*.

Najah-Imane Bentabet, Rémi Juge, Ismail El Maarouf, Virginie Mouilleron, Dialekti Valsamou-Stanislawski, and Mahmoud El-Haj. 2020. The Financial Document Structure Extraction Shared task (FinToc 2020). In *The 1st Joint Workshop on Financial Narrative Processing and MultiLing Financial Summarisation (FNP-FNS 2020, Barcelona, Spain*.

Leo Breiman. 2001. Random forests. *Machine Learning*, 45(1):5–32, October.

Mahmoud El-Haj, Paul Rayson, Paulo Alves, Carlos Herrero-Zorita, and Steven Young. 2019. Multilingual financial narrative processing: Analysing annual reports in English, Spanish and Portuguese. *Multilingual Text Analysis: Challenges, Models, And Approaches*, page 441.

Emmanuel Giguet and Gaël Lejeune. 2019. Daniel@ FinTOC-2019 shared task: TOC extraction and title detection. In *Proceedings of the Second Financial Narrative Processing Workshop (FNP 2019)*, pages 63–68.

Abhijith Athreya Mysore Gopinath, Shomir Wilson, and Norman Sadeh. 2018. Supervised and unsupervised methods for robust separation of section titles and prose text in web documents. In *Proceedings of the 2018 Conference on Empirical Methods in Natural Language Processing*, pages 850–855.

Pavel Král Tomas Hercig. 2019. UWB@ FinTOC-2019 shared task: Financial document title detection. In *Proceedings of the Second Financial Narrative Processing Workshop (FNP 2019)*, pages 74–78.

Anthony Kay. 2007. Tesseract: An open-source optical character recognition engine. *Linux J.*, 2007(159):2, July.

Thi-Tuyet-Hai Nguyen, Antoine Doucet, and Mickaël Coustaty. 2017. Enhancing table of contents extraction by system aggregation. In *14th IAPR International Conference on Document Analysis and Recognition, ICDAR 2017, Kyoto, Japan, November 9-15, 2017*, pages 242–247. IEEE.

Ke Tian and Zijun Peng. 2019. Finance document extraction using data augmentation and attention. In *Proceedings of the Second Financial Narrative Processing Workshop (FNP 2019), September 30, Turku Finland*, number 165, pages 1–4. Linköping University Electronic Press.

Daniel@FinTOC '2 Shared Task:
Title Detection and Structure Extraction

Emmanuel Giguet[1]
Normandie Univ, UNICAEN,
ENSICAEN, CNRS, GREYC
14000 Caen, France

Gaël Lejeune[2]
STIH, EA 4509
Sorbonne University
75006 Paris, France

Jean-Baptiste Tanguy[2]
OBVIL/STIH, EA 4509
Sorbonne University
75006 Paris, France

[1]`firstname.lastname@unicaen.fr`   [2]`firstname.lastname@sorbonne-universite.fr`

Abstract

We present our contributions for the FinTOC'2 Shared Tasks: Table of Content (ToC) extraction in English and French documents. For ToC Extraction, we propose to combine information from multiple sources: ToC itself, wording of the document, and lexical domain knowledge. For title detection, we compare surface features to character-based features on various training configurations. We show that title detection results are very sensitive to the training dataset used.

1 Introduction

The Fintoc'2 Financial Document Structure Extraction competition (Bentabet et al., 2020) proposed to evaluate two tasks : *Title Detection* and *ToC Structure Extraction*. Structure Extraction is an important issue for Natural Language Processing and Document Analysis. Rich logical structures can be exploited for document classification and clustering (Doucet and Lehtonen, 2007; Ait Elhadj et al., 2012). In the Document Analysis field, ToC generation aims to retrieve or extract a ToC from documents where the logical structure is not explicitly marked. ToC makes it easier to access information, in particular in Digital Humanities where documents can be long and structured in parts, chapters, appendices. Title Detection plays an important role for extracting the structure by helping to get candidates to populate the ToC. Furthermore, the position of sentences with respect to titles is used to improve the results in some NLP tasks: text classification (Lejeune et al., 2013), Terminology Acquisition (Daille et al., 2016) or Keyphrase Extraction (Florescu and Caragea, 2017). The paper is organized as follows. Section 2 gives a quick background for both subtasks. Section 3 describes our contribution to *ToC Extraction* and Section 4 our contribution to *Title Detection*. We give some words of conclusion in Section 5.

2 Background

Usually, the logical structure of natural language data is not explicitly encoded within a PDF document, it is the case for most financial prospectuses. The organization of the information has to be inferred from the layout and the style of text blocks. Positional and contrastive features allows the recovery of the underlying structure. Recovering the global structure of a document is an important process to achieve for information extraction. In this regard, document structure analysis certainly precedes sentence analysis. By the way, neither one of them can be seen as preprocessing stage. Both are fully part of a natural language processing system. These processes relate to *skimming* and *scanning* reading techniques. While skimming allows a reader to get a first glance of a document, scanning is the process of searching for a specific piece of information. Different parts of the document may be spotted by the reader and sought for specific information using a zoom-in/zoom-out strategy (Andrew et al., 2019). Concerning global structure, important information is found in the titles and subtitles, making the detection of titles important for improving web indexation (Changuel et al., 2009) or downstream NLP tasks (Huttunen et al., 2011; Tkaczyk et al., 2018). We can see two main strategies for ToC extraction: detecting the ToC pages and relying on the book content. The ICDAR Book Structure Extraction competitions results (Doucet et al., 2013) showed that hybrid systems are promising which is consistent with more recent results from (Nguyen et al., 2017) who combined different systems to get better results.

Proceedings of the 1st Joint Workshop on Financial Narrative Processing and MultiLing Financial Summarisation, pages 174–180
Barcelona, Spain (Online), December 12, 2020.

3 Contribution to the ToC Extraction Shared Task

3.1 From Table of Content Extraction to Document Structure Extraction

In previous INEX Book Structure Extraction Competitions, we used to consider the whole wording of the document (Giguet and Lucas, 2010a; Giguet and Lucas, 2010b; Giguet et al., 2009). This is a minority approach, it is more common to rely on the recognition and the parsing of the ToC since most books contain one that is usually quite easy to locate. Taking into account the whole wording of the document presents several advantages. First, it allows to consistently handle documents with and without ToC. Second, it permits to extract titles that are not included in the ToC, such as lower-level titles or preliminary titles. Third, it avoids having to process erroneous ToCs. Indeed, the ToC of a document may not be accurately synchronized if the authors forgot to update it. It may also contain entries that are not titles, for instance a paragraph incorrectly labelled as a title, or wrong page numbers. These cases often occur when documents are published without the supervision of an editorial board.

In FinTOC'1 (Giguet and Lejeune, 2019) our strategy relied on the detection of the ToC combined to a simple fallback strategy when no ToC is found. Our expectations was to have a good precision and a low recall due to missing or incomplete ToCs. ToCs belong to the category of index lists like list of figures or list of tables. Index lists together form a network of links starting from the periphery and pointing to the inner content. These links facilitate direct access to information and enable alternative reading strategies. They provide an "at-a-glance" snapshot of the complexity of the structure. While Document Structure Extraction do not consist in ToC extraction, it would be unfortunate to get rid of the information contained in the ToCs. Therefore, ToC recognition and parsing is integrated to our extraction method. Linking ToC entries to headings of the main text stream is the first step of our integration process.

3.2 Title Extraction from the Whole Content

As documents do not all contain ToCs, alternative ways have to be found to capture the hierarchy of headings. The main stream of content is the most natural source of information. However, it needs to be accurately and reliably detected. The task is not straightforward since the content is fragmented into pieces of texts. In order to retrieve the main text stream from the document content, page layouts have to be inferred in order to exclude the headers and the footers which break the linearity of the main text stream. Floating objects such as figures, tables, graphics and framed texts have to be excluded as well.

With financial documents, we solely focus on table detection and removal: they are the most frequent floating objects. Table removal reduces the search space and prevents considering table content when searching title candidates, thereby reducing the number of false positives. The table detection module parses the PDF vectorial shapes that are extracted by the `pdf2xml` command (Déjean, 2007). Text background and framed content are first inferred. The algorithm then builds table grids from adjacent framed content interpreted as possible table cells. Once the main text stream is extracted, titles are located with the help of two complementary strategies: Numbered List Detection and Salient Text Detection.

The *Numbered List Detection* strategy detects coherent series of numbered lines that may correspond to numbered titles. We exploit various features of text lines: the numbering style type (i.e., decimal, lower/upper-latin, lower/upper-roman), the numbering pattern (e.g., prefixes such as Chapter, Section, hierarchical numbering system such as A.2, 3.1.b). The *Text Saliency Detection strategy* is a contrastive approach to title detection. Titles are salient objects that stands out from the surrounding background. The background corresponds to text blocks (i.e., paragraphs, list items) that share common stylistic properties (i.e., font properties, line spaces, background, alignment). Title candidates are searched among the salient remaining text lines. A text line is salient if its stylistic properties generates enough contrasts with the surrounding text background. Salient texts sharing identical stylistic properties are clustered in order to build sets of titles acting at the same level of the hierarchy.

3.3 Taking advantages of Prospectus Document Model and Specific Document Models

The structure of financial prospectuses is driven by strong expectations from potential buyers and authorities. Thus, a model tends to emerge among the producers of financial information: across organizations, prospectuses tend to share common features in terms of macro structure. Certain sections and subsections

	Xerox measures				Inex08 measures					Error count		
	P	R	F1	Title	P	R	F1	Title	Level	Pb Title	Pb Level	Err
French	89.6	53.6	64.4	62.0	40.7	25.7	30.5	45.4	9.3	1765	3061	461
English	89.8	63.9	70.3	68.8	50.0	35.8	39.7	54.5	29.9	2713	4256	974

Table 1: Results obtained on the train dataset

Team	Inex F1
DNLP	0.37
taxy.io	0.32
Baseline	0.32
Daniel 2	0.22

Team	Inex F1
DNLP	0.34
Daniel 2	0.28
taxy.io	0.24
Amex 1	0.23
Baseline	0.18

(a) Results for the test dataset (French)　　　　(b) Results for the test dataset (English)

Table 2: Official results (Inex F1) for the ToC extraction task

are expected and are present with an expected naming. Moreover, prospectuses issued by an organization tend to share the same structure over products and over years. Moreover they also often share exact or similar document or page layout models. It is interesting to take benefit of these features, whether they are related to the genre or related to a specific organization. In this regard, titles from the training set are stored as lexical entries and reused as an external knowledge source for title detection.

3.4 Results

Table 1 exhibits the results obtained on the train dataset. We performed better than our first contribution (Giguet and Lejeune, 2019) which mainly relied on the ToC detection and extraction. The current version still demonstrates good precision and considerably improves recall. The choice to favour precision is much more sensitive with the Xerox metrics than with the Inex08 metrics. Our results on the test set are given in Table 2. One can see that, contrary to other systems, it performed better on the English data than on the French data. This in accordance with the results obtained on the train set.

4 Contribution to the Title Detection Shared Task

4.1 Datasets

The training and testing sets of the shared task are composed of segments labelled *Title* or *Not Title*. We also used the Fintoc-2019 (https://wp.lancs.ac.uk/cfie/shared-task/) corpus for improving English title detection and the DEFT-2011 (https://deft.limsi.fr/2011/) for French. In order to observe the impact of adding training data, we kept the split in training and testing sets. Both the FinTOC-2019 and the DEFT-2011 corpora are made up of segments labelled as *Title* or *Not Title*. A segment in the FinTOC-2019 corpus (as in the Fintoc-2020 corpus) refers to a physical component that is, in practice, a line. In the DEFT-2011 corpus, a segment refers to a logical component : a Title, a section, a subsection, etc. We must be clear that DEFT-2011's documents are scientific papers. We experiment several training sets combinations in order to assess the impact of the language and the text genre. To test the models, we selected randomly 20% of each dataset to use it as development data (see details in Appendices).

4.2 Methods: surface features and character n-grams

Baselines　Three group of features are used to get six baselines (Table 3): **basic** (five booleans: IS-BOLD, ISITALIC, IS ALLCAPS, BEGINSWITHCAPS and BEGINSWITHNUMBER and the page number, the **length** (in characters) and **stylo** (frequency of punctuation signs, numbers and capitalized letters).

***n*-gram method**　It consists in vectorizing the segments by counting the frequency of character n-grams. We explore different values for n_{min} and n_{max} minimum and maximum size of the n-grams.

For both methods we use a Random Forest with 50 estimators since it outperformed other classifiers.

B1	basic
B2	basic + length
B3	stylo
B4	stylo + basic
B5	stylo + length
B6	basic + stylo + length

Table 3: Baselines features description.

4.3 Results

	(i)				(ii)				(iii)				(iv)		
	P	R	F		P	R	F		P	R	F		P	R	F
B1	.628	.634	.631	B1	.627	.631	.629	B1	.802	.641	.689	B1	.819	.642	.694
B2	.586	.727	.614	B2	.586	.726	.615	B2	.744	.789	.764	B2	.814	.763	.786
B3	.585	.656	.607	B3	.585	.655	.607	B3	.720	.612	.646	B3	.809	.570	.608
B4	.581	.734	.608	B4	.588	.751	.617	B4	.797	.792	.795	B4	.849	.777	.808
B5	.592	.787	.624	B5	.593	.790	.625	B5	.768	.728	.746	B5	.840	.675	.729
B6	**.639**	**.801**	**.684**	B6	**.643**	**.808**	**.688**	B6	**.821**	**.855**	**.837**	B6	**.881**	**.822**	**.849**

Table 4: Baseline results on the F-2020-en-dev dataset, learned from: (i) F-2019-en-TRAIN, (ii) F-2019-en-TRAIN+TEST, (iii) F-2019-en-TRAIN+TEST + F-2020-en-TRAIN and (iv) F-2020-en-TRAIN

	(i)				(ii)				(iii)				(iv)		
	P	R	F-m		P	R	F-m		P	R	F-m		P	R	F-m
B1	.460	.500	.479	B1	.460	.500	.479	B1	.812	.724	.759	B1	.811	.724	.758
B2	.579	.658	.592	B2	.590	.679	.606	B2	.813	.772	.791	B2	.828	.769	.794
B3	.572	.681	.572	B3	.578	.699	.581	B3	.821	.650	.699	B3	.846	.633	.683
B4	.579	.672	.590	B4	.581	.678	.593	B4	.857	.822	.838	B4	.881	.821	.848
B5	.584	**.699**	.594	B5	.590	**.714**	.602	B5	.781	.744	.761	B5	.839	.710	.756
B6	**.589**	.682	**.606**	B6	**.591**	.687	**.608**	B6	**.873**	**.844**	**.858**	B6	**.888**	**.845**	**.865**

Table 5: Baseline results on the F-2020-fr-dev dataset, learned from: (i) D-2011-TRAIN, (ii) D-2011-TRAIN+TEST, (iii) D-2011-TRAIN+TEST + F-2020-fr-TRAIN and (iv) F-2020-fr-TRAIN

From the results obtained with the baselines (Table 4 for English and Table 5 for French) we observe that B6 gives the best results in all cases. This result is in accordance with the observations we made in previous edition (Giguet and Lejeune, 2019). Regarding the training datasets, we can observe that the Fintoc-2020 train set gives the best results. We observe the same pattern for the character n-gram method (heatmaps are given in appendixes), the F score does not achieve 80% without this data. We also observed that using bilingual datasets does not improve results (see appendixes).

5 Conclusion

In this article we proposed approaches for two shared tasks of FinTOC 2020. Regarding the ToC Extraction Shared Task, we propose a hybrid approach. It consists in combining the output of multiple modules dedicated or related to title detection. Title candidates are extracted from the table of contents thanks to a ToC Detection and Extraction module. Candidates are also extracted from the main text stream with the help of two complementary modules: a Numbered List detection module and a Text Saliency Detection module. In order to enrich the approach, titles from the training set are used to detect domain-specific titles. The title candidates are merged to generate a complete Table of Contents. For the Title Detection task, we proposed to use two types of features: surface features and character n-grams. We showed that stylometric features (frequency of punctuation, numbers and capitalized letters) combined with visual characteristics (bold, italic...) achieve better results than the character n-gram approaches.

References

Ali Ait Elhadj, Mohand Boughanem, Mohamed Mezghiche, and Fatiha Souam. 2012. Using structural similarity for clustering XML documents. *Knowledge and Information Systems*, 32(1):109–139, juillet.

Judith Jeyafreeda Andrew, Stéphane Ferrari, Fabrice Maurel, Gaël Dias, and Emmanuel Giguet. 2019. Model-driven Web Page Segmentation for Non Visual Access. In *16th International Conference of the Pacific Association for Computational Linguistics (PACLING 2019)*, Hanoï City, Vietnam, October.

Najah-Imane Bentabet, Rémi Juge, Ismail El Maarouf, Virginie Mouilleron, Dialekti Valsamou-Stanislawski, and Mahmoud El-Haj. 2020. The Financial Document Structure Extraction Shared task (FinToc 2020). In *The 1st Joint Workshop on Financial Narrative Processing and MultiLing Financial Summarisation (FNP-FNS 2020*, Barcelona, Spain.

Sahar Changuel, Nicolas Labroche, and Bernadette Bouchon-Meunier. 2009. A general learning method for automatic title extraction from html pages. In Petra Perner, editor, *Machine Learning and Data Mining in Pattern Recognition*, pages 704–718, Berlin, Heidelberg. Springer Berlin Heidelberg.

Béatrice Daille, Evelyne Jacquey, Gaël Lejeune, Luis Felipe Melo, and Yannick Toussaint. 2016. Ambiguity Diagnosis for Terms in Digital Humanities. In *Language Resources and Evaluation Conference*, Portorož, Slovenia, May.

Hervé Déjean, 2007. *pdf2xml open source software*. Last access on July 31, 2019.

Antoine Doucet and Miro Lehtonen. 2007. Unsupervised classification of text-centric xml document collections. In *Comparative Evaluation of XML Information Retrieval Systems, Fifth International Workshop of the Initiative for the Evaluation of XML Retrieval, INEX 2006*, volume 4518 of *Lecture Notes in Computer Science*, pages 497–509. Springer.

Antoine Doucet, Gabriella Kazai, Sebastian Colutto, and Günter Mühlberger. 2013. Overview of the ICDAR 2013 Competition on Book Structure Extraction. In *Proceedings of the Twelfth International Conference on Document Analysis and Recognition (ICDAR'2013)*, pages 1438–1443, Washington DC, USA, August.

Corina Florescu and Cornelia Caragea. 2017. PositionRank: An unsupervised approach to keyphrase extraction from scholarly documents. In *Proceedings of the 55th Annual Meeting of the Association for Computational Linguistics (Volume 1: Long Papers)*, pages 1105–1115, Vancouver, Canada, July. Association for Computational Linguistics.

Emmanuel Giguet and Gaël Lejeune. 2019. Daniel@fintoc-2019 shared task: Toc extraction and title detection. In *The Second Financial Narrative Processing Workshop (FNP 2019)*, pages 63–68, Turku, Finland, September.

Emmanuel Giguet and Nadine Lucas. 2010a. The book structure extraction competition with the resurgence software at caen university. In Shlomo Geva, Jaap Kamps, and Andrew Trotman, editors, *Focused Retrieval and Evaluation*, pages 170–178, Berlin, Heidelberg. Springer Berlin Heidelberg.

Emmanuel Giguet and Nadine Lucas. 2010b. The book structure extraction competition with the resurgence software for part and chapter detection at caen university. In *Comparative Evaluation of Focused Retrieval - 9th Workshop of the Initiative for the Evaluation of XML Retrieval (INEX 2010), Revised Selected Papers*, pages 128–139.

Emmanuel Giguet, Alexandre Baudrillart, and Nadine Lucas. 2009. Resurgence for the book structure extraction competition. In Shlomo Geva, Jaap Kamps, and Andrew Trotman, editors, *INEX 2009 Workshop Pre-Proceedings*, pages 136–142.

Silja Huttunen, Arto Vihavainen, Peter von Etter, and Roman Yangarber. 2011. Relevance prediction in information extraction using discourse and lexical features. In *Proceedings of the 18th Nordic Conference of Computational Linguistics (NODALIDA 2011)*, pages 114–121.

Gaël Lejeune, Romain Brixtel, Charlotte Lecluze, Antoine Doucet, and Nadine Lucas. 2013. Added-value of automatic multilingual text analysis for epidemic surveillance. In *Artificial Intelligence in Medicine (AIME)*, pages 284–294.

Thi-Tuyet-Hai Nguyen, Antoine Doucet, and Mickael Coustaty. 2017. Enhancing table of contents extraction by system aggregation. In *2017 14th IAPR International Conference on Document Analysis and Recognition (ICDAR)*, volume 01, pages 242–247, Nov.

Dominika Tkaczyk, Andrew Collins, and Joeran Beel. 2018. Who did what?: Identifying author contributions in biomedical publications using naïve bayes. In *Proceedings of the 18th ACM/IEEE on Joint Conference on Digital Libraries*, JCDL '18, pages 387–388, New York, NY, USA. ACM.

Appendices

	Lang.	Number of segments	Nb *Title*	Nb *Not Titles*
F-2019-en-TRAIN	English	75,625	10,271	65,354
F-2019-en-TRAIN+TEST	English	90,441	11,159	79,282
F-2020-en-TRAIN	English	148,940	5,463	143,477
F-2019-en-TRAIN+TEST + F-2020-en-TRAIN	English	239,381	16,622	222,759
D-2011-TRAIN	French	15,771	1,666	14,105
D-2011-TRAIN+TEST	French	22,531	2,415	20,116
F-2020-fr-TRAIN	French	54,483	4,233	50,250
D-2011-TRAIN+TEST + F-2020-fr-TRAIN	French	77,014	6,648	70,366
F-2020-en-DEV	English	37,234	1,322	35,912
F-2020-fr-DEV	French	13,620	1,076	12,544

Table 6: Size and composition of each training configuration used (F: FinTOC, D: DEFT)

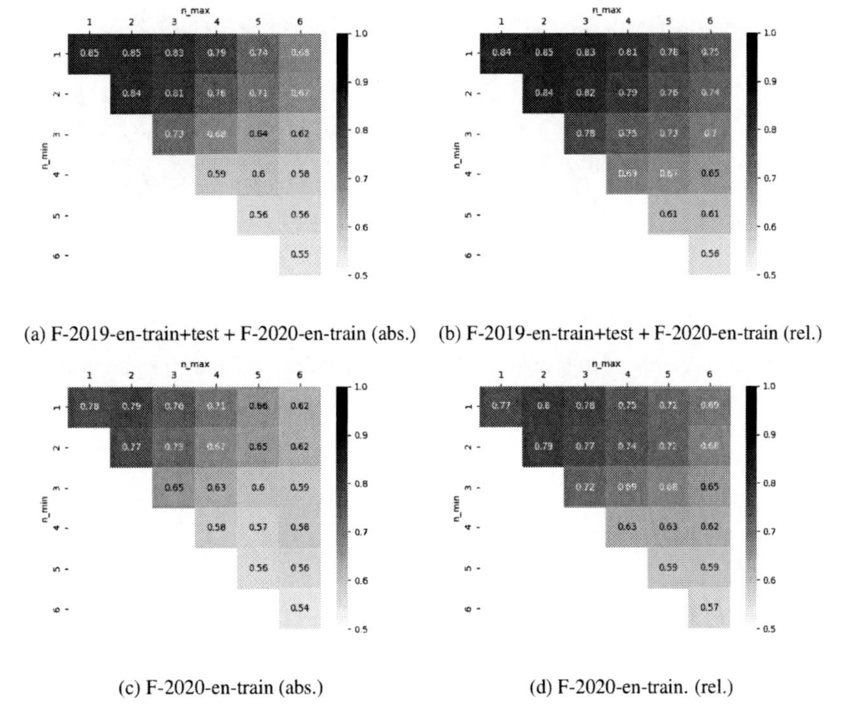

(a) F-2019-en-train+test + F-2020-en-train (abs.) (b) F-2019-en-train+test + F-2020-en-train (rel.)

(c) F-2020-en-train (abs.) (d) F-2020-en-train. (rel.)

Figure 1: English n-grams models results with various training sets and absolute or relative counts

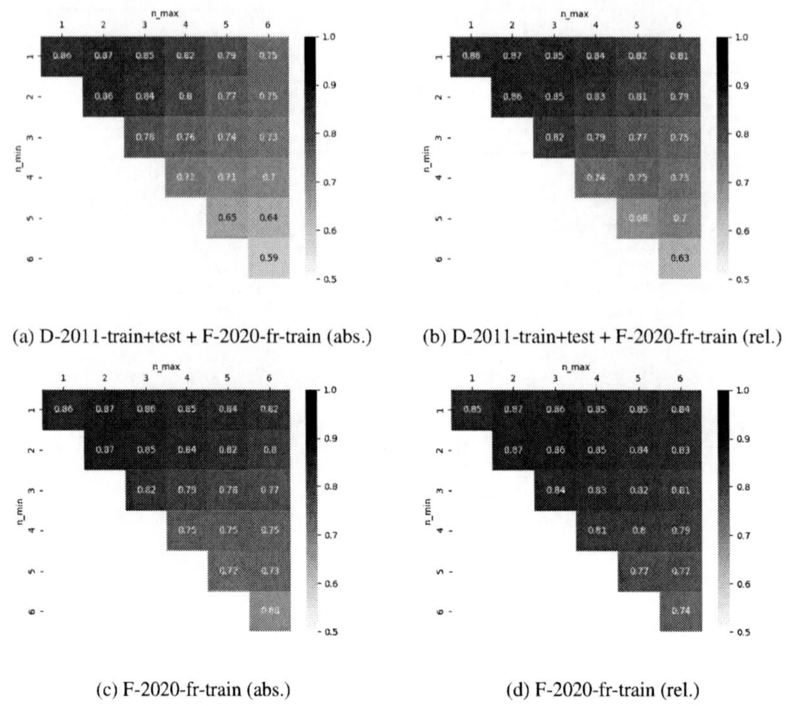

(a) D-2011-train+test + F-2020-fr-train (abs.)   (b) D-2011-train+test + F-2020-fr-train (rel.)

(c) F-2020-fr-train (abs.)   (d) F-2020-fr-train (rel.)

Figure 2: French n-grams models results with various training sets and absolute or relative counts

	FinTOC-2020-en-dev				FinTOC-2020-fr-dev		
	P	R	F-m		P	R	F-m
B1	.774	.657	.698	B1	.801	.626	.670
B2	.736	.775	.754	B2	.770	.734	.750
B3	.723	.597	.633	B3	.806	.618	.662
B4	.788	.789	.789	B4	**.841**	.789	.812
B5	.759	.719	.737	B5	.800	.728	.758
B6	**.809**	**.839**	**.824**	B6	.838	**.829**	**.833**

Table 7: Results on F-2020-fr-dev of the baseline methods, learned from the bilingual training set (F-2019-en-train+test + F-2020-en-train + D-2011-train+test + F-2020-fr-train).

A Computational Analysis of Financial and Environmental Narratives within Financial Reports and its Value for Investors

Felix Armbrust[1], **Henry Schäfer**[1] and **Roman Klinger**[2]
[1]Institute of Business Administration
[2]Institut für Maschinelle Sprachverarbeitung
`{felix.armbrust,henry.schaefer}@bwi.uni-stuttgart.de`
`roman.klinger@ims.uni-stuttgart.de`

Abstract

Public companies are obliged to include financial and non-financial information within their corporate filings under Regulation S-K, in the United States (SEC, 2010). However, the requirements still allow for manager's discretion. This raises the question to which extent the information is actually included and if this information is at all relevant for investors. We answer this question by training and evaluating an end-to-end deep learning approach (based on BERT and GloVe embeddings) to predict the financial and environmental performance of the company from the "Management's Discussion and Analysis of Financial Conditions and Results of Operations" (MD&A) section of 10-K (yearly) and 10-Q (quarterly) filings. We further analyse the mediating effect of the environmental performance on the relationship between the company's disclosures and financial performance. Hereby, we address the results of previous studies regarding environmental performance. We find that the textual information contained within the MD&A section does not allow for conclusions about the future (corporate) financial performance. However, there is evidence that the environmental performance can be extracted by natural language processing methods.

1 Introduction

Understanding the textual information in corporate disclosures is an important part of financial accounting research. It provides additional information about numerical financial data and aids the reader to understand the managerial information sets. In addition, the manager's communication patterns can reveal certain behavioral traits – e.g., in case the company provides truthful and meaningful information or if the company tries to obfuscate or withhold information. The textual information can, hence, guide users of corporate disclosures to better understand the firm's behavior and decisions (Li, 2010b, p. 143–144) – in particular, when information asymmetries exist (Fields et al., 2001, p. 256). However, corporate disclosures often tend to be boilerplate (Palmiter, 2015; Bloomfield, 2008; SEC, 2003). As a consequence, the Securities and Exchange Commission (SEC, 2003), concerned that a substantial part of the corporate disclosures includes generic language and immaterial detail, issued a guideline to elicit more meaningful disclosure. In 2010, the SEC further published an interpretive release on climate change related disclosures "to remind companies of their obligations under existing federal securities laws and regulations to consider climate change and its consequences as they prepare disclosure documents", (SEC, 2010, p. 6297). Therefore, the company's disclosures should not only consist of financial narratives but also contain information about the environmental aspects concerning the firm. Whether these corporate disclosures are truly informative (Li, 2010a, p. 1050) or are just boilerplate generic disclosures (Wasim, 2019; Palmiter, 2015; Li, 2010b) remains an empirical question, which we address in this paper.

While in the financial domain, the financial narratives of corporate reports have been analysed with respect to dictionary-based approaches or standard classification methods like naïve Bayes (Kearney and Liu, 2014, p. 174), little research has focused on more sophisticated methods (Gentzkow et al., 2019,

Proceedings of the 1st Joint Workshop on Financial Narrative Processing and MultiLing Financial Summarisation, pages 181–194
Barcelona, Spain (Online), December 12, 2020.

p. 569). This equally applies for studies analysing the non-financial information[1] content (Kölbel et al., 2020, p. 8). The most common methods for analysing the non-financial, narrative information content still remain a manual- or dictionary-based approach (Berkman et al., 2019; Matsumura et al., 2018; Reverte, 2016; Verbeeten et al., 2016; Clarkson et al., 2008; Cormier and Magnan, 2007, i.a.). Also, only few studies concerning non-financial information focus on the actual *narrative* information content, and rather address the *quantity* of non-financial information published (Hummel and Schlick, 2016).

In this paper, we analyse the information content of the Management's Discussion and Analysis of Financial Conditions and Results of Operations (MD&A) section of 10-K and 10-Q filings with respect to the financial performance and environmental performance using a variety of natural language processing (NLP) methods. Our contributions are that we, (1), evaluate if the MD&A section contains information that can be used to predict financial and environmental performance in a machine learning setting, (2), analyse if the environmental information complements the financial information in explaining the future financial performance.[2] As more than 2000 studies have linked non-financial performance to financial performance (Friede et al., 2015), we assume that the narrative *per se* also contributes to the financial performance. Hence, we directly train the classifier on the financial performance and the environmental performance using a sentence-wise BERT- and word-wise GloVe-embedding model, instead of regressing a certain measure on a disclosure-score previously derived from either a manually constructed word-list or a tfidf-weighting scheme, like most other studies.

The hypothesese we discuss in this paper are: (H1) Corporate disclosures, particularly the MD&A section, contain information regarding the company's financial performance. (H2) Corporate disclosures, particularly the MD&A section, contain information regarding the company's environmental performance. (H3) Narrative, non-financial information within the MD&A section, complements narrative financial information in explaining the financial performance, i.e., environmental performance serves as a mediator for financial performance.

2 Background on Financial and Non-Financial Disclosures and Related Work

2.1 Computational Linguistics in the Financial Domain

The field of computational linguistics has made enormous progress in converting text into meaningful representations for computational use (Gentzkow et al., 2019, p. 537). Content analysis – a technique that allows users to objectively and systematically identify specific characteristics from a text (Stone et al., 1966) – can lead to interesting insights to transparently analyse text and provide evidence for (economic) theories. A field of research includes the application of content analysis to efficiently examine the level of corporate disclosures (Grüning, 2011). However, in the financial domain, applications of more recently developed methods are rather in their early stages (Gentzkow et al., 2019). The most common methods still remain a dictionary-based approach or comparably, straightforward naïve Bayes approaches (Kearney and Liu, 2014, p. 174) or dictionary-based methods which lack coverage.

A complementary strain of research in computer science does use state-of-the-art methods, however, with applications in financial data which tend to primarily focus on news articles predicting stock prices in the short-term (Mishev et al., 2019; Dodevska et al., 2019; Day and Lee, 2016; Curme et al., 2015; Li et al., 2014, i.a.). Only recently, more advanced methods also find their way into the financial domain (Kölbel et al., 2020; Luccioni and Palacios, 2019, i.a.).

2.2 Financial Narratives

In the United States, all public companies are required to prepare audited financial statements, which have to be filed with the SEC and need to be accompanied by a narrative explanation to aid the users in

---

[1] While the terms business sustainability, corporate social responsibility (CSR) or environmental, social, governance information (ESG) are often used interchangeably in the financial literature (Rezaee, 2015, p. 2), we generally refer to it as non-financial information in this paper. However, in our specific case, we only consider the environmental aspect of non-financial information.

[2] Similarly suggested by Reverte (2016) and Semenova et al. (2010). Considering the direct and indirect effect of non-financial reporting, Reverte (2016) finds that the integration of non-financial information into financial investment analysis provides a richer understanding of the companies' long-term performance. Further, evidence from Semenova et al. (2010) indicates that environmental and social performance are value-relevant and complement financial information.

assessing the company's situation (Yang et al., 2018, p. 45). The SEC had recognized that a numerical presentation alone might be insufficient for investors (SEC, 1987).

One of the most read components of the corporate filings include the MD&A section (Tavcar, 1998). It provides investors with a company's long- and short-term analysis from the management's point of view including narratives on past performance as well as potential future prospects (Muslu et al., 2008; Griffin, 2003). This analysis should also include prospective matters, known material[3] trends and uncertainties relevant to the company (SEC, 2003).

The Regulation S-K and the SEC's guidelines make the MD&A section mandatory. However, the MD&A sections of the 10-K and 10-Q filings do not need to be audited (Hüfner, 2007), and the requirements for the MD&A section still allow for management discretion (Li, 2010a, p. 1053). Managers could withhold unfavourable information below a critical disclosure level (Verrecchia, 1983), or provide imprecise information. However, companies might face litigation risk when making misleading or fraudulent disclosures, which in turn serves as a disciplining tool (Li, 2010a; Kothari et al., 2009). As Kothari et al. (2009, p. 1643) notes, "the disciplining forces might be less operative when disclosures are qualitative and long-term in nature (e.g., discussion in MD&A section) rather than quantitative [...] and short-term".

Several studies have analysed the impact of corporate disclosures with respect to the financial information using the narrative information content: There is evidence for the disclosures affecting company's risk (Kravet and Muslu, 2013; Kothari et al., 2009; Li, 2006), future earnings (Moreno-Sandoval et al., 2019; Athanasakou and Hussainey, 2014; Li, 2010a), and, ultimately, firm value (Campbell et al., 2014; Jegadeesh and Wu, 2013; Feldman et al., 2008).[4] However, nearly all previous work relies purely on a word-count, word-phrase count or comparably, straightforward approaches. Thus, we hypothesise that the extraction of the information content will improve by using more advanced embedding methods or applying convolutional neural networks. While most studies tend to derive some kind of disclosure-score from the text and subsequently regress the score on financial performance or some other measure, we propose a deep-learning classifier being able to find relevant patterns in the text that provide conclusions about the financial (and environmental) performance.

2.3 Non-Financial Narratives

Recent efforts by standard-setting institutions reflect the increasing demand for decision-useful, climate-related information (IMP, 2020; TCFD, 2019) and, also, various surveys have shown that institutional investors value climate-relevant information (Ilhan et al., 2019; Amel-Zadeh and Serafeim, 2018; CFA Institute, 2017). While climate-change related factors are also a risk to the company, manager's awareness and proper handling represent an opportunity for financial gain (Wasim, 2019; Jung et al., 2018).

The 2010 guideline on climate-change related disclosures highlights the importance of non-financial information within corporate reports, often referred to as environmental, social, and governance information (ESG) (Eccles and Stroehle, 2018; Eccles et al., 2012). The SEC mandates material factors to be disclosed within the MD&A section, the risk factors section, legal proceedings and the description of business (Eccles et al., 2012, p. 68). However, the principle-based approach the SEC applies makes companies autonomously responsible to identify the relevant risks and factors. Passages that address climate-change related disclosures are hard to identify (Luccioni and Palacios, 2019) and, thus, the disclosure requirements have been criticized as to be lax and ineffective (Wasim, 2019; Palmiter, 2015). Nevertheless, corporate disclosures slightly improved after the 2010 guidance (Palmiter, 2015).

The theory of discretionary-based disclosures (Verrecchia, 2001) applies to non-financial information as well (Hummel and Schlick, 2016; Clarkson et al., 2008). Previous studies found only a small percentage of companies explicitly mention climate-change in their annual report (Palmiter, 2015; Hirji, 2013). While some companies are disclosing information apart from the SEC's required disclosure regimes, these do not substitute the SEC mandated disclosures. Without a mandatory standardized framework, not all issuers will disclose, and a lack of reliability and comparability exists (Lee, 2020). However, authors

---

[3]Materiality refers to the relevance of an item to users of financial statements. For a more detailed discussion on materiality see Eccles et al. (2012).

[4]We refer the interested reader to other publications for more details (Kearney and Liu, 2014; Loughran and McDonald, 2016; Loughran and McDonald, 2019).

have shown that voluntary, standalone non-financial disclosures are positively associated with market value and negatively with cost of equity capital (Verbeeten et al., 2016; De Villiers and Marques, 2016; Reverte, 2016; Plumlee et al., 2015; Dhaliwal et al., 2014; Clarkson et al., 2013).[5] For 10-K forms, similar dictionary based risk measures indicate a negative association with firm value and a positive association with implied cost of capital (Berkman et al., 2019). As Matsumura et al. (2018) show, firms disclosing material factors have a lower cost of equity. Kölbel et al. (2020) provide evidence that disclosures on climate risk within the 10-K risk section affects the spreads of credit default swaps, by training a sentence-wise BERT algorithm on sample reports from the task force on climate-related financial disclosures, supported by humanly annotation. We, thus, hypothesize that the MD&A section provides similar valuable information for investors, which can be retrieved by directly training classifiers on the text without human interference.

3   Study Design and Research Methodology

Our aim is to examine whether NLP methods can capture the meaning of the MD&A section of corporate disclosures with respect to financial and non-financial narratives. If we find evidence, this is an indicator that such information is contained, if not, this is an indicator that this information might not be available, which, however, would motivate future work to investigate this further. Therefore, we directly train classifiers on the text in the MD&A section to predict financial *and* environmental performance.

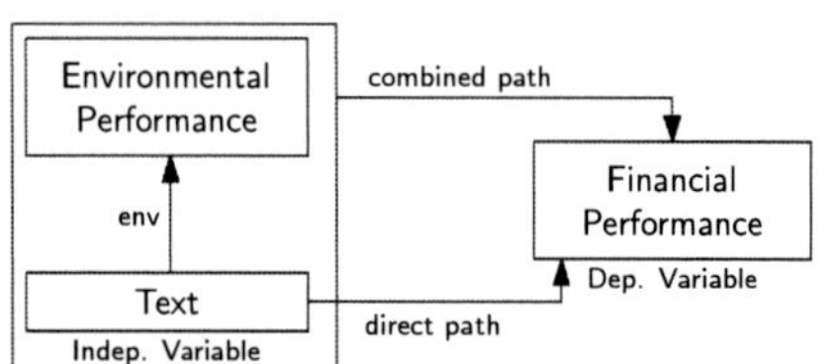

Figure 1: Our model predicts financial performance under consideration of environmental performance.

Figure 1 elicits our approach: First, we predict the financial performance from the MD&A section, i.e., *Direct Path*. Second, we predict the environmental performance from the text, represented by path *env*. Third, we build an extended model, which predicts the financial performance from the text while also considering the (predicted) environmental performance, i.e., *Combined Path*. In case all paths show a meaningful relation to their labels and the *Combined Path* shows an improved F_1-score compared to the *Direct Path*, we conclude that the environmental narrative complements the financial narrative in explaining the financial performance.

While the company might provide information in a timely fashion through other communication channels, e.g., ad-hoc messages, press releases and twitter posts, the MD&A section gives companies a more comprehensive way to discuss their future prospects and operating strategy. On top, the dissemination in the MD&A section is for free. Hence, we assume companies also provide previously released information within their MD&A (in more detail).[6] Furthermore, we assume that any material information from sustainability reports will also be published in the MD&A section.

Nevertheless, the impact of the financial information content of the 10-K and 10-Q filings might be quite limited since companies typically make an earnings announcement that includes information on their earnings, cash flows, and other key performance indicators approx. three weeks before disclosing the filings (Muslu et al., 2008; Lansford, 2006; Schrand and Walther, 2000). Hence, the majority of quantitative information is not expected to provide much information content to investors. However, the *narrative* information content probably will.

3.1   Data and Preprocessing

Our sample consists of S&P500 firms for the five-year period from the beginning of 2014 to the end of 2018 for which we are able to calculate all class labels (see Section 3.2).[7] To minimise survivorship bias,[8]

---

[5]For an overview see, for example, Verbeeten et al. (2016, p. 1363-1365).

[6]For a confirmation of these assumptions see Muslu et al. (2008).

[7]The time horizon is limited by the ESG data available on Bloomberg since for most companies the sustainability data was not available before the beginning of 2014.

[8]By including *only* companies that were part of the S&P500 *throughout* the years 2014 till 2018, one would neglect poor performing companies that did not fulfil the S&P500 criteria at any point in time during the time horizon – namely having a too

we also include all companies that were constituents at any time during the observation period. This adds up to 615 companies under consideration, for which the 10-K and 10-Q reports were retrieved from the Notre Dame Software Repository for Accounting and Finance (SRAF) website (McDonald, 2019; Loughran and McDonald, 2016).[9] The files taken from SRAF are the entire reports containing all sections. We manually filter to the MD&A sections and only include the "Quantitative and Qualitative Disclosures About Market Risk" (QQD) section in addition, due to the fact that most companies include the QQD within the MD&A section. We opted against an automatic parsing procedure to avoid downstream errors, which would have been possible due to some companies reporting sections titled item 7 (MD&A) and 7A (QQD), but still include the *actual content* in a later part of the filing, e.g., in exhibit 13 or exhibit 99.1 – an additional attachment to the filings (Center, 2014). We lose a total of 2815 observations due to missing data. The final sample consists of 8772 observations (554 unique firms). The corpus includes 2.914.623 sentences and 56.063.378 tokens in total (45.872 unique tokens).[10]

3.2 Class Labels

As financial performance can be measured in several ways, we consider two sources for labels for the *Direct Path*. The first one uses the change in earnings per share as the according label[11] and the second one uses buy-and-hold returns as the class label (Barber and Lyon, 1997, p. 344)[12]. While earnings do not directly allow conclusions about the relevance of the filings to investors, it measures the informativeness of the MD&A section, i.e., how much information is actually conveyed that affects the future financial performance of the company. We denote this first label as $\Delta\mathrm{EPS}_{i,q}$, which is calculated as the difference in quarterly earnings previously reported and earnings published in the subsequent quarter. Here, q is the quarterly change and i denotes to a particular firm. For the buy-and-hold returns, we use the compounded SP500 index return, which we subtract from the contemporaneous, compounded return of the company under consideration.[13] Compared to Loughran and McDonald (2011) and Jegadeesh and Wu (2013), who use primarily a 3-day event window for the buy-and-hold-returns, we extend the period to 30 days to match the change in environmental performance ratings. This is important for the *Combined Path*, when considering the environmental narrative as well as the financial narrative. We denote the buy-and-hold-returns as $\mathrm{BHAR}_{i,t}$, which indicates how the information is perceived by investors (i again denotes the company, t denotes the 30-day period).

To measure the information conveyed by environmental narratives, we employ ESG data from Sustainalytics accessed via Bloomberg.[14] The ESG data is adjusted on a monthly basis. To match the earnings class label, we use a three-month time horizon for the environmental narrative. Hence, the first environmental class label is the change in the ESG percentile score denoted as $\Delta\mathrm{Env}_{i,q}$ and calculated as the change in the environmental percentile score over the subsequent quarter – measured by the time it takes the company to file the next report with the SEC. Index i is again for the company i and q denotes the quarterly change. The second class label for the environmental narrative uses a one-month change to match the second financial class label. The calculation is done in a similar fashion as for the quarterly environmental performance label and denoted as $\Delta\mathrm{Env}_{i,t}$ with i for the company and t for the day period. We calculated the label as the difference in the previously available percentile score on the filing date and the subsequent score available.

Again, the first class labels on financial and environmental narratives consider the quarterly change and the second labels the monthly impact of the MD&A section. Hence, we construct a long-term and a short-term model. While the long-term model considers the general informativeness and significance

---

small market capitalization in any of the years between 2014 till 2018. This would lead to logical errors and one would create biased statistics (see e.g., Carpenter et al. (1999), Brown et al. (1992)).

[9]Files and pre-processing description at `https://sraf.nd.edu/data/stage-one-10-x-parse-data/` (accessed 15.03.2020); unprocessed files are at `https://www.sec.gov/Archives/edgar/Feed/`

[10]The token number for BERT varies, as BERT uses its own tokenizer, see Devlin et al. (2019).

[11]Similar to Li (2010a).

[12]Similar to Loughran and McDonald (2011) and Jegadeesh and Wu (2013).

[13]The t-test $t_{\mathrm{BHAR}} = \frac{\overline{\mathrm{BHAR}_{i,t}}}{\sigma(\mathrm{BHAR}_{i,t})/\sqrt{n}}$ showed that BHAR are significant to the 1%-significance level.

[14]To proxy environmental performance, other studies have also used data from KLD (today MSCI), Asset4, Viegeo Eiris, or single emission data.

of corporate disclosures, the second model considers the informativeness of corporate disclosures with respect to investors. We binary encode all labels, i.e., converting positive $BHAR_{i,t}$, $\Delta EPS_{i,q}$, $\Delta Env_{i,t}$ and $\Delta Env_{i,q}$ to 1 and negative values to 0, respectively. The idea for the *Combined Path* is to predict the environmental class label first and then using the environmental label to predict the financial label from text.

3.3 Model Architecture and Feature Extraction

We use five different feature extraction methods and model architectures: (1) **BOW**: Bag-of-words in a maximum entropy classifier. (2) **TF-IDF**: Bag-of-words weighted with TF-IDF in a maximum entropy classifier. (3) **GloVe**: Embeddings (Pennington et al., 2014) in a maximum entropy classifier. (4) **CNN**: GloVe embeddings with a convolutional neural network, following the architecture by Zhang and Wallace (2017) (three convolutional layers, each followed by max-pooling, each with drop-out, followed by dense layer with drop-out and a sigmoid output layer; filter sizes of 2, 3, 4; 2 filters for each length; dropout rate 0.5). (5) **BERT**: BERT sentence-embeddings followed by a Bidirectional-GRU, a relu layer, an attention layer with drop-out and a fully-connected sigmoid layer. For the BERT embeddings, we split each document into sentences using NLTK (Bird et al., 2009), encode each sentence with the required [CLS]-token using the BERT tokenizer and do a feed-forward pass to the BERT base network (Devlin et al., 2019).[15] The resulting [CLS]-tokens can be considered a vector representation of the sentences (Alammar, 2019, i.a.). Due to BERT base model input length restrictions of 512-tokens (Devlin et al., 2019), we limit each sentence to the first 200 tokens.[16] For models (1), (2), (3) and (4), we remove stop words using NLTK (Bird et al., 2009), non-alphabet characters and words that are shorter than two characters. Since BERT can make use of sentences that are grammatically correct, we do not remove any tokens for BERT. For all models, we use the adam optimizer (Kingma and Ba, 2015) and binary cross-entropy as a loss function. All models are fit using *50* epochs and a batch size of 32, except for the BERT model, which is trained for only *10* epochs. For hyperparameter optimization, we evaluate the following settings: We use dense layers with sizes of {50, 100} for each model with an additional dense layer and set the drop-out probabilities to a probability of {40%, 50%, 60%}. For the CNN, we also applied both l1 and l2-regularization with regularization weights of {1, 0.1, 0.01}. The optimal set of parameters are dense layers of size 50 and drop-out probabilities of 50%. The reported CNN models apply 0.01-weighted l2-regularization. The size of each max-pooling window was set to 32 and GloVe word-embeddings are of size 100. For BERT, the GRU are of size 50 and the attention layer size is 100. The data is split into 10% test, 10% validation, and 80% training data.[17] We chose the epoch of the best performing model with the validation data. Since larger companies tend to obtain a higher ESG-rating (Doyle, 2018, p. 9), we control path *env* models for size. Size is measured by the logarithm of the market capitalization. The geographical bias is comparably small, since we only consider stocks listed within the United States. To account for any potential industry bias, we also use the Standard Industrial Classification (SIC) to find the according division responsible,[18] which we include in path *env* models as one-hot-encoded input before the sigmoid output layer. Hence, path *env* models include a concatenate layer before the sigmoid layer to control for size and industry.

3.4 Evaluation

We assume that if the classifier is able to capture the meaning of the disclosures, i.e., has a high F_1-score, then the evidence that the MD&A section is associated with the class labels is consistent with the hypotheses that managers are truthfully disclosing information in the MD&A section and that corporate filings have information content.[19] However, if the MD&A section, based on the classifier, is not associated

---

[15]For BERT, we consider a maximum of 1,000 sentences per document, as the median and arithmetic mean of sentences per document is 270 and 332.26, respectively. We then pad each document to the same length before doing the feed-forward pass.

[16]To build our models, we use the Python library Keras (Chollet and others, 2015) using the tensorflow backend (Abadi et al., 2015). To leverage the classifiers, we use the Scikit-learn library (Pedregosa et al., 2011). To implement BERT, we use the Hugging Face transformer library (Wolf et al., 2019).

[17]Our python code is available at: `https://github.com/ForgeFin/Fin-Env-Narrative`

[18]See `https://www.osha.gov/pls/imis/sic_manual.html` (accessed 05.06.2020) for divisions.

[19]This is equivalent to Li (2010a).

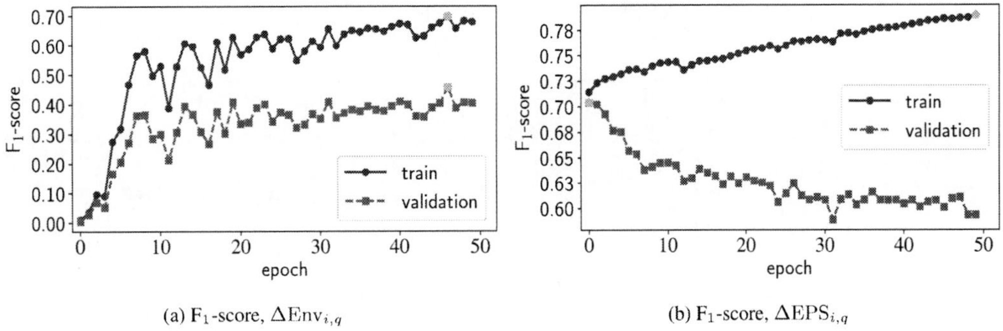

(a) F$_1$-score, $\Delta\mathrm{Env}_{i,q}$ (b) F$_1$-score, $\Delta\mathrm{EPS}_{i,q}$

Figure 2: Exemplary F$_1$-score curve for the tfidf-classifier on $\Delta\mathrm{Env}_{i,q}$ and $\Delta\mathrm{EPS}_{i,q}$

with the class labels, then we cannot reject the hypothesis that the MD&A section has no information content because the result could be due to the low power of the classifier. Nevertheless, this might be an indicator that this is eventually the case.

We compare our model's performances to a majority baseline (i.e., always predict class 1, namely "improving"). If a model has a substantially higher F$_1$-score than the baseline, we are able to predict financial and environmental improvements more precisely compared to always assuming an improvement. In a next step, we compare the F$_1$-score of the *Direct Path* with the F$_1$-score of the *Combined Path* using a Bootstrap approach. If the *Combined Path* – considering both environmental performance and text – is significantly better than the *Direct Path*, it indicates that the environmental performance contributes to the relationship between text and financial performance.

4 Empirical Results

Table 1 shows the results of *path env*, the *Direct Path* and the *Combined Path* on the test data as well as the baseline for each classifier. All classifiers do not show a substantial improvement compared to the baseline, meaning always guessing an improvement in environmental or financial performance performs at least as good as a trained classifier. Hence, we plotted the F$_1$-score for all classifiers to analyse the results further – exemplary shown for **TF-IDF** in Figure 2. While the curve increases for $\Delta\mathrm{Env}_{i,q}$ on the validation data (see Fig. 2a), the model does not show any meaningful increase for $\Delta\mathrm{EPS}_{i,q}$ on the validation data (Fig. 2b). Both graphs show that the classifiers learn from the training data. However, generalisation remains low as the predictive power for the validation data remains low and the F$_1$-score remains below the baseline. Additionally, we observe that the loss curve (not shown) declines in all instances for the training data but the validation loss decreases only slightly for the first few epochs. Shortly thereafter, loss increases for the validation data indicating an overfit for each model. The results for other classifiers (not shown here) indicate a similar pattern. While there is no classifier for the earnings or the buy-and-hold return label that shows an increasing F$_1$-score with a decreasing loss function on the validation data, there is a slight improvement for the long and short-term environmental performance. For the environmental classifiers on the validation data, recall mostly improves during training while precision remains relatively constant. This applies for both short-term and long-term environmental performance. Even so, the classifiers remain below the baseline. For the financial performance, the classifiers do not learn from the data. Although, the training F$_1$-score increases for both financial labels, the results cannot be generalized (similar to Figure 2b). This might be due to low information content, generic language or due to our small sample. Although, the performance of all classifiers remained below expectations, we present the *Combined Path* with the original environmental performance (see Table 1 Task Combined). As could be expected from the previous results, no model proves to be better than the baseline. Further, some models showed that the best model is indeed always guessing class 1.

Model	Task	$\Delta\text{EPS}_{i,q}$			$\text{BHAR}_{i,t}$			$\Delta\text{Env}_{i,q}$			$\Delta\text{Env}_{i,t}$		
		P	R	F_1	P	R	F_1	P	R	F_1	P	R	F_1
Baseline		.53	1	.70	.49	1	.65	.44	1	.61	.37	1	.54
BOW	Single	.56	.89	.69	.51	.75	.61	.46	.64	.54	.40	.56	.46
BOW	Combined	.58	.81	.68	.51	.76	.61						
TF-IDF	Single	.54	1	.70	.49	.63	.55	.47	.45	.46	.50	.22	.31
TF-IDF	Combined	.54	1	.70	.48	.59	.53						
GloVE	Single	.54	.96	.69	.50	.89	.64	.44	.92	.59	.39	.57	.46
GloVE	Combined	.54	.94	.69	.49	1	.65						
CNN	Single	.53	1	.70	.49	1	.65	.46	.51	.48	.39	.16	.22
CNN	Combined	.53	1	.70	.49	1	.65						
BERT	Single	.54	1	.70	.48	1	.65	.44	.52	.48	.39	.10	.16
BERT	Combined	.54	1	.70	.52	.39	.44						

Table 1: Model results with precision, recall, and F_1, respectively. Task *Single* shows *Direct Path* and path *env* for each model. Task *Combined* presents *Combined Path* for each model.

5 Analysis and Discussion

Analysing the reports revealed that the MD&A section varies largely in content and size. While 10-Q reports are rather short and often refer to the 10-K report for more detail, the 10-K reports tend to be rather extensive, with some reports ranging up to more than 100 pages. However, the heterogeneity of 10-K reports make inter-comparisons quite challenging. For our sample, we could not show that the MD&A sections have information content with respect to financial or environmental performance. Given our sample, we cannot reject the null hypothesis for H1, H2, and H3 and, hence, conclude that the MD&A section is not informative with respect to financial and environmental information. However, this can be due to the low performance of the classifiers. As performance of trained classifiers could not be generalised, it is likely that there is not sufficient, material environmental and financial information within the MD&A section, i.e., reports tend to be boilerplate.

Analysing the top 200 weights of the tfidf-classifier, we observe that particularly for the environmental labels the majority of words can be related to the Pharmaceutical or Chemical Industry. The top 200 weights show that for the short-term environmental performance 25 words can be related to the Pharmaceutical or Chemical Industry (12.5%) and 41 words for the long-term environmental performance (20.5%). Filtering for reports which include at least 5 of these words reveals that these reports are related to the Manufacturing division (particularly SIC showing pharmaceutical preparations; surgical&medical instruments; biological products industry etc.). This indicates that the classifier rather learns industries instead of environmental performance, even as we are controlling for industry and market capitalization. However, it is important to note that including at least five of these words in a report does not necessarily result in a performance improvement. While for $\Delta\text{EPS}_{i,q}$ 21 words can be categorized as financial words, the top 200 words appear to be quite random for $\text{BHAR}_{i,t}$.

6 Conclusion

In this paper, we analysed the information content of the MD&A section with respect to financial and environmental narratives employing various NLP methods. We proxy environmental performance with the change in ESG rating percentile scores and the financial performance with earnings and buy-and-hold-returns. Although, we sought to implement a model that uses the predicted environmental performance and text to predict financial performance, results proved to be not as promising. Therefore, we implemented the model with the original environmental performance data instead of the predicted data. We find that our classifiers are not able to surpass a baseline model of always guessing an improvement in financial and environmental performance. As a consequence, we were not able provide evidence that the MD&A

section has information content with respect to financial and environmental narratives, and the section appears to be rather boilerplate. This asks for more structured reports with respect to volume and content as well as the inclusion of more material information. However, it is clearly a limitation of this study to focus solely on one ESG rating provider. As rating construction among providers varies, this raises general data quality concerns (Eccles and Stroehle, 2018) and limits the generalisability of our study. Although other information sources were neglected, corporate disclosures should be by itself useful, informative and reliable. While one could argue that the information is already priced into stock prices shortly after dissemination, the general information content with respect to earnings remains remarkably low. Surprisingly, the usefulness of the MD&A section appears to be quite limited with respect to future corporate performance. An explanation are the reports ambiguity and low polarization. As other researchers have shown, specific word lists are more likely to capture the specific context in this setting. Alternatively, a larger sample could overcome the distinctions of the reports for classification purpose. Future research might use different rating providers, support the classifiers by humanly annotation, or apply BERT models specific for the financial domain, like the recently published FinBert (Yang et al., 2020).

Acknowledgements

This research paper was made possible through the help and support from Christoph Klein at ESG Portfolio Management and our former colleague Sven Raith. Further, we would like to thank Laura Oberländer for her fruitful discussions and suggestions.

References

Martín Abadi, Ashish Agarwal, Paul Barham, Eugene Brevdo, Zhifeng Chen, Craig Citro, Greg S. Corrado, Andy Davis, Jeffrey Dean, Matthieu Devin, Sanjay Ghemawat, Ian Goodfellow, Andrew Harp, Geoffrey Irving, Michael Isard, Yangqing Jia, Rafal Jozefowicz, Lukasz Kaiser, Manjunath Kudlur, Josh Levenberg, Dandelion Mané, Rajat Monga, Sherry Moore, Derek Murray, Chris Olah, Mike Schuster, Jonathon Shlens, Benoit Steiner, Ilya Sutskever, Kunal Talwar, Paul Tucker, Vincent Vanhoucke, Vijay Vasudevan, Fernanda Viégas, Oriol Vinyals, Pete Warden, Martin Wattenberg, Martin Wicke, Yuan Yu, and Xiaoqiang Zheng. 2015. TensorFlow: Large-scale machine learning on heterogeneous systems. Software available from tensorflow.org.

Jay Alammar. 2019. A visual guide to using BERT for the first time. `http://jalammar.github.io/a-visual-guide-to-using-bert-for-the-first-time/`. (accessed: 2020-01-09).

Amir Amel-Zadeh and George Serafeim. 2018. Why and how investors use ESG information: Evidence from a global survey. *Financial Analysts Journal*, 74(3):87–103.

Vasiliki Athanasakou and Khaled Hussainey. 2014. The perceived credibility of forward-looking performance disclosures. *Accounting and business research*, 44(3):227–259.

Brad M. Barber and John D. Lyon. 1997. Detecting long-run abnormal stock returns: The empirical power and specification of test statistics. *Journal of financial economics*, 43(3):341–372.

Henk Berkman, Jonathan Jona, and Naomi S. Soderstrom. 2019. Firm-specific climate risk and market valuation. Available at SSRN 2775552. `https://papers.ssrn.com/sol3/papers.cfm?abstract_id=2775552`.

Steven Bird, Ewan Klein, and Edward Loper. 2009. *Natural language processing with Python: analyzing text with the natural language toolkit*. O'Reilly Media, Inc.

Robert Bloomfield. 2008. Discussion of "annual report readability, current earnings, and earnings persistence". *Journal of Accounting and Economics*, 45(2-3):248–252.

Stephen J. Brown, William Goetzmann, Roger G. Ibbotson, and Stephen A. Ross. 1992. Survivorship bias in performance studies. *The Review of Financial Studies*, 5(4):553–580.

John L. Campbell, Hsinchun Chen, Dan S. Dhaliwal, Hsin-min Lu, and Logan B. Steele. 2014. The information content of mandatory risk factor disclosures in corporate filings. *Review of Accounting Studies*, 19(1):396–455.

Jennifer N. Carpenter and Anthony W. Lynch. 1999. Survivorship bias and attrition effects in measures of performance persistence. *Journal of financial economics*, 54(3):337–374.

Reynolds Center. 2014. 10-K filings guide: Traps and mistakes. `https://businessjournalism.org/2014/02/10-k-filings-guide-traps-and-mistakes/`. (accessed: 2020-04-09).

CFA Institute. 2017. ESG survey: Global perceptions of environmental, social, and governance issues in investing. `https://www.cfainstitute.org/en/research/survey-reports/esg-survey-2017`.

François Chollet et al. 2015. Keras. `https://keras.io`.

Peter M. Clarkson, Yue Li, Gordon D. Richardson, and Florin P. Vasvari. 2008. Revisiting the relation between environmental performance and environmental disclosure: An empirical analysis. *Accounting, organizations and society*, 33(4-5):303–327.

Peter M. Clarkson, Xiaohua Fang, Yue Li, and Gordon Richardson. 2013. The relevance of environmental disclosures: Are such disclosures incrementally informative? *Journal of Accounting and Public Policy*, 32(5):410–431.

Denis Cormier and Michel Magnan. 2007. The revisited contribution of environmental reporting to investors' valuation of a firm's earnings: An international perspective. *Ecological economics*, 62(3-4):613–626.

Chester Curme, H. Eugene Stanley, and Irena Vodenska. 2015. Coupled network approach to predictability of financial market returns and news sentiments. *International Journal of Theoretical and Applied Finance*, 18(07):1–26.

Min-Yuh Day and Chia-Chou Lee. 2016. Deep learning for financial sentiment analysis on finance news providers. In *2016 IEEE/ACM International Conference on Advances in Social Networks Analysis and Mining (ASONAM)*, pages 1127–1134. IEEE.

Charl De Villiers and Ana Marques. 2016. Corporate social responsibility, country-level predispositions, and the consequences of choosing a level of disclosure. *Accounting and Business Research*, 46(2):167–195.

Jacob Devlin, Ming-Wei Chang, Kenton Lee, and Kristina Toutanova. 2019. BERT: Pre-training of deep bidirectional transformers for language understanding. In *Proceedings of the 2019 Conference of the North American Chapter of the Association for Computational Linguistics: Human Language Technologies, Volume 1 (Long and Short Papers)*, pages 4171–4186, Minneapolis, Minnesota, June. Association for Computational Linguistics.

Dan Dhaliwal, Oliver Zhen Li, Albert Tsang, and Yong George Yang. 2014. Corporate social responsibility disclosure and the cost of equity capital: The roles of stakeholder orientation and financial transparency. *Journal of Accounting and Public Policy*, 33(4):328–355.

Lodi Dodevska, Viktor Petreski, Kostadin Mishev, Ana Gjorgjevikj, Irena Vodenska, Ljubomir Chitkushev, and Dimitar Trajanov. 2019. Predicting companies stock price direction by using sentiment analysis of news articles. *Computer Science and Education in Computer Science*, pages 37–42.

Timothy M. Doyle. 2018. Ratings that don't rate: The subjective world of ESG ratings agencies. Report, American Council for Capital Formation. `https://accfcorpgov.org/wp-content/uploads/2018/07/ACCF_RatingsESGReport.pdf`.

Robert G. Eccles and Judith C. Stroehle. 2018. Exploring social origins in the construction of ESG measures. Available at SSRN 3212685. `https://papers.ssrn.com/sol3/papers.cfm?abstract_id=3318225`.

Robert G. Eccles, Michael P. Krzus, Jean Rogers, and George Serafeim. 2012. The need for sector-specific materiality and sustainability reporting standards. *Journal of Applied Corporate Finance*, 24(2):65–71.

Ronen Feldman, Suresh Govindaraj, Joshua Livnat, and Benjamin Segal. 2008. The incremental information content of tone change in management discussion and analysis. Available at SSRN 1126962. `https://papers.ssrn.com/sol3/papers.cfm?abstract_id=1126962`.

Thomas D. Fields, Thomas Z. Lys, and Linda Vincent. 2001. Empirical research on accounting choice. *Journal of Accounting and Economics*, 31(1-3):255–307.

Gunnar Friede, Timo Busch, and Alexander Bassen. 2015. ESG and financial performance: aggregated evidence from more than 2000 empirical studies. *Journal of Sustainable Finance & Investment*, 5(4):210–233.

Matthew Gentzkow, Bryan Kelly, and Matt Taddy. 2019. Text as data. *Journal of Economic Literature*, 57(3):535–74.

Paul A. Griffin. 2003. Got information? investor response to form 10-K and form 10-Q EDGAR filings. *Review of Accounting Studies*, 8(4):433–460.

Michael Grüning. 2011. Artificial intelligence measurement of disclosure (aimd). *European Accounting Review*, 20(3):485–519.

Zahra Hirji. 2013. Most U.S. companies ignoring SEC rule to disclose climate risks. Inside-Climate News. https://insideclimatenews.org/news/20130919/most-us-companies-ignoring-sec-rule-disclose-climate-risks.

Bernd Hüfner. 2007. The SEC's MD&A: does it meet the informational demands of investors? *Schmalenbach Business Review*, 59(1):58–84.

Katrin Hummel and Christian Schlick. 2016. The relationship between sustainability performance and sustainability disclosure–reconciling voluntary disclosure theory and legitimacy theory. *Journal of Accounting and Public Policy*, 35(5):455–476.

Emirhan Ilhan, Philipp Krueger, Zacharias Sautner, and Laura T. Starks. 2019. Institutional investors' views and preferences on climate risk disclosure. Swiss Finance Institute Research Paper. No. 19-66.

IMP. 2020. Statement of intent to work together towards comprehensive corporate reporting. https://www.impactmanagementproject.com/structured-network/statement-of-intent-to-work-together-towards-comprehensive-corporate-reporting/.

Narasimhan Jegadeesh and Di Wu. 2013. Word power: A new approach for content analysis. *Journal of Financial Economics*, 110(3):712–729.

Juhyun Jung, Kathleen Herbohn, and Peter Clarkson. 2018. Carbon risk, carbon risk awareness and the cost of debt financing. *Journal of Business Ethics*, 150(4):1151–1171.

Colm Kearney and Sha Liu. 2014. Textual sentiment in finance: A survey of methods and models. *International Review of Financial Analysis*, 33:171–185.

Diederik P. Kingma and Jimmy Ba. 2015. Adam: A method for stochastic optimization. Proceedings of the 3rd International Conference on Learning Representations (ICLR). Contribution to International Conference on Learning Representations, May 7-9, 2015, San Diego.

Julian F. Kölbel, Markus Leippold, Jordy Rillaerts, and Qian Wang. 2020. Does the CDS market reflect regulatory climate risk disclosures? Available at SSRN 3616324. https://papers.ssrn.com/sol3/papers.cfm?abstract_id=3616324.

Sabino P. Kothari, Xu Li, and James E. Short. 2009. The effect of disclosures by management, analysts, and business press on cost of capital, return volatility, and analyst forecasts: A study using content analysis. *The Accounting Review*, 84(5):1639–1670.

Todd Kravet and Volkan Muslu. 2013. Textual risk disclosures and investors' risk perceptions. *Review of Accounting Studies*, 18(4):1088–1122.

Benjamin Lansford. 2006. Strategic coordination of good and bad news disclosures: The case of voluntary patent disclosures and negative earnings surprises. Available at SSRN 830705. https://papers.ssrn.com/sol3/papers.cfm?abstract_id=830705.

Allison Herren Lee. 2020. "modernizing" regulation S-K: Ignoring the elephant in the room. https://www.sec.gov/news/public-statement/lee-mda-2020-01-30.

Xiaodong Li, Haoran Xie, Li Chen, Jianping Wang, and Xiaotie Deng. 2014. News impact on stock price return via sentiment analysis. *Knowledge-Based Systems*, 69:14–23.

Feng Li. 2006. Do stock market investors understand the risk sentiment of corporate annual reports? Available at SSRN 898181. https://papers.ssrn.com/sol3/papers.cfm?abstract_id=898181.

Feng Li. 2010a. The information content of forward-looking statements in corporate filings—a naïve bayesian machine learning approach. *Journal of Accounting Research*, 48(5):1049–1102.

Feng Li. 2010b. Textual analysis of corporate disclosures: Survey of the literature. *Journal of accounting literature*, 29:143–165.

Tim Loughran and Bill McDonald. 2011. When is a liability not a liability? textual analysis, dictionaries, and 10-Ks. *The Journal of Finance*, 66(1):35–65.

Tim Loughran and Bill McDonald. 2016. Textual analysis in accounting and finance: A survey. *Journal of Accounting Research*, 54(4):1187–1230.

Tim Loughran and Bill McDonald. 2019. Textual analysis in finance. Available at SSRN 3470272. `https://papers.ssrn.com/sol3/papers.cfm?abstract_id=3470272`.

Alexandra Luccioni and Hector Palacios. 2019. Using natural language processing to analyze financial climate disclosures. In *Proceedings of the 36th International Conference on Machine Learning, Long Beach, California*.

Ella Mae Matsumura, Rachna Prakash, and Sandra C Vera-Muñoz. 2018. Capital market expectations of risk materiality and the credibility of managers' risk disclosure decisions. Available at SSRN 2983977. `https://papers.ssrn.com/sol3/papers.cfm?abstract_id=2983977`.

Bill McDonald. 2019. Software repository for accounting and finance. `https://sraf.nd.edu/`. (accessed: 2020-04-09).

Kostadin Mishev, Ana Gjorgjevikj, Irena Vodenska, Ljubomir Chitkushev, Wataru Souma, and Dimitar Trajanov. 2019. Forecasting corporate revenue by using deep-learning methodologies. In *2019 International Conference on Control, Artificial Intelligence, Robotics & Optimization (ICCAIRO)*, pages 115–120. IEEE.

Antonio Moreno-Sandoval, Pablo Alfonso Haya Ana Gisbert, Marta Guerrero, and Helena Montoro. 2019. Tone analysis in spanish financial reporting narratives. In *Proceedings of the Second Financial Narrative Processing Workshop (FNP 2019)*, pages 42–50.

Volkan Muslu, Suresh Radhakrishnan, KR Subramanyam, and Dongkuk Lim. 2008. Causes and consequences of forward looking disclosures in the management discussion and analysis (MD&A). Technical report, Working Paper.

Alan R. Palmiter. 2015. Climate change disclosure: A failed SEC mandate. Available at SSRN 2639181. `https://papers.ssrn.com/sol3/papers.cfm?abstract_id=2639181`.

F. Pedregosa, G. Varoquaux, A. Gramfort, V. Michel, B. Thirion, O. Grisel, M. Blondel, P. Prettenhofer, R. Weiss, V. Dubourg, J. Vanderplas, A. Passos, D. Cournapeau, M. Brucher, M. Perrot, and E. Duchesnay. 2011. Scikit-learn: Machine learning in Python. *Journal of Machine Learning Research*, 12:2825–2830.

Jeffrey Pennington, Richard Socher, and Christopher D. Manning. 2014. Glove: Global vectors for word representation. In *Proceedings of the 2014 conference on empirical methods in natural language processing (EMNLP)*, pages 1532–1543.

Marlene Plumlee, Darrell Brown, Rachel M. Hayes, and R. Scott Marshall. 2015. Voluntary environmental disclosure quality and firm value: Further evidence. *Journal of accounting and public policy*, 34(4):336–361.

Carmelo Reverte. 2016. Corporate social responsibility disclosure and market valuation: evidence from spanish listed firms. *Review of Managerial Science*, 10(2):411–435.

Zabihollah Rezaee. 2015. *Business sustainability: Performance, compliance, accountability and integrated reporting*. Greenleaf Publishing.

Catherine M. Schrand and Beverly R. Walther. 2000. Strategic benchmarks in earnings announcements: The selective disclosure of prior-period earnings components. *The Accounting Review*, 75(2):151–177.

SEC. 1987. Securities act release no. 6711. april 24. Washington, DC. `https://www.sec.gov/rules/interp/33-6835.htm`.

SEC. 2003. Commission guidance regarding management's discussion and analysis of financial condition and results of operations. `https://www.sec.gov/rules/interp/33-8350.htm`.

SEC. 2010. Commission guidance regarding disclosure related to climate change. `http://www.sec.gov/rules/interp/2010/33-9106.pdf`.

Natalia Semenova, Lars Hassel, and Henrik Nilsson. 2010. The value relevance of environmental and social performance: Evidence from swedish six 300 companies. *The Finnish Journal of Business Economics*, 3:265–292, 01.

Philip J. Stone, Dexter C. Dunphy, and Marshall S. Smith. 1966. The general inquirer: A computer approach to content analysis. MIT press.

Lawrence R. Tavcar. 1998. Make the MD&A more readable. *The CPA Journal*, 68(1):10.

TCFD. 2019. Task force on climate-related financial disclosures: 2019 status report. `https://www.fsb-tcfd.org/wp-content/uploads/2019/06/2019-TCFD-Status-Report-FINAL-053119.pdf`.

Frank HM Verbeeten, Ramin Gamerschlag, and Klaus Möller. 2016. Are CSR disclosures relevant for investors? empirical evidence from germany. *Management Decision*.

Robert E. Verrecchia. 1983. Discretionary disclosure. *Journal of Accounting and Economics*, 5:179 – 194.

Robert E. Verrecchia. 2001. Essays on disclosure. *Journal of Accounting and Economics*, 32(1-3):97–180.

Roshaan Wasim. 2019. Corporate (non) disclosure of climate change information. *Columbia Law Review*, 119(5):1311–1354.

Thomas Wolf, Lysandre Debut, Victor Sanh, Julien Chaumond, Clement Delangue, Anthony Moi, Pierric Cistac, Tim Rault, R'emi Louf, Morgan Funtowicz, and Jamie Brew. 2019. Huggingface's transformers: State-of-the-art natural language processing. arXiv: 1910.03771. `https://arxiv.org/abs/1910.03771`.

Fang Yang, Burak Dolar, and Lun Mo. 2018. Textual analysis of corporate annual disclosures: a comparison between bankrupt and non-bankrupt companies. *Journal of Emerging Technologies in Accounting*, 15(1):45–55.

Yi Yang, Mark Christopher Siy UY, and Allen Huang. 2020. Finbert: A pretrained language model for financial communications.

Ye Zhang and Byron C. Wallace. 2017. A sensitivity analysis of (and practitioners' guide to) convolutional neural networks for sentence classification. In *Proceedings of the Eighth International Joint Conference on Natural Language Processing (Volume 1: Long Papers)*, pages 253–263.

Appendix

A Data preprocessing details

For matching the environmental ratings with the filing date, we apply the following process: Reports are usually filed sometime during the month, e.g., 11.02.2016. However, the ESG data available on Bloomberg is adjusted on a monthly basis at the end of each month, e.g., 28.02.2016. To measure a change in the rating data, we need to match each filing date with the previous months rating. This means a file published on the 11.02.2016 is assigned the ESG percentile score of the 31.01.2016 – provided that a rating exists. Subsequently, the according change in the percentile score is calculated. For reports that were published in February 2014 or March 2014, it is likely that no prior data on the environmental rating is available, hence, the report is not considered. This also applies to some companies that are not rated at all.

B Label calculation

The first financial class label is the change in earnings per share. It serves as a measure of the informativeness of the MD&A section and is defined as $\Delta\text{EPS}_{i,q} = \text{EPS}_{i,q+1} - \text{EPS}_{i,q}$, where the change in earnings per share $\Delta EPS_{i,q}$ is measured as the difference in the earnings reported in the next period $q+1$ and the previously reported earnings for company i.

For the second financial class label, we use buy-and-hold returns and classify the 10-K and 10-Q filings based on the sign of the buy-and-hold returns, $\text{BHAR}_{i,t} = \prod_{t=0}^{t}[1 + R_{it}] - \prod_{t=0}^{t}[1 + R_{mt}]$, where R_{it} and R_{mt} are the returns on stock i and on the SP500 index on date t. Barber and Lyon (1997) state that BHAR are particularly suited for longer periods compared to other measures. BHAR indicates how the information is perceived by investors.

For the first label on the environmental narrative, we use the quarterly change in the environmental percentile score to match the according $\Delta\text{EPS}_{i,q}$ label. The change in the percentile score can be formally expressed as $\Delta\text{Env}_{i,q} = \text{Env}_{i,q+1} - \text{Env}_{i,q}$, with q indicating the according quarter for company i.

The second class label on the environmental narrative uses a one months time horizon to match the $\text{BHAR}_{i,t}$ label. $\Delta\text{Env}_{i,t}$ is the change in the environmental percentile score over the subsequent month, formally expressed as $\Delta\text{Env}_{i,t} = \text{Env}_{i,t+1} - \text{Env}_{i,t}$, with the previously available percentile score being $\text{Env}_{i,t}$ for company i on the filing date and $\text{Env}_{i,t+1}$ being the next environmental score available.

Information Extraction from

Federal Open Market Committee Statements

Oana Frunza
Morgan Stanley
oana.frunza@morganstaley.com

Abstract

We present a novel approach to unsupervised information extraction by identifying and extracting relevant concept-value pairs from textual data. The system's building blocks are domain agnostic, making it universally applicable. In this paper, we describe each component of the system and how it extracts relevant economic information from U.S. Federal Open Market Committee[1] (FOMC) statements. Our methodology achieves an impressive 96% accuracy for identifying relevant information for a set of seven economic indicators: household spending, inflation, unemployment, economic activity, fixed investment, federal funds rate, and labor market.

1 Introduction

While there are many information extraction approaches described in the literature (Niklaus et al. 2018; Jeanhee and Shawn, 2005), there are few that can extract targeted concept-value pairs with sentiment scores and are universally applicable to various data types. In addition, many systems require training data or additional corpora to draw meaningful statistics from. We built a framework that does not make use of predefined language patterns or any additional training data to extract targeted concept-value pairs with sentiment scores, across various data types. In addition, the framework provides a means to derive a semantic representation of unstructured data along with supporting sentiment analysis. We applied it to extract a set of economic concepts and their associated values in FOMC statements.

Financial events and information relevant to stakeholders are disseminated at constantly, yielding massive amounts of textual data. In recent years, unstructured textual data has become an important source of information for various financial systems, (Xing et al. 2018). While some textual data is created at high frequencies, *e.g.*, news headlines, others as-necessary, *e.g.* SEC[2] filings, others are generated at pre-defined time intervals, *e.g.* FOMC statements.

The statements appear roughly every 6 weeks but if special circumstances arise, like the Covid-19 pandemic at the beginning of 2020, additional statements are released accordingly. Each FOMC statement lays out the direction of U.S. monetary policy. These statements include the federal funds rate, one of the most important economic indicators. In addition, they contain information about inflation, unemployment, economic growth, and monetary supply. The language used in these statements is carefully selected; every word included is intentional due to the market moving effects of these statements.

---

[1] https://www.federalreserve.gov/monetarypolicy/fomccalendars.htm
[2] https://www.sec.gov/

Proceedings of the 1st Joint Workshop on Financial Narrative Processing and MultiLing Financial Summarisation, pages 195–203
Barcelona, Spain (Online), December 12, 2020.

Changes in wordings have shown to bring major effects on markets (Gurkaynak et al., 2005) and directions of market movements have shown to be correlated with statement sentiment scores (Rosa, 2011).

In essence, the most important economic aspects in the statement are federal funds rate, household spending, inflation, unemployment, economic activity, fixed investment, and labor market conditions. Identifying and extracting these concepts along with what is said about them would not only provide a semantic representation of the statement but give rise to a fast integration, as soon as release time, of crucial economic data. Results can be easily and timely integrated into decision making processes, without any human effort. They can be used to derive short- and long-term interest rates, foreign exchange rates, employment rates, economic output, and the supply of credit and demand for investment.

Furthermore, providing sentiment analysis for each economic concept will make the extracted information more valuable to both humans and financial systems.

In the next sections we are going to present our information extraction system, each of its components, and how we applied it to extract economic concept-value pairs from FOMC statements.

2 Problem Statement

In this study we propose an unsupervised information extraction framework that is able to extract concept-value pairs from textual data. In addition, our approach differentiates itself from other methods in that it also assigns a sentiment score to each extracted pair. Unsupervised extraction refers to the fact that no training set was provided to the system at the time it was built.

We built this system to extract seven economic concepts and their values from FOMC statements. While the framework is universal and can be applied to any other unstructured textual data without further tuning, we anchor the system's description around FOMC statements. To show that we can apply the framework to other types of data, in the Results section we present system outputs on a sample of short news articles. Table 1 provides an example of an expected output for the information extracted.

FOMC statement	Expected output
January 29, 2020 Federal Reserve issues FOMC statement For release at 2:00 p.m. EST Share Information received since the Federal Open Market Committee met in December indicates that the labor market remains strong and that economic activity has been rising at a moderate rate. Job gains have been solid, on average, in recent months, and the unemployment rate has remained low. Although household spending has been rising at a moderate pace, business fixed investment and exports remain weak. On a 12-month basis, overall inflation and inflation for items other than food and energy are running below 2 percent. Market-based measures of inflation compensation remain low; survey-based measures of longer-term inflation expectations are little changed. Consistent with its statutory mandate, the Committee seeks to foster maximum employment and price stability. The Committee decided to maintain the target range for the federal funds rate at 1-1/2 to 1-3/4 percent. The Committee judges that the current stance of monetary policy is appropriate to support sustained expansion of economic activity, strong labor market conditions, and inflation returning to the Committee's symmetric 2 percent objective. The Committee will continue to monitor the implications of incoming information for the economic outlook, including global developments and muted inflation pressures, as it assesses the appropriate path of the target range for the federal funds rate. In determining the timing and size of future adjustments to the target range for the federal funds rate, the Committee will assess realized and expected economic conditions relative to its maximum employment objective and its symmetric 2 percent inflation objective. This assessment will take into account a wide range of information, including measures of labor market conditions, indicators of inflation pressures and inflation expectations, and readings on financial and international developments. Voting for the monetary policy action were Jerome H. Powell, Chair; John C. Williams, Vice Chair; Michelle W. Bowman; Lael Brainard; Richard H. Clarida; Patrick Harker; Robert S. Kaplan; Neel Kashkari; Loretta J. Mester; and Randal K. Quarles. Implementation Note issued January 29, 2020	**household spending**: have moderated **inflation**: 2 percent **unemployment**: has stayed low **economic activity**: has been rising at a moderate rate **fixed investment**: have moderated from their strong fourth-quarter readings **federal funds rate**: 1-1/2 to 1-3/4 percent **labor market**: has continued to strengthen

Table 1. Example of an FOMC statement with expected output.

Investigating the expected output in Table 1, the problem we address is a concept-value or key-value pair extraction task. One important aspect to mention is that while we know that we aim to extract values for a targeted set of economic factors it is not necessarily true that the exact factor *e.g.* "economic activity" is present in the statement. More so, when the concept is present it can appear in many places and the system must choose which occurrence to output. As an example, there are many places where "inflation" is mentioned in the above statement, "*survey-based measures of longer-term inflation expectations are little changed, on balance*", "*but the Committee is monitoring inflation developments closely*", "*Inflation on a 12-month basis is expected to move up…*" etc., but the only mention that is of interest is the one that contains the rate, "*have continued to run below 2 percent*".

As mentioned earlier, our approach does not stop at just identifying and selecting key-value pairs. It also assigns a sentiment score to the pair. The sentiment score reflects the tone of the language used to describe the factor, either positive or negative with values between -1 and 1. The sentiment does not take into account the financial aspect but is lexically driven. For example, "unemployment: has stayed low", has a negative score since the language used to describe the factor uses words associate with a negative sentiment, even though economically speaking, a low unemployment rate is a positive economic outcome. However, this can be easily remedied by flagging the factors for which the sentiment scores need to be inversed. As a result, the score of the above example will change polarity to become positive.

In summary, we tackle a concept-value pair information extraction task with sentiment analysis. We focus the task on FOMC statements but build a universal solution for any unstructured textual data.

The following sections describe the building blocks that constitute our methodology.

3   Related Work

While there is a rich body of literature on information extraction, (Saidul and Vincent Ng, 2014; Chung and Murphy, 2005) there are not many studies that address a concept-value pair extraction task with sentiment analysis for financial text. Sentiment analysis for financial data has been a hot research interest for both natural language processing and finance fields. There is a large body of literature on how to perform this task with solutions falling in two main categories: lexical resource-based, (Loughran and McDonald, 2011; Ke et al., 2019) and machine-learning based, (Zhang et al., 2018). The financial domain tends to prefer the former mainly due to ease of use and efficiency, (Kearney and Liu, 2014).

Our methodology, unlike related research, makes use of the extraction layer to derive better sentiment scores. We have tried off-the shelf solutions for adding sentiment scores but none of the options were acceptable, (Tang et al., 2009). A large majority of off-the-shelf solutions are built on product reviews, making them unsuitable for financial data, mostly due to poor coverage and resulting neutral sentiment scores. The literature, mostly on identification of features of product reviews (Zhang and Liu, 2014) makes use of similar building blocks, but our methodology does not heavily rely on problem constraints *e.g.,* use of opinion or sentiment words for aspect identification or it does not yield as comprehensive output as ours. Also, systems that return sentiment scores for very short texts, even for financial data are not widely supported. While we make use of a pre-existing lexical resource, we enhance it with a graph-based methodology to weigh in the importance of each word a technique we have not seen previously. Therefore, the end-to-end architecture that we propose becomes a complete coherent solution.

In terms of FOMC sentiment analysis our method stands out in comparison to other research for the fact that we assign a sentiment score to individual economic concepts rather than to the statement as a whole (Cannon. 2015). We provide individual sentiment scores for the most salient economic aspects mentioned in the statement, giving users more powerful decision tools.

While there is a considerable body of literature around FOMC analysis, a substantial amount is focused on mining meeting notes rather than the statement itself, e.g., identify covered topics in minutes (Hansen et al., 2015) and predict economic indicators like equity and interest rate volatilities (Boukus and Rosenberg, 2006). Compared to other studies on FOMC statement analysis, our solution brings improvements in terms of both methodology and granularity of the information it extracts.

4   Methodology

To this point, we have laid the groundwork of the solution proposed and the problem tackled. In this section, we are going to detail our proposed methodology and each building block it contains. Our concept-value pair information extraction system is rooted in dependency parsing outcome, with each subsequent step making use of the previous one, all leading up to a sentiment analysis and a concept-value pair filtering step. In a nutshell, the main components our framework makes use of are as follows:

1. Dependency parsing
2. Concept-value pair extraction

3. Sentiment analysis
4. Concept-value pair filtering

While the end results are relevant concept-value pairs, the input data for our system is the .html file of the statement. The textual body is extracted using the BeautifulSoup[3] package.

Figure 1 depicts an overview of our proposed methodology.

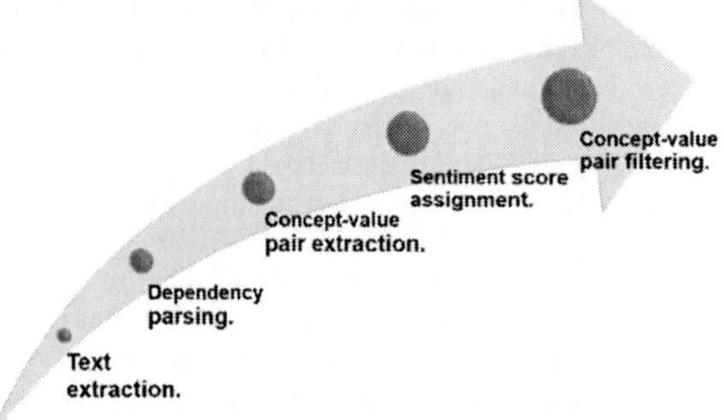

Figure 1. Methodology overview.

In the following subsections we describe each individual component of the system.

4.1 Dependency parsing information and concept-value pair extraction

While we build our framework on top of a few textual analysis components, syntactic dependency information represents the central part of the methodology we propose. We decided to do this because in the absence of any labeled data, syntactic information is a rich source of knowledge. Also, the language used is grammatically correct resulting in highly accurate parsed data. Finally, sentences tend to be short and factual, allowing for important information to be captured by primary dependency relations.

We obtain dependency parsing information by using the Stanford CoreNLP[4] engine on the entire body of a statement. After we retrieve parsed data, the system begins to build concept-value pairs by identifying each "**nsubj**" relation. With all relations identified, the next steps focus on adding targeted dependents, in a recursive manner, to each component of the relation. The below steps highlight the way our methodology makes uses of dependency information:

1. Run each sentence of the statement through the parser.
2. Identify subject-verb relation, "**nsubj**", where **POS=NN***.
3. For both **Subject** and **Governor** entities in the "**nsubj**" relation:
   a. Attach right dependents, if their syntactic relation is part of a *pre-defined set*.
   b. Attach left dependents, if their syntactic relation is part of a *pre-defined set*.
   c. If the **POS** of any added dependents is part of a *pre-defined set*, re-run the steps in 3.

There are few pre-defined sets of syntactic information we mention in the above algorithm, syntactic relations for left and right dependents, these are two different sets, and POS information for when to recursively call the algorithm. While our method is unsupervised, the sets of syntactic relations mentioned above were fine-tuned from a process that manually analyzed system results on 3 years of FOMC statements, 2013 through 2015, a total of around 15 statements. We started with lists derived by using the meaning of the syntactic relations then adjusted them by analyzing the results.

Figure 2 shows the parse result of a sentence, the starting point of the process.

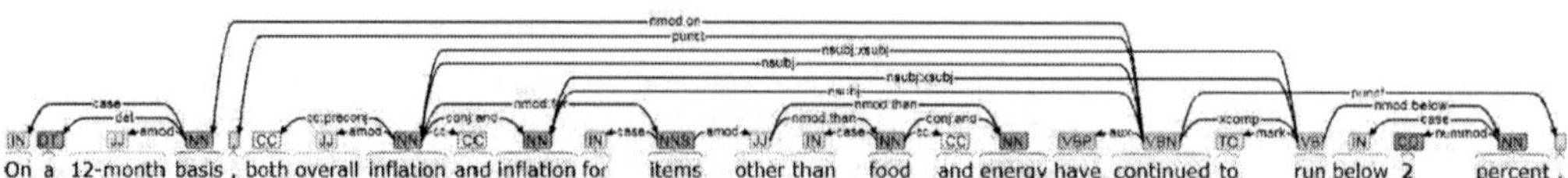

Figure 2. Dependency parsing output.

[3] https://www.crummy.com/software/BeautifulSoup/bs4/doc/
[4] https://stanfordnlp.github.io/CoreNLP/

The outcome of running the algorithm consists of a list of concept-value pairs, rooted in **nsubj** relations. The **key** is the **Subject** with its chosen dependents and the **value** is the **Governor** with its dependents. For a better understanding of the pair extraction step, we added an example bellow.

The concept-pair extraction steps are as follows:

1. **Subject relations:**
    1. "inflation" – "continued"
    2. "inflation" – "continued"
2. **Subject relations dependents:**
    1. "inflation" – "continued"
        1. **"inflation"** -> [both overall **inflation** and inflation [for] $_2$ items]$_1$
        2. **"continued"** -> [have **continued** [to]$_2$ run [below 2]$_3$ [percent]$_2$]$_1$
    2. "inflation" – "continued"
        1. **"inflation"** -> [**inflation**]$_1$
        2. **"continued"** -> [have **continued** [to]$_2$ run [below 2]$_3$ [percent]$_2$]$_1$
3. **Extracted key-value pairs:**
    1. **both overall inflation and inflation for items - have continued to run below 2 percent**
    2. **inflation - have continued to run below 2 percent**

4.2 Sentiment analysis

Subsequent to the dependency parsing module is the sentiment analysis step. Each concept-pair extracted in the previous step will receive a sentiment score.

Since we tried off-the-shelf tools, without being able to successfully capture the sentiment of the language used in the statements, the vast majority of scores turn neutral, we decided to perform this step with a custom-based solution. In fact, it is well known that sentiment analysis tools that are trained on customer product reviews, like the vast majority of available tools, are not suitable for financial texts. Loughran and McDonald (2011) found out that a large majority of negative words aren't negative if used in financial contexts. As an example, the word "bond" in non-financial data carries a positive connotation, but in finance is just a financial instrument that carries an objective charge.

Our proposed solution is rooted in SentiWordNet, (Esuli Andrea and Sebastiani, 2010) a lexical resource based on WordNet[5]. In SentiWordNet, each word is associated with three scores: objective, positive, and negative. These scores are obtained using a statistical model. We decided to use this resource to leverage the lexical and semantic nature of WordNet and the part-of-speech information. It provided superior results even though it is not specifically tuned for financial data. It also allowed us to derive custom sentiment scores and to easily and efficiently perform a sentiment analysis step.

To make our sentiment score more meaningful we accounted for, only the words that belong to the top key phrases extracted by the TextRank algorithm, (Mihalcea and Tarau, 2004). The algorithm identifies the most central key phrases in the text by using a rank-based graph method.

Given the above observations around our sentiment analysis component, the approach we implement to derive a sentiment score for the value of each concept-pair is as follows:

1. Run the TextRank algorithm on the statement to identify top keyphrases
2. For each value word that belongs to the selected keyphrases, calculate the (positive – negative) SentiWordNet score, taking into account POS information.
    a. If negation present, negate value.
3. Compute concept-value pair sentiment score as the average of the scores from step 2.

Using the approach described above, below are some examples of assigned scores:

- *advanced: 0.1406*
- *remains elevated: 0.0729*
- *continued to advance: 0.0417*
- *declined: -0.0893*

---

[5] https://wordnet.princeton.edu/

- *has stayed low: -0.2051*

From these examples we can observe how our method is able to capture various nuances of the language: *"declined"* has a lower score than *"has stayed low"*. At the end of this step, our framework assigns a sentiment score for each extracted pair with values ranging from -1 to 1.

4.3   Concept-value pair filtering

The last component we implement is a selection step where we only select one concept-value pair for each of the economic factors of interest from all extracted concept-value pairs. The ultimate goal is to expose the one concept-value pair that captures the right information, as presented in Table 1.

The way we conduct this phase is by implementing a set of functions that act as adjustable knobs. One function is aimed to filter and identify relevant pairs by searching the economic factor in either the key, the value, or both parts of a pair. Another function supports a search step that allows for both string and embedding-based matching. Here, an embedding space of the implementer's choice can be used.

Besides the availability of robust search strategies, we also defined and implemented a set of targeted constraints a pair needs to follow *e.g.*, should contain numbers, returns only the shortest pair, etc. While the method has some default behavior and returns the best shortest match it also supports the return of the entire set of best matches.

One of the most robust features of the system is the fact that it is very easy to enhance it to target additional economic factors *e.g.*, job status. In order to achieve this, simply name a new factor of interest and if necessary, define which constraints the pairs need to follow.

Below are some examples of extracted pairs that show the language variations the method is able to capture. The text in bold represents the concept part of the pair while the underlined text is the value.

- *On a 12-month basis, overall **inflation** and the measure excluding food and energy prices have declined and <u>are running below 2 percent</u>.*
- ***Labor market conditions** <u>improved</u>, with the **unemployment rate** <u>declining further</u>.*
- *Recent data suggest that **growth of household spending** <u>moderated from its strong fourth-quarter pace</u>, while **business fixed investment** <u>continued to grow strongly</u>.*
- ***Household spending** <u>has continued to rise moderately</u> while **business fixed investment** <u>has remained soft</u>.*

The filtering module is the last step, at the end of which the best concept-value pairs are identified.

5   Results

For each given statement and for each economic factor, the system will return a single best concept-value pair with a sentiment score. When measuring the system's performance on how well it is able to identify and extract the correct pairs, both precision and recall stand at **96%**. These results are manually obtained on a dataset of 30 statements of 5 years, 2016 to 2020, inclusive.

The cases where the method is not identifying or extracting the correct information are mostly due to one of the following reasons: the quality of the parsing output, search match, *e.g.* while the method extracts the pair *"investment - advanced more quickly in recent months"* the filtering step fails to select it due to missing string match with "fixed investment", and occasionally large variations in the language of the statement that do not allow the method to extract the complete relevant value.

The default system output is an .xlsx file that contains the extracted concept-value pairs and their sentiment scores. This format can be easily integrated with automatic systems. In addition, to show how the extracted information can be used for human consumption, Figure 3 presents results obtained over a period of 8 years, 2013 to 2020, for two of the economic factors. We used bars to represent federal-funds rates, one of the most important economic information, and labels to depict economic factors values. We color coded the bars to reflect the sentiment scores, red color encodes a positive sentiment while blue a negative one. Sentiment intensity is reflected in the darkness of the color. In addition, the lower part of the plot captures the sentiment score throughout the years providing users with a historic view of how the sentiment of an economic factor changes and how it is correlated with the federal funds rate.

As we can observe, our method is not only able to identify and surface the right information but also provides a sentiment analysis history for the economic factors. This aspect in itself represents a

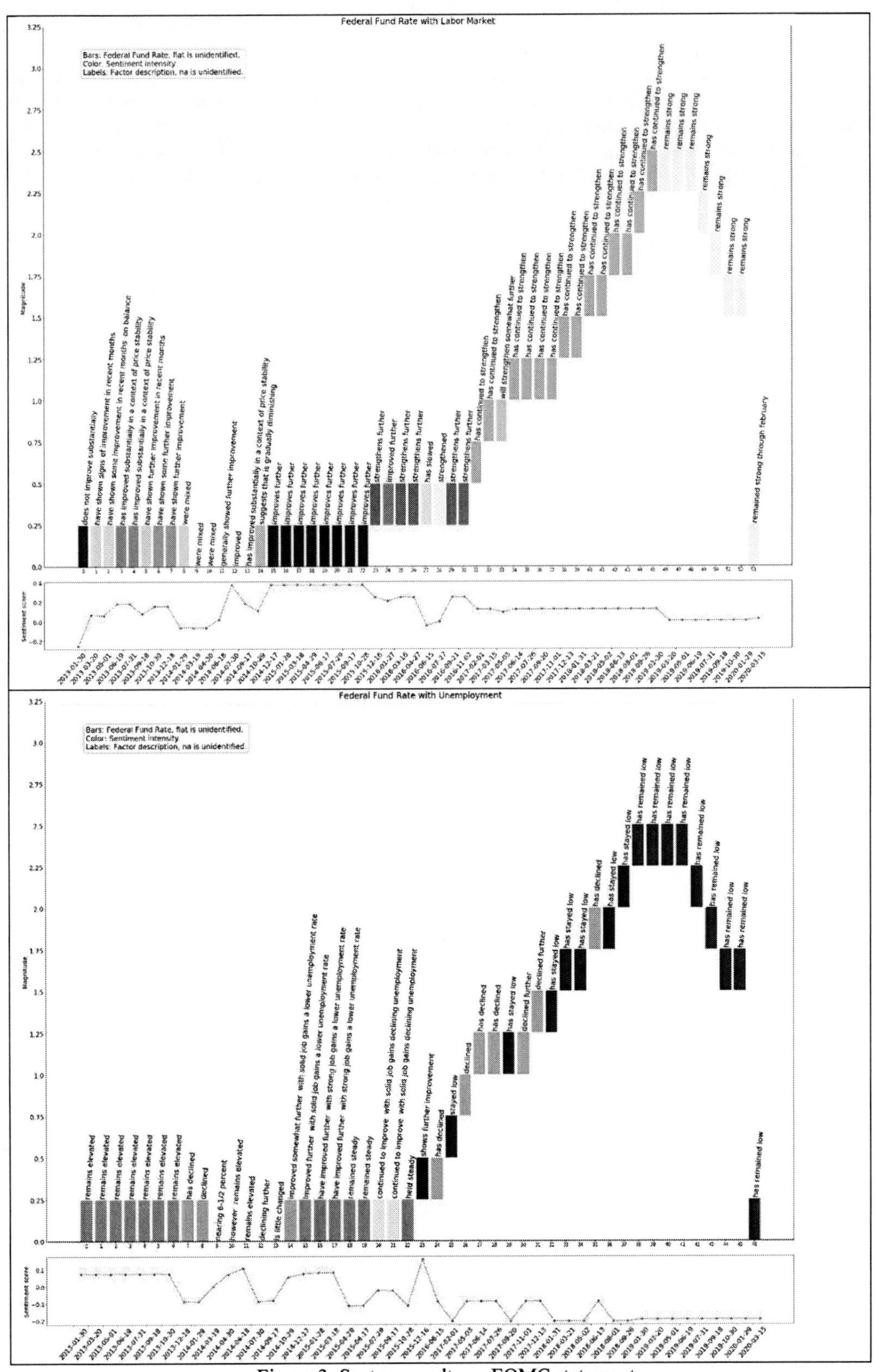

Figure 3. System results on FOMC statements.

valuable source of information for financial systems that try to predict the type of economy we could expect. More so, the extracted concept-value pairs can provide a semantic representation of an FOMC statement given that it captures the most salient information. Revealing such a semantically charged representation allows both humans and financial systems to easily compare and contrast how various economic aspects change throughout the years.

For a more complete analysis we run our methodology on news articles. Figure 4 presents results on the following news body *"The U.S. dollar declined against most major foreign currencies yesterday, although the drop was softened when bond prices failed to advance Tuesday's rally. The dollar began weakening in Europe as interest rates fell there for dollar deposits. The decline continued in New York trading, which was thin, although the dollar recovered slightly when bond prices began falling. Lower bond prices translate into higher long-term interest yields, which make dollar denominated investments more attractive. The bond market later closed little-changed from Tuesday. 'This is the first time in a while that we've gone back to trading off interest rates, and my feeling is it will continue between now and the (U.S.) election,' said Daniel Holland, an assistant vice president at Discount Corp., New York. In late New York trading, the dollar fell to 3.0210 West German marks from 3.0318 marks on Tuesday. The British pound rose to $1.2223 from $1.2155. In early Tokyo trading Thursday, the dollar strengthened against the Japanese currency, to 245.45 yen from 245.13 yen late yesterday in New York."*[6]

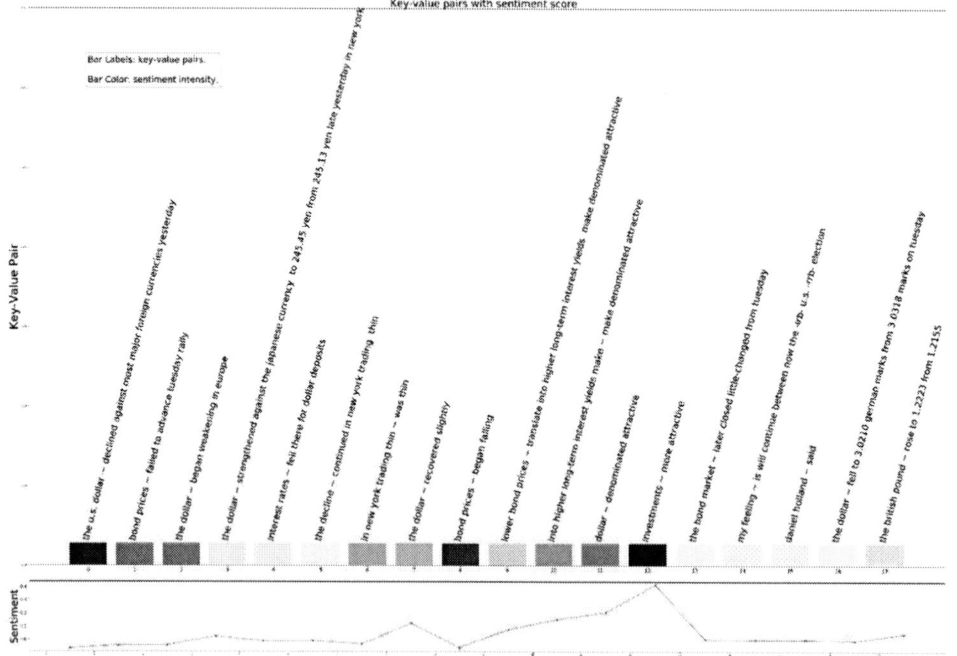

Figure 4. System results on news.

The extracted key-value pairs show that we can easily obtain a semantic summary of what has been mentioned in the body along with the sentiment it conveys. Results support the fact that our methodology extracts important information from a variety of textual data.

6 Conclusions

In this study we presented a novel unsupervised information extraction system with sentiment analysis. Our proposed architecture is robust, as it can be extended to support new targeted concepts, it can easily adapt to user-defined constraints, and it can be tuned to vary the amount of information it returns. We achieve 96% accuracy at extracting relevant concept pairs from FOMC statements and we show that we can use the same methodology on completely different data than the one used for tuning.

---

[6] https://www.figure-eight.com/data-for-everyone/

Acknowledgements

I would like to thank Morgan Stanley head of Transformation Division, MD Sigal Zarmi and the head of the Montreal, Canada office, MD Alan Vesprini for their support.

References

San Cannon. 2015. Sentiment of the FOMC: Unscripted. Federal Reserve Bank of Kansas City Economic Review (Fourth Quarter).

Jeanhee Chung, Shawn Murphy. 2005. Concept-value pair extraction from semi-structured clinical narrative: a case study using echocardiogram reports. AMIA Annual Symposium Proceedings, 2005:131–135.

Andrea Esuli and Fabrizio Sebastiani. 2010. Sentiwordnet 3.0: An enhanced lexical resource for sentiment analysis and opinion mining. In *Proceedings of the Seventh International Conference on Language Resources and Evaluation (LREC'10)*, pages: 2200–2204, Valletta, Malta.

Chung Jeanhee and Murphy Shawn. 2005. *Concept-Value Pair Extraction from Semi-Structured Clinical Narrative: A Case Study Using Echocardiogram Reports.* AMIA Annual Symposium proceedings / AMIA Symposium. AMIA Symposium 2005, pages: 131-5.

Refet S. Gurkaynak, Brian Sack, and Eric T. Swanson. 2005. *Do actions speak louder than words? The response of asset prices to monetary policy actions and statements.* Intl J Central Banking 1(1). May 2005.

Hasan Kazi Saidul and Vincent Ng. 2014. Automatic Keyphrase Extraction: A Survey of the State of the Art. In *Proceedings of the 52nd Annual Meeting of the Association for Computational Linguistics*, 2014, pages 1262–1273, Baltimore, Maryland, USA.

Colm Kearney and Sha Liu. 2014. *Textual sentiment in finance: A survey of methods and models.* International Review of Financial Analysis, 33:171-185.

Tim Loughran, and Bill McDonald. 2011. When a liability is not a liability? Textual analysis, dictionaries, and 10-Ks. *The Journal of Finance* 66(1): 35-65.

Pekka Malo, Ankur Sinha, Pyry Takala, Pekka Korhonen, Jyrki Wallenius. 2014. Good Debt or Bad Debt: Detecting Semantic Orientations in Economic Texts. *Journal of the American Society for Information Science and Technology,* 65, 4, pp. 782-796.

Rada Mihalcea and Paul Tarau. 2004. Textrank: Bringing order into texts. In *Proceedings of the Conference on Empirical Methods in Natural Language Processing*, pages 404–411, Barcelona, Spain.

Christina Niklaus, Matthias Cetto, André Freitas and Siegfried Handschuh. 2018. A Survey on Open Information Extraction. In *Proceedings of the 27th International Conference on Computational Linguistics*, pages 3866–3878, Santa Fe, NM, USA. 33.

Carlo Rosa. 2011. Words that shake traders: the stock markets reaction to central bank communication in real time. *Journal of Empirical Finance Volume 18, Issue 5, 2011, pages 915-934.*

Huifeng Tang, Songbo Tan, and Xueqi Cheng. 2009. A survey on sentiment detection of reviews. Expert Systems with Applications (ELSEVIER), 2009, 36:10760–10773.

Zheng Tracy Ke, Bryan T. Kelly, and Dacheng Xiu. 2019. *Predicting Returns with Text Data.* Cambridge, MA: NBER Working Paper Series.

Bikesh Upreti, Philipp Back, Pekka Malo, Oskar Ahlgren, and Ankur Sinha. 2019. Knowledge-Driven Approaches for Financial News Analytics. In: *Network Theory and Agent-Based Modeling in Economics and Finance.* Springer, Singapore: pages 375-404, Springer, Singapore.

Frank Xing, Erik Cambria, and Roy Welsch. 2018. Natural language based financial forecasting: A survey. Artificial Intelligence Review. 2018, doi:10.1007/s10462-017-9588-9.

Lei Zhang and Bing Liu. 2014. Aspect and entity extraction for opinion mining. In *Data Mining and Knowledge Discovery for Big Data*, Volume 1, pages 1-40. Springer.

Lei Zhang, Shuai Wang, and Bing Liu. 2018. Deep learning for sentiment analysis: A survey. In *Wiley Interdisciplinary Reviews: Data Mining and Knowledge Discovery*, page e1253. Wiley Online Library.

Mitigating Silence in Compliance Terminology during Parsing of Utterances

Esme Manandise
Intuit Futures
2600 Marine Way
Mountain View, CA 94043
USA
esme_manandise@intuit.com

Conrad De Peuter
Intuit
2600 Marine Way
Mountain View, CA 94043
USA
Conrad_DePeuter@intuit.com

Abstract

This paper reports on an approach to increase multi-token-term recall in a parsing task. We use a compliance-domain parser to extract, during the process of parsing raw text, terms that are unlisted in the terminology. The parser uses a similarity measure (Generalized Dice Coefficient) between listed terms and unlisted term candidates to (i) determine term status, (ii) serve putative terms to the parser, (iii) decrease parsing complexity by glomming multi-tokens as lexical singletons, and (iv) automatically augment the terminology. We illustrate a small experiment with examples from the tax-and-regulations domain. Bootstrapping the parsing process to detect out-of-vocabulary terms at runtime increases parsing accuracy in addition to producing other benefits to a natural-language-processing pipeline, which translates arithmetic calculations written in English into computer-executable operations.

1 Introduction

The task of extracting multi-token terms [1], i.e. terminological units which denote concepts and entities in a domain, is a core task of Natural Language Processing (NLP). Within the tax-and-regulations domain, some terms are compositional (Nunberg et al., 1994; Baldwin, 2006; Krcmar et al., 2013; Boguraev et al., 2015) [2] in meaning and/or in form, such as *unmarried college student* or *estimated tax payment*; others are mixed instances of compositionality such as *taxable sick leave pay* or *cannabis duty payable*. In addition, terms can correspond either to the canonical form of the concept or to variant forms of concepts' names as in *spouse or common-law partner credit* versus *spouse's or common-law partner's credit*, or *spouse amount* versus *spousal amount* (Park et al., 2002).

From the perspective of parsing raw text, having multi-token terms not only simplifies the input by grouping multi-tokens as singletons but also removes syntactic complexity as the internal structure of these expressions remains opaque to parsing (Korkontzelos et al., 2010; Wehrli, 2014; Boguraev et al., 2015; Nerima et al., 2017). In addition, having multi-token terms allows parsers to output structurally-similar parses for sentences that are constituent-wise similar even if the intra-phrasal complexity of multi-token terms vary.

One major issue in term extraction, known as *silence*, is the failure to extract terms that appear infrequently in a domain-corpus but that domain-specialists would include in a term lexicon. An example of *silence* is when terms such as *inventory valuation* or *combination money purchase* do not make it into the terminology because they occur infrequently in our domain corpus [3]. In the tax-and-regulations domain, the problem with terminology *silence* is particularly acute, as there are many instances of rules and arithmetic calculations concerning a specific entity which is mentioned once in the entire corpus. While

---

[1] We are not focused on single-token terms. These were extracted in a separate base lexicon.

[2] Compositionality whereby the meaning of an expression is a function of the meaning of its immediate constituents and the syntactic rules used to combine them.

[3] Our corpus consists of a collection of tax forms and instructions for Canada (https://www.canada.ca/en/revenue-agency/services/forms-publications.html) and the United States (https://www.irs.gov/forms-instructions). Approximately 20,000 multi-token terms were automatically extracted. The terms are not vetted by human experts. The parser itself is tasked with choosing the best listed terms for the raw utterance being parsed.

Proceedings of the 1st Joint Workshop on Financial Narrative Processing and MultiLing Financial Summarisation, pages 204–212
Barcelona, Spain (Online), December 12, 2020.

the entity is not mentioned enough to be highly scored by collocation-based measures during the term extraction process, for the purposes of automatically interpreting and representing tax-and-regulations content, it is essential the entity be treated the same as other items in its class by the parser.

This paper describes a simple method for extracting automatically multi-token terms that are not listed in the compliance terminology at the start of the parsing process of unlabelled utterances. The compliance terminology for taxes and regulations is the result of prior work on identifying, given the domain corpus, concepts and entities by means of co-occurrence/collocation-based surface statistical measures. In addition, linguistic-rule-based filters exclude a set of ill-formed terms from the final list. Because out-of-vocabulary (OOV) terms are tax-and-regulations–specific, we cannot rely on external lexical resources as these expressions are unlikely to be listed in general-purpose, financial or business lexicons. In our approach, the detection of OOV terms takes place during parsing. We use Generalized-Dice-Coefficient-based (GDC) metrics [4] to estimate the degree of similarity between established terms and OOV term candidates. When the GDC-based detection of multi-token terms is enabled during parsing of utterances, experiments show improvements of 93% in parsing accuracy for utterances with OOV terms at the start of the parsing process.

2 Motivation

The goal of the compliance-domain parser is to output, in a simplified logical form (SLF) (Wang et al., 2015, Constant et al., 2016), a semantic representation of utterances taken from tax forms written in English [5]. Of particular interest, are utterances that express entire or partial arithmetic calculations. Downstream components of our NLP pipeline interpret the SLFs and automatically transform them into executable operations.

In our compliance domain, the language of arithmetic calculations written in English is distributed along a continuum of syntactic complexity. Table 1 lists some pairs of utterances and their corresponding SLF (terms are denoted by the underscore) [6].

No.	Calculation Utterances	SLF
1	Enter the sum of exclusion of income from Puerto Rico and form 4563 line 15.	add(exclusion_of_income(puerto_rico),form(4563,line(15)))
2	Enter $1,195 or the total of your employment income you reported on lines 101 and 104 of your return, whichever is less.	min(1195, employment_income(add(line(101),line(104))))
3	Enter $75,300 if married filing jointly or qualifying widow(er)	ifte(or(eq(filing_status(taxpayer),married_filing_jointly), eq(filing_status(taxpayer),qualifying_widow(er))),75300)

Table 1: Calculation utterances and corresponding SLF.

The SLF of utterance 1 is an addition between the amount denoted by the multi-token term *exclusion of income* and the amount on a specific line of a specific form. Utterance 2 is about a choice: the smallest amount of two amounts (*min* operator). The notion of *smallest* is conveyed by a discontinuous dependency as a relative clause at the end of the utterance, namely, *whichever is less*. The first amount for the choice is a dollar constant amount; the second is an addition of the amounts denoted by the term *employment income*, expressed by *total ... on lines 101 and 104*. In utterance 3, inputting the constant

---

[4]The Generalized Dice coefficient is a similarity measure used in lexicography and term extraction to compute the lexical cohesion of multi-token term candidates. Park et al., 2002 and Kozakov et al., 2004 discuss at length the Dice-Coefficient and the Generalized-Dice-Coefficient statistical measures.

[5]We use a lexical-functional-based parser developed in-house for the compliance domain. In particular, it is tailored to interpret unannotated utterances that express arithmetic calculations written in English

[6]*ifte* in SLFs is a token to denote Boolean branching conditions.

amount of *$75,300* to a calculation is conditional on satisfying one of the disjuncts (*or* operator) for the filing status of the taxpayer, expressed by the multi-token terms *married filing jointly* and *qualifying widow(er)*.

When multi-token terms are missing from the terminology, the task of the parser is to determine the dependencies between the individual tokens that make up the utterances. With more available tokens to parse, the chance of an inaccurate parse increases. Note that, with a large terminology (over 20,000 lexical entries), the prior acquisition of multi-token expressions that are in fact not multi-token domain-concepts is a possibility [7]. If multi-token terms contain pieces of calculations that should be discrete, the parser will not accurately break down the calculation into its constituents, since multi-token terms are monolithic literal strings to the parser–regardless of how many spaces there are between the tokens of a term.

Consider the expressions *married and retired* versus *tuition and fees*. The first expression is not a term; it describes a Boolean operation, where the NLP pipeline must check separately whether the taxpayer is both *married* and *retired*. In contrast, the second expression is a term describing a single entity which is only specific to educational-related forms and instructions. *Tuition and fees* does not occur frequently-enough in our corpus to have made it into the terminology. Extracting, during parsing, the OOV expression *tuition and fees* as a GDC-based term candidate prevents interpreting *tuition and fees* as a Boolean operation. The method identifies the OOV term *tuition and fees* as *similar* to *pensions and annuities*-a term in the existing terminology. Additional examples are provided in Table 2 [8].

GDC Term Candidate	POS Pattern	POS GDC Score	Token GDC Score	Similar Listed Term
investor tax credit	[NN, NN, NN]	1.00	0.67	input tax credit
mining exploration tax credit	[NN,NN,NN,NN]	1.00	0.75	mineral exploration tax credit
universal child care	[JJ, NN, NN]	0.67	0.67	specified child care
unused Ontario tuition	[JJ, NNP, NN]	0.80	0.60	unused federal tuition

Table 2: GDC-based term candidates and similarity to terms in terminology.

Finally, the interpretation of utterances with and without OOV terms is reflected in the corresponding SLF. Contrast utterances in Table 3.

No.	Term	Utterances	SLF
1	Yes	amount for an eligible dependant, claim $85.00	ifte(eligible_dependant,85.00)
2	OOV	amount for a qualified dependant, claim $85.00	ifte(dependant(qualified),85.00)
3	Yes	amount for a single parent's qualified dependant, claim $64.00	ifte(single_parent_qualified_dependant,64.00)
4	OOV	amount for a single parent's eligible dependant, claim $64.00	ifte(eligible_dependant(single_parent),64.00)

Table 3: Utterances and SLF with/without terms.

Utterances 1 and 2 differ by the tokens *eligible* versus *qualified* where *eligible* is part of the term *eligible dependant* in utterance 1. While 3 contains the single four-token term *single parent qualified dependant*, utterance 4 counts two separate two-token terms, namely, *single parent* and *eligible dependant*. In the case of utterances 2 and 4 with OOV terms, the parser parses *qualified* and *single parent*

---

[7] Extraction of invalid term candidates is called *noise*–the opposite of *silence*.

[8] The part-of-speech (POS) names are Penn tags where JJ stands for adjective, NN for singular noun, and NNP for proper noun.

as left modifiers of the head of the noun phrase. In SLFs, the modifiers are enclosed in parentheses as arguments to the predicates, respectively *dependant* in utterance 2 and *eligible_dependant* in utterance 4.

Intuitively, each of the utterances in Table 3 should be of the form *if X, Y* where *X* is a multi-token term with no internal structure for the parser to consume. Otherwise, there is a discrepancy in predicate-argument relations across syntactically- and/or semantically-similar utterances [9].

The SLFs of utterances 2 and 4 of Table 3 should be as in Table 4 below such that their SLFs align with those of utterances 1 and 3 of Table 3 (repeated in Table 4).

No.	Term	Utterances	SLF
1	Yes	amount for an eligible dependant, claim $85.00	ifte(**eligible_dependant**,85.00)
2	Yes	amount for a qualified dependant, claim $85.00	ifte(**qualified_dependant**,85.00)
3	Yes	amount for a single parent's qualified dependant, claim $64.00	ifte(**single_parent_qualified_dependant**,64.00)
4	Yes	amount for a single parent's eligible dependant, claim $64.00	ifte(**single_parent_eligible_dependant**,64.00)

Table 4: SLF unification.

Even with an increase in the size of the domain corpus, there is no guarantee that the OOV terms *qualified dependant* or *single parent eligible dependant* of Table 3 will occur frequently-enough to make it into a term lexicon (as the result of a terminology extraction process)[10]. When processing arithmetic calculations automatically from utterances in English, our compliance system has one shot at outputting SLFs for each calculation such that downstream components can interpret them and transform them into executable operations. SLFs need be accurate. Bootstrapping parsing with a method that detects, on-the-fly, OOV term candidates increases parsing accuracy for these utterances.

3 Experiment

In order to measure the impact of detecting GDC-based terms at runtime on the success of the NLP pipeline that extracts and interprets arithmetic calculations in the tax-and-regulations domain, we ran the following experiment.

3.1 Functional Setup

We used, as a baseline lexical resource, the latest version of the terminology created by our term-extraction process. Separately, we fitted the parser with a preprocessing module to generate multi-token terms from each input utterance. In effect, the preprocessor functions as a chunker with a small grammar to define nominal phrases in English. The grammar sanctions the sequences of adjacent single-token words, which are grouped on the basis of linguistic properties (POS, semantic features, and/or WordNet-based similarity traits); in other words, the grammar rules out non-linguistic *n-gram* word sequences. For instance, for the utterance *Capital gains on gifts of property to qualified donees*, the preprocessor will generate two nominal multi-token term candidates *capital gain* and *qualified donees* [11].

For each term candidate generated by the preprocessor, the process retrieves, from the existing terminology, all terms that share a similar POS pattern. POS patterns need not be identical to allow for complimentary variance like *spouse* versus *spouse's* versus *spousal* in terms such as *spouse amount*, *spouse's amount*, and *spousal amount*. For instance, the POS pattern [NN, NN] is a permissible match with [JJ, NN]. Table 5 lists further matches [12].

To compute the lexical cohesion of the OOV multi-word candidate terms detected during parsing, we

---

[9]Boguraev et al (2015) make a similar observation about ESG, the parser used in IBM Watson.

[10]Note that, in the examples discussed in Table 3, term extraction did not detect a four-token term with *eligible* but did detect

POS Pattern	Permissible Matches
[NN, NN]	[NN. NN]
	[NNP, NN]
	[NNPS, NN]
	[JJ, NN]
	[JJR, NN]
	[JJS, NN]
	[VBG, NN]
	[VBN, NN]

Table 5: Permissible POS-pattern matches.

used the GDC statistical measure (Park et al.2002, Kozakov et al. 2004)[13]. The idea was to measure the *termness* of the n-gram candidate terms formed at the onset of parsing with the term-generation preprocessor. Further, the GDC-values could help indicate whether, even weakly-associated n-gram word sequences with at least one identical anchor-token between the candidate and related terms in the terminology, can be extracted as candidate terms to use for parsing of the utterance. We can extract candidate terms whose combined tokens are lexically-cohesive to a certain limit.

The GDC metrics used:

1. all of the terms listed in the terminology that have similar POS patterns.

2. all of the POS patterns from the terms retrieved from the terminology.

3. all of the terms with at least one token shared between a preprocessor-generated term candidate and the terms retrieved from the terminology.

4. on all of the single tokens of the terms retrieved from the terminology.

5. on all of the dictionary values associated with each of the single tokens that make up the terms retrieved from the terminology.

Table 6 below lists some examples of GDC-based terms, scores and closest-related term from the terminology.

When parsing of an utterance completes, GDC-based terms, if any, are added to the terminology. Note that the compliance terminology does not consist merely of a list of terms, but rather the terminology is a dictionary of pairs like [key:values]. The GDC-based terms are added as new entries augmented with a set of default values from established related terms already in the terminology. Adding GDC-based terms to the terminology upon completion of the parsing of an utterance makes the terms immediately available to the utterances that remain, if any, in the parser's queue.

3.2   Steps for Detecting OOV Terms

1. Tokenize utterance.

2. For each single token, do morphological stemming and return base forms of individual tokens.

3. Look up each base form in the single-token base lexicon. Retrieve all lexical data of base form.

4. Generate POS-based term candidates (all legal combinations from left to right) that resolve in a nominal phrase of preset length.

---

eligible in a two-token term. With *qualified*, it is the reverse–a four-token term but no two-token term.

[11]The preprocessor rules out patterns that include multiple prepositions. For a discussion on term extraction and the nature of terms, see Boguraev et al., 2015.

[12]The Penn tags NN, NNP, NNPS, JJ, JJR, JJS, VBG and VBN correspond to, respectively, singular noun, singular proper noun, plural proper noun, adjective, comparative adjective, superlative adjective, gerund/present participle and past participle.

[13]Park et al., 2002 and Kozakov et al., 2004 discuss at length the statistical measures

GDC Term Candidate	POS Pattern	GDC Score for POS Pattern	GDC Scores for Token Relatedness	Related Listed Term
qualified small business corporation	[VBN,JJ,NN,NN]	1.00	0.25	qualified principal residence indebtedness
total qualified expenditures	[JJ,VBN,NNS]	0.67	0.33	total municipal bonds
qualified expenditures	[VBN, NNS]	0.50	0.50	qualified education
qualified resource	[VBN, NN]	1.00	0.67	qualified education
qualified resource property	[VBN,NN,NN]	1.00	0.33	qualified retirement plan

Table 6: New terms containing *qualified* detected at runtime.

5. For each term candidate generated in step 4, check current baseline terminology for possible matches. If term candidate exists in terminology, remove candidate from term-candidate list generated in step 4.

6. For each term candidate generated in step 4, retrieve all terms that have similar POS patterns. Retrieve the terms as [key:values] pairs.

7. Compute all the GDC metrics as described in subsection 3.1 above.

The terms in the leftmost column of Table 6 are terms produced by our approach.

3.3 Evaluation

The goal of our evaluation was two-fold:

- Determine the number of new multi-token terms extracted on-the-fly during parsing.

- Evaluate the impact of GDC-based terms on parsing accuracy.

In one experiment, we created a corpus of unlabelled utterances collected from tax forms and instructions published in 2017 by the Internal Revenue Service of the United States. We further narrowed the focus to utterances that included the token *qualified*. The test set counted 6,553 utterances with the token *qualified* .

First, we parsed each utterance in the test set only with the latest version of the terminology to create a baseline consisting of utterances paired with their corresponding SLF; the output name is *BTPrun* [14]. Second, we parsed each utterance in the test set with the baseline terminology used in *BTPrun* but with GDC-based-extraction enabled; the output is called *BTGDCrun* [15].

In the BTPrun, 1099 multi-token terms with *qualified* were detected. In contrast, at the end of BTGDCrun, 1,380 terms were extracted– a gain of 281 new multi-token terms extracted during parsing (or 4.3%) (see Table 7).

Finally, we had two human annotators perform a quality assessment of the SLFs with GDC-based terms acquired during parsing. A comparison of the SLFs output by each of the runs yielded 724 changes in the output of the BTGDCrun. The annotation schema was simple: given the utterance, is the new SLF correct? The evaluation was binary: 1 for correct SLF, 0 for ill-formed SLF. Even with a stringent schema for manual evaluation, annotators may judge outcomes differently. However, for this task, judgments were close. Averaging the numbers of SLFs judged as having been corrected through the detection of terms during parsing, we saw a 93% improvement in parsing accuracy for the test set (see Table 8 below).

---

[14]BTPrun stands for parsing with baseline terminology and baseline parser with **no** GDC-built-in method.

[15]BTGDCrun stands for parsing with baseline terminology and with parser where GDC-based extraction is enabled.

	Total of Utterances in Test Set	Total of *qualified* terms	Percentage of *qualified* terms
BTPrun	6,553	1,099	16.7%
BTGDCrun	6,553	1,380	21%

Table 7: Totals and percentages of terms detected during parsing of utterances in test set.

	Total of Utterances in Test Set	Total of modified SLFs in BTGDCrun	Number of Improved SLFs
	6,553	724	
Annotator 1			669
Annotator 2			675

Table 8: Manual evaluation of modified SLFs in BTGDCrun.

In addition, for each improvement, the annotators were asked to classify the changes in the modified SLFs according to at least one of the following three categories:

- Term matching

- SLF well-formedness

- SLF generation

Consider the three cases of Table 9.

No.	Partial Utterances	SLF in BTPrun	SLF in BTGDCrun
1	qualified reimbursements	reimbursement(qualified)	qualified_reimbursement
2	qualified production activities income	income(qualified_production)	qualified_production_activities_income
3	voluntary employee contributions to a qualified retirement plan (including the federal thrift savings plan)	UNSPECIFIED	voluntary_employee _contribution(and(qualified_retirement _plan, federal_thrift_savings_plan))

Table 9: SLF improvements with GDC-based terms.

In examples 1-3 of the BTGDCrun, the SLFs include novel multi-token terms. The SLF of example 2 is more accurate as *activities* is included as a content-bearing token of the term. In example 3 of the BTGDCrun, the detection of the OOV term *qualified retirement plan* enables the parser to push one possible interpretation for the content in the parenthetical material. Note that, in the BTPrun, the parser did not output any SLF, which is indicated by the convention *UNSPECIFIED*.

Table 10 summarizes the classification by each of the human annotators. Interestingly, the annotators' judgments about the class of improvements by GDC-based terms on SLFs align.

4 Additional Downstream Benefits

An additional advantage for this method occurs further downstream in the NLP pipeline, where elements of parsed phrases are matched to an internal data model. When executing the calculation for *ifte(qualified_dependant,85.00)*, we use a custom-built entity-recognition system to determine the value of *qualified_dependant*. One of the features of this entity recognition system is consecutive token

	Improved SLFs	**Term Matching**	**SLF Well-Formedness**	**SLF Generation**
Annotator 1	669	597	49	23
Annotator 2	675	603	49	23

Table 10: Classification of modified SLFs in BTGDCrun.

matches. As the internal named entity has a description of *IsQualifiedDependant*, having the parser output *ifte(qualified_dependent,85.00)* instead of *ifte(dependent(qualified),85.00)* increases the likelihood of predicting the correct entity.

5   Conclusion

In this paper, we have described a method which increases term recall and improves parsing accuracy of utterances with OOV terms at the start of the parsing process. In addition, multi-token terms detected at parsing runtime are automatically added to the existing terminology. We use a parser fitted with a term-generation preprocessor to identify similarity between OOV multi-token term candidates and multi-token terms listed in the terminology. We observe improvements not only in the interpretation and representation of the utterances by our parser but also in the transformation of the SLFs into executable operations in downstream components of our NLP pipeline.

This method is best suited for domains where precision in a term lexicon, which has been automatically extracted, is important and where the problem with term *silence* can be severe [16] In the future, we would like to experiment with beginning the parsing process by using a terminology manually curated by domain experts. Because the method is domain-agnostic, we do not believe the discovery of OOV terms and augmentation of a domain-specific terminology (as long as there is a preexisting terminology at outset of a parsing task) is constrained to our example domain.

This work has shown that it is possible to overcome term *silence* by adding functionality to a parser with a preprocessor to discover OOV terms on the fly.

Acknowledgements

We gratefully acknowledge the comments by three anonymous reviewers. Not everyone agreed with everything but each comment and suggestion helped the co-authors clarify points in the paper and start a TODO list for future development and testing.

References

Timothy Baldwin. 2006. Compositionality and multiword expressions: Six of one, half a dozen of the other? In *Proceedings of the Workshop on Multiword Expressions: Identifying and Exploiting Underlying Properties*, page 1, Sydney, Australia, July. Association for Computational Linguistics.

Branimir Boguraev, Esme Manandise, and Benjamin Segal. 2015. The bare necessities: Increasing lexical coverage for multi-word domain terms with less lexical data. In *Proceedings of the 11th Workshop on Multiword Expressions*, pages 60–64, Denver, Colorado, June. Association for Computational Linguistics.

Stephen Cohen. 2005. Words! words! words!: Teaching the language of tax. *Journal of legal education*, 55, 12.

Matthieu Constant, Joseph Le Roux, and Nadi Tomeh. 2016. Deep lexical segmentation and syntactic parsing in the easy-first dependency framework. In *Proceedings of NAACL-HLT 2016*, pages 1095–1101. Association for Computational Linguistics, June.

Michael Curtotti and Eric McCreath. 2011. A corpus of Australian contract language: Description, profiling and analysis. pages 199–208, 06.

---

[16]Our method can introduce *noise*, i.e. wrongly glom a multi-token expression as a single term. However, the individual tokens of a candidate term created by the preprocessor remain available to the parser, which relies on additional corpus-based decision heuristics to rank SLF parses with or without GDC-based terms.

Jacob Devlin, Ming-Wei Chang, Kenton Lee, and Kristina Toutanova. 2018. Bert: Pre-training of deep bidirectional transformers for language understanding.

Isabella Distinto, Nicola Guarino, and Claudio Masolo. 2013. A well-founded ontological framework for modeling personal income tax. 06.

Ioannis Korkontzelos and Suresh Manandhar. 2010. Can recognising multiword expressions improve shallow parsing? In *Human Language Technologies: The 2010 Annual Conference of the North American Chapter of the Association for Computational Linguistics*, pages 636–644, Los Angeles, California, June. Association for Computational Linguistics.

Lev Kozakov, Youngja Park, Tong-Haing Fin, Youssef Drissi, Yurdaer Doganata, and Thomas Cofino. 2004. Glossary extraction and utilization in the information search and delivery system for ibm technical support. In *IBM SYSTEMS JOURNAL*, pages 546–653. IBM.

Lubomír Krcmár, Karel Jezek, and Pavel Pecina. 2013. Determining compositionality of word expressions using word space models. In *MWE@NAACL-HLT*.

Esme Manandise. 2019. Towards unlocking the narrative of the United States income tax forms. In *Proceedings of the Second Financial Narrative Processing Workshop (FNP 2019)*, pages 33–41, Turku, Finland, September. Linköping University Electronic Press.

Luka Nerima, Vasiliki Foufi, and Eric Wehrli. 2017. Parsing and mwe detection: Fips at the parseme shared task. In *Proceedings of the 13th Workshop on Multiword Expressions (MWE 2017)*, pages 54–59, Valencia, Spain, April. Association for Computational Linguistics.

Geoffrey Nunberg, Ivan A. Sag, and Thomas Wasow. 1994. Idioms. In Stephen Everson, editor, *Language*, pages 491–538. Cambridge University Press.

Youngja Park, Roy Byrd, and Branimir Boguraev. 2002. Automatic glossary extraction: Beyond terminology identification. In *Proceedings of the 19th International Conference on Computational Linguistics*, pages 60–64, Denver, Colorado, January. Association for Computational Linguistics.

Yushi Wang, Jonathan Berant, and Percy Liang. 2015. Building a semantic parser overnight. In *Proceedings of the 53rd Annual Meeting of the Association for Computational Linguistics and the 7th International Joint Conference on Natural Language Processing (Volume 1: Long Papers)*, pages 1332–1342, Beijing, China, July. Association for Computational Linguistics.

Eric Wehrli. 2014. The relevance of collocations for parsing. In *Proceedings of the 10th Workshop on Multiword Expressions (MWE)*, pages 26–32, Gothenburg, Sweden, April. Association for Computational Linguistics.

Hierarchical summarization of financial reports with RUNNER

Marina Litvak
Shamoon College of
Engineering (SCE)
Beer-Sheva
Israel
marinal@ac.sce.ac.il

Natalia Vanetik
Shamoon College of
Engineering (SCE)
Beer-Sheva
Israel
natalyav@sce.ac.il

Tzvi Puchinsky
Shamoon College of
Engineering (SCE)
Beer-Sheva
Israel
tzvipu@ac.sce.ac.il

Abstract

With the constantly growing amount of information, the need arises to automatically summarize this written information. One of the challenges in the summary is that it's difficult to generalize. For example, summarizing a news article is very different from summarizing a financial earnings report. This paper reports an approach for summarizing financial texts, which are different from the documents from other domains at least in three parameters: length, structure, and format. Our approach considers these parameters, it is adapted to hierarchical structure of sections, document length, and special "language". The approach builds a hierarchical summary, visualized as a tree with summaries under different discourse topics. The approach was evaluated using extrinsic and intrinsic automated evaluations, which are reported in this paper. As all participants of the Financial Narrative Summarisation (FNS 2020) shared task, we used FNS2020 dataset for evaluations.

1 Introduction

The area of text summarization exists for several decades, since the first work of Luhn (Luhn, 1958). Since then, the summarization approaches evolved from simple and straightforward extractive unsupervised approaches to abstractive supervised methods, using deep learning language models (Liu, 2019). However, the most advanced seq2seq models (transformers) are very limited in input size and, therefore, are inapplicable to long texts. Also, only few of state-of-the-art summarizers consider hierarchical structure of the input documents (Yang and Wang, 2008; Zhang et al., 2019), their key concepts (Ouyang et al., 2009) or topics (Wang et al., 2013; Akhtar, 2017) and build a hierarchical summary (Christensen et al., 2014; Akhtar et al., 2019). Usually, hierarchical summary is built per document collection. The top level of hierarchy provides a general overview and users can navigate the hierarchy to drill down for more details on topics of interest.

There is a growing interest in the application of automatic and computer-aided approaches for extracting, summarising, and analysing both qualitative and quantitative financial data, as a series of FNP and related workshops (El-Haj, 2019; El-Haj et al., 2018) recently demonstrates. However, summarization of documents in financial domain is usually limited to summarization of financial news (Filippova et al., 2009; Yang and Wang, 2003; de Oliveira et al., 2002; Baralis et al., 2016; Zhang et al., 2018) which are not very different from the general news in length and format. Only few attempts were made to summarize financial reports (Isonuma et al., 2017), which are different from the news articles in at least four parameters: length, structure, format, and lexicon.

This paper reports an approach for hierarchical summarization of financial reports. Financial annual reports in the data of Financial Narrative Summarisation (FNS 2020) shared task[1](El-Haj et al., 2020) are long, have many sections, and are written in "financial" language using many special terms, numerical data, and tables. Our system for hieRarchical sUmmarization fiNaNcial rEpoRts (shortly RUNNER) considers discourse and topic hierarchical structure and builds a hierarchical view of the summarized

---

[1]http://wp.lancs.ac.uk/cfie/fns2020/

Proceedings of the 1st Joint Workshop on Financial Narrative Processing and MultiLing Financial Summarisation, pages 213–225
Barcelona, Spain (Online), December 12, 2020.

report with interactive user interface. In contrast with the previous works on hierarchical summarization, our approach considers the internal hierarchical structure of a document and its topics instead mapping it to a global hierarchy of entire corpus.

2 Hierarchical Summarization with RUNNER

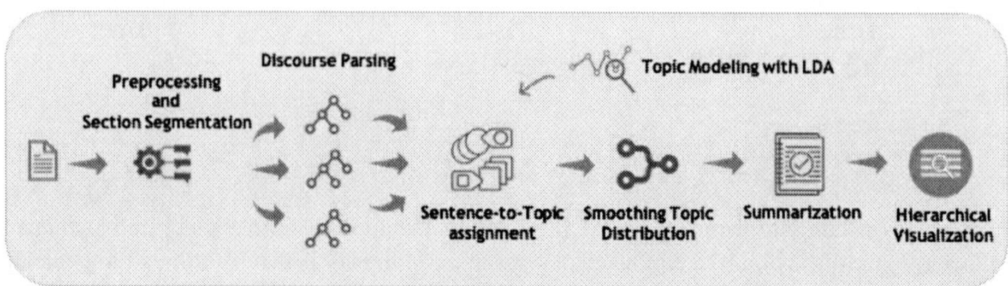

Figure 1: RUNNER pipeline

RUNNER utilizes two main methods: topic modeling (TM) and discourse parsing (DP). The pipeline of the proposed methodology is depicted in Figure 1 and includes the following steps:

Text preprocessing, that includes text cleaning, sentence splitting and tokenization. We developed our own tool that cleaned text before segmenting it to sentences and tokens. Financial reports usually contain a lot of sections, figures, and tables. Because the text files in the FNS-2020 dataset were obtained by converting pdf files to plain texts, these texts contain a lot of "noise" left from broken tables and meta-data such as section and page numbers. We cleaned the noise by measuring the ratio between text and numbers and ratio between number of words and whitespaces. Lines with ratio less than 0.4 were removed. Then, regular expressions were applied to find and mark such entities as URL, phone number, date, time, email. Finally, non-Unicode characters were filtered out. Figure 2 demonstrates the example of text before and after preprocessing.

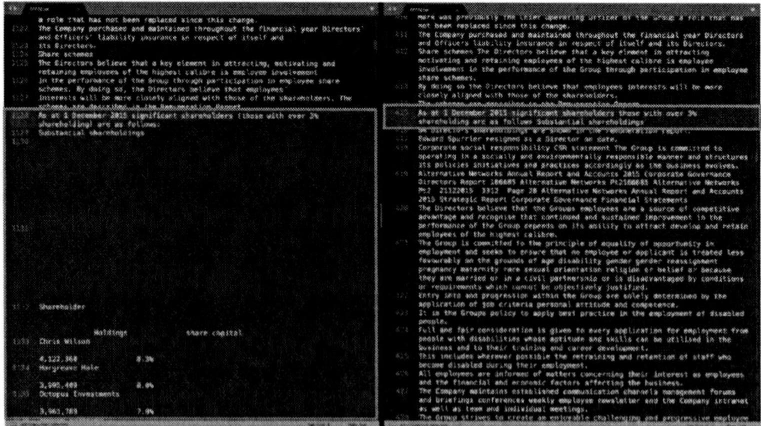

Figure 2: Text before and after preprocessing.

Section segmentation, where section headers are identified and a document is segmented into sections. The section titles were extracted following the heuristic rules saying that (1) each title appears in a separate line, (2) does not end with period mark, and (3) contains only few (up to 5) words with (4) each word either starting with capital case letter or containing only upper case letters. The extracted

214

candidates were then compared against the list of 13 manually edited titles[2]. The candidate that obtained Jaccard similarity above 0.4 to one of the titles from the list was extracted as a title. The text body between two consequent titles was marked as a section.

Discourse parsing of each section. For discourse parsing we used the CODRA parser (Joty et al., 2015). CODRA parser performs two-part process: (1) a discourse segmenter creates a segmentation analysis on the sentence level and EDU's for the discourse parsing process and (2) a discourse parser parses the text on sentence level and document level to identify relations between parts of sentences and sentences in the document. Figure 3 shows an example discourse tree. Leaf node stands for a sentence or a part of a sentence. The rhetorical analysis of the parser starts from a breaking a text into Elementary Discourse Units (EDUs). Because EDUs do not span across multiple sentences, this segmentation task finds EDUs inside the sentence boundaries. As a result, some sentences (actually, most, according to our observations) are split into EDUs. Every EDU is marked as a *nucleus* (an essence part) or a *satellite* (a complementary part of the related nucleus), based on the relation that they are connected to. Internal (relation) nodes represent different inter-sentence relations: elaboration, same-unit, etc.

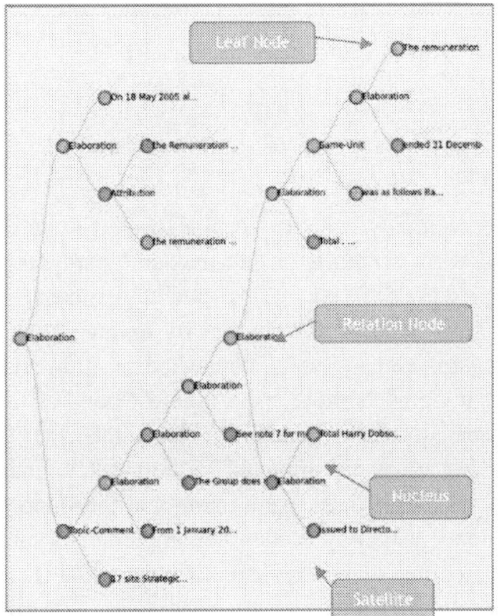

Figure 3: Discourse tree for sentences from "remuneration report" section of document 17941.txt in FNS-2020 dataset.

Topic modeling. For topic modeling we applied Latent Dirichlet Allocation (LDA) model (Blei et al., 2003). It was applied on all files in the FNS-2020 dataset with predefined number of topics[3].

Topic-to-text assignment, where each sentence (or sentence part) represented by a leaf node of the discourse tree, is assigned to one of the topics obtained by LDA. We refer topic probabilities $p(t|w)$ for all sentence S words $w \in S$ as their topic-related importance scores. Therefore, we extract a dominant topic ($t \in T$) for each sentence S, as a topic with the maximal normalized sum of topic probabilities for all sentence words $w \in S$: $\max_{t \in T} \frac{\sum_{w \in S} p(t|w)}{\sum_{w \in S} 1}$. Figure 4 shows an example of a topic-to-sentence assignment.

Topic distribution smoothing. We noticed that after single text nodes (that stand for sentences or

---

[2]Titles that appear in almost every report in FNS-2020 dataset, such as: 'chairman statement', 'chief executive officer CEO review', 'chief executive officer CEO report', 'governance statement', 'remuneration report', 'business review', 'financial review', 'operating review', 'highlights', 'auditors report', 'risk management', 'chairman governance introduction', 'corporate social responsibility CSR disclosures'.

[3]We experimented with 4, 6, and 10 topics, and finally decided to keep 10 topics as best performing value. After reviewing word clusters representing topics, we found that they most probably represent key information from the different sections of the financial report

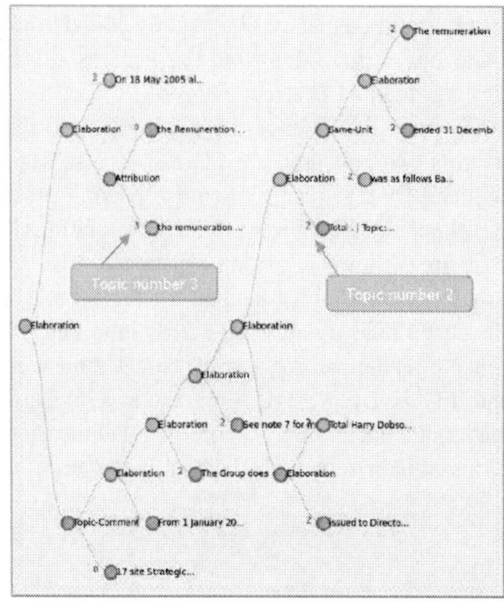

Figure 4: Topic-to-text assignment.

sentence parts) are assigned to topics, we can get unexpected topic distribution where two parts of the same sentence or two adjacent sentences inside the same paragraph and/or belonging to the same discourse relation are assigned to different topics, and transition from one topic to another is not coherent.[4] We decided to smooth topic distribution by extrapolating one dominant topic on entire block of adjacent sentences and sentence parts, connected by a direct discourse relation. We denote nodes with at least one leaf node as "simple" (see Figure 5) and all leaves in its sub-tree are finally assigned to one dominant topic, so that a "random" noise is left out. The implement this approach as follows. We know that all leaf nodes are arranged in the natural sequential order of their texts from right-to-left (top-down) in a discourse tree. We assume that the important information usually comes first (important part of a sentence usually precedes its complementary part, and a sentence stating some fact usually precedes a sentence that elaborates more about this fact) and, therefore, upper right nodes and nucleuses should propagate their topics on their siblings. According to this assumption and our empirical observations on each parameter's influence, the final impact factor NI of node n is calculated as follows. $NI(n) = \sum_{i=1}^{3} w_i \times f_i(n)$, where:

- f_1 is a relative depth feature $rd(n) = \frac{h(t)+1-d(n)}{h(t)+1}$, $h(t)$ is a tree height, $d(n)$ is n's depth

- f_2 is a position feature $pos(n) = \begin{cases} 1, \text{if } n \text{ is on right} \\ 0, \text{else} \end{cases}$

- f_3 is a discourse label feature $l(n) = \begin{cases} 1, \text{if } n \text{ is nucleus} \\ 0, \text{else} \end{cases}$

- $w_1 = 0.5$, $w_2 = 0.3$, and $w_3 = 0.2$

Then, the final dominant topic for a "simple" sub-tree is calculated as follows: $\max_{t \in T} \{\sum_{n \in leaves} NI(n) * score_{t,n}\}$. After topic-to-sentence assignment (at previous stage), every leaf node has non-zero value for only one dominant topic, other topics have $score_{t,n} = 0$.

We also experimented with the *second strategy* of assignment topics to sentences, where we do not assign a dominant topic to each leaf but operate their vectors of topic weights $\vec{v_n} = (w_{t_1}, w_{t_2}, \ldots, w_{t_{|T|}})$,

---

[4]We assume that in a natural topic distribution, that is usually observed in general domains, topics must flow from one paragraph (or sections or cluster of sentences) to another, without mix of topics inside clusters.

where w_{t_i} is a normalized sum of topic t_i probabilities for all sentence words, as calculated in previous stage. The dominant topic is assigned to entire sub-tree (under the "simple" node) by summing the topic distribution vectors multiplied by the importance score of their nodes and choosing a topic with a maximal score. Formally, the dominant topic is assigned as follows: $\max_{t \in T} \sum_{n \in leaves} \vec{v_n} \times NI(n)$.

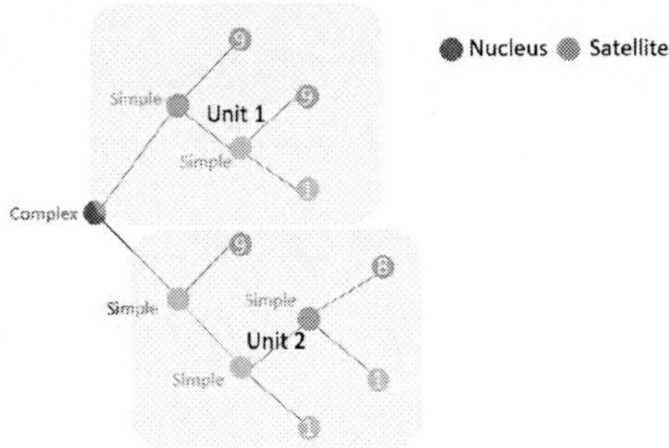

Figure 5: Example of "simple" sub-trees with initial LDA-based sentence-over-topics distribution. Based on this distribution and discourse structure, one dominant topic is finally calculated for each "simple" sub-tree. Given the initial topic assignment to leaves, the dominant topic of the first (upper) sub-tree is finally assigned to 9.

Summarization of entire report (regardless visualization) and of each section (for visualization needs) was performed by two different greedy strategies:

(1) All topics t are ranked by their importance $TI(t)$ (normalized sum of their probabilities for all document/section words). Then, summaries are created by extraction of nucleuses from each topic, in the topics' importance order, until the maximum length limit is reached. As for entire report a summary should not exceed 1000 words according to the shared task instructions, we limit a section summary to 100 words.

(2) All nucleuses are ranked by their importance. An importance score of nucleus m, represented by a node n in the discourse tree, is calculated as $NI(n) \times TI(dt)$, where dt is a dominant topic assigned to m. Then, in a greedy manner, summaries are created by extraction of nucleuses in their importance order, until the maximum length limit is reached.

We report the results for both strategies in the Experiments section.

Hierarchical visualization. At this stage RUNNER creates an interactive html file with the data from all the stages for a user to browse. The file contains the following sections: (1) original text; (2) processed XML text after cleaning and section segmentation; (3) discourse trees for all the sections; (4) sentences (nodes) with assigned topics after smoothing; (5) the final hierarchical tree with the section summaries, and (6) a general report summary. For visualization and interactive user's navigation, the following tree structure of a document is built and present to a user: root represents an entire document and points to its sections, each section is split to major topics inside this section after smoothing, and each topic points to a summary of this particular section focused on the chosen topic. Visualization is performed in interactive manner, upon a user's request. Figure 6 shows an example of such a tree. Demo video[5] demonstrates all interactive options provided by the system.

3 Experiments

We performed two types of evaluation for our summarization method[6]: extrinsic and intrinsic. Extrinsic evaluation can help judge the quality of the summaries based on how they affect the completion of specific task, while intrinsic evaluation estimates the quality of the generated output directly, usually by comparing it to the human-generated content.

---

[5]`https://drive.google.com/file/d/14qMRUhZIwaVoSltaLPSiH6NZx13M_9ue/view`

[6]Only general summaries were evaluated, due to limitations of gold standard summaries provided with a test set.

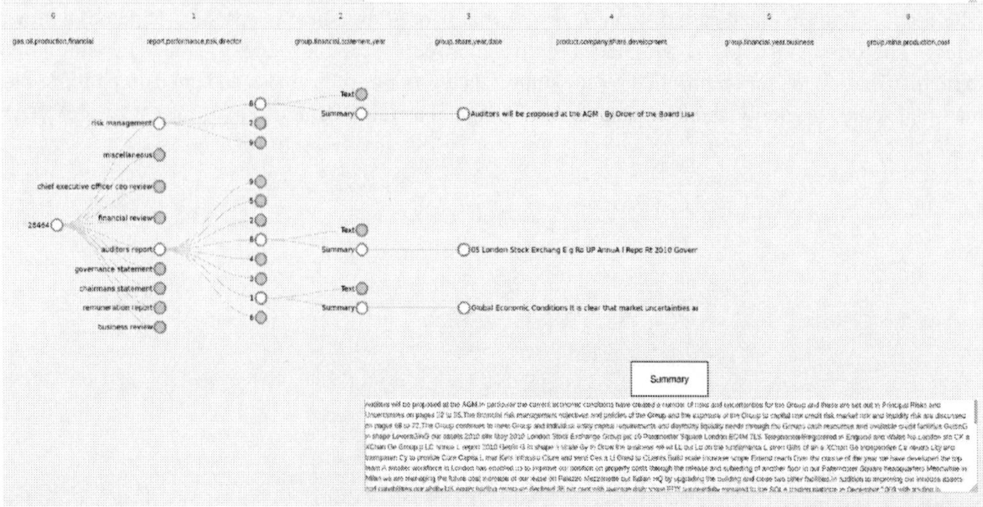

Figure 6: Visualization summary tree.

3.1 Dataset

The Financial Narrative Summarisation (FNS 2020) shared task aims to demonstrate the value and challenges of applying automatic text summarisation to financial text written in English, usually referred to as financial narrative disclosures. The task dataset has been extracted from UK annual reports published in PDF file format. UK annual reports are lengthy documents with around 80 pages on average, some annual reports could span over more than 250 pages, while the summary length should not exceed 1000 words. The training set includes 3,000 annual reports, with 3-4 human-generated summaries as gold standard. For the evaluation process the test set of 500 files were provided. To address the time limitations and processing long files[7] the project reduced the length of the original files (to 15000 characters) to be able to process in feasible time limit (20 minutes per file at most). Table 1 contains the dataset statistics. Please note that our method is unsupervised and does not require a training set. Therefore, we calculated average statistics only for the documents of the test set.

# documents	avg words	avg sentences	avg sections	avg words/section
500	63583.7	40	5.3	13452.6

Table 1: FNS 2020 dataset statstics. Test set.

3.2 Evaluated methods

We evaluate four variations of our approach (denoted by RUNNER_{ij}), which are combinations of two strategies for node importance calculation ($i \in \{1, 2\}$) and two strategies of summarizaion ($j \in \{1, 2\}$), and compare their results with two baseline methods—MUSE (Litvak et al., 2010) and POLY (Litvak and Vanetik, 2013). MUSE is a supervised approach based on a genetic algorithm, it was trained on 30 randomly selected gold standard summaries provided with FNS-2020 dataset. POLY is unsupervised approach based on linear programming, it was applied with Maximal Weighted Term Sum (OBJ1 in (Litvak and Vanetik, 2013)) objective function.

3.3 Extrinsic evaluation

We decided to utilize clustering as an evaluated task and see how similar the clustering of summaries is to that of the original reports. For this purpose, K-means (Lloyd, 1982) was applied on original reports and

---

[7]mostly, due to a very time-consuming discourse parsing

then on their summaries. Different clustering quality metrics were calculated on both clustering results and compared. As preprocessing before K-Means application, we performed corpus vectorization with tf-idf and Principal component analysis (Pearson, 1901) to reduce dimensionality. Number of clusters was set to three. In order to compare between clustering results we used the following metrics: Davies-Bouldin index (DBI) (Davies and Bouldin, 1979), Dunn index (DI) (Dunn, 1974), Silhouette coefficient (SC) (Rousseeuw, 1987), inter-cluster distance (inter-CD—sum of the square distance between each cluster centroid), intra cluster distance (intra-CD—sum of the square distance from the items of each cluster to its centroid), maximum radius (MR—largest distance from an instance to its cluster centroid), and average radius (AR—sum of the largest distances in each cluster divided by the number of clusters). Since algorithms that produce clusters with high intra-cluster similarity and low inter-cluster similarity will have a low DBI, the clustering algorithm that produces a collection of clusters with the smallest DBI is considered the best algorithm. Dunn index is defined as the ratio between the minimal inter-cluster distance to maximal intra-cluster distance. Therefore, algorithms that produce clusters with high DI are more desirable. Silhouette coefficient contrasts the average distance to elements in the same cluster with the average distance to elements in other clusters. Objects with a high SC value are considered well clustered, objects with a low value may be outliers. We also measured Precision, Recall, and Purity for all clusters of summaries, assuming that clusters of reports are ground truth.

Table 2 shows the comparative results. The best scores are marked in bold and the second best are marked by grey background. It can be seen that clustering of reports gains better scores than clustering of summaries in most metrics. However, smaller intra-cluster similarity and radius mean that clusters of summaries are smaller and more distant from each other. Also, as MUSE SC score shows, the summaries clusters may contain less outsiders. As it can be seen, RUNNER produces summaries with second best scores for sever (out of ten) metrics, meaning that it succeeds to keep the most representative information and filter out the redundant one in its summaries. The most important, that despite close results, clustering of summaries took much less time (16 times faster) than clustering of entire reports—2 versus 33 seconds for entire test set of 500 documents.

corpus	DBI	DI	SC	inter-CD	intra-CD	MR	AR	P	R	Purity
Reports	**0.702**	**0.558**	0.498	**0.331**	0.112	0.370	0.316	**1.000**	**1.000**	**1.000**
MUSE	0.673	0.456	**0.542**	0.278	0.091	0.253	**0.196**	0.407	0.492	0.602
POLY	0.857	0.318	0.414	0.206	**0.080**	0.307	0.277	0.396	0.369	0.504
$RUNNER_{11}$	0.909	0.321	0.386	0.223	0.097	0.281	0.252	0.303	0.284	0.682
$RUNNER_{12}$	0.847	0.461	0.403	0.218	0.089	0.231	0.200	0.388	0.337	0.412
$RUNNER_{21}$	0.884	0.335	0.383	0.223	0.090	0.322	0.273	0.599	0.569	0.636
$RUNNER_{22}$	0.834	0.469	0.408	0.219	0.089	**0.224**	0.204	0.430	0.377	0.420

Table 2: Clustering results.

3.4 Intrinsic evaluation

Intrinsic evaluation was performed using ROUGE metrics (Lin, 2004) which work by comparing an automatically produced summary against a set of reference summaries (typically human-produced). We applied three ROUGE metrics—ROUGE-1, ROUGE-2, and ROUGE-L. Table 3 show the results, with recall, precision, and F-measure for each metric. It can be seen that RUNNER performs better than POLY (both are unsupervised), and even outperforms MUSE (which is supervised) in one metric (ROUGE-L, Precision), meaning that its summaries are less "scattered" and more coherent (and therefore probably more readable) then other summaries. The comparative results with other systems participating in the FNS 2020 shared task can be seen in Appendix, Tables 4-7.[8]

3.5 Tools and runtime environment

For LDA, we used the Python gensim4 package. Corpus tf-idf vectorization and K-means clustering were performed by the Python sklearn package. For running Rouge, we used ROUGE 2.05 java pack-

---

[8] Only one variation of RUNNER was submitted to the task evaluations, which is the closest to $RUNNER_{11}$. However, since then RUNNER's code was significantly updated, therefore the scores are not the same.

system	R-1 R	R-1 P	R-1 F	R-2 R	R-2 P	R-2 F	R-L R	R-L P	R-L F
MUSE	**0.483**	**0.413**	**0.433**	**0.311**	**0.198**	**0.234**	**0.486**	0.381	**0.419**
POLY	0.324	0.253	0.274	0.147	0.088	0.105	0.270	0.182	0.212
RUNNER$_{11}$	0.290	0.396	0.324	0.150	0.153	0.144	0.290	**0.396**	0.324
RUNNER$_{12}$	0.358	0.337	0.337	0.181	0.127	0.144	0.331	0.285	0.299
RUNNER$_{21}$	0.293	0.392	0.324	0.151	0.151	0.144	0.294	0.325	0.300
RUNNER$_{22}$	0.358	0.337	0.337	0.181	0.127	0.144	0.331	0.285	0.299

Table 3: Rouge results.

age (Ganesan, 2018). Our approach was implemented in Python and run on Intel Pentium Gold G5400 with 16GB memory server with 40GB swap file configured.

4 Conclusions and Future Work

This paper describes a new method for hierarchical summarization of financial reports, based on integrating the discourse structure and topic modeling. In future, we intend to apply this method and its extension to educational materials, which also have highly hierarchical structure and an evolving flow of topics in a discourse. Hierarchical summarization can help to organize those materials in a hierarchical structure and provide users with interactive navigation to the topics of interest. RUNNER's source code is available[9] and can be run using the provided instructions[10].

Acknowledgements

We would like to thank Alla Kitaeva for supporting this project in a scope of the final undergraduate project.

References

Nadeem Akhtar, Hira Javed, and Tameem Ahmad. 2019. Hierarchical summarization of text documents using topic modeling and formal concept analysis. In *Data Management, Analytics and Innovation*, pages 21–33. Springer.

Nadeem Akhtar. 2017. Hierarchical summarization of news tweets with twitter-lda. In *Applications of Soft Computing for the Web*, pages 83–98. Springer.

Elena Baralis, Luca Cagliero, and Tania Cerquitelli. 2016. Supporting stock trading in multiple foreign markets: a multilingual news summarization approach. In *Proceedings of the Second International Workshop on Data Science for Macro-Modeling*, pages 1–6.

David M Blei, Andrew Y Ng, and Michael I Jordan. 2003. Latent dirichlet allocation. *Journal of machine Learning research*, 3(Jan):993–1022.

Janara Christensen, Stephen Soderland, Gagan Bansal, et al. 2014. Hierarchical summarization: Scaling up multi-document summarization. In *Proceedings of the 52nd annual meeting of the association for computational linguistics (volume 1: Long papers)*, pages 902–912.

David L Davies and Donald W Bouldin. 1979. A cluster separation measure. *IEEE transactions on pattern analysis and machine intelligence*, (2):224–227.

Paulo Cesar Fernandes de Oliveira, Khurshid Ahmad, and Lee Gillam. 2002. A financial news summarization system based on lexical cohesion. In *Proceedings of the International Conference on Terminology and Knowledge Engineering, Nancy, France*.

Joseph C Dunn. 1974. Well-separated clusters and optimal fuzzy partitions. *Journal of cybernetics*, 4(1):95–104.

Mahmoud El-Haj, Paul Rayson, and Andrew Moore. 2018. The first financial narrative processing workshop (fnp 2018). In *Proceedings of the LREC 2018 Workshop*.

---

[9] https://github.com/Tzvi23/Hierarchical-Summarization-Part1
[10] https://drive.google.com/drive/folders/1YxnNQ-9ebPX1Gtd6Dmr0to6UIBgudflC

Mahmoud El-Haj, Ahmed AbuRa'ed, Nikiforos Pittaras, and George Giannakopoulos. 2020. The Financial Narrative Summarisation Shared Task (FNS 2020). In *The 1st Joint Workshop on Financial Narrative Processing and MultiLing Financial Summarisation (FNP-FNS 2020*, Barcelona, Spain.

Mahmoud El-Haj. 2019. Multiling 2019: Financial narrative summarisation. In *Proceedings of the Workshop MultiLing 2019: Summarization Across Languages, Genres and Sources*, pages 6–10.

Katja Filippova, Mihai Surdeanu, Massimiliano Ciaramita, and Hugo Zaragoza. 2009. Company-oriented extractive summarization of financial news. In *Proceedings of the 12th Conference of the European Chapter of the ACL (EACL 2009)*, pages 246–254.

Kavita Ganesan. 2018. Rouge 2.0: Updated and improved measures for evaluation of summarization tasks. *arXiv preprint arXiv:1803.01937*.

Masaru Isonuma, Toru Fujino, Junichiro Mori, Yutaka Matsuo, and Ichiro Sakata. 2017. Extractive summarization using multi-task learning with document classification. In *Proceedings of the 2017 Conference on Empirical Methods in Natural Language Processing*, pages 2101–2110.

Shafiq Joty, Giuseppe Carenini, and Raymond T Ng. 2015. Codra: A novel discriminative framework for rhetorical analysis. *Computational Linguistics*, 41(3):385–435.

Chin-Yew Lin. 2004. Rouge: A package for automatic evaluation of summaries. In *Text summarization branches out*, pages 74–81.

Marina Litvak and Natalia Vanetik. 2013. Mining the gaps: Towards polynomial summarization. In *Proceedings of the Sixth International Joint Conference on Natural Language Processing*, pages 655–660.

Marina Litvak, Mark Last, and Menahem Friedman. 2010. A new approach to improving multilingual summarization using a genetic algorithm. In *Proceedings of the 48th annual meeting of the association for computational linguistics*, pages 927–936.

Yang Liu. 2019. Fine-tune bert for extractive summarization. *arXiv preprint arXiv:1903.10318*.

Stuart Lloyd. 1982. Least squares quantization in PCM. *IEEE transactions on information theory*, 28(2):129–137.

Hans Peter Luhn. 1958. The automatic creation of literature abstracts. *IBM Journal of research and development*, 2(2):159–165.

You Ouyang, Wenjie Li, and Qin Lu. 2009. An integrated multi-document summarization approach based on word hierarchical representation. In *Proceedings of the ACL-IJCNLP 2009 Conference Short Papers*, pages 113–116.

Karl Pearson. 1901. Liii. on lines and planes of closest fit to systems of points in space. *The London, Edinburgh, and Dublin Philosophical Magazine and Journal of Science*, 2(11):559–572.

Peter J Rousseeuw. 1987. Silhouettes: a graphical aid to the interpretation and validation of cluster analysis. *Journal of computational and applied mathematics*, 20:53–65.

Chi Wang, Xiao Yu, Yanen Li, Chengxiang Zhai, and Jiawei Han. 2013. Content coverage maximization on word networks for hierarchical topic summarization. In *Proceedings of the 22nd ACM international conference on Information & Knowledge Management*, pages 249–258.

Christopher C Yang and Fu Lee Wang. 2003. Automatic summarization for financial news delivery on mobile devices. In *WWW (Posters)*.

Christopher C Yang and Fu Lee Wang. 2008. Hierarchical summarization of large documents. *Journal of the American Society for Information Science and Technology*, 59(6):887–902.

Yong Zhang, Erdan Chen, and Weidong Xiao. 2018. Extractive-abstractive summarization with pointer and coverage mechanism. In *Proceedings of 2018 International Conference on Big Data Technologies*, pages 69–74.

Xingxing Zhang, Furu Wei, and Ming Zhou. 2019. Hibert: Document level pre-training of hierarchical bidirectional transformers for document summarization. *arXiv preprint arXiv:1905.06566*.

Appendix

system	R-1 R	R-1 P	R-1 F
SRIB2020-SYSTEM3	0.612	0.393	0.466
SRIB2020-SYSTEM2	0.611	0.392	0.465
SUMSUM-BASE	0.494	0.481	0.462
SUMSUM-BERT	0.450	0.530	0.460
KG-SUMMAR-NN	0.568	0.381	0.445
SUMSUM-01	0.447	0.511	0.442
HULAT-1	0.536	0.393	0.441
KG-SUMMAR-SVM	0.495	0.416	0.438
KG-SUMMAR-S-LSTM	0.506	0.406	0.438
MUSE	0.483	0.413	0.433
CIST-BUPT-RUN3	0.434	0.449	0.428
SUMTO-SUMMARY-3PE	0.447	0.426	0.424
SUMTO-SUMMARY-2PE	0.441	0.427	0.422
SUMTO-SUMMARY-1PE	0.431	0.437	0.421
CIST-BUPT-RUN2	0.418	0.440	0.416
AMEX-ENSEMBLE	0.442	0.408	0.412
AMEX-BILSTM	0.436	0.406	0.409
FORTIA-SYSTEM1	0.428	0.431	0.407
HULAT-2	0.503	0.352	0.402
CIST-BUPT-RUN1	0.405	0.423	0.401
FORTIA-SYSTEM2	0.394	0.410	0.384
FORTIA-SYSTEM3	0.365	0.370	0.352
UOB-NLP-SECOND-SUMMARIES	0.307	0.315	0.301
SCE-SUMMARY (RUNNER)	0.288	0.399	0.297
UOB-NLP-THIRD-SUMMARIES	0.296	0.316	0.296
AMEX-TEXTRANK	0.353	0.271	0.295
UOB-NLP-FIRST-SUMMARIES	0.296	0.315	0.295
SRIB2020-SYSTEM1	0.241	0.378	0.283
POLY	0.324	0.253	0.274
LEXRANK-SUMMARY	0.337	0.269	0.264
TEXTRANK-SUMMARY	0.414	0.118	0.172

Table 4: Comparative results. Rouge-1.

system	R-2 R	R-2 P	R-2 F
SUMSUM-BERT	0.365	0.295	0.306
SUMSUM-BASE	0.398	0.259	0.294
SRIB2020-SYSTEM3	0.451	0.222	0.289
SRIB2020-SYSTEM2	0.448	0.220	0.288
SUMSUM-01	0.358	0.277	0.286
FORTIA-SYSTEM1	0.299	0.282	0.274
HULAT-1	0.412	0.200	0.261
SUMTO-SUMMARY-3PE	0.296	0.228	0.249
CIST-BUPT-RUN3	0.288	0.233	0.248
KG-SUMMAR-SVM	0.357	0.199	0.247
KG-SUMMAR-NN	0.402	0.184	0.246
KG-SUMMAR-S-LSTM	0.360	0.193	0.243
FORTIA-SYSTEM2	0.247	0.263	0.241
SUMTO-SUMMARY-1PE	0.270	0.225	0.237
CIST-BUPT-RUN2	0.272	0.224	0.237
SUMTO-SUMMARY-2PE	0.276	0.217	0.235
MUSE	0.311	0.198	0.234
HULAT-2	0.375	0.177	0.233
CIST-BUPT-RUN1	0.258	0.206	0.220
AMEX-ENSEMBLE	0.264	0.192	0.214
AMEX-BILSTM	0.260	0.190	0.211
FORTIA-SYSTEM3	0.207	0.222	0.202
SCE-SUMMARY (RUNNER)	0.159	0.157	0.138
UOB-NLP-SECOND-SUMMARIES	0.149	0.110	0.121
LEXRANK-SUMMARY	0.193	0.107	0.120
AMEX-TEXTRANK	0.184	0.097	0.120
SRIB2020-SYSTEM1	0.114	0.138	0.118
UOB-NLP-THIRD-SUMMARIES	0.140	0.108	0.117
UOB-NLP-FIRST-SUMMARIES	0.140	0.107	0.116
POLY	0.147	0.088	0.105
TEXTRANK-SUMMARY	0.229	0.044	0.070

Table 5: Comparative results. Rouge-2.

system	R-L R	R-L P	R-L F
SRIB2020-SYSTEM3	0.605	0.376	0.456
SRIB2020-SYSTEM2	0.603	0.377	0.455
MUSE	0.470	0.370	0.407
SUMTO-SUMMARY-3PE	0.410	0.395	0.394
SUMTO-SUMMARY-1PE	0.406	0.385	0.387
HULAT-1	0.444	0.357	0.386
SUMTO-SUMMARY-2PE	0.403	0.382	0.385
FORTIA-SYSTEM1	0.397	0.397	0.381
AMEX-ENSEMBLE	0.408	0.365	0.378
AMEX-BILSTM	0.402	0.360	0.372
HULAT-2	0.392	0.358	0.364
FORTIA-SYSTEM2	0.374	0.373	0.362
FORTIA-SYSTEM3	0.341	0.339	0.331
CIST-BUPT-RUN3	0.324	0.348	0.329
SUMSUM-BASE	0.332	0.350	0.324
CIST-BUPT-RUN2	0.311	0.352	0.324
SUMSUM-BERT	0.304	0.389	0.322
KG-SUMMAR-NN	0.389	0.278	0.318
KG-SUMMAR-S-LSTM	0.344	0.307	0.317
CIST-BUPT-RUN1	0.294	0.361	0.317
SUMSUM-01	0.304	0.375	0.313
KG-SUMMAR-SVM	0.340	0.303	0.312
AMEX-TEXTRANK	0.246	0.245	0.237
SRIB2020-SYSTEM1	0.213	0.254	0.225
SCE-SUMMARY (RUNNER)	0.225	0.286	0.223
LEXRANK-SUMMARY	0.210	0.263	0.218
UOB-NLP-THIRD-SUMMARIES	0.227	0.202	0.208
UOB-NLP-FIRST-SUMMARIES	0.226	0.203	0.208
UOB-NLP-SECOND-SUMMARIES	0.223	0.204	0.207
TEXTRANK-SUMMARY	0.235	0.197	0.206
POLY	0.260	0.177	0.205

Table 6: Comparative results. Rouge-L.

system	R-SU4 R	R-SU4 P	R-SU4 F
FORTIA-SYSTEM1	0.344	0.332	0.318
SUMSUM-BERT	0.406	0.268	0.302
FORTIA-SYSTEM2	0.299	0.313	0.290
SUMSUM-BASE	0.442	0.236	0.288
SRIB2020-SYSTEM3	0.508	0.209	0.288
SRIB2020-SYSTEM2	0.506	0.208	0.286
SUMSUM-01	0.398	0.253	0.282
HULAT-1	0.464	0.193	0.264
SUMTO-SUMMARY-3PE	0.353	0.223	0.264
SUMTO-SUMMARY-1PE	0.332	0.218	0.254
MUSE	0.375	0.201	0.253
FORTIA-SYSTEM3	0.263	0.271	0.253
SUMTO-SUMMARY-2PE	0.340	0.211	0.252
CIST-BUPT-RUN3	0.346	0.209	0.251
KG-SUMMAR-SVM	0.411	0.188	0.248
KG-SUMMAR-S-LSTM	0.417	0.182	0.245
CIST-BUPT-RUN2	0.330	0.204	0.243
KG-SUMMAR-NN	0.464	0.170	0.242
HULAT-2	0.430	0.173	0.239
AMEX-ENSEMBLE	0.328	0.194	0.235
AMEX-BILSTM	0.325	0.192	0.232
CIST-BUPT-RUN1	0.315	0.190	0.228
SCE-SUMMARY (RUNNER)	0.208	0.164	0.158
UOB-NLP-SECOND-SUMMARIES	0.214	0.123	0.150
SRIB2020-SYSTEM1	0.165	0.149	0.149
UOB-NLP-THIRD-SUMMARIES	0.203	0.122	0.146
UOB-NLP-FIRST-SUMMARIES	0.203	0.121	0.145
AMEX-TEXTRANK	0.250	0.108	0.144
LEXRANK-SUMMARY	0.253	0.117	0.140
POLY	0.213	0.105	0.135
TEXTRANK-SUMMARY	0.302	0.048	0.079

Table 7: Comparative results. Rouge-SU4.

Predicting Modality in Financial Dialogue

Kilian Theil and **Heiner Stuckenschmidt**
Data and Web Science Group
University of Mannheim, Germany
{kilian, heiner}@informatik.uni-mannheim.de

Abstract

In this paper, we perform modality prediction in financial dialogue. To this end, we introduce a
new dataset and develop a binary classifier to detect strong or weak modal answers depending
on surface, lexical, and semantic representations of the preceding question and financial features.
To do so, we contrast different algorithms, feature categories, and fusion methods. Perhaps
counter-intuitively, our results indicate that the strongest features for the given task are financial
uncertainty measures such as market and individual firm risk.

1 Introduction

In this paper, we predict the modality of answers depending on their preceding question and other features in financial dialogue. Modality is an important concept in principal–agent settings of asymmetric
information such as the stock market, since it can be used as a strategic tool by company executives:
Using modality markers such as "probably" or "certainly," investor expectations can be managed or the
effect of negative news can be mitigated without having to commit to false statements. Loughran &
McDonald (2016, p. 1224) suggest to examine the hypothesis that larger shares of modal words in conference calls might worsen stock or operating performance. Subsequently, Dzieliński *et al.* (2019) found
that executive modality is indeed predictive of stock price as well as analyst's earnings forecasts and firm
valuations (Dzieliński et al., 2019). Although different to past work, we explore causes, not effects, of
modality in the financial domain, this shows that modality prediction has potential down-stream uses in
return, risk, and analyst forecast prediction. Specifically, modality prediction models could be employed
for intra-day return prediction.

1.1 Modality

Linguistic modality, a concept related to politeness (Danescu-Niculescu-Mizil et al., 2013) and hedging (Lakoff, 1973; Hyland, 1998), is most commonly categorized into *dynamic*, *priority*, and *epistemic
modality* (Portner, 2009, p. 47). In this work, we focus on epistemic modality, which expresses a
speaker's confidence in the truth of their proposition [*ibid.*]: a high epistemic modality (variously expressed through markers such as "certainly," "must") describes a high confidence and a low modality
("probably," "might") stands for a low degree of confidence. While past socio-linguistic research has
shown that a manual annotation of modality on a 5-item scale is a comparably hard task for humans
(Rubin, 2007), past work in the financial domain indicates that the task seems to be easier for a binary
distinction and a broader definition of uncertainty (Theil et al., 2018a). As manual annotation is costly
and time-consuming, we were interested in automatically creating a silver standard dataset based on an
established lexicon of modality markers (Loughran and McDonald, 2011) in the financial domain. To
the best of our knowledge, there is no study investigating the determinants of modality in dialogue using
natural language processing.

Proceedings of the 1st Joint Workshop on Financial Narrative Processing and MultiLing Financial Summarisation, pages 226–234
Barcelona, Spain (Online), December 12, 2020.

1.2 Earnings Calls

Earnings calls—the textual form we analyze in this paper—are quarterly public teleconferences or webcasts in which companies present the financial results of the ending business quarter. Past literature has examined indirectness (Crawford Camiciottoli, 2009), persuasion (Crawford Camiciottoli, 2011; Crawford Camiciottoli, 2018), and deception (Larcker and Zakolyukina, 2012) in earnings calls. Earnings calls typically consist of two parts: first, the company management (usually the CEO and/or CFO) as well as investor relations representatives hold a scripted presentation which closely follows the accompanying press release. Second, the call is opened to investors and banking analysts, which pose questions to the management in a Q&A session. Together with the information asymmetry, this unscripted kind of interaction makes the Q&A part especially suitable for our modality prediction task. Hence, we were motivated to extract question–answer pairs from the Q&A and to predict the modality of an answer depending on the content of the preceding question.

1.3 Contributions

We provide the following contributions to the community:

- We publish a dataset of 5K question–answer pairs for modality prediction.

- We introduce the first modality classifier including semantic information and learning from heterogeneous features.

- We provide interpretable results by visualizing the importance and effect of the used features.

2 Related Work

In the financial domain, the task of modality or vagueness detection is closely related to risk and return prediction. Loughran & McDonald (2011) handcrafted a set of sentiment lexica based on frequent terms in a sample of 60K 10-Ks. These lexica (from now on: LM) span the categories *positive*, *negative*, *uncertain*, *litigious*, *strong modal*, and *weak modal* and have been shown to possess predictive power of risk. Subsequent work in the NLP community automatically expands said lexica by adding semantically similar terms according to word embedding models for predictions of risk in form of return volatility (Tsai and Wang, 2014; Rekabsaz et al., 2017) or correlations with it (Theil et al., 2018b; Theil et al., 2020).

Štajner *et al.* (2017) perform speculation detection in the monetary policy domain as a binary sentence classification task. They use a list a list of uncertainty triggers extracted from the CoNLL-2010 shared task's training set (Farkas et al., 2010), the LM *uncertain* lexicon, and an own list of speculation triggers tailored to the task. Theil *et al.* (2018a) train a binary sentence classifier predicting the linguistic uncertainty of 1K sentences randomly sampled from a dataset of earnings calls. They use lemmatized bag-of-words (BoW) vectors, part-of-speech tags, a set of handcrafted syntactic rules, the CoNLL-2010 list of uncertainty triggers (Farkas et al., 2010), and the LM *uncertain* lexicon. Their results indicate that BoW vectors and the LM lexicon are the strongest features, which is why we include them in our classifier, too. Note that different to these works, we do not aim to predict the uncertainty of a sentence given its content, but rather the uncertainty of an answer given the content of the preceding question. Furthermore, we explore additional feature categories, such as semantic or financial features.

Using a set of 120K earnings calls, Dzieliński *et al.* (2019) find that the modality of executive utterances is correlated with post-call stock price, analyst's earnings forecasts, and firm valuation. Keith and Stent (2019) gather 12K earnings call transcripts and find that pragmatic and semantic features are moderately predictive of analysts' price forecast targets following the call dates. Their pragmatic feature set contains a dictionary of uni- and n-gram hedges (Prokofieva and Hirschberg, 2014) as well as the LM dictionary (Loughran and McDonald, 2011); however, they find the influence of semantic features (BoW and doc2vec (Le and Mikolov, 2014) vectors) to be stronger. Theil *et al.* (2019) collect a dataset of 90K earnings calls and develop an attention-based neural model to predict financial risk (i.e. return volatility) given the transcripts and several financial features. We include their financial features in our classifier,

types	tokens	sentences	utterances
7.7K	232.1K	15.1K	5.0K

Table 1: Descriptive statistics of our dataset.

as past research suggests a correlation between linguistic modality and financial risk. Different to these works, we do not predict external financial measures based on linguistic features. Instead, we aim to predict a linguistic variable (modality) as we are interested in uncovering its determinants in financial Q&A settings.

3 Methodology

We begin by introducing a new dataset for modality prediction in financial dialogue (cf. Section 3.1), proceed by defining different features sets (cf. Section 3.2), and finally introduce a classifier for our binary classification task (cf. Section 3.3).

3.1 Dataset

We obtain 20K earnings call transcripts from SeekingAlpha[1] and sample all question–answer (Q&A) pairs from them. Numbers are identified with SpaCy's named entity recognizer and replaced with uniform placeholder tokens. We remove Q&A pairs with inaudible parts, audiogaps, or multiple speakers talking at once.

We use the established LM dictionary (Loughran and McDonald, 2011) as a basis to induce the binary modality label of the answers, thus forming a silver standard dataset used in the subsequent classification. To this end, we focus on the two categories *weak* and *strong modality* and extract the answers with the highest share of these words—to avoid ambiguous labels, we require the *weak modal* answers to contain zero *strong modal* words and vice versa:

- The *weak modality* lexicon contains 27 tokens conveying vagueness such as "maybe" and "possibly." We take the 2.5K answers with the highest share of weak modal tokens and assign them a *weak modal* label.

  Example: "Well, the numbers might suggest that."

- The *strong modality* lexicon contains 20 tokens conveying certainty such as "always" and "undoubtedly." We take the 2.5K answers with the highest share of these tokens and assign them a *strong modal* label.

  Example: "It will. That's right, it will."

This yields a balanced dataset of 5K (2.5K *weak* and 2.5K *strong modal*) instances; Table 1 describes this set in terms of surface features. For the subsequent experiments, we apply an $80 : 20$ training–test split. Both our dataset and code can be found online.[2]

3.2 Features

Since we aim to predict the modality of an answer given the preceding question, all features are extracted from the questions. In total, we evaluate four different feature categories, which are partly motivated by the previous literature (cf. Section 2).

3.2.1 Surface Features

In the SURFACE feature set, we explore the following:

---

[1] `seekingalpha.com` is a crowd-sourced provider of data and research on financial markets. We comply with their reproduction policy of not quoting more than 400 words of any given transcript.

[2] `https://www.uni-mannheim.de/dws/people/researchers/phd-students/kilian-theil`

- **Length** is once represented by the number of sentences and once by the number of tokens in the respective question.

- **Positivity** and **negativity** are the share of tokens according to the respective LM lexica. These are defined by 354 positive tokens such as "breakthrough" or "win" and 2,355 negative tokens such as "decline" and "worsen."

- **Strong** and **weak modality** of a question could influence the modality of the respective answer. Examples of strong and weak model tokens according to the LM lexicon are given in Section 3.1.

- **Uncertainty** is again measured by the respective LM lexicon which contains 297 tokens referring to linguistic imprecision or risk, e.g. "hypothesis" and "volatility."

3.2.2 Lexical (Semantic) Features

In the LEXICAL category, we compare tf and tfidf vectors, which have been shown to perform strong for an uncertainty detection task (Theil et al., 2018b). To reduce sparsity, we apply singular value decomposition (SVD) and experiment with dimensions $d_{BoW} \in \{100, 200, ..., 1000\}$. Additionally, to expand the LEXICAL feature set with semantic information, we train word embedding models with word2vec (Mikolov et al., 2013) on the entire earnings call corpus (cf. Section 3.1). We evaluate dimensions $d_{w2v} \in \{100, 200, 300\}$ with both the continuous bag-of-words (CBOW) and the skip-gram (SG) architecture. Finally, we represent all questions as embedding centroids. Our results indicate that out of all previously mentioned representations, tfidf vectors with $d_{BoW} = 300$ are optimal for the given task.

3.2.3 Semantic Features

We use the Latent Dirichlet Allocation (LDA) algorithm to obtain topic models forming our SEMANTIC feature set. To find an optimal number of topics n, we evaluate the sensitivity of the log-likelihood l and the perplexity P to $n \in \{5, 10, ..., 45, 50\}$ in a five-fold cross validation setup on our training set. Our results indicate that an optimal l and P are obtained for $n = 5$.[3]

3.2.4 Financial Features

We use the FINANCIAL feature set proposed by Theil et al. (2019) to contrast the predictive power of linguistic features to that of performance measures about the firm or the overall economy:

- **Firm volatility**, measured by the standard deviation of stock returns, is the most important measure for financial risk. We include the volatility in the preceding business quarter as this feature should have an impact on investor and manager confidence.

- **Market volatility** as gauged by the CBOE Volatility Index (VIX),[4] reflects the overall market uncertainty and should have a similar (albeit more global) impact as firm volatility.

- **Firm size** or market value is the number of outstanding shares multiplied by the stock price and is a well-known driver of risk (Fama and French, 1992).

- **Book-to-market** reflects the firm value according to the balance sheet divided by the market value and thus reflects the degree of over- or undervaluation. Similar to the preceding measures, this ratio is considered to be a major risk driver (Fama and French, 1992).

- **Earnings surprise** reflects the deviation from the actual earnings per share figure from the mean of previous analyst forecasts. Negative surprises tend to decrease stock returns (Price et al., 2012) which may lead the executives to manage investor expectations.

- **Industry** dummies are obtained from the established Fama–French 12-industry scheme,[5] which distinguishes between e.g. "energy" or "healthcare."

---

[3] $l = -145218.44$ and $P = 1782.15$.

[4] http://www.cboe.com/vix

[5] http://mba.tuck.dartmouth.edu/pages/faculty/ken.french/data_library.html

Features	Weak Modal			Strong Modal			Average		
	P	R	F	P	R	F	P	R	F
SURFACE	0.52	0.55	0.53	0.51	0.48	0.50	0.52	0.52	0.52
LEXICAL	0.57	0.60	0.59	0.56	0.53	0.54	0.57	0.57	0.57
SEMANTIC	0.51	0.52	0.51	0.49	0.47	0.48	0.50	0.50	0.50
FINANCIAL	**0.89**	**0.95**	**0.92**	**0.95**	0.87	**0.91**	**0.92**	**0.91**	**0.91**
ALL$_{early}$	0.86	**0.95**	0.90	0.94	0.85	0.89	0.90	0.90	0.90
ALL$_{late}$	**0.89**	0.85	0.87	0.85	**0.89**	0.87	0.87	0.87	0.87
Random	0.50	0.50	0.50	0.50	0.50	0.50	0.50	0.50	0.50

Table 2: Classification results per class (*weak* and *strong modal*) and on average.

3.3 Classifier

Since we are interested in examining the influence of different features on an answer's modality, we select a set of algorithms with interpretable weights. In sum, we consider: (Gaussian) Naïve Bayes, Logistic Regression, Support Vector Machines (with RBF kernel), Decision Trees, Random Forest, and XGBoost (Chen and Guestrin, 2016). The classifier is implemented and evaluated using `sklearn 0.21.2` and `xgboost 0.90`.

3.3.1 Feature Fusion

To fusion our four feature categories, we use the following methods: (1) Early fusion involves representing all feature categories in the same vector space; (2) late fusion (or "stacking") implies that for each feature category, a separate classifier is trained—the predicted labels of these classifiers are then used as feature inputs for a meta-classifier predicting the final label. Our results show that, when representing all features in one vector space (early fusion), the XGBoost classifier outperforms all other algorithms. We furthermore find that the Gaussian Naïve Bayes algorithm performs best as meta-classifier for the late fusion approach.

3.3.2 Evaluation

We evaluate the performance of our classifiers with precision, recall, and F-score metrics. Furthermore, to quantify relative feature importance in case of the early fusion approaches, we use SHAP (SHapley Additive exPlanations) values, which were introduced by Lundberg and Lee (2017) and subsequently adapted for tree-based learners (Lundberg et al., 2020):

$$\phi_i(f_x) = \sum_{R \in \mathcal{R}} \frac{1}{M!} [f_x(P_i^R \cup i) - f_x(P_i^R)], \tag{1}$$

where ϕ_i is the SHAP value for feature i, f_x is the model output, $\mathcal{R}$ is the set of all feature orderings, P_i^R is the set of all features preceding feature i in ordering R, and M is the total number of features.

4 Results and Discussion

4.1 Feature Performance

Table 2 shows the results of our classification task in terms of precision (P), recall (R), and F-score (F) for both the *strong* and the *weak modal* class as well as on average. The early fusion approach uses an XGBoost classifier trained on a single vector containing all features; the late fusion approach additionally uses a Gaussian Naïve Bayes meta-classifier stacked upon two XGBoost classifiers trained separately on the linguistic and financial features. Since the binary labels are evenly distributed, a useful classifier should exceed a value of 0.50 across all measures. The SURFACE, LEXICAL, SEMANTIC, and FINANCIAL feature sets are defined as outlined in Section 3.2 and the fused features are represented by ALL with separate subscripts for the *early* and the *late* fusion approach.

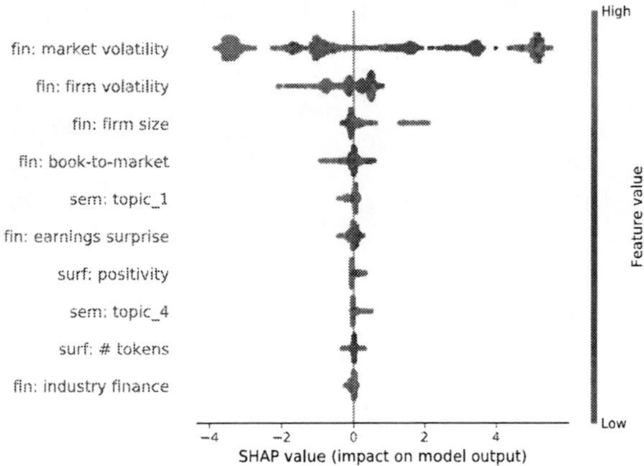

Figure 1: Violin plot of SHAP values for the top-10 features in the binary classification with early fusion.

All feature sets (with the exception of SEMANTIC for the *strong modal* class) improve over a random prediction. Furthermore, although late fusion improves slightly in terms of precision on the *weak modal* class (P = 0.89 vs. 0.86) and in terms of recall on the *strong modal* class (R = 0.89 vs. 0.85), the overall performance is slightly worse than that of an early fusion approach. When looking at individual features sets, we find that, perhaps counter-intuitively, the financial feature set alone has the strongest performance—even when compared to the more complex fusion approaches. This suggests that e.g. market or firm risk have a comparably larger influence on the modality of executive answers than the content of the preceding question. Therefore, while past literature asserts a comparably small impact of textual information for correlations with financial risk (Loughran and McDonald, 2011; Theil et al., 2018b), the same seems to apply when predicting a linguistic variable such as modality. Furthermore, this motivates to explore whether the effect persists when featuring a larger context window of textual information (perhaps including the earnings call presentation or prior questions and answers) or different methods of textual representation.

4.2   Feature Importance

One advantage of the early fusion approach is its interpretability: since all features are represented in the same vector, we can obtain a notion of relative feature importance quantitatively. To do so, we calculate the SHAP values (cf. Section 3.3.2) for all features and present the results in Figure 1. The intuition behind these values is to compare the contribution of a feature value to the difference between the actual and the mean prediction.

The strongest feature is market volatility, followed by firm volatility, and firm size. Interestingly, a high market and firm volatility positively impact the model output (and vice versa), implying that risky economic conditions may prompt managers to create a sense of security by committing to *strong modal* answers more frequently. Apart from two topical features, the strongest linguistic feature is positivity: Less positive questions tend to decrease the modality of an answer which could be attributed to their unsettling impact on manager confidence.

In addition, we were interested to explore the importance of individual linguistic types for the final prediction. To this end, we ranked the average SHAP values of all components of the purely LEXICAL model. In addition, we ran SpaCy's part-of-speech tagger on the ranked terms to explore the prevalence of different word classes. The vocabulary size of the complete dataset is 7,679 types. Out of these, only 153 terms have an average SHAP value > 0, i.e. are important for the final prediction. We found that the majority of terms are nouns (63), followed by verbs (47), adjectives (21), and adverbs (10). The top-20 terms according to their average SHAP value can be found in Table 3. Questions with numerical content (e.g. containing the token "number" or the placeholder tokens "DATE," "MONEY," "CARDINAL" for

term	SHAP in %	term	SHAP in %
DATE	5.67	share	0.94
okay	4.61	obviously	0.91
really	2.37	CARDINAL	0.89
number	1.85	color	0.88
MONEY	1.71	doing	0.85
does	1.46	tax	0.81
capex	1.44	charge	0.79
opportunity	1.26	performance	0.77
opportunities	1.13	stores	0.69
timing	1.12	given	0.68

Table 3: Average SHAP values for the top-20 terms. Uppercase terms represent placeholder tokens for the respective numerical named entity types identified with SpaCy.

dates, monetary values, and cardinal numbers) appear to influence an answer's modality. Likewise, business jargon terms such as "capex," "share," or "tax" are important for modality prediction.

Lastly, we were motivated to compare the feature distributions of the 434 misclassified instances to the total population of 1K test instances. For example, systematically higher VIX values in the misclassified instances compared to the rest of the population would motivate further experiments with a different weighting/sampling procedure of this feature in the training process. To do so, we checked for significant differences in the SURFACE and FINANCIAL feature sets across both misclassified and test instances using independent t-tests. Although none of the features showed significant differences in mean for $p \in \{0.05, 0.01, 0.001\}$, we found that the p-value for question uncertainty approaches conventional levels for significance ($p = 0.144$). This indicates that, apart from the increased context window mentioned above, future work could deeper explore the measurement of and prediction based on uncertainty for the given task—perhaps building on prior work on modality, hedging, or uncertainty detection presented in Section 2.

5   Conclusion

In this paper, we present a new dataset for modality prediction in financial dialogue and introduce a binary classifier to address this task. In our experiments, we contrast the performance of various algorithms, feature sets, and fusion methods. Interestingly, we reach a counter-intuitive result indicating that financial features (most prominently market and firm risk) possess a higher predictive power for answer modality than linguistic features (such as bags-of-words, topic models, or word embeddings) of the preceding question. In future work, it would be interesting to explore whether this effect persists when using a larger context window for the textual representations.

Acknowledgements

We would like to thank the anonymous reviewers for their helpful comments.

References

Tianqi Chen and Carlos Guestrin. 2016. XGBoost: A Scalable Tree Boosting System. In *Proceedings of ACM SIGKDD*, pages 785–794.

Belinda Crawford Camiciottoli. 2009. "Just Wondering if You Could Comment on That": Indirect Requests for Information in Corporate Earnings Calls. *Text & Talk*, 29(6):661–681.

Belinda Crawford Camiciottoli. 2011. Ethics and Ethos in Financial Reporting: Analyzing Persuasive Language in Earnings Calls. *Business Communication Quarterly*, 74(3):298–312.

Belinda Crawford Camiciottoli. 2018. Persuasion in Earnings Calls: A Diachronic Pragmalinguistic Analysis. *International Journal of Business Communication*, 55(3):275–292.

Cristian Danescu-Niculescu-Mizil, Moritz Sudhof, Dan Jurafsky, Jure Leskovec, and Christopher Potts. 2013. A Computational Approach to Politeness with Application to Social Factors. In *Proceedings of ACL*, pages 250–259.

Michał Dzieliński, Alexander Wagner, and Richard J. Zeckhauser. 2019. Straight Talkers and Vague Talkers: The Effects of Managerial Style in Earnings Conference Calls. *Swiss Finance Institute Research Paper Series*, 17(13).

Eugene F. Fama and Kenneth R. French. 1992. The Cross Section of Expected Stock Returns. *Journal of Finance*, 47(2):427–465.

Richárd Farkas, Veronika Vincze, György Móra, János Csirik, and György Szarvas. 2010. The CoNLL-2010 Shared Task: Learning to Detect Hedges and their Scope in Natural Language Text. In *Proceedings of CoNLL: Shared Task*, pages 1–12.

Ken Hyland. 1998. *Hedging in Scientific Research Articles*. John Benjamins, Amsterdam/Philadelphia.

Katherine A. Keith and Amanda Stent. 2019. Modeling Financial Analysts' Decision Making via the Pragmatics and Semantics of Earnings Calls. In *Proceedings of ACL*, pages 493–503.

George Lakoff. 1973. Hedges: A Study in Meaning Criteria and the Logic of Fuzzy Concepts. *Journal of Philosophical Logic*, 2:458–508.

David F. Larcker and Anastasia A. Zakolyukina. 2012. Detecting Deceptive Discussions in Conference Calls. *Journal of Accounting Research*, 50(2):494–540.

Quoc Le and Tomas Mikolov. 2014. Distributed Representations of Sentences and Documents. In *Proceedings of ICML*, pages 272–280.

Tim Loughran and Bill McDonald. 2011. When Is a Liability Not a Liability? Textual Analysis, Dictionaries, and 10-Ks. *The Journal of Finance*, 66(1):35–65.

Tim Loughran and Bill McDonald. 2016. Textual Analysis in Accounting and Finance: A Survey. *Journal of Accounting Research*, 54(4):1187–1230.

Scott M. Lundberg and Su-in Lee. 2017. A Unified Approach to Interpreting Model Predictions. In *Proceedings of NIPS*, pages 1–10.

Scott M. Lundberg, Gabriel Erion, Hugh Chen, Alex DeGrave, Jordan M. Prutkin, Bala Nair, Ronit Katz, Jonathan Himmelfarb, Nisha Bansal, and Su-In Lee. 2020. From Local Explanations to Global Understanding with Explainable AI for Trees. *Nature Machine Intelligence*, 2(1):56–67.

Tomas Mikolov, Kai Chen, Greg Corrado, and Jeffrey Dean. 2013. Efficient Estimation of Word Representations in Vector Space. *arxiv:1301.3781*.

Paul Portner. 2009. *Modality*. Oxford University Press.

S. McKay Price, James S. Doran, David R. Peterson, and Barbara A. Bliss. 2012. Earnings Conference Calls and Stock Returns: The Incremental Informativeness of Textual Tone. *Journal of Banking and Finance*, 36(4):992–1011.

Anna Prokofieva and Julia Hirschberg. 2014. Hedging and Speaker Commitment. In *International Workshop on Emotion, Social Signals, Sentiment & Linked Open Data*. LREC.

Navid Rekabsaz, Mihai Lupu, Artem Baklanov, Allan Hanbury, Alexander Duer, and Linda Anderson. 2017. Volatility Prediction Using Financial Disclosures Sentiments with Word Embedding-Based IR Models. In *Proceedings of ACL*, pages 1712–1721.

Victoria L. Rubin. 2007. Stating with Certainty or Stating with Doubt: Intercoder Reliability Results for Manual Annotation of Epistemically Modalized Statements. In *Proceedings of NAACL HLT 2007*, pages 141–144.

Sanja Štajner, Goran Glavaš, Simone Paolo Ponzetto, and Heiner Stuckenschmidt. 2017. Domain Adaptation for Automatic Detection of Speculative Sentences. In *Proceedings of the International Conference on Semantic Computing*, San Diego.

Christoph Kilian Theil, Sanja Štajner, Heiner Stuckenschmidt, and Simone Paolo Ponzetto. 2018a. Automatic Detection of Uncertain Statements in the Financial Domain. In *Proceedings of CICLing*, pages 642–654. Springer.

Christoph Kilian Theil, Sanja Štajner, and Heiner Stuckenschmidt. 2018b. Word Embeddings-Based Uncertainty Detection in Financial Disclosures. In *Proceedings of the ACL Workshop on Economics and Natural Language Processing (ECONLP)*, pages 32–37.

Christoph Kilian Theil, Samuel Broscheit, and Heiner Stuckenschmidt. 2019. PRoFET: Predicting the Risk of Firms from Event Transcripts. In *Proceedings of IJCAI*, pages 5211–5217.

Christoph Kilian Theil, Sanja Štajner, and Heiner Stuckenschmidt. 2020. Explaining Financial Uncertainty through Specialized Word Embeddings. *ACM/IMS Transactions on Data Science*, 1(1).

Ming-Feng Tsai and Chuan-Ju Wang. 2014. Financial Keyword Expansion via Continuous Word Vector Representations. In *Proceedings of the EMNLP*, pages 1453–1458.

Extracting Fine-Grained Economic Events from Business News

Gilles Jacobs   **Véronique Hoste**
Language and Translation Technology Team
Ghent University, 9000 Gent, Belgium
`firstname.lastname@ugent.be`

Abstract

Based on a recently developed fine-grained event extraction dataset for the economic domain, we present in a pilot study for supervised economic event extraction. We investigate how a state-of-the-art model for event extraction performs on the trigger and argument identification and classification. While F_1-scores of above 50% are obtained on the task of trigger identification, we observe a large gap in performance compared to results on the benchmark ACE05 dataset. We show that single-token triggers do not provide sufficient discriminative information for a fine-grained event detection setup in a closed domain such as economics, since many classes have a large degree of lexico-semantic and contextual overlap.

1 Introduction

We present a pilot study on a novel dataset annotated with economic and financial events in English company-specific news. Event processing automatically obtains the "what, who, where and when" of real-world events described in text. Event extraction consists of identifying event triggers, i.e. the tokens that express an event of a predetermined type, and identifying participant arguments, i.e. the tokens that express prototypical participant roles.

Event extraction is typically an upstream step in pipelines for financial applications: it has been used for news summarization of single (Lee et al., 2003; Marujo et al., 2017) or multiple documents (Liu et al., 2007; Glavaš and Šnajder, 2014), forecasting and market analysis (Nassirtoussi et al., 2014; Bholat et al., 2015; Nardo et al., 2016; Zhang et al., 2018; Chen et al., 2019), risk analysis (Hogenboom et al., 2015; Wei et al., 2019), policy assessment (Tobback et al., 2018; Karami et al., 2018), and marketing (Rambocas and Pacheco, 2018). This work aims to enable these information extraction tasks in the financial domain by making available a dataset and fine-grained event extraction model for company-specific news by classifying economic event triggers and participant arguments in text.

Our SENTiVENT dataset of company-specific events was conceived to be compatible with fine-grained event representations of the ACE benchmark corpora as to enable direct application of advances in the field. In our pilot study, we investigate the portability of an existing state-of-the-art model for event extraction, named DYGIE++ (Wadden et al., 2019b), to the task of financial event extraction.

2 Related Research

Our work on economic event extraction is accommodated within the rich history of automatic event detection. The ACE (Automatic Content Extraction) annotation scheme and programme was highly influential in event processing. Periodically, "Event Detection and Recognition" evaluation competitions were organized where event extraction corpora were released (Consortium, 2005; Walker et al., 2006) to enable automatic inference of entities mentioned in text, the relations among entities, and the events in which these entities participate (Doddington et al., 2004). Some years later, the ERE (Entities, Relations, Events) standard was conceived as a continuation of ACE with the goal of improving annotation consistency and quality. Our annotation scheme is inspired by the Rich ERE Event annotation schemes

Proceedings of the 1st Joint Workshop on Financial Narrative Processing and MultiLing Financial Summarisation, pages 235–245
Barcelona, Spain (Online), December 12, 2020.

(Linguistic Data Consortium, 2016; Linguistic Data Consortium, 2015a; Linguistic Data Consortium, 2015b) as to provide compatibility with on-going research in event extraction, where the ACE and ERE datasets remain dominant benchmarks.

Many approaches to the detection of economic events are *knowledge-based and pattern-based* (Arendarenko and Kakkonen, 2012; Hogenboom et al., 2013; Du et al., 2016; Chen et al., 2019). These use rule-sets or ontology knowledge-bases which are largely or fully created by hand and do not rely fully on manually annotated supervised datasets for machine learning. The Stock Sonar project (Feldman et al., 2011a) notably uses domain experts to formulate event rules for rule-based stock sentiment analysis. Their approach has been successful in formulating trading strategies (Ben Ami and Feldman, 2017) and in assessing the impact of events on the stock market (Boudoukh et al., 2016). Along the same line, Hogenboom et al. (2013) rely on a hand-crafted financial event ontology for pattern-based event detection in the economic domain and incorporates lexicons, gazetteers, PoS-tagging and morphological analysis.

Several *semi- or distantly supervision* approaches exist in which seed sets are manually labeled or rule-sets are used to generate or enhance training data (Qian et al., 2019; Rönnqvist and Sarlin, 2017; Ein-Dor et al., 2019). For Chinese, Yang et al. (2018) and Chen et al. (2019) rely on a knowledge-base of rules for extracting ACE-like events in stock market prediction. Han et al. (2018) describe a hybrid approach to ACE-like event extraction by labeling triggers, argument types, and event types for Chinese news articles with 8 economic event types using an automatically expanded trigger dictionary and used a pattern-matching approach for argument extraction.

Few strictly *supervised approaches* exist due to the lack of human-annotated ground-truth data. Malik et al. (2011) annotated Dividend and Profit figure slots and detected these types with high precision by combining supervised learning with rule post-processing. The English and Dutch SentiFM business news corpus (Van De Kauter et al., 2015) contains token-span annotations of 10 event types with only one type of relation. Sentence-level event detection experiments have been conducted (Lefever and Hoste, 2016; Jacobs et al., 2018), but supervised fine-grained extraction of triggers and roles as presented here. We are not aware of any other published fine-grained ACE-like event extraction approaches for the economic domain.

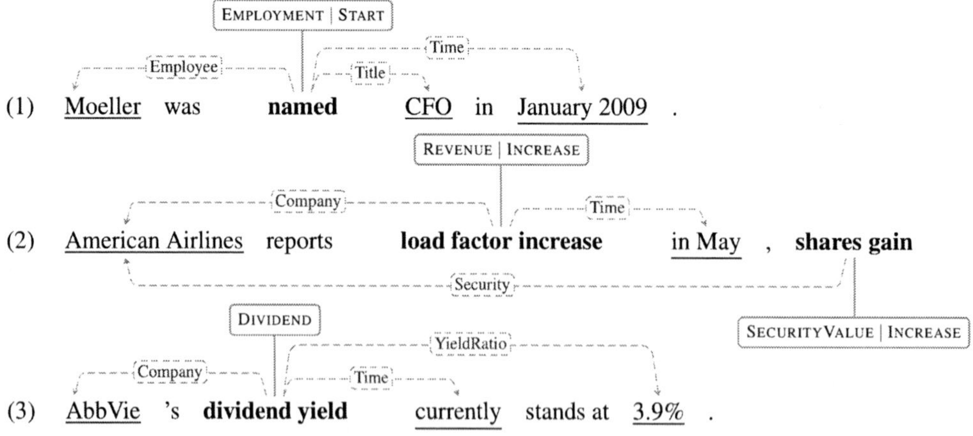

Figure 1: Examples of annotated economic event schemata with argument roles. **Boldface** indicates event trigger spans. Underlining indicates argument spans.

3 Dataset

We define economic events as '*textually reported real-world occurrences, actions, relations, and situations involving companies and firms*'. Fine-grained events in our dataset are operationalized as *event triggers*, i.e. the minimal span of text (a single word or a phrase) that most succinctly expresses the occurrence of an event type, and *event arguments*, i.e., participating entities involved in the event by filling a certain prototypical semantic role. Figure 1 shows examples of annotated event triggers with their TYPE | SUBTYPE label linked to argument with their roles.

We annotated 288 documents with structured events containing event types and subtypes, arguments and event attributes (i.e., negation, modality & event co-reference). The news article pertain to 30 S&P500 companies spread over different industries and time between June 2016 to May 2017 to avoid topical specialization. These companies were selected as a starting point for scraping because market data (e.g., key financials, spot prices, dividend, earnings and P/E ratio) for these are readily available, enabling market research. For a full description of the data collection, annotation process, dataset properties, and agreement study, we refer to Jacobs and Hoste (2020). The event typology contains 18 event main types with 42 subtypes for which 48 possible argument roles exist. Not every main event type has subtypes and the arguments "Time", "Place", and "Capital" can belong to any event. The typology was iteratively developed on a sample corpus in which news events were evaluated by financial domain experts. Starting with the set of event types in previous literature (Feldman et al., 2011b; Boudoukh et al., 2019; Hogenboom et al., 2013; Van De Kauter et al., 2015; Du et al., 2016), types were removed and added based on frequency and cohesion of categories. Relevant argument roles were also added in this process of iterative refinement. For a full description of the types and subtypes, we refer to the annotation guidelines (Jacobs, 2020b). Here is a list of main Types → unique Arguments:

- CSR/BRAND → Company
- DEAL → Goal, Partner
- DIVIDEND → Amount, Company, HistoricalYieldRatio, YieldRatio
- EMPLOYMENT → Amount, Employee, Employer, Replacer, Replacing, Title
- EXPENSE → Amount, Company, HistoricalAmount
- FACILITY → Company, Facility
- FINANCIALREPORT → Reportee, Result
- FINANCING → Amount, Financee, Financer
- INVESTMENT → CapitalInvested, Investee, Investor
- LEGAL → Allegation, Adjudicator, Complainant, Defendant, Sentence
- MACROECONOMICS → AffectedCompany, Sector
- MERGER/ACQUISITION → Acquirer, Cost, Target
- PRODUCT/SERVICE → Producer, Product/Service, Trialer
- PROFIT/LOSS → Amount, HistoricalAmount, Profiteer
- RATING → Analyst, HistoricalRating, Security, TargetPrice
- REVENUE → Amount, Company, DecreaseAmount, HistoricalAmount, IncreaseAmount
- SALESVOLUME → Amount, Buyer, GoodsService, HistoricalAmount, Seller
- SECURITYVALUE → DecreaseAmount, HistoricalPrice, IncreaseAmount, Price, Security

The types PROFIT/LOSS, REVENUE, EXPENSE, and SALESVOLUME represent major metrics in financial reporting on the income statement. Of all financial metrics, we found these types to be commonly and generally reported in business news. Other metrics such as debt ratios or cash flow statements as well as highly industry-specific indicators were collected under the FINANCIALREPORT type. Discussion of asset performance are captured by RATING and SECURITYVALUE. MACROECONOMICS is a broad category pertaining to events that do not involve decisions or interactions of specific companies. While this category is not company-specific, it was devised to capture discussions of sector trends, economy-wide phenomena, and governmental policy. In the event extraction pilot study, we only experiment with classifying main event types and not the subtypes.

Table 1 shows the counts of annotation units in our SENTiVENT corpus compared to the benchmark ACE2005-English-Events corpus (henceforth ACE05) (Walker et al., 2006) for the training, development and test set splits used in the pilot experiments.

An important difference in event trigger annotation with ACE05 is the tagging of discontinuous, multi-word triggers (e.g., "upgraded ... to buy", "cut back ... expenses", "EPS decline"). In ACE05, triggers are always single-word and any multi-word idiomatic expressions are joined into one token (e.g. "kick

	SENTiVENT				ACE05			
	Train	Dev	Test	Total	Train	Dev	Test	Total
Documents	228	30	30	288	529	28	40	597
Events	4,603	618	982	6,203	4,202	450	403	5,055
Sentences	5,475	681	727	6,883	17,172	923	832	18,927
Arguments	10,052	1,327	2,296	13,675	4,859	605	576	6040
Entities	12,732*	1,739*	1,441*	15.912*	29,006	2,451	3,017	34,474

	SENTiVENT	ACE05
Domain	Business News	Geo-Political
Entity cat.	-*	7
Trigger cat.	18	33
Argument cat.	48	22

Table 1: Properties for our SENTiVENT dataset and ACE05 in totals, as well as for the training, development and the test evaluation sets. * indicates that SENTiVENT contains no manually annotated entities.

the bucket" becomes "kick_the_bucket"). For SENTiVENT, 42% of triggers are multi-word and 13% are both discontinuous and multi-word.

Comparing annotation counts in ACE05 to our annotations, SENTiVENT has less documents but a higher density of event annotations. This reflects a difference in annotation approach in which events are less constrained by syntactic rules than in ACE05. Unlike ACE, we did not annotate entity tags and do not restrict event arguments definition by entity type. Not restricting events by syntactic rules or entity type results in a conceptually simplified annotation process. It also decreases to degree to which lexico-semantically present events are not tagged because of restrictive rules. Furthermore, the generality of geo-political event types in ACE05 compared to the domain-specific economic events in business news entails that more relevant events will be present. Due to the absence of entity annotations in our dataset, we also have significantly more arguments as in ACE05 argument roles are restricted by specific entity labels. Our argument role annotation is any span within the event scope that expresses the argument role and is thus semantically motivated.

4   Experimental Setup

Task definition   Event extraction concerns identifying event triggers and their event types, event arguments and event roles. The input documents are represented as a sequence of tokens D from which the model constructs the set of all possible within-sentence spans $S = \{s_1, ..., s_T\}$ in the document (limited by a threshold-length). Each token d_i is assigned an event type label t_i. Then, for each trigger d_i, event arguments are assigned by predicting and argument role a_{ij} for all spans s_j in the same sentence as d_i.

Evaluation   For ACE05, we follow the evaluation splits (cf. Table 1) and method commonly used in previous research (Nguyen et al., 2016; Sha et al., 2018; Zhang et al., 2019). All reported precision (P), recall (R), and F_1-scores (F_1) are micro-averaged. Our experiments involve the following four subtasks:

Trigger identification (Trig-ID) is the subtask of identifying if a token position matches a ground-truth reference trigger. *Trigger classification (Trig-C)* determines the type of the identified trigger. A trigger is correct when it is correctly identified and its type label matches the reference.

Argument identification (Arg-ID) is the subtask of identifying if a text span belongs to a certain event type. An argument is correctly identified when the span matches and the event type is correct. *Argument classification (Arg-C)* determines the *role* (e.g. "Employee") of an identified argument. An argument is correctly classified if it is correctly identified and its role label matches the ground-truth reference.

Data pre-processing   All documents were sentence split and tokenized before annotation. As our event triggers are multi-token spans similar to Rich-ERE triggers, we transformed these multi-token spans into single-token triggers to allow us to use the DYGIE++ implementation in its basic configuration. For argument spans this pre-processing step is not needed as arguments are annotated as continuous, multi-token spans in both ACE05 and SENTiVENT. We selected single tokens by dependency parsing the triggers and selecting verbal and nominal root token within the trigger span using Spacy NLP library (Honnibal and Montani, 2017). When filtering multiple tokens to a single trigger, we use syntactic priority criteria based on PoS in which nominal tokens are prefered over verbal tokens which are prefered over other types. Search for these parts-of-speech goes one level down into the parse tree from the original trigger's root token, defaulting to the original root token if no nominal of verbal child is found. Examples of this pre-processing applied to original multi-token triggers:

- PROFIT/LOSS   "improve margins"   → "margins"
- FACILITY   "operating on-site gas stations"   → "stations"
- SALESVOLUME   "attracting the greatest volume" → "volume"

This priority chain was empirically determined on a subsample of 15% of all triggers by comparing other selection criteria.

The DYGIE++ model also allows the use of named entity labels as features in training the trigger and argument subtasks. Unlike ACE05, our dataset does not include entity annotations (argument roles are unconstrained by entity types). To test if silver-standard entity labels improve identification and classification, we used entity label predictions of a trained entity model on the ACE05 dataset (Entity F_1-score: 90.7%).

Event extraction model   For the event extraction pipeline we relied on the state-of-the-art DYGIE++ information extraction framework (Wadden et al., 2019b; Wadden et al., 2019a). As a current state-of-the-art model on ACE event extraction and other information extraction tasks, DYGIE++ is a good candidate for establishing a baseline on our new dataset.

DYGIE++ relies on graph propagation of contextualized embeddings of text spans in the local and global context to jointly model event triggers and arguments. The model enumerates candidate text spans and encodes them using pretrained contextual language models (such as BERT (Devlin et al., 2019)) and task-specific message updates passed over a text span graph. BERT embeddings are encoded at the subword-level by the WordPiece algorithm (Kudo, 2018) and to obtain token-level representations WordPieces are pooled. Tokens are encoded with frozen BERT embeddings using a sliding window, feeding each sentence to BERT together with a size-L window of surrounding sentences. Spans of text are enumerated and constructed by concatenating the tokens together with a learned span width embedding. With event propagation enabled, a graph is generated based on the model's best guess at the relations present among spans in the document. The event graph has two types of nodes: trigger nodes and argument nodes. Trigger nodes pass messages to their likely arguments updating those argument representations and arguments pass messages to their probable triggers. The re-contextualized representations are input into a two-layer feedforward neural net (FFNN) for each subtask. For a trigger token g_i, the final prediction is computed by $\text{FFNN}_{\text{trig}}(g_i)$ and for argument role prediction the relevant pair of embeddings is concatenated and $\text{FFNN}_{\text{arg}}([g_i, g_j])$ computed.

Model variations   We experiment with two main variations in the model architecture: **BERT+LSTM** feeds pretrained BERT embeddings to a bi-directional LSTM layer, while the LSTM parameters are trained jointly with a task specific layer. **BERT Finetune** uses supervised fine-tuning of the BERT model on the end-task. We relied on the BERT implementations provided by the AllenNLP framework (Gardner et al., 2018): $\text{BERT}_{\text{Base}}$ with 12 layers (transformer blocks), 12 attention heads, and 110 million parameters. and $\text{BERT}_{\text{Large}}$ with 24 layers, 16 attention heads and, 340 million parameters. In initial testing, we found $\text{BERT}_{\text{Large}}$ improved performance in the LSTM variant over $\text{BERT}_{\text{Base}}$. For finetuning, we relied on the smaller $\text{BERT}_{\text{Base}}$ due to memory restrictions.

We examine the impact of **disabling the NER** subtask in the DYGIE++ event extraction pipeline. The SENTiVENT dataset does not contain manually annotated ground-truth entity labels. The labels used in experiments with joint training on the NER subtask are predictions from a pretrained ACE05 model.

We also **enable event propagation** where graph updates between triggers and arguments are computed. The base approach (BERT+LSTM) with event propagation bypasses trigger-argument span updates and directly feeds the embedded span representations from the Bi-LSTM layer to the feedforward scoring layer.

Additionally, we experimented with replacing the pretrained BERT general language model with the in-domain **FinBERT** model (Araci, 2019) as previous state-of-the-art systems have shown in-domain pretraining to increase performance on text classification and information extraction tasks (Howard and Ruder, 2018; Wadden et al., 2019b). FinBERT further pretrains BERT on the TRC2-financial corpus of news articles published by Reuters between 2008 and 2010 resulting in a model that outperforms regular BERT on financial sentiment analysis tasks.[1]

5 Results and Discussion

	SENTiVENT			ACE05		
Task	P	R	F_1	P	R	F_1
Trig-ID	48.23	58.10	52.71	70.22	83.33	76.22
Trig-C	38.86	46.81	42.46	67.04	79.56	72.76
Arg-ID	40.46	38.56	39.49	60.73	63.35	62.01
Arg-C	38.95	37.12	38.01	55.17	57.55	56.33

Table 2: Micro-avg. precision (P), recall (R), and F_1-score of the best system (BERT-Large + LSTM) on SENTiVENT and ACE05 for comparison.

Table 2 shows the results for the best configuration of the SENTiVENT model. The best model configuration was selected by the highest mean F_1-score on the Trig-C and Arg-C subtasks. The scores for the best model variant with similar configuration trained on ACE05 is given as comparison. The best model variation on the different SENTiVENT event subtasks is BERT + LSTM with the NER subtask enabled (Table 3). The same architecture also was best for ACE05.[2]

For our task, using the in-domain FinBERT did not improve performance over BERT on any task. In line with (Wadden et al., 2019b), fine-tuning decreases performance for both BERT and FinBERT configurations. This is likely due to the sensitivity of both the optimization hyper-parameters and BERT finetuning as the trigger detector begins overfitting before the argument detector is finished training. Event propagation also does not improve scores, likely due to the asymmetric relationship between triggers and arguments.

Disabling the NER subtask in which predicted entity labels are used as features lowers performance, showing that the silver-standard entity labels do provide useful features in training.

Variation	Trig-ID	Trig-C	Arg-ID	Arg-C
FinBERT+LSTM	50.97	41.78	37.04	35.44
FinBERT Finetune	49.96	42.34	30.24	29.19
BERT Finetune	50.37	42.22	30.75	29.41
BERT+LSTM	**52.71**	**42.46**	**39.49**	**38.01**
+EventProp	49.54	41.13	32.85	31.61
−NER	49.92	40.03	34.56	33.64

Table 3: Micro-avg. F_1-scores for model variations on the SENTiVENT-Event subtasks.

Interestingly, there is a large gap in performance on the two datasets while similar model settings were used and while a outwardly similar text genre (news text) was under investigation. We believe there

---

[1] The model weights were obtained from https://github.com/ProsusAI/finBERT.

[2] The ACE05 scores differ from those reported in Wadden et al. (2019b) as we did not use ensembles. We did use all the same data pre-processing, splits, and single-model settings provided by the authors.

might be several reasons for this performance gap. First of all, the drop in performance can to a certain extent be explained by the DYGIE++ requirement for single-token triggers, which is the unit of investigation in the ACE05 dataset. Many trigger types in our SENTiVENT corpus are differentiated lexically by the combination of a nominal and verbal phrase. In order to obtain single token triggers, a dependency parsing approach was taken in which the syntactic head noun or verb was preferred, introducing ambiguity. A multi-token trigger such as "conquer consumer spending" for SALESVOLUME would then lead to a more general and ambiguous trigger "spending" which is common in event type EXPENSE). We hypothesize that single-token triggers delineate general-domain ACE05 geo-political event types (LIFE.BE-BORN, LIFE.MARRY, MOVEMENT.TRANSPORT, TRANSACTION.TRANSFER-MONEY) better than our company-specific events.

Finally, due to the higher event-sentence density of our data (cf. Table 1), there is less global context to learn from, as well as a higher likelihood of overlap in the lexical context (local and global) of triggers and arguments.

Error analysis   Table 4 shows the frequency of errors made by the BERT+LSTM system. For event triggers, missing identified triggers (51.7%) constitutes the largest error and 13.6% involves misclassified cases where a trigger was identified but the event type was mistaken (e.g., a REVENUE event is assigned PROFIT/LOSS). Missing event arguments is the largest error type (70.8%) for arguments with misclassification playing a minor role (1.3%). Spurious triggers or arguments account for 34.7% and 27.9%, respectively and they occur when token spans are assigned a label where none is present.

Error type	Missing	Spurious	Misclassified
TRIGGER	51.7%	34.7%	13.6%
ARGUMENT	70.8%	27.9%	1.3%

Table 4: Frequency of error types of the best system on the test set.

Trigger Error Type	Specialized/Creative Language	Lexical Sparsity	Plausible Spurious	Ambiguous Trigger	Single-Token Pre-processing
Freq.	12.4%	9.1%	16.4%	20.1%	34.1%

Table 5: Frequency of trigger errors in manual assessment.

We also manually reviewed half of the evaluation test set documents and annotated the errors in more detail (Table 5). *Lexical sparsity errors* where triggers are missing or misclassified because they are rare or unseen in training is less of a problem (associated with 9% of errors). *Highly specialized contexts or creative language use* introduces contextual lexical sparsity. This occurs more frequently with company-specific news than general news because industry, product, or company-specific terminology is used; e.g., *"Besides its **track-tested** suspension and race-ready seats, the Edge ST's looks take a dark turn..."* → true: PRODUCT/SERVICE, pred.: Missing. *Ambiguous triggers* are also a common source of errors, e.g., "growth" is often used for various types related to financial metrics such as PROFIT/LOSS, REVENUE, EXPENSE, etc.: e.g., *"Expect strongest **growth** from services and Asia."* → true: FINANCIALREPORT, pred.: SALESVOLUME. *"Apple **made** $64.1 billion before taxes in fiscal 2017."* → true: PROFIT/LOSS, pred: REVENUE. Another example is "buy", which is a trigger often used for MERGER/ACQUISITION but often misclassified as a 'buy/hold/sell' RATING. Better capturing the long context and event co-reference should resolve ambiguous trigger mentions as often the preceding context specifies the metric. A large amount of errors (34%) were due to the *pre-processing* step of converting our ground-truth multi-token triggers into single-tokens. This discards discriminative information regarding type and causes many spurious and missing errors. e.g., *"... organic sales **growth** projections for this year ..."* where "sales growth" is the original annotated SALESVOLUME trigger reduced to "growth" introducing class ambiguity which has evidently not been resolved by local or global context. Spurious triggers that *plausibly* express an event but are absent in the ground-truth are also fairly common (16%). This is not an artifact of low-quality annotations but occurs with non-salient mentions of events which are generic or unspecific in nature and for which a more concrete example is annotated in the direct vicinity. Our conceptualization of economic events includes specificity and relevancy in annotation, which is not well-captured by the model, e.g., in *"Below is an analysis of Apple's App Store revenue..."* "revenue" is a spurious REVENUE prediction that is not in the ground-truth because it is a generic mention followed by a series of fully-realized events.

6 Data availability and replication

This work's source code, preprocessed replication data in DYGIE-format, and the winning trained model are publicly available at `https://osf.io/j63h9` (Jacobs, 2020a). The original dataset will be freely downloadable at the end of the SENTiVENT project through this repository. Up until then, the fully annotated corpus is available on request for academic research purposes.

7 Conclusion and Future Work

Event extraction is a required step in many data-driven financial tasks in which factual information is needed to capture changes in the real-world. Various general domain fine-grained event extraction corpora are freely available but no economically focused corpus exists. We presented a pilot study on a novel dataset enabling supervised fine-grained extraction of economic events as trigger and argument classification. Using a state-of-the-art information extraction pipeline based on span-based graph propagation of pretrained contextual embeddings, we observed a large drop in performance on our dataset compared to the benchmark ACE05 dataset. After error analysis, we found this is largely caused by missing predictions. For event triggers, many errors are due to ambiguity introduced by the requirement of the DYGIE++ model implementation for single-token triggers. We hypothesize that single-token triggers for the SENTiVENT corpus do not provide sufficient discriminative information for detecting classes which have a large degree of semantic and contextual overlap.

Hence, in future work we will focus on event extraction methods that model arbitrary length triggers. Currently on-going, we are adding "investor sentiment" annotations on top of events as well as separate sentiment expression annotations with their targets. These sentiment annotations will allow us to jointly process the "common-sense" sentiment of events. We will investigate how extracted event schemata can be used upstream from aspect-based sentiment analysis.

Acknowledgements

This work was supported by the Research Foundation Flanders (FWO) under a Ph.D fellowship grant for the SENTiVENT project. We would like to thank anonymous reviewers for their helpful suggestions, as well as David Wadden for publishing and maintaining their model source code and answering questions about the model.

References

Dogu Araci. 2019. Finbert: Financial sentiment analysis with pre-trained language models.

Ernest Arendarenko and Tuomo Kakkonen. 2012. Ontology-Based Information and Event Extraction for Business Intelligence. In *Artificial Intelligence: Methodology, Systems, and Applications*, volume 7557 of *Lecture Notes in Computer Science*, pages 89–102. Springer.

Zvi Ben Ami and Ronen Feldman. 2017. Event-based trading: Building superior trading strategies with state-of-the-art information extraction tools. SSRN Working Paper 2907600.

David Bholat, Stephen Hansen, Pedro Santos, and Cheryl Schonhardt-Bailey. 2015. Text mining for central banks. *Available at SSRN 2624811*.

Jacob Boudoukh, Ronen Feldman, Shimon Kogan, and Matthew P Richardson. 2016. Information, trading, and volatility: Evidence from firm-specific news. SSRN Working Paper 2193667.

Jacob Boudoukh, Ronen Feldman, Shimon Kogan, and Matthew Richardson. 2019. Information, trading, and volatility: Evidence from firm-specific news. *The Review of Financial Studies*, 32(3):992–1033.

Deli Chen, Yanyan Zou, Keiko Harimoto, Ruihan Bao, Xuancheng Ren, and Xu Sun. 2019. Incorporating fine-grained events in stock movement prediction. In *Proceedings of the Second Workshop on Economics and Natural Language Processing*, pages 31–40, Hong Kong, November. Association for Computational Linguistics.

Linguistic Data Consortium. 2005. Ace (automatic content extraction) english annotation guidelines for events version 5.4.3.

Jacob Devlin, Ming-Wei Chang, Kenton Lee, and Kristina Toutanova. 2019. Bert: Pre-training of deep bidirectional transformers for language understanding. In *Proceedings of the 2019 Conference of the North American Chapter of the Association for Computational Linguistics: Human Language Technologies, Volume 1 (Long and Short Papers)*, pages 4171–4186.

George R Doddington, Alexis Mitchell, Mark Przybocki, Lance Ramshaw, Stephanie Strassel, and Ralph Weischedel. 2004. The automatic content extraction (ace) program–tasks, data, and evaluation. In *Proceedings of the Fourth International Conference on Language Resources and Evaluation (LREC'04)*.

Mian Du, Lidia Pivovarova, and Roman Yangarber. 2016. PULS: natural language processing for business intelligence. In *Proceedings of the 2016 Workshop on Human Language Technology*, pages 1–8.

Liat Ein-Dor, Ariel Gera, Orith Toledo-Ronen, Alon Halfon, Benjamin Sznajder, Lena Dankin, Yonatan Bilu, Yoav Katz, and Noam Slonim. 2019. Financial Event Extraction Using Wikipedia-Based Weak Supervision. In *Proceedings of the Second Workshop on Economics and Natural Language Processing*, pages 10–15, Stroudsburg, PA, USA. Association for Computational Linguistics.

Ronen Feldman, Benjamin Rosenfeld, Roy Bar-Haim, and Moshe Fresko. 2011a. The stock sonar sentiment analysis of stocks based on a hybrid approach. In *Twenty-Third IAAI Conference*.

Ronen Feldman, Benjamin Rosenfeld, Roy Bar-Haim, and Moshe Fresko. 2011b. The Stock Sonar — Sentiment Analysis of Stocks Based on a Hybrid Approach. *Iaai*, pages 1642–1647.

Matt Gardner, Joel Grus, Mark Neumann, Oyvind Tafjord, Pradeep Dasigi, Nelson F. Liu, Matthew Peters, Michael Schmitz, and Luke Zettlemoyer. 2018. AllenNLP: A deep semantic natural language processing platform. In *Proceedings of Workshop for NLP Open Source Software (NLP-OSS)*, pages 1–6, Melbourne, Australia, July. Association for Computational Linguistics.

Goran Glavaš and Jan Šnajder. 2014. Event graphs for information retrieval and multi-document summarization. *Expert Systems with Applications*, 41(15):6904–6916.

Songqiao Han, Xiaoling Hao, and Hailiang Huang. 2018. An event-extraction approach for business analysis from online Chinese news. *Electronic Commerce Research and Applications*, 28:244–260.

Alexander Hogenboom, Frederik Hogenboom, Flavius Frasincar, Kim Schouten, and Otto Van Der Meer. 2013. Semantics-based information extraction for detecting economic events. *Multimedia Tools and Applications*, 64(1):27–52.

Frederik Hogenboom, Michael de Winter, Flavius Frasincar, and Uzay Kaymak. 2015. A news event-driven approach for the historical value at risk method. *Expert Systems with Applications*, 42(10):4667–4675.

Matthew Honnibal and Ines Montani. 2017. spacy 2: Natural language understanding with bloom embeddings, convolutional neural networks and incremental parsing. *To appear*, 7(1). Dependency parsing model used: en_core_web_lg v2.3.1.

Jeremy Howard and Sebastian Ruder. 2018. Universal language model fine-tuning for text classification. In *Proceedings of the 56th Annual Meeting of the Association for Computational Linguistics (Volume 1: Long Papers)*, pages 328–339.

Gilles Jacobs and Véronique Hoste. 2020. SENTiVENT: Enabling supervised information extraction of company-specific events in economic and financial news. *Manuscript submitted for publication*.

Gilles Jacobs, Els Lefever, and Véronique Hoste. 2018. Economic event detection in company-specific news text. In *Proceedings of the First Workshop on Economics and Natural Language Processing*, pages 1–10.

Gilles Jacobs. 2020a. Replication data for extracting fine-grained economic events from business news, Oct.

Gilles Jacobs. 2020b. SENTiVENT Event Annotation Guidelines v1.1. Technical report, LT3, Ghent University, jun.

Amir Karami, London S Bennett, and Xiaoyun He. 2018. Mining public opinion about economic issues: Twitter and the us presidential election. *International Journal of Strategic Decision Sciences (IJSDS)*, 9(1):18–28.

Taku Kudo. 2018. Subword regularization: Improving neural network translation models with multiple subword candidates. In *Proceedings of the 56th Annual Meeting of the Association for Computational Linguistics (Volume 1: Long Papers)*, pages 66–75, Melbourne, Australia, July. Association for Computational Linguistics.

Chang Shing Lee, Yea Juan Chen, and Zhi W Jian. 2003. Ontology-based fuzzy event extraction agent for Chinese e-news summarization. *Expert Systems with Applications*, 25(3):431–447.

Els Lefever and Véronique Hoste. 2016. A classification-based approach to economic event detection in Dutch news text. In *Proceedings of the Tenth International Conference on Language Resources and Evaluation (LREC'16)*, pages 330–335, Portorož, Slovenia, May. European Language Resources Association (ELRA).

Linguistic Data Consortium. 2015a. DEFT Rich ERE Annotation Guidelines: Argument Filler V2.3. Technical report, Linguistic Data Consortium, 11.

Linguistic Data Consortium. 2015b. DEFT Rich ERE Annotation Guidelines: Events V3.0. Technical report, Linguistic Data Consortium, 11.

Linguistic Data Consortium. 2016. Rich ERE Annotation Guidelines Overview V4.2. Technical report, Linguistic Data Consortium. Accessed: 2018-09-05.

Maofu Liu, Wenjie Li, Mingli Wu, and Jun Hu. 2007. Event-based extractive summarization using event semantic relevance from external linguistic resource. *Proceedings - ALPIT 2007 6th International Conference on Advanced Language Processing and Web Information Technology*, pages 117–122.

Hassan H. Malik, Vikas S. Bhardwaj, and Huascar Fiorletta. 2011. Accurate information extraction for quantitative financial events. *International Conference on Information and Knowledge Management, Proceedings*, pages 2497–2500.

Luís Marujo, Ricardo Ribeiro, Anatole Gershman, David Martins de Matos, João P. Neto, and Jaime Carbonell. 2017. Event-based summarization using a centrality-as-relevance model. *Knowledge and Information Systems*, 50(3):945–968.

Michela Nardo, Marco Petracco-Giudici, and Minás Naltsidis. 2016. Walking down wall street with a tablet: A survey of stock market predictions using the web. *Journal of Economic Surveys*, 30(2):356–369.

Arman Khadjeh Nassirtoussi, Saeed Aghabozorgi, Teh Ying Wah, and David Chek Ling Ngo. 2014. Text mining for market prediction: A systematic review. *Expert Systems with Applications*, 41(16):7653–7670.

Thien Huu Nguyen, Kyunghyun Cho, and Ralph Grishman. 2016. Joint event extraction via recurrent neural networks. In *Proceedings of the 2016 Conference of the North American Chapter of the Association for Computational Linguistics: Human Language Technologies*, pages 300–309, San Diego, California, June. Association for Computational Linguistics.

Yu Qian, Xiongwen Deng, Qiongwei Ye, Baojun Ma, and Hua Yuan. 2019. On detecting business event from the headlines and leads of massive online news articles. *Information Processing and Management*, 56(6):102086.

Meena Rambocas and Barney G Pacheco. 2018. Online sentiment analysis in marketing research: a review. *Journal of Research in Interactive Marketing*.

Samuel Rönnqvist and Peter Sarlin. 2017. Bank distress in the news: Describing events through deep learning. *Neurocomputing*, 264:57–70.

Lei Sha, Feng Qian, Baobao Chang, and Zhifang Sui. 2018. Jointly extracting event triggers and arguments by dependency-bridge rnn and tensor-based argument interaction. In *AAAI Conference on Artificial Intelligence*.

Ellen Tobback, Hans Naudts, Walter Daelemans, Enric Junqué de Fortuny, and David Martens. 2018. Belgian economic policy uncertainty index: Improvement through text mining. *International Journal of Forecasting*, 34(2):355 – 365.

Marjan Van De Kauter, Diane Breesch, and Véronique Hoste. 2015. Fine-grained analysis of explicit and implicit sentiment in financial news articles. *Expert Systems with Applications*, 42(11):4999–5010.

David Wadden, Ulme Wennberg, Yi Luan, and Hannaneh Hajishirzi. 2019a. Dygie++: Span-based system for named entity, relation, and event extraction. https://github.com/dwadden/dygiepp.

David Wadden, Ulme Wennberg, Yi Luan, and Hannaneh Hajishirzi. 2019b. Entity, relation, and event extraction with contextualized span representations. In *Proceedings of the 2019 Conference on Empirical Methods in Natural Language Processing and the 9th International Joint Conference on Natural Language Processing (EMNLP-IJCNLP)*, pages 5784–5789, Hong Kong, China, November. Association for Computational Linguistics.

Christopher Walker, Stephanie Strassel, Julie Medero, and Kazuaki Maeda. 2006. Ace 2005 multilingual training corpus.

Lu Wei, Guowen Li, Jianping Li, and Xiaoqian Zhu. 2019. Bank risk aggregation with forward-looking textual risk disclosures. *The North American Journal of Economics and Finance*, 50:101016.

Hang Yang, Yubo Chen, Kang Liu, Yang Xiao, and Jun Zhao. 2018. Dcfee: A document-level chinese financial event extraction system based on automatically labeled training data. In *Proceedings of ACL 2018, System Demonstrations*, pages 50–55.

Xi Zhang, Siyu Qu, Jieyun Huang, Binxing Fang, and Philip Yu. 2018. Stock market prediction via multi-source multiple instance learning. *IEEE Access*, 6:50720–50728.

Tongtao Zhang, Heng Ji, and Avirup Sil. 2019. Joint entity and event extraction with generative adversarial imitation learning. *Data Intelligence*, 1(2):99–120.